There's a
STORM
Coming

The Journey to Rescue and Save My Father

Tributes and Acknowledgement

I dedicate this book to all those who may seem to the rest of us to be absent or invisible in the world, but who are actually still very much alive and yearn to be valued participants in it. I also dedicate it to those caregivers who recognize this and patiently and lovingly seek ways to help them retain their purpose and dignity.

I express my appreciation for the diligence and patience of my formatter and designer, Bart Dawson. Though I have always been considered to be "pickier" than most about product quality, the subject of this particular book commanded an even greater awareness that it be as correct as possible because it is intended to honor God and my father. Bart matched my own concern for quality from text revision to cover design.

"Occasionally, in a man's life, there is a book or manuscript that comes his way that is so far out of the 'norm' and so deep beyond expectation that it requires thought, prayer, and time to assimilate the information through meditation. *There's a Storm Coming*, Kathryn Huddleston's book on the subject of her father's experience with Alzheimer's disease and her passion to help him be the very best he could be physically, mentally and spiritually, is incredible. The journey with glimpses into the family life through the eyes of a person with medical insight, and ultimately, through a spiritual lens, allows us to take a peek behind the veil of one of the most difficult and tough situations facing many Americans today. This book is an incredible read for those who care about the condition of their fellow human beings. I highly recommend *There's a Storm Coming* because for each of us on this journey in life, until that day we see Him as He is, there is a storm coming."

Maury Davis, Senior Pastor, Cornerstone Church, Nashville, TN
Maury Davis Ministries

"God brings hope to us in stormy times. Through these dark years, compassion and care for loved ones is always first. This could not be more true than in this book."

Michelle Stein, Executive Director, Alzheimer's Solutions Project
Center for Health Transformation, Washington, D.C.

"The author captures the reader's attention by recounting in narrative form how she attempted to overcome the many challenges and trials in her 'stormy family' in order to lessen her father's turbulence and bring him peace in the last phase of his life. In an unassuming, authentic way, the author illustrates how she ensured her father remained a valued participant in the world. By giving caregivers concrete ideas on how she helped her father make decisions, ensured up-close and personal interaction with others, and recognized the importance of tone, spirit, and listening to what was 'not said,' they should receive a sense of hope."

E.L. Shoenfelt, Ph.D., Professor of Psychology,
Western Kentucky University, Performance Psychologist

"Kathryn Huddleston believes that while in the midst of other life storms God gave her the gift to care for her father. Here she shares that journey in a very personal, detailed, and honest fashion. Not only is this a wonderful handbook for the Alzheimer's caregiver, Kathryn's story affirms my experience of God's daily walk with those who appear to be absent. While we may see our loved ones as fading way, in reality, they may be living the old gospel hymn, 'Just a Closer Walk with Thee.' This book gives the caregiver, or any reader, great spiritual hope."

Chaplain R. Gene Lovelace, Alive Hospice, Nashville, TN

There's a
STORM
Coming

The Journey to Rescue and Save My Father

Helping my Father Reach His
Physical, Mental, and Spiritual Potential
During His Alzheimer's Disease

Kathryn Huddleston, Ph.D.

*This publication is designed to provide accurate information with regard to the subject matter
covered gleaned from personal experience and authoritative sources. Some of the names have been
changed to protect parties involved in this work of nonfiction.*

*All Scripture quotations are taken from the Holy Bible, King James Version
Cover and Layout by Bart Dawson*

WestBow Press books may be ordered through booksellers or by contacting:

*WestBow Press
A Division of Thomas Nelson
1663 Liberty Drive
Bloomington, IN 47403
www.westbowpress.com
1-(866) 928-1240*

*Because of the dynamic nature of the Internet, any Web addresses or links contained in
this book may have changed since publication and may no longer be valid. The views
expressed in this work are solely those of the author and do not necessarily reflect the
views of the publisher, and the publisher hereby disclaims any responsibility for them.*

*ISBN: 978-1-4497-0597-8 (sc)
ISBN: 978-1-4497-0599-2 (dj)
ISBN: 978-1-4497-0598-5 (e)*

Library of Congress Control Number: 2010935862

Printed in the United States of America

WestBow Press rev. date: 9/30/2010

WESTBOW
PRESS
A DIVISION OF THOMAS NELSON

TABLE OF CONTENTS

PREFACE

Weathering the many battles throughout the five year journey with my father gave me answers about my father's life and mine that I would never have known otherwise. I came to know the truth about why both of us had to endure estrangement and alienation, even before my father became afflicted with the symptoms of the Alzheimer's disease.

I am not even certain that my father had what is technically today known as Alzheimer's, even though it was diagnosed as such, because of the physical and environmental factors at work in his life before the diagnosis. Because he had lived in a fairly cloistered, controlled environment throughout most of it, had for years suffered from aortic stenosis, which restricted the amount of oxygen going into the brain, and because there was no autopsy performed after his death, it is really impossible to know whether he had "Alzheimer's," or another form of severe dementia. And whether it was his frontal lobe that was primarily damaged, or whether it was the temporal lobe which was primarily affected, I cannot say. Researchers disagree anyway on the behavioral differences between the two. I do not attempt to discuss the competing biological theories about the condition because I am not a physician and have no expertise with which to address these issues. In a few instances, I do draw general comparisons between what happens in the brains of those with severe dementia and in the operating systems of more familiar objects, like computers.

What this work does present is an understanding of the impact of this condition on the physical, mental, and spiritual life of a person afflicted with it from a totally up-close and personal view. The intent is to offer suggestions and lessons learned from my own experience. Because I alone took care of my father at home during the last phase of his life, I came to different conclusions about his behavior than some researchers who have studied the disease. The journey my father and I traveled was different than the typical one made by most people who have family members afflicted, not only because he was not institutionalized, but because of the impact of another family member who exhibited symptoms of a more damaging disorder than my father had, but one that was never technically diagnosed by a physician. So destructive was the impact of this disorder that I began to see it more as an evil force which she could not ultimately control. The "storm," which threw its force against both my father and me, prompted me to use every conceivable resource to enable us to survive. My father's reference to the "storm" in responding to the hospital chaplain's question in the last phase of his life appeared to be his word for the overall turbulence from which there was only one escape. When asked what he would wish for if he could have anything, my father replied, "You've got this storm coming, and what you've got to is to get your family together into church, and then God will come and save you." Whether at this time he was thinking of the turbulent family situation, I cannot say. But he knew there was only one refuge.

Pragmatically this book is intended to provide concrete ideas to those caregivers who may be going through some semblance of this journey and feeling alienated and hopeless themselves so they might know the "next" thing to do to survive their own "storms." Hopefully the strategies on how to communicate with, manage, and gain from those whose minds which have become reprogrammed from their original ones as well as those who have always been mentally ill will make the caregiver's road smoother than mine. Responding to the subconscious of the Alzheimer's victims and sensing what is not said at times are far more important than the conscious, logical reasoning and explanations. Caregivers simply have to enter the Alzheimer's world, and if they are able to do this, I believe their path will be less rocky. The great dividend will be that the victim will have a greater dignity and purpose – and so will the caregiver.

Woven throughout the sociological and psychological journey is the major focus of the book, the spiritual journey. And it was this element that ultimately overcame the storm's impact. I came to believe that God intended my entire life to be a training ground for this very journey, in spite of the fact that my family, except for my grandmother, had given me the clear message that I was not a valuable part of it, indeed, that I had no place. Evidently, His purpose for my life was to love the unloved and to care for the unwanted, and I came to finally accept this high calling. My many obstacles had prepared me for and culminated in what I thought at the time was one final great mission: to care for my father in the last phase of his life – after he had lost his other mind and personage. There was no one else who could possibly value this other different person, just as there had been no one else who had been able to love many who crossed my path previously. Ironically, during the past two years, God has reminded me that this mission may not be over after all, because just in these years He has placed others in my path who have been either abandoned, alienated, mentally challenged, and or just who had so many other steep hills to climb that everyone else has run from them. But the stormy journey with my father was a huge one that demanded all my energy, resources, and faith to navigate through it. The waves were high, the waters troubled and long. But the Word of God was steady and helped me get through it more than anything else. Though I took it on to transform my father, it also transformed me. It enabled me ultimately to regain the belief that, even though my father died, God's will for my life did not.

I received clear evidence that God's sovereign plan really *will* be accomplished, in spite of evil attempts to thwart it.

I became Daddy's "partner in Christ" to help him on his journey to heaven. I believe that God enabled my father and me to become connected primarily so that Daddy's beliefs about God and the Kingdom would be reconfirmed and that he would no longer have to suppress his beliefs in Christ and his hope of eternity for fear of enraging my mother. He would have someone who believed him when he said, "Jesus comes into my room every night." From his dying lips, I gained the awareness that I had accomplished this.

But I continue to struggle with the obliqueness of the statement that God has a reason for everything. I still strive to fully believe God has not forgotten me and to recover from this feeling of abandonment. Though understanding the "why" of so many actions helped me endure the "how," throughout this journey with my father, this understanding did not, as I expected, delete the hurt or create total peace because my losses continued after his death. I am still grieved for not being more a part of my father's life before this period and not having the courage to stay with him and hold his hand in his dying minutes. But God knows I was afraid of provoking my mother's ire and creating conflict in the atmosphere surrounding Daddy's death bed in that moment when my father went to be with the Lord. If I make it to heaven, hopefully I'll get the chance to tell Daddy why I didn't stay with him until he took his last breath and maybe I can hold his hand – and not just for a moment.

I pray for the time when my overwhelming burst of grief is calmed into the gentle tear of recollection, when all my anguish about what might have been is overcome by a pensive meditation on all that was. It has begun to happen. But I should not forget or deny the darkness. Perhaps it was sent to illustrate the feeling of abandonment that Christ felt from "His own who received him not," and even that He felt from God for a brief moment on the cross.

In order to *totally* emerge from this passage of grief, from the dark time of isolation, I must question, inquire, and interpret the events that transpired during this five-year journey with my father, however painful reliving it may be, and compare those years with what has happened before and since that journey.

One way to accomplish at least partial peace and bring some order out of the chaos of those years is by integrating and interpreting notes I took each night for over five years about each day's events and then examining them in light of what has happened since. Every night, after my father went to sleep, I wrote down the activities and my thoughts surrounding them at the time. That was about the only way I was able to keep any of my own sanity in the midst of my mother's insanity and my father's confusion. At the time I didn't compare them with previous encounters in my life or analyze them, but just let my jumbled feelings come to the surface, being so determined that this journey with my father would not be lost forever. From time to time, I became aware of many different story lines which could be developed. It seemed that each week during those five years brought another piece of the puzzle, another revelation. It has taken me several years to finally bring that order, to understand what all those notes really meant in the context of my entire life and to put all the pieces together into one coherent piece. Nothing I have ever written before came out of a darker period, and it has taken me this long to have the fortitude to re-live the journey.

Recent events, which only could have come from God, have re-kindled in me the notion that God intends for me to continue to work through the storms, to continue to love the unlovable, the invisible, and those who can never love me back. Now, however, I have some assurance that I will secure safe passage through them. They have given me a sense of urgency to complete this work. Perhaps I can better bind up others' wounds than I did with my father and mother. The journey with both of them helped me to better understand and communicate not just with those who are powerless, but with those who have various mental disabilities, whose brains may be wired differently from mine, because of what *they* have been through. The result, hopefully, will be a book which will demonstrate the strength, courage, honor, and value of my father, a man of God, and how his and my faith in our heavenly Father gave us a common bond with which to build some sort of relationship, regardless of how our brains functioned. Daddy will no longer be invisible. Also I hope it will verify to others that our most important personal mission must be to align our actions with *God's* will for our lives.

PART I

STEPPING INTO TROUBLED WATERS

M any super-achievers are hidden hypomanics. Throughout history there have been many great minds who have suffered from manic depression and mood swings, from Lincoln to Churchill. But the manic depression did not prevent them from accomplishing good results. Sometimes manic activity has served people very well, as in the case of Theodore Roosevelt, who pursued every subject with an insatiable thirst for knowledge and experience, perhaps as a defense against depression. He apparently was a happy manic, who talked incessantly, and his condition seemed partially responsible for his incredibly – almost abnormal – high energy. All these men evidently had enough highs to perform great feats, or their manic depression was mild, lacking the bizarre, excruciating symptoms of those whose manic depression takes over their lives and destroys others in the process.

But my family was not famous, or wealthy. And the manic behaviors of one member were severe enough to take over the life of that afflicted member and, rather than achieving good results, destroy other lives as well. These behaviors, including symptoms of manic depression, paranoia, narcissism, and schizophrenia, became so overwhelming that I couldn't distinguish the difference between them and pure evil. And even now, I can't really tell the difference between the force that appeared to take over my mother's life, which I came to see as a satanic influence, and just her "mental illness," which others who were not around her very much called it. Because she refused to ever admit that she might have *any* problem, except being stuck with my father and me, she resisted suggestions for counseling and just increased her drinking to make herself feel better. The combination of alcohol and these mental conditions resulted in a behavior so bizarre and vitriolic that by the time my father received the Alzheimer's diagnosis, I knew she was not capable of caring for him. Her self-absorption alone left her incapable of considering the needs of anyone but herself. So it was up to me, who had rarely dared admit even to myself that she had any mental disorders, making excuses for her my entire life, to finally face a hidden past and save my father from its effects. When I was very young, all I knew to do was run for cover when one of her raging "fits" began, and once I began an adult, I just tried to stay away from my family much of the time, since I had only mainly been considered a commodity anyway. But after my father was diagnosed with Alzheimer's, God compelled me to take on a new important mission that I had not counted on, to intervene and grope my way through the morass of a tangled past which no longer could be ignored but must be dealt with to save his life.

CHAPTER 1

God is my strength and power; and He is making my way perfect.

—2 Samuel 22:3

INTRODUCTION

About seven years have passed since my father's death, and I still suffer great anguish and pain. This pain is different from the pain that results when people lose parents who protected them throughout their lives. In my case, it results mainly from feeling that *I* didn't do enough to protect my *parent*. My nightmares continue of trying to save my father from some horrible dark evil. We both try to flee, and I wake up exhausted. I had so hoped that the blocked, dark, and hopeless passages my father and I encountered during the last phase of his life would by now be transformed into open, light paths, filled with new possibilities and the assurance that my father had finally attained the peace and love he was denied through most of his life. I had also prayed and hoped that God would let me know that I had done all that was possible to restore some of his dignity and help him along to the gates of heaven. Though over these years there have been brief moments when God has sent me little signs of assurance, until recently I have remained dubious. In some ways these past seven years have been as difficult as those previous five ones because I have mostly felt abandoned by Him.

Repeatedly I had been told by my family through the years that I had no rights and didn't belong. And then, after my father died, no longer did anyone have to keep up any pretenses. On the day of his little memorial service, I admit that I, too, actually breathed a sigh of relief because I would no longer be compelled to pander or cater to a family to which I had always only been a convenient commodity when things needed to be done and paid for. I could at least place a dash, if not a period, to a very dark and painful past.

I thought I would now have peace. I could rest and reflect on our journey which I know was intended by God to get me back on the straight and narrow gate to eternity. And I could get back to work, work that for years had largely defined me. Immediately following my father's death, I was almost convinced that God would help me recover some of my past life's activities, confident that He would help my pain subside and decrease my losses after so many years of suffering for His sake and trying to attend to those who had no one else. However, the opposite happened.

Death, though freeing my father from this world, did not free me from it. Until the past couple of years, the shadow of darkness actually grew greater. I lost all contact with my family. And I never expect to have it again because I had been my father's advocate. Doing battle on his behalf was evidently an error in their minds for which I will never be forgiven. On the day of my father's service, seven years ago, I had the sense that it wouldn't be long before I was totally dumped from the family album because I had never really been considered a part of it. But it still seems a little surreal that anyone can be just deleted from an entire family and town, much like one would, with the click of a key, empty the trash bin of a computer. Therefore, it is beyond me why my bookcases and walls are still dotted with pictures of the entire family – pictures of people I probably will never see again – as I perpetuate the charade of one time belonging to a family. While I have never felt really at home in this world, still I have allowed it to batter and shape me into thinking that everyone should belong to someone while here.

Throughout most of my life, I had felt like unclaimed baggage, and so I thought I was pretty much immune from the effects of feeling "excommunicated" from my family after my grandmother died 30 years ago. However, apparently I was more affected than I realized. While I was still able to work full-time, my focus on my business masked the deeper pain of alienation. Perhaps this inordinate pain and grief I have always felt for others who are alienated and whose plights appear hopeless is rooted in my own abandonment from an earthly family.

But for years after my father's death, I was challenged to again feel the importance of purpose found in caring for and truly identifying with the pain of others who have no one else. I shied away from it, in part because I had become too absorbed in my own losses, in part because it called up too heavily the suffering during the journey with him, and in part because I didn't have as much physical stamina to cope with it as I once had. Surely, I had done enough for God and thought that He would now help *me* get back *my* life.

So immediately after my father's death I sought to find another venue for at least some of my training and professional speaking work which in large part had defined me for many years, hoping to discover assignments which might mirror this "real" work and help me forget the previous traumatic five years. I didn't allow any time to transition from the world I had left behind but was just determined to get on with it. So those forces which should have been unleashed in the grieving period were just contained. If I let them out, then I would have to relive that chaotic and dark time. This refusal to take time to grieve probably contributed to my unsuccessful attempts to work where

I could again use my skills and knowledge employed in my training business. Those who interviewed me may have sensed my artificial exuberance. Consequently, the failure to land these parallel jobs exacerbated my post-traumatic stress, consequent physical pain, and continuing financial stress of the previous years. As time passed, this frustration mushroomed and, with it, my physical and mental pain.

Instead of "getting on with my life," subsequent events just sent me into a greater depression which lasted for years, including the discovery that my father's will had been tampered with right after he died and my inheritance taken as a partial penalty for taking care of him. This was my mother's final confirmation that I was never really considered a part of the family. My only activities were the continued teaching of Bible classes, which I must admit had become almost bothersome, a little volunteer work for the elderly and disabled, and teaching a couple of college writing classes. None of these reflected the 23 year business which had provided me with the sense of really making a difference in people's lives and enough money to help those who had fewer material possessions than me.

My lack of success seemed to suggest that God had no more use for me either and really cared little about *my* life. I felt totally abandoned by Him. Though I had been able to manage being deleted from my earthly family, it was different with God. He had been the one to whom I had always clung. He alone had enabled my father and me to weather the many storms and confront so much evil during the last five years of his life. For years following his death, this feeling of abandonment increased as I continued to suffer major financial and personal losses.

Only during the past two years have I begun to believe that maybe just the fact that I still *long* to be claimed by God may be some evidence that He *does* claim me. Also becoming connected with various people dropped by the wayside – and then by my side – has confirmed what evidently has always been God's priority mission for my life.

Maybe this priority mission was *not* providing leadership training that I had done for 23 years, *not* fighting for accountability and higher standards in the teaching profession as I had done for 30 years, and *not* working as a political activist that I had been for over 25 years. Perhaps it was becoming connected with various ones who have reminded me of the aim of much of my "other" activities, which had little to do with corporate America or government. These activities existed before the journey with my father. They existed before becoming a teacher, beginning my training business, and becoming politically involved. Those whom God has recently placed in my path, just like those He placed in my life before my journey with my father, have either become invisible in our society, been abandoned by family and friends, or suffered terrific hardships. Yet they have either retained or regained their faith in God. Those times of interaction with them, as well as with my father, were periods when I felt closest to God. They have compelled me to get back on *His* track. They have reminded me to be grateful for having a bed to sleep in, or enough to eat.

They have reminded me that God's long-term objectives for us may be very different from those which we develop, and if we believe the admonitions of Jesus, our primary focus shouldn't be on financial and achievement objectives this world promotes anyway. Actually those goals and activities we may have deemed as "asides," which often come under the "Additional Information" heading on our resumes, may turn out to be the most important ones when we get to our interview with God. They may be God's "Selection Standards."

Often our conscious ideas conflict with that inner urge to become what God intends us to be and do. Before the journey with my father, I had accomplished what I thought were important business objectives. During the journey with him, I came to see those as relatively insignificant compared to the sense of urgency I came to have surrounding the new mission God handed me. My sense of purpose resulted from ensuring that my father regained a piece of his dignity and knew that there was at least one person in the world who saw his value. The journey with him compelled me to get back on the track I was on before my business became successful, to remember all those who had crossed my path who had no one else but me to love and care for them. But then he died, and so with his death went that sense of purpose.

What I failed to realize is that this journey with my father was only the major *component* in God's mission for my life. I have since concluded those activities which had virtually no relationship to my gainful work for 23 years *did* relate to what evidently was and still is God's priority for my life: to love the unloved, the neglected, the invisible, the alienated, the helpless. Only years after Daddy's death did other people, whom God placed before me, compel me to remember this primary mission. These connections have not been coincidences. Only God could have been responsible for bringing me into their lives to help them reach their potential because evidently no one else had noticed their plight, or if they had, they had run away from it. I had prayed so hard to be rid of the torment of regretting that earlier in my life I had not made more of an effort to attend to my father's wounded heart, and though some of that torment remains, it has begun to lessen because God is giving me the chance to make up that deficit. He has also verified through them that

God may claim me after all.

It was up to me and me alone to really listen to my father, to try to restore some dignity and self-esteem that had become eroded over the years. It was my job to love him unconditionally – when no one else ever could. I am thankful that I came to know and understand a man who even none of my immediate family appeared to really know or value. Obviously, I came to a different conclusion about his life than they did. As my dividend, I came to know his sweetness, a sweetness that was recovered from his earlier years – before he became sullen and dour, as a result of having been beaten down and unable to control his fate. Over our five year journey together, my friends, who became Daddy's friends, saw only a gentle spirit. Some remarked about the "light" that shone from him. And other friends and relatives from his earlier days, whom we visited, thought he was very much like he had always been.

That memory remains, and for that I am grateful.

We created our own world, my father and I, more out of the spiritual and unconscious than the conscious. That world held its own language, its own inhabitants, and its own meaning. Our communication was authentic because it involved a personal commitment. Our world was one in flux because every conversation and every action changed both our brains, and every conversation and action was a little different from every other one. There were fragments that were similar, but the whole was never the same.

The truth is supposed to set us free, and the answers to many questions garnered throughout the journey to rescue and save my father did seem to set me free from much imposed evil and create some peace. But was the sacrifice of losing any further communication with my family worth the battle to save my father? Was it worth losing my inheritance? Was it worth losing my business? Was it worth losing much of my physical health? At the time of my father and mother's deaths, my answer to these questions was "yes." I came to believe that my father really did love me all along. Not long before he died, when most of his faculties had failed him, he said clearly, "I always loved you; I don't care what the rest of them said about you." He had never dumped that love in any trash bin of his brain. Contrary to what had seemed to me to be the opposite throughout my life, all along and even during his dying days, he said he had loved me. And now he had nothing to fear from anyone else for acknowledging what I had come to suspect in our journey together – that even in the late stage of his Alzheimer's condition, he had not adopted what my mother, brother, and nephews had said and thought of me.

My father and I compressed two lives into a few short years. I know that death tends to bury errors. I know my father had defects. Perhaps he should have been able to stand up *for* me and up *to* his wife during the years preceding this final phase of his life. But God gave me answers as to why he couldn't. In the only way he knew how, Daddy saved me. He saw to it that I became protected by one of God's angels, Daddy's mother, and God finally allowed me to finally care for her by caring for her son.

At the beginning of our journey together, I had already come to realize that for any mission to be successful, one must envision the ultimate goal. I did know the aim was to rescue my father, but I did not fully understand from what, nor did I know the rules or what we would have to endure for the desired end. After my father's death, I knew what the "next thing" was that I must do: relive our journey and remember how we had become connected in spite of the Alzheimer's and a lifelong absence from each other, through a commonality that transcended the mind and years, a belief in God and a trust in His will. Even though at times I really had to work to keep this trust and unrelenting determination to keep on "keeping on," God enabled me to continue. I knew I had to finish my writing I had started when I first began my mission of rescuing Daddy. It would be painful, but it must be done. We must keep track of the stories of our lives because they remind us of who we have been - and perhaps still may be. Writing about them reminds us where we have come from, so we may have a greater appreciation of where we are going. Perhaps the lessons about God and His power and the understanding I had gained about my father that this journey had given me could be passed to others who might better know the "next" thing to do.

This journey is not so important because it belongs just to my father and me, but parts of it may be recognizable to others and therefore help them.

My hope is that my inner darkness I suffered will not be a stumbling block to others, but instead translate into the realization that a person can still accomplish God's work in spite of it. Darkness can be a good thing because it forces us to feel the darkness that Christ was bound to have felt many times. Furthermore, "feelings" are subordinate to Truth. How we "feel" about what God thinks of us isn't necessarily what is true. Even though Christ's face may become blurred and hidden during very difficult times, one must believe God's Word, which is Truth for the Christian, which tells us that He's still around - as long as we haven't been overcome with evil. I pray that my interior suffering from becoming alienated from family and *feeling* alienated from God will *not* lead the reader to the conclusion that I ever lost my love for Him or my inner belief that all things work together for *His* purposes, not mine.

I have attempted to record the many small favors others did for my father and me to illustrate that during that journey, I was given confirmation that

God had not left us. Since his death, especially recently, I have been overwhelmed with grief for others whom I have barely known, and perhaps this response is a sign that the Holy Spirit *continues* to abide in me. Maybe the pain and darkness I experienced in my journey with my father even intensified my anguish for others. Certain events recorded in the last chapter confirm that my life-long mission has not quite ended, and I am once again realizing I can perform God's work in spite of the doubt about what He thinks of me.

CHAPTER 2

For now we see through a glass, darkly; but then face to face: now I know in part; but then shall I know even as also I am known.

–1 Corinthians 13:12

FACING PAINFUL TRUTHS

It was 1998, and somehow in spite of a volatile mother apparently afflicted with various mental conditions, who seemed to hold utter disdain for me, and a father who seemed to consider me non-existent, I had been able to build a relatively successful teaching and training career. This career consisted of conducting training for corporations and the Department of the Army for the prior 22 years. I had authored a book a few years before and had gained credibility for my work in the quality and leadership area. However, here I was at middle age in my life, being forced to face uncomfortable, painful truths that would put an end to this career and almost make me totally forget my identity I had built up over the years.

The first painful truth was that I was *still* controlled and manipulated by my mother. I was still fearful of her rage, still pacifying and accommodating her. I was still postponing my life to take care of her. It was depressing and scary to realize that there was little difference in the way I reacted to my mother at this point in my life and the way I reacted to her when I was ten.

However, there *was* one difference. If my fear did make me a victim (and, contrary to my denial of it, the few who knew a little about my life insisted that I was a primary victim of a mentally ill family), now my fear took on a greater dimension, and led to the second painful truth. Daddy was clearly a more helpless victim than I was and more helpless than he had been earlier in his life. His life was actually now at risk due to his deteriorating health. I realized with horror that the manic disorders, or just plain evil, which had overtaken my mother's life, could, as it had already done in other ways, manifest itself in even more malevolent behavior towards him. With every step I took, I had to consider the impact of my mother's rage on his helpless condition.

So the time had come to totally shift my priorities. Though it seemed to me and others that I had always placed my mother's welfare above everything else, I still had managed not to be around her too much during my adult life. But about five and a half years before Daddy's death I made the decision to intervene in order to attempt to restore some of his dignity and health, which had been taken from him. I will always remember the day of that decision because it was a day which would change my own life forever.

I was visiting my parents' home about 180 miles from mine. My mother had mentioned that she had taken Daddy to a doctor in a nearby city, and he was given a series of tests. The diagnosis was Alzheimer's. Oh, no, not Alzheimer's! Anything but this. Then I didn't know that the symptoms of "Alzheimer's" were not very different from the symptoms of other forms of dementia which in earlier times had been given other names. I didn't know that Alzheimer's can't really be diagnosed until *after* death through an autopsy. I didn't know that all Alzheimer's victims don't exhibit the same behaviors. I had always known elderly people who had become senile, or who had what some called, "hardening of the arteries," or who had some form of dementia. But at this time, I really didn't know much of anything about Alzheimer's – except that it was a dreaded word such as "cancer" used to be. I was aware that Daddy's major artery, his aorta, had been restricted for years, and I had often wondered if this blockage was affecting the amount of oxygen his brain received. I had also read that the part of the brain that doesn't get the oxygen becomes starved for it and might manifest itself in some type of stroke, which is why I had often urged my mother to allow my father to have the surgery to unblock this artery. But, until the previous year, when my father's habits and behaviors began to slightly change, and his short-term memory became a little fuzzier, I had never really considered that the part of the brain which could be affected would be the portion of the brain that holds the short-term memory and result in a diagnosis of Alzheimer's.

Even though I had noticed some increased confusion in Daddy and some subtle changes toward me during that past year, I rationalized it away as stress resulting from all the many years of living with my mother. "Please, God, don't let this be the case with Daddy," I begged. "Let there be some mistake." I knew Daddy had always been powerless against my mother, so perhaps he just couldn't pass whatever test the doctor had given him, for fear he would not give the right answers in front of her. So I telephoned the doctor myself, thinking I might give her a little history of the situation to ascertain if there could be some other explanation. The doctor spoke indifferently and coldly, as she defined the part of the brain that was non-functioning and confirmed the diagnosis. She offered no encouragement whatsoever.

This diagnosis was the nightmare that I had long dreaded. My mother was the last person in the world who would ever be willing *or able* to make adjustments needed for an Alzheimer's victim. What in the world would or could Daddy or I do now? This was the beginning of the end of Daddy's life.

But I did not fully realize at the time that I was about to embark upon the biggest battle of my *own* life, ensuring that what life my father had left had some quality and purpose. Nor did I know at the time that it was also the beginning of the end of my life as it had been: the end of my career, my financial security, my interaction with nieces and nephews, my social life, and much of my own health.

After this diagnosis, I knew that things were bound to get much worse for my father, as if they hadn't been bad enough already. I realized I must begin traveling to East Tennessee to visit my parents more often. The very thought of having to do this made my mouth dry and my stomach queasy. I really didn't want to do it.

For the previous thirty years, I had lived about three hours driving time from them and thus had an excuse not to visit too frequently. Though I had continued to imagine that each trip to see them might be productive and good, the trips always turned out to be dark and depressing. Those trips took me days - even weeks - to recover from. Nor had sending my mother on trips, giving her gifts, and revising my work schedule to accommodate her demands been successful in achieving any happiness for her because they had not lessened her anger at feeling that somehow life had dealt her a bad deal.

My mother was always and forever the victim. I never really knew the origin of this feeling, just that I had tried throughout my life to make her feel less deprived. But because my efforts almost always ended in a feeling of futility, I tried to put her out of my mind during the actual conduct of my work. Years ago I learned to effect the notion that everything was great in my own life, because if I hinted otherwise, I would receive the responses, "You're killing me," and "You're worrying me to death." So when I was hospitalized, or I had lost a contract or job or boyfriend, my mother never knew about it.

Up until this point, my father had been almost a non entity to me. My mother had ensured that we had never in our entire lives had the opportunity to know each other directly, without her intervention, and to be together. I telephoned their home frequently, but even these telephone calls had never given me the chance to talk to my father. I will always regret that I hadn't figured out a way to just see him more before he had developed this condition - without the interference of my mother.

It hadn't mattered that much to me up until now, as I had been able to put both of them out of my mind when I was working.

It mattered now.

Even before the diagnosis, I came to believe that things had gotten worse in that house. About a year before the Alzheimer's condition was discovered, my father began answering the phone. I thought this was odd, as my mother had always guarded it. On one of these occasions, I asked him how he was, and he whispered, "I don't know where she is." On another one, he whispered, "She's laying out there drunk...shhh." Though I realized that Alzheimer's victims often exhibit some paranoid delusions, something about this statement rang true. Later, after I came to know Daddy directly, I became tormented that I hadn't figured out even then that he was crying out for help.

During my first visits, my father expressed how grateful he was to have me come and begged me not to leave. "Why don't you stay with us all summer?" he pleaded. Something had definitely changed for the worse, and whatever it was, it had negatively affected him. Gradually he began to make statements that implied more cry for help. He stated several times, "You can't imagine how she treats me." I, however, occasionally having heard varying versions of this idea before, was afraid to think much about what this could actually mean now. Most would have thought that this statement was typical of someone in the beginning phases of Alzheimer's, and I at that time actually wanted to believe that it was. But because I knew all too well my mother's rage and some sort of mania, I realized there could be more to it. I also knew that I myself had never been able to do anything about it.

My father was forced to endure much more of my mother's irritability and rage than I, since he had had to live with it for well over 50 years. But how in the world could I change that now? He had always placed her needs and wishes above everyone, especially himself, because he had loved her so much. Even when I had gently tried to take up for him in earlier times, Mother would begin screaming, and Daddy then would appear to want me to leave. Besides, I rationalized, until recently he could get away, at least for short periods of time. He could drive to the local Dairy Queen, golf course, or to the hardware store. I also rationalized that since my mother had for so long also complained about Daddy, maybe the traits of both parents had increased. Since old age had set in, they were bound to have a greater impact on them than previously.

After this diagnosis, though, I stopped rationalizing. I couldn't turn a deaf ear to what God had shown me. I realized it was up me alone to effect any change in the situation, since my brother didn't want to hear any of it, when I tried talking with him. Like my mother, he never wanted to hear anything that would make him uncomfortable or interfere with his activities. I actually had discovered this before the Alzheimer's diagnosis. So, even though I dreaded doing so, I knew I had to visit more often. However stressful the trips already had been for me, after I spoke to the doctor, I realized that I would have to make them to really get a glimpse of what was happening.

So I framed them as a benefit to my mother. "Mother, I know it's so tough for you. I would like to come and stay one or two nights a week and make them coincide with your bridge days."

I was forced to confront a reality I had actually known on some level for many years. As a child, I had experienced my mother's wrath and narcissism, but as an adult I had been able to get away from it. Now, once again, I had to face it head on and deal with it, along with my mother's different personalities, since I knew there was no one else to save my father. Would my behavior resemble the helpless ten-year old again? Would I become insane myself in the process? I shuddered at that prospect.

I had also known for many years that my mother had controlled Daddy as long as I could remember, and that he, fearing her rage, had allowed himself *to be* controlled. But when his mind was intact, he could get in *his* car and leave for a little while to get away from her anger. Now it was different. He had become more helpless as my mother and brother had conspired to take all control away from him. I later learned that they had wrested his property and assets away from him years before the Alzheimer's diagnosis. My mother had gained power of attorney, and my brother had become alternate power of attorney by manipulating Daddy into signing the document, rationalizing it as an action done because of his heart condition. I had realized that my brother had become totally critical of my father and totally supportive of my mother – regardless of how wrong her actions were. However, I did not know the degree of deception until later. I came to learn that Daddy was aware of this power being taken from him, but he was powerless against the two of them. I still hear his refrain in my head, "They've taken everything from me." It will not go away.

The trips verified that my mother's resentment and anger had worsened and had begun to manifest itself in insidious ways against Daddy, who by this time was well on his way to becoming totally helpless against her. My mother was not missing greeting my father in the morning, asking him for advice, or having a conversation with him, as many who lose their loved ones to Alzheimer's. She had *never* really interacted with him in these ways. What *was* missing was his ability to take care of *her*. I did not doubt that my father had begun to exhibit some unusual behaviors, but my mother refused to consider his behavioral changes as a direct consequence of the disease when he resisted being controlled, or wanted something different to eat than he had always eaten. She could not accept that he usually was not in control of these changes. These visits also confirmed that her schizophrenic traits had deepened.

On my mother's bridge day, I traveled early on that morning from

Nashville to get there in time for her to have lunch with her friends before the bridge game. "What in the world am I going to do for several hours with Daddy?" I worried. He doesn't know me, and I don't know him. Cookeville. That was the answer. He always wanted to go visit the town he grew up in where people had respected and remembered him, and did still. So I began these sojourns by driving Daddy to his beloved Cookeville, the small town about 80 miles from their home that he talked about so much and where most of his relatives lived and where his parents were buried. It was during these trips that I became aware of still more painful truths.

For example, quite by accident I discovered that Daddy was virtually blind. He was unable to read a road sign on the interstate since he couldn't make out the letters. Since this discovery had occurred after his Alzheimer's diagnosis, I wondered how much of the first test for Alzheimer's was valid. I realized that he would not have been able to read the print. It was also on one of these trips that Daddy began to speak a little about his money. "They have taken all my money," he stated quite clearly. At this time my father's cognitive skills had only begun to deteriorate, and he understood what had been done to him, making the concealed actions more painful. I tried not to think too much about that statement then.

During these little journeys, I realized more and more that my life was going to be radically altered for the next several years. My work, travel requirements, friends, and schedule: all would have to come second to rescuing and saving my father.

About six months following my discovery of his physical and mental problems, I began more aggressively trying to overcome some of them. Always trying to think of ways to reduce my mother's anger, I had a thought that might accomplish both purposes. At the very least perhaps it would reduce her sense of deprivation.

I telephoned one of my mother's friends to get her idea on what I might give my mother for Mother's Day that would make her happy. I had already thought of a short trip for her and a few of her close friends so that she might get away and that I might have an opportunity to spend time just with my father. The friend thought it would be a grand idea and offered to drive. "That sounds great; I think she would like that." I then arranged the mini-vacation to North Carolina, prepaying the hotel and meal expenses for the four of them. Over the phone I mentioned it to my mother. "Mother, I know you do so much, and I would like to give you this trip. I'll come and stay at the house with Daddy...." Cutting me off, she resisted the idea at first, insisting that Daddy would never stay with me without her. But on second reflection, she decided she wanted the trip more than she wanted control for a couple of days.

Before they left, I asked my mother if there was anything particular she would like me to do. She said there was nothing. Realizing by now it had been a long time since my father had seen a dentist, I asked her if I might take him to have his teeth cleaned. She actually agreed! Since their dog had been suffering for a while, I also mentioned that I could take the dog to the vet to see if he could get some relief. Mother just shrugged her shoulders and sighed, "You can do this, but he's old. I don't want to spend any money on him." "You won't have to Mother," I responded as quietly as possible.

In my memory, those days were the first time ever that I had been allowed to have direct interaction with my father, without the company of my mother. It was the first time I had realized how starved Daddy was for affection. Though it was an awkward time, it was significant because I discovered so much about his state of mind and the degree of neglect he had suffered. He was in the early stages of Alzheimer's - or something akin to it - and I had not been alone with him at all since the diagnosis. I had not yet figured out the reasons for the difference in behavior towards me in the presence of and away from my mother through the years and was therefore a little concerned about the interaction between us. Keenly aware that Daddy had always seemed to want to express some affection to me in my mother's absence, I was somewhat wary about being alone with him. Therefore I planned a bunch of activities: work in the yard, trip to the vet, a trip to a little Amish settlement - anything to keep his attention off me. And I was confident that I could manage any unexpected behaviors.

On the way back from an Amish settlement on the first day, out of the blue Daddy asked, "Will you be my wife?" A little nervous about this question because of previous encounters, and because I hadn't yet figured everything out, I quickly responded, "God probably wouldn't like that." And Daddy quickly and silently responded, "Oh, I'm sorry; that's right." He continued, "Jenny Dillon won't even let me hold her hand. She won't let me kiss her. One time when we were in bed, and I tried to kiss her, she kicked me. That's why my arm has always hurt." He had had a lot of pain in one of his arms over the years, and this was the first time I understood the reason. For a while I thought he was talking about his sister, when he said that "Jenny Dillon" wouldn't even touch his hand because that was the name of his sister who had shown mainly disdain for him and had finagled some of his father and mother's property and assets from him many years prior. But I thought it was a little strange that she could have kicked him in the arm when they were in bed together, unless he was talking about a time when they were little children. Soon afterwards I realized this was the name he had transferred to his wife. By this time, he seemed to have co-mingled his sister and his wife. Or maybe not. Actually, he could have known exactly what he was doing because for many years my mother despised his sister and would never have wanted to be thought of as being like her. So it could have been my father's way of showing my mother that he knew the two had become alike. At that time, given the little contact I had had with him, I could not be certain what Daddy thought, because, though his senses remained keen, he had difficulty verbally expressing what he really thought. Although he had rarely expressed his own needs and wants earlier, at least he had the capacity to. Now he had lost much of that ability.

He had asked me a few times over the past year if I would just hold his hand since "Jenny Dillon" wouldn't. Oh, this pain was becoming greater to bear. By then I knew how important affection and touch are to people with Alzheimer's and how little my father was obviously getting. This man had been so starved for any crumb of attention and affection. So much of the past was gushing out. His words tore my heart in two.

Still, on the first night, I felt a little trepidation about going to sleep because this was the first time in my entire life when Daddy and I had been alone during the night, and I didn't know how he would behave with me in the house after bedtime. I was moving in unchartered territory. Before I drifted off, I heard him tiptoe into my room. He began to climb into bed with me. I didn't know if he forgot and thought it was my mother's bed, or something else was going on in his brain. If I had known then how deprived he had been of affection and how much he needed it, I probably would have just let him lie there and at least hold his hand for a little while. But at the time I had not really fully known how needy he was for it from my mother, or just anybody. My uncertainty about what was really going on prompted me to ask, "Daddy, don't you think you'll be more comfortable in your own room?" He didn't say anything, but I just led him back. The next night he stayed in his room; later I hated to think my behavior might have reflected my mother's.

These few days gave me the opportunity to begin to try to overcome some of Daddy's neglect. I took him to an optometrist who confirmed what I had suspected: that he was virtually blind. The doctor found that he had sustained an injury on one of his eyes that made it un-correctable, and he had a cataract so big on the other that there was very little sight out of that one either. His cataract could be corrected, but one eye had been so badly injured and consequently had so much scar tissue that it was irreparable, even with surgery. Daddy said that "Jenny Dillon" had damaged his eye when she kicked him as he tried to kiss her. This may or may not have been the same incident when she had kicked his arm, but the point is that it appeared my mother had aggressively resisted my father's affections, and probably many times over because Daddy often referred to her unwillingness to hold his hand.

I immediately purchased him some glasses from the prescription written by the optometrist who also recommended an ophthalmologist at a nearby town. The glasses would help him a little until my mother might allow Daddy to have surgery on the one eye. I knew it would be an uphill battle to convince her, and it would take some time. Up until then, Daddy had been trying to read with Wal-Mart glasses. I recalled my mother's exasperated tone when she insisted, "He's not interested in reading anymore." She had read just enough of the Alzheimer's literature to be really dangerous. No wonder his interest in reading had left him!

The next day I took him to have his teeth cleaned. Daddy had always been so proud of his teeth; he still had them all and hardly ever had any cavities, even though the Coumadin had yellowed them. But since it had been a couple of years since they had been cleaned, this trip gave me the opportunity to get this done. I figured my mother might have a fit about me addressing his teeth *and* eyes, but I hoped that her anger would abate since neither would cost her any money. I knew I must capitalize on the freedom we had during these days.

While my mother and her friends were gone, Daddy and I also cleaned up the yard, cleaned out the utility room, and took the dog to the vet. I had dinner prepared upon their return. That day I said to Daddy, "Mother's going to be in such a good mood." He sadly and quietly replied, "Don't count on it."

When my mother and friends pulled into the driveway, Daddy and I went out to greet them. I invited her friends in to eat, but they declined. I thought, with my mother's friends present, this might be the safest time to mention that I had taken Daddy to the optometrist who had recommended an ophthalmologist. I knew they would know the doctor who was recommended and might confirm his credibility. There would be a much greater chance of Mother accepting the word of her friends rather than mine. "Yes, of course, Dr. Reid; he performed my surgery. He is one of the best," declared Rachael, who had driven them on their trip. I breathed a sigh of relief. My mother might at least take her friend's word; I knew there wasn't much chance she would take mine.

As my mother, father and I walked into the house, my optimism quickly disappeared. "Mother, how was your trip?" I asked. Mother began complaining about the hotel they had stayed in, the length of the trip, Rachael's driving, and various and sundry other conditions that were less than perfect. Oh, no, not a good sign. Daddy was right. I hoped, however, she might cheer her up by telling her what Daddy and I had accomplished.

This was absolutely the worst thing I could have done. Immediately Mother complained, "All you want to do is come up here and take control of everything!" Always fearing doing anything without first getting permission from her, I asked her to smell some milk in the refrigerator that I noticed had spoiled. I hadn't dared throw it away without asking her. I thought this would show her that she really had control again. She jerked the milk carton out of my hand and threw it at me. I later thought this over-the-top behavior even for my mother was the result of my taking Daddy to have his eyes examined. She had not given me the permission to do this.

I swallowed hard, took a deep breath, and quickly changed the subject. I mentioned that I had found out at the vet that their dog had a very severe bone problem and bad arthritis. The veterinarian had suggested a medicine for those problems, which I had purchased. And since the dog was eaten up with fleas, I let them give him a treatment and purchased a two months' supply of that medicine as well.

Her voice rising, Mother scolded, "You had no business taking the dog to the vet....He's old, what do you expect?" Um, I thought. This was the exact same statement she usually said about Daddy if I alluded to anything which might be hurting him. "What did *that* cost?" she screamed. She almost always screamed. "Mother, it didn't cost you anything." Again, she accused, "All you want to do is control everything." She seemed to spit out the words, as she rolled her eyes. Though I had told her that I would be taking the dog to the vet, I concluded that either one of her other personalities was at work at the time or her bi-polar tendencies were running at high speed, since she denied she had ever consented to this action.

Although I hated leaving Daddy alone with that anger, I thought it best to get out of her path. I said as objectively as I could that I might drive over to see my brother and sister-in-law who lived only a few miles away. My mother said nothing. I could feel my tears well up as I noted the expression on Daddy's face. I simply had to get out of there before she could see any of them. Throughout my life, she always seemed triumphant when she made me cry.

Upon returning, I found Daddy in bed even though it wasn't even dark. Over the years he had to frequently retreat to his little room when he just couldn't take his wife's tirades any more, just as I had to retreat to mine for the same reasons. His eyes were red; he obviously had been crying. My heart was broken for him. He was so proud of what he and I had accomplished, but he knew her even better than I did. I went into his room. He didn't say a word but simply shook his head and took my hand. At that moment I realized what he had suffered throughout all those married years. I wondered how many times he had wanted to speak candidly to me but was afraid of what she might do to both of us if he did.

Though I had come to sense some difference in my father's behavior – especially towards me – others in the family had denied it. Perhaps because Mother had always told him what to do, what to say, what to eat, and what to be, it was hard to tell any difference. And because he had rarely ever complained about anything, one had to be sensing enough to figure out the gap. This was not a trait members in this self-absorbed family were prone to possess. The reality was that no one had noticed that a silent death had taken place in his head.

UNDERSTANDING PAST ACTIONS

Things were beginning to clear up for me, things I had not dared think about before. The clarity was creating more internal pain. Not really understanding why throughout my life my father had not come to my defense, I began to realize that he indeed had tried to protect me in his own way. He alone knew of the potential of Mother's rage. I now understood my grandmother's statements. She had raised me, and she had rarely ever said anything negative about anyone. But she had dropped hints about the problem along the way with occasional statements such as, "No one will ever know what your father has had to go through" or "A woman needs to learn how to control her temper." The second comment had been made when she noticed red marks on my cheek after I had been slapped. Up until this time I had hoped that the first comment was just a mother empathizing with her son. Now I can only imagine how many times she had to bite her lip to keep from saying anything when she observed my mother's behaviors and their impact on my father. I was beginning to think that some dark force had been holding Mother as victim. I was learning many answers to many questions, and they were all very disturbing.

The next several years were to teach me more painful truths about the tragic life my father had led. My family's policy was "Don't ask, don't tell, and don't feel." I had been vaguely aware that my father had suffered through some of the same bluster and volatility that I had, but because the memories were so painful, I had not faced his suffering head-on until recent discoveries.

I began to realize how neglected and abused he had been. I began to think that if I could reduce my mother's anger and take greater responsibility for him, she might somehow remember how much her husband had cared for *her* over the years. That realization might lessen her intent to carry out her plan which I was just beginning to get wind of, to dispose of Daddy in some facility.

So I thus embarked on a mission to help both parents more by giving Daddy opportunities he had never had the chance to have and to save him from my mother's own mental disorders. And by getting him away from my mother, I might also reduce the burden on her. As a life-long advocate of elderly rights, and care giver for some elderly orphans, I had taken several into my home, and I began to be tormented by the fact that I was being forced to stand by and watch my own father lose everything. Hopefully it was not too late to give him back some of his eroded self-respect and peace. I found myself racing against time to restore both. I am still grieved that my father led such an isolated and unloved life before I became a part of it and that he had never had the chance to really know a person who could truly value him.

I had read that those who are alienated and have little social interaction are more prone to dementia. To this day, I blame myself for not helping him many years ago to get away from this situation. But I also knew that until the five years preceding his death my mother had prevented me from any direct involvement with him outside of her presence.

So with each awareness, I became more determined to make up for my father's life of sacrifice and suffering and give him some degree of comfort, dignity, and joy in his last days. I was also compelled to step up my efforts to change my mother's attitude about my father. I realized it would mean new sacrifices from me, but I had to be willing for one more helpless.

During those years, I had many opportunities to witness my father's courage and bravery. It had only been during the Alzheimer's years that I had had the chance to know him, apart from my mother. How ironic and painful to finally come to know your father after he's begun losing his mind! But as with everything, I had begun to realize that God had finally given me this opportunity to discover truths which I had never known, and it's all about His timing, His agenda, not our own.

CHAPTER 3

Thou hast seen it; for thou beholdest mischief and spite, to requite it with thy hand: the poor committeth himself unto thee; thou art the helper of the fatherless.

—Psalms 10:14

IT'S DADDY'S TURN

I had spent most of my life trying to accommodate, placate, and satisfy Mother. Though I intellectually realized she may have had some type of mental disorder which rendered her incapable of thinking of others' needs, I was still worn out with trying to parent what I had emotionally come to just see as a bratty demanding child. Gifts, trips, rearranging my work and my personal life: all had been done in an effort to get her to become less angry and more joyful. And I must admit the few moments when I had managed to create a little momentary happiness for her had been moments of my own greatest happiness. My social worker and my grief counselor have often asked me why I thought that was. I don't know. But I do know they were fleeting moments, and nothing had worked for very long. So finally, after many years of unsuccessfully trying to make her happy, I was going to take the advice of friends and get on with my own life.

But God had other plans. With the painful realization of Daddy's predicament, I realized it was now time for him. My grandmother had rescued me, and I would now rescue her son. "God help me to walk bravely," I prayed. Mustering up the courage to again pose the possibility of Daddy's sight problem to my mother, she again resented the question and sighed with her dismissive rubber stamp remark: "He's old...What do you expect? I'm the one who needs cataract surgery."

This response forced me to remember the countless times I heard my mother tell Daddy what to do and what to say. I thought about the extent of ridicule inflicted on him through the years. "I've taken care of him for the past twenty five years," she frequently complained to her friends in front of him. That in itself was bad enough, but the worst part was that it was a lie. Daddy had always taken care of Mother - longer than I had. He had cajoled, pampered, pandered to, and endured her. He had cooked for her and cleaned the house. He had fixed anything that was broken. He had built her a sunroom and an extra bathroom. He was always willing to let her go and do anything she wanted. He appeared to have adored her.

But he also feared her, and that fear had increased during recent years. Two years previously, when Mother had gone to bed for the night, Daddy said, "You know, she could kill both of us." Most people might again think that this response was typical of a paranoid Alzheimer's patient, but I had come to realize that at least in my father's case, his harbored thoughts were beginning to come out. Though I made light of the remark, I knew deep down it was true. No one but Daddy and I knew how dangerous my mother really could be.

Despite Mother's resistance, I had managed to convince her to allow Daddy to have cataract surgery on one eye. So I obtained and got an appointment with the reputable ophthalmologist recommended by the optometrist, who confirmed the diagnosis. We set about preparing the way for him to have laser surgery. Any benefit to Daddy had to be strategized, and it always required a third party. I kept wondering how my brother could overlook this neglect, especially since he knew that his father also had a major heart condition. But I had begun to accept that Donald just didn't want to be bothered. After all, he had his own life. I had tried to telephone and talk to him, but he would hear none of it. "Stay out of this... Leave us alone...This is none of your business..." I received the same responses I typically received from my mother. He went on a vacation to Florida the day before Daddy's surgery and never phoned about how he made it through. At the time I had not realized the degree to which alcohol may also have been affecting his behavior.

Throughout the visits and surgery, Mother became testier and more resentful of the attention Daddy was receiving. On the day after his laser surgery, as I sat with Daddy in their home, I could feel my mother's resentment as I remained by his lounge chair to keep him from rubbing his bandage. Because his short term memory was rapidly decreasing, I knew he wouldn't remember why he had the patch on his eye and might therefore try to strip it off. With every drop I put into Daddy's eye that first day and night, I could feel my mother's resentment grow. To offset it, I tried a bit of small talk with her, but it didn't work, and after several tries, I just sat there and said nothing. Minutes seemed like hours. When I asked Mother if she could turn the television down a little, she began one of her tantrums and shrieked, "Nobody cares about me. I'll just leave." I gave my usual, "It's okay, Mother; we don't need the TV turned down." I caught Daddy's non-bandaged eye as he looked at me and closed it. He knew. Together he and I had contributed to this behavior. I hated my timidity, but I had brought much of it on myself through pandering and accommodation through the years.

"You *don't* have to be here," Mother complained; "I can put in the drops." She always threw out some kind of threatening statement to me to control situations. I had no trust at all that she would do that. As difficult as it was to stay in the same house with my unstable mother, I knew that if I didn't, Daddy's eye surgery might have to be repeated.

One of the neighbors came by to see how Daddy was doing, and Mother whined, "I need eye surgery too, and I am going to get it." I joined in with the neighbor in confirming that this was a good idea.

Unfortunately, for my mother, there was never any ultimate "profit" in her self-absorption. Instead, the standard of her expectations became higher the next go-around. She never really became satisfied, and the result was often just a vexation of her spirit.

About a year after his eye surgery, Daddy's irregular heart beat had worsened, this condition resulting in an increased shortness of breath and weakness. I had begged my mother for years to allow Daddy to have pacemaker surgery, but she had resisted. Finally on one particular evening when I was at their home, his breath became extremely short, and he was experiencing pains around his heart. My mother acknowledged that they needed to go to the hospital, so I urged her to let me drive. "You are *not* going to drive. This doesn't concern *you*," she snapped." So she drove. I sat in the back seat like an impotent child, not daring to utter a word.

When we arrived at the emergency room, still thinking it was my responsibility to help in some way, I approached the front desk to inform the person at the desk of Daddy's situation. Mother literally shoved me aside. Feeling foolish and like the powerless ten-year old child again, I followed her into an ER room where the medical personnel had Daddy. The emergency room physician was crass and abrupt with him. Upon the doctor leaving the room and my father being transported to another room, I quietly mentioned to my parents that Daddy really needed his own cardiologist. Mother began screaming for me to get out of there, that none of this was my business, and followed it with the usual, "You are upsetting your father." As always, because Daddy had always feared the consequences of not doing so, he echoed her. He closed his eyes and shook his head from side to side. Mother slammed the door in my face and would not allow me in the room when the doctor talked with her. And that was that.

However difficult that evening was, an ultimate good resulted. My father's records from that evening were sent to my parents' internal medicine physician, and he suggested a cardiologist, who in turn recommended pacemaker surgery. So my mother finally agreed partially because other doctors now knew how serious Daddy's heart condition was and partially because Daddy had become so weak he could hardly walk, his frailty causing her more inconvenience.

Also, by this point she had begun realizing that dumping her husband in a facility might not be that easy. She had told her friends and neighbors that *she* had finally convinced Daddy to have the surgery. Of course, it didn't matter; the main thing was that Daddy was given the opportunity to have it.

This surgery was performed, and it enabled Daddy to breathe and walk better – at least for a couple of years. Once again, I was concerned that Mother would not give him the attention he needed after the surgery. By this point, his Alzheimer's condition had worsened, and I knew that he wouldn't remember the surgery and would consequently not remember why he was sore, or to only lift his arm up so far. I realized my mother would not help him bathe, dress, or eat, or if she did, she would constantly complain to others in front of Daddy about all she was forced to do So there was nothing else to do than try to figure out how to bring Daddy home with me again for a few days, though at that point he had been alone with me at my home only one other time. I could reschedule what little work I had tried to continue. Therefore I told Mother that I knew she needed a break.

"Mother, I know this has been hard on you. Would you consider allowing Daddy to come home with me for a few days?" "I don't care, but he'll never come," she sighed. "You can't help him BATHE!" "Mother, remember when he stayed with me for a couple of days a few months ago when you and your friends went to North Carolina?" "That was different; he was here, then," she snapped. "He'll never go with you. He won't go anywhere without me," she insisted with exasperation. I tried again in an almost whispery timid voice, which I detested. "But Mother, he also went home with me last month for a couple of days. Do you remember?" She appeared to not know what I was referring to and just frowned.

On that occasion, the previous month, Mother had responded in this same way when, for the first time ever, I had asked her – with my brother present – if I might try taking Daddy home with me for the weekend. "Daddy, how would you like to go home with me for a couple of days?" "I'm ready right now. I've got to get out of here," he quickly responded. This had been on one of my visits when I discovered he had become more depressed than usual. I found him in my mother's bedroom, looking at the window. "She's taken everything from me," he said quietly. "Look at her out in the yard....She does that just to upset me." He turned from the window and stood in front of the mirror, combing his hair, as he pointed out the window. Mother was mowing the grass. This was the first time I had realized the extent to which her control had stripped him of all dignity. I also realized that even though my father might have difficulty remembering what may have just happened, or how to articulate his thoughts, he nonetheless was exhibiting a deep sense of awareness which had heretofore gone unspoken.

Daddy's Alzheimer's diagnosis had given my mother the opportunity to take on a greater victim role, as she had removed the opportunity for Daddy to mow the yard, rake the leaves, clean out the gutters, and perform all those other activities he had always done outside the house, and at that time, still could. It gave her the opportunity to show the neighbors that she now had to do everything. "I have it all to do," she frequently whimpered, refusing to allow my father any role in taking care of the house or yard, in order to garner pity. Several times in previous weeks, when I had telephoned, Daddy answered. "She's out there; she won't let me mow...." I could hear the helplessness and depression in his voice. At that point, Daddy knew he still could mow the yard, and he also realized why his wife was not letting him do it. This awareness of the appearance of his impotence to others made it all the more embarrassing and difficult on him, but he just had to swallow his frustration.

So he was just about ready to go with just about anyone just about anywhere. But even that trip home with me was a little challenging for both of us, since it was the first time ever he had been at any other place other than his house without my mother. He was confused and clearly distrusted me because he assumed my motives were the same as my mother's – to make him "relocate" from his home.

This time, following the pacemaker surgery, then, would be only the second time we would have direct interaction together at somewhere other than his home. And now there would be an added challenge, since I would need to more attentive because of his surgery. Still, it would be much less difficult for him and me without my mother's presence.

By the time of this surgery I knew my mother was missing some of her freedom to go and come as she pleased. So I figured she might ultimately allow my father to go with me, especially since she would have to stay closer to him to keep him from raising his arm "What about if we just try it," I urged one more time. She finally acquiesced. "Oh, well, but he won't stay," she sighed. I was grateful.

I telephoned my brother and asked his wife if they would come over and be there again when we left the house. Knowing how frequently Mother changed her mind, I was afraid that as we went out the door, she might try to stop us.

Before the Alzheimer's diagnosis, Mother had already given Daddy's tools to their grandson, along with his golf clubs and other possessions. At the time I first began intervening, I had not realized this. But for years after I became involved with his life, he frequently talked about losing his tools, and I think that loss depressed him almost as much as losing his car. His skill with them was one of those things which gave his life purpose and dignity. He had used them to build houses for others in the Habitat for Humanity Program; he had built the den, sunroom, and bathroom at their own house with them. He had used them to help build their earlier house in Cookeville. He had used them to fix just about anything that needed repairing for his wife and for others. The family had saved so much in plumbing bills because of Daddy's facility with his tools. When everything else was taken away, for a long time he had been able to hang on to his tools. Now he had lost *them*.

But losing the opportunity to drive upset my father almost as much as thinking he was losing his home. Driving for all of us means independence and freedom. But when my mother took away my father's car keys, she took away his ability to escape from wrath, volatility, and isolation.

There was also the matter of the increasingly closing aorta. For many years I had also tried suggesting to my mother that she consider valve surgery for my father, since his arteries were so clogged and constricted and I knew there might be a connection between this condition and his memory loss. Again, Mother's response was the same old refrain, "He's old; what do you expect?" It was depressing to realize that if she had allowed this surgery, perhaps the blood would have flowed more easily to his brain, and he might not have developed dementia.

Little by little, as Daddy's physical and mental health declined, Mother more often allowed me to bring him home with me. I began to scale back my business even more so that I could do this, never doubting that God intended me to now perform this more important role. I came to discover with horror that he was fed only minimally at Mother's house, had virtually no engagement from anyone, and was getting weaker with each trip. The longer visits were necessary to "beef him up" in order for him to make it until the next time I went to get him.

About a year later when Daddy's motor skills had deteriorated to such a degree that his "ups" and "downs" and "lefts" and "rights" were all turned around, his cognitive skills had appreciably dropped, and he had begun to lose control of some of his bodily functions, my mother finally allowed me to keep him four days every week. Or that was one plan. So I began driving about ten hours every week - five hours up to their house and back to get him and five hours up and back to return him - to help reduce Daddy's anguish and pain during what I had begun to realize was the last phase of his life.

During those days that I had my father, I tried very hard to make up the deficits in his life - the food deficit, the companionship deficit, the love deficit. It was so tricky at first, since he had never really known me except through his wife's lenses. Still, he always told his doctors and my friends, as he would point to me, "She feeds me good." I always cringed. To this day, that response pains me almost as much as anything I heard from him during those final years.

I found myself spending most of my time when he was at my mother's trying to think of ways to stimulate and engage him when he was at my house, including music and church events, especially where children would be present. I was determined to develop his trust, reduce his paranoia, and create some joy so that he would know someone was in his corner and that he would look forward to coming down to my house. True love requires surrendering our lives for others. We simply have to be willing to take their place, as Christ did for us.

CHAPTER 4

*Even the spirit of truth; whom the world cannot receive, because it seeth him not,
neither knoweth him: but ye know him; for he dwelleth with you, and shall be in you. I
will not leave you comfortless: I will come to you.*

—John 14:17-18

MORE ANSWERS TO
UNANSWERED QUESTIONS

B ecause Alzheimer's patients have lost their short term memory and
have difficulty articulating their thoughts, most people assume that
they have little awareness of anything. I came to realize the opposite
is true. In some ways Daddy's senses were heightened. Or at least, if he had
always had them, they were no more suppressed.

Actually it was through my father and my father's relatives that I gained
considerable insight and many answers to previously unanswered questions
about my mother, father, and brother's conditions during the five years preceding Daddy's death. These were answers that up until now I didn't want
uncovered, and they were tough to swallow.

I had always known that my mother was beautiful when she was young.
"She was the prettiest girl in town" was the typical response from people over
the years. To this day people remark on her beauty. Indeed, Mother's claim to
fame had always been her beauty. Being beautiful had been a major part of her
business, her art, and her delight. It had taken her a long way and had earned
her dividends. She had often mentioned that the portrait studio in her hometown had used her as a model to sell its product. She had always believed that
she could have had any man in town. When I was a young girl, she had talked
me into collecting movie star photographs, and she bought me a scrapbook to
keep them in. Eva Gardner and Elizabeth Taylor were her role models. There
was a glamorous movie star posed picture of her that hung in my father's little
bedroom of their house. My mother loved movie stars.

Even during recent years before this new involvement she often mentioned to me what others said to her about her beauty. Throughout my life
the only sentences I could remember being allowed to finish when talking
with her were extensions of compliments others had given her. She usually

either talked over any other statement about anything other than herself, or immediately changed the subject to herself. Only later did I understand that she could not do otherwise.

My mother was still prettier than most women, even in her old age, although wrinkles had definitely increased with her increased alcohol intake. And the increased wrinkles increased her anger, which in turn increased the wrinkles. It was a vicious circle. It was almost like a multi-millionaire who had outlived her money. Conversations with relatives and people in the town who knew her in earlier days helped me piece together the reasons for Mother's self-absorption and to figure out what could have prompted such rage. In such conversations, I usually heard an extension to the response: "She was the prettiest girl in town. It was "and she knew it." She was not able to wear her beauty with grace and meekness. It was not innocently possessed. But at least she was happy with it. When that beauty began to fade, so did her primary asset. She excoriated the ravages of old age and never accepted this different person as an inevitable consequence of growing old. She just became angrier.

My few friends who had been around my mother thought the root of her resentment of me was competition and jealousy. This was ridiculous, because I was aware that I was never beautiful, never tried to be, and really never placed too much value on that trait. I always thought, "Since I'm not pretty, I'll just be smart enough to make it through life." And I always figured that my boyfriends' statements about any attractiveness they perceived stemmed from my ability to discuss political, economic, and religious issues. The tape of my inferiority relative to my mother played loudly and clearly in my head. Others had always told me that I could not take compliments. "No, I'm not pretty; my mother is" became my habitual response. Whether it was because my mother's claim to fame had been her beauty, and I was determined that no one would think of me like they thought of her, or just merely being afraid that the idea would somehow become known by my mother and therefore take the spotlight away from her, I rejected any suggestion that I might also be the least bit pretty.

Rather, I preferred to remember my grandmother's words, "Beauty is as beauty does...Be a good girl." She valued a beautiful mind and heart. She had also reminded me many times, "No one can take your education away from you." That statement now seems prophetic since eventually just about everything would be eventually taken from me, *except* my education. My core values had come from my grandmother, and did not, in any way, reflect those of my mother. Once in great while when a tendency or a fleeting thought did pop up in me reminiscent of my mother, I squashed it immediately.

I came to discover that Mother had various boyfriends, a couple after she had married my father. She loved a party and continued to go out after she and Daddy married, and after Daddy had enlisted as a marine in World War II. She frequently made comments to me, suggesting that she had been denied opportunities to have another man who would have given her more. Statements such as "No one should ever marry anyone who is going off to war" and "I married the wrong man" were frequently made. When these remarks were made, I thought that actually she had married the right man because no one else would ever have endured the complaining, demands, and volatility. She had always painted my father as such a dullard, though he always worked hard, did double shift work so she could have more money, cooked for her, cleaned the house, and overall treated her like a princess. He had enabled her self-absorption – but in large part to protect his children for fear of her rage.

After I became an adult and began teaching, my mother showed me her diamond earrings that her "secret admirer" had given her. At that time she was working at a bank, and I figured it must have been someone there. But I didn't know what the appropriate response was to give to something like that. I just told her they were pretty. At that time, I had not yet dared to think about what my father had been through during his life, just regarding this issue alone. She had always insinuated that she could have had so many men, but that she had gotten stuck with him.

It was only at Daddy's memorial service that someone who had attended school with my father had come up and told me that he had been the president of his senior class and scholastically and athletically outstanding. I knew he had been quite an athlete, and everyone in Cookeville remarked about how good looking and nice he was to everyone. But my mother's portrayal of him through the years had created in my own mind a perception of him as a dullish young man. This was an image also painted to those in the town to which they had moved when I was in the seventh grade. After my father's death when I studied photographs of this young man, I tried to recreate how he was before he married my mother. But the original contexts of those family albums had been severed, and thus this effort was rendered futile. After his death, I asked my brother for the medals Daddy had earned during the war. He didn't know where they were. Nor did he know where the letters were that Daddy had sent my mother when he was in the Theater of the Pacific. I had begun to realize that Daddy, like me, was almost invisible to the rest of the family.

I came to believe that while she probably wasn't raped, the fact that she had had at least one affair while her husband was at war was a repressed thought that had started coming to the surface of Daddy's brain, as is often the case with Alzheimer's victims. In the beginning phases of his condition, Daddy often whispered to me, "She's out on the back porch; drunk...Ten men raped her last night...shhhh!" I began to wonder if my father had been doubtful about the timing of my mother's pregnancy with me, and the only acceptable way for him to justify it was to frame it this way in his head. I did know that he had not seen me until I was several months old, but I had heard from his earlier friends that Daddy, on leave, had gotten Mother pregnant to put an end to her "dating" while he was in service. In any event, what I did know was that my father's suspicions about his wife's behavior were still very much in his head until the end of his life, and partially responsible for his continuing question, "Who's taking care of her?"

But I believe there was more. He still loved her. Even in his scrambled brain, Daddy retained his care and concern about his wife because he felt responsible for her and for her behavior. It was almost as if he had been willing to be a victim to give himself totally to her – and to protect her. And in this way, he was emulating Christ, far more than I was who couldn't excuse her behavior even if her mental condition had caused it. Yes, I was far less forgiving than my father – and demonstrating less of a Christian's duty.

CHAPTER 5

For the which cause I also suffer these things: nevertheless I am not ashamed: for I know whom I have believed, and am persuaded that he is able to keep that which I have committed unto him against that day.

—2 Timothy 1:12

LET'S TRY AGAIN

About a year and a half after discovering my father's plight, I conceived a way to get Daddy away from Mother for longer periods of time, mainly to get Daddy away from the chaos and noise in their house. Any individual who has dementia becomes more anxious and stressed with increased noise and needs a non-threatening, calming environment to resist trying to escape or becoming combative. As usual, I framed the request to show a benefit to her. "Mother, I know you need rest. I know how difficult all this is on you..." But before I could continue, Mother tearfully responded, "No you don't; no one knows. My life is over and no one is doing anything to help me." After some time, Mother finally paused for breath, and I continued, "How about if I begin bringing Daddy home with me for a few days at least every other week?" "He would never stay with you. He depends on me too much," she smugly insisted again, as if saying it over and over made it so, even though he had already come home with me for brief periods. Her statement had some validity, since the dependency on her was heavy. But eventually, she relented, as her liberty was beginning to be as important as her victim status she had successfully gained with her friends.

I frequently thanked God when she agreed upon some kind of schedule for my getting Daddy, but even so, there was never a *constant* plan with her. Something would inevitably happen to disrupt any plan that might appear to be workable: Mother might feel she was losing that victim status with her friends; she might just block out what she had originally told me; or sometimes she would just simply change her mind. Regardless of the real reason, her unpredictability always kept me on edge and from ever being able to confidently plan any work schedule for myself. Sometimes I would drive about three hours to her home, only to be forced to turn around in the driveway and leave, because she had changed her mind about allowing Daddy to go home with me. Occasionally she sniped, "I didn't ask you to come up here and get him." Maybe the alcohol really had blacked out what she had earlier said; maybe it was one more way of punishing me. The result was the same. Although I had cancelled work so that I might help out, I had to return to my home without Daddy – and without work for that particular week.

Upon telephoning Mother one day about 18 months after I had begun intervening, I once again heard a desperate, "I can't take this anymore. You've got to do something." Fearful of what she might do to Daddy, in my typical fashion, I quickly responded with, "Mother, I'll fix this. Give me a little time. I'll make some phone calls." I continually found myself in an urgent state to keep my mother pacified and calmer so she wouldn't execute her plan to institutionalize Daddy. I was still hanging on to some of my work, and I thought I might discover a plan which would enable me to continue it. Surely I could discover a way to help the family survive with the least pain and still allow me to retain a little of my work because I needed at least *some* income.

It is one thing when a person with Alzheimer's doesn't appear to know the difference in people or place. It is quite another when the awareness still exists. A supportive and caring environment can make such a difference in the progression of the disease, and I knew my father was getting neither.

So I spent the rest of that day and the next telephoning various facilities – assisted living and other senior living places – to discover some alternatives. I concentrated on those in the town where Daddy grew up and where he wanted to be. I managed to discover one that was recommended by Daddy's relatives and made an appointment the following day to my parents there. It was located about 100 miles from my home.

I arrived before my mother to lay the groundwork and talk to the administrator. Upon my parents' arrival, my mother came into the facility, rolling her eyes and sighing. She complained, "He won't get out of the car. He says he *has* a home." I knew this was a natural response of anyone who had realized he was being manipulated out of his home and possessions. I later came to discover that my mother had already started a process for placing him in a facility. I responded, "I'll go out and talk with him."

When I got to the car, Daddy wouldn't open the door. I finally asked him if I could sit in the back seat. "I don't care *what* you do," he responded quietly and sarcastically. Finally he emphatically stated, "I've been controlled by women all my life." That was it, probably the first time in his life he had let that out.

I began to talk with him, about nothing really. Actually I wasn't talking *with* him, since there was no reply. But I just kept on. Realizing by now that he had become paranoid about leaving his home, sensing that there was a plan to remove him from it (and his home was just about the only thing he had left at this point – or so I had thought), I understood that any other facility in his mind would be threatening.

"Daddy, what about just taking a look at this place? We are in Cookeville and there might be people you know inside. It's your choice, of course." "I'm not your daddy," he quietly stated, head bowed. I was never quite certain if what he said was something coming up from the past, or whether it was truth in the present. But I thought this might be a good time to get an answer to a question I had always wondered about. "Who *is* my daddy?" I nonchalantly asked. There was no answer. The moment had passed. His fear of the answer to that question was back.

Eventually, after sitting there a little while and saying nothing, I asked again, "Daddy, would you like to go inside and get a coke?" "Okay," he said impassively. And we got out of the car. This was a different moment.

My mother continually told her friends and relatives that her husband was different when he was around me and implied that he was deliberately so. That in itself was threatening to her. "He's a different person around you; *they* always turn on their caregivers." She often read only just enough litera-ture about anything to use the parts of it as ammunition when she needed it, and she had read in one brochure that Alzheimer's patients "mistreat their caregivers." I mused that if that happens, it's probably because the "caregivers" are mainly caring about themselves. Many don't understand that one has to enter the Alzheimer patient's world. And that world *is* frightening, because the brain is a scrambled morass, and it's a terrible feeling not to feel in control of your life. It's also frightening for the caregiver, because it's a totally new ter-ritory. Every time I had an interaction with my father, my own brain became slightly altered, and in some ways perhaps fractured. "You don't know what he's like," Mother pouted, bottom lip out. It was stated as an accusation. Mother could never have faced why this was true, and I wasn't about to sug-gest the reason. Indeed, he was different, because he tended to take on the mood and the spirit of the person he was around and to respond in the way the other person was treating him.

As we toured the assisted living facility, Mother discovered there were several people living there whom she knew, and so she was off socializing with them. This was helpful because it gave Daddy and me the chance to interact with some folks there, and we didn't have to worry about the focus being shifted from my mother. When Daddy and I were around others, I served merely as a facilitator. I might say, "Daddy, this is Mrs. So-and-So." To the oth-ers, I would say, "This is my father, and he used to live in Cookeville." This would be enough usually to prompt some conversation from him. It might not make a lot of sense, but he felt a part of the dialog. He was engaged. I came to learn how significant to Alzheimer's patients it is to *feel* engaged and a part of whatever activity was going on. If I turned to another person and had any conversation excluding Daddy, he became extremely depressed and wanted to leave.

My mother returned from visiting some of her friends, and the three of us were taken on a tour. "This might be a possibility," I mused. They would be in Cookeville where Daddy wanted to be, and Mother would be able to talk with people she knew. I was a little skeptical since the women there were somewhat older than her and less agile, and my mother never wanted to think of herself as old. Still, I was hopeful since there was an available apartment, and it was one of those deals where you could just sign up for a month at a time. It was only later that I realized that these friends of my mother had known her in earlier days – before she reinvented herself in East Tennessee – and this knowledge about her could be threatening.

My parents returned to their home, and I returned to Nashville. Immediately upon entering my house, I telephoned Mother to make certain they had arrived safely. I asked what she thought. She actually sounded upbeat as she offered, "I mentioned that we might stay there through the winter months and consider it like a winter vacation." A wonderful idea I thought. "That would be terrific. How did Daddy respond?" I asked. "He loved it and kept saying over and over that this was a good idea...that he would be in Cookeville." This was such a blessing for a couple of reasons. This was one of the few times that Mother was actually showing some empathy about him and Daddy was enthused about something. I was thrilled and just thought it might be an answer to prayers. "Thank you God."

But that moment passed. The next day another personality came on the scene. When I telephoned Mother and suggested they might want to proceed with renting the place for just a month (and offered to pay for that month myself), she was out of the mood. "I would suffocate in that place...My friends are here; I don't have anything in common with them." So that was it again. That brief moment when she placed someone else's needs above her own was gone. "Are you sure, Mother? You could just try it for a little while; you might be surprised," I begged. "No one ever cares about what I want," she whined.

Another time when I was on a work assignment in Baltimore, I telephoned her only to hear the familiar desperate-sounding response, "I just can't take this anymore." And again, I panicked, wondering what she might do before I could return to get my father. So I conceived of the idea of renting the house that had been theirs in Cookeville, having earlier heard that it was up for lease and thinking that maybe Daddy and I could live there. He would be next door to my grandmother's house and in the house that once was his, and in Cookeville! I hadn't thought far enough along to consider the financial impact on me, but I telephoned my mother back and mentioned it, thinking this might decrease her anger and give her an answer she had not thought about. She actually listened and said this might be a possibility. However, once I had made a dozen or so long-distance calls to work this out, Mother denied to me that she had ever considered allowing such a thing to happen. Perhaps she had been drinking at the time and really didn't remember ever hearing this idea.

One major reason neither of these ideas ultimately was acceptable to her was that she realized that the Cookeville people knew some of her past. They knew, for example, that my father had taken care of *her* for many years. They knew him to be patient and sacrificing. They were not as vulnerable to the victim role that had been propagated in the town they lived in now. Later I realized she had to have been a tormented soul, and maybe she couldn't help her mood shifts. Now I can muster up a little pity for her. Then, however, I could only feel fatigue from this total and complete disinterest in the impact of her behavior on anyone else.

CHAPTER 6

For we wrestle not against flesh and blood, but against principalities, against powers, against the rulers of the darkness of this world, against spiritual wickedness in high places.

—Ephesians 6:12

THE SCHEME BEGINS

I had always been terrified of my mother's rage and volatility, but until those last few years after I had begun intervening on Daddy's behalf, I had not allowed myself to imagine the impact of her rage on him. I had come to learn that my mother had used my father's diagnosis of Alzheimer's as a license to strip him of everything – his possessions, his opportunity to work around the house, his freedom to get away from her when she became enraged, which was frequently, and consequently, his dignity. Even with all this, I had not realized the extent of her cunning and deception.

Mother, I came to learn, was beginning to develop a plan. If she could get veterans funds to have him put away, then she could be free. So she began to put her plan into action. And I had even thought early on that if the facility were a good one, perhaps it would be better than being with her. At this time, I was still trying to conduct some training to pay my basic bills, and I had not yet quite let myself imagine that I would need to give up all work.

Up until after my father *and* my mother's deaths, I assumed my mother and brother gained power of attorney right *after* the Alzheimer's diagnosis. I was sickened even at that since they immediately took away his opportunity to do simple tasks – which he desperately wanted to do – and his possessions which had given him purpose. It was only years later that I learned the depth of deception within this family. Actually, they had taken much of his life long before then. Things started to make sense to me, including why Daddy had been so sad even before the onset of Alzheimer's. When I had given him a big party on his 79th birthday in 1994, some four years before his Alzheimer's diagnosis, many of his relatives from long distances away attended. I arranged for it to be held at the old country club in the town where Daddy grew up and had pre-paid a goodly sum of money for all the food to be catered. I expected Daddy to be jubilant to have so many of his kinfolks there. Instead, he sat in a corner, hardly saying a word. He seemed so depressed. I didn't see him smile once. Not realizing what had just transpired before that time, I said, "Daddy, I know it's depressing to be in pain so much of the time." I had assumed it was his heart condition that made him so sullen. Because he was with Mother, he didn't dare say what the real reason was. He just nodded. I should have picked up on this unusual reaction to seeing all his relatives there because normally this would have made him happy.

It was not until after his death that I learned that shortly before this event and years before his Alzheimer's began, Daddy had been coerced into signing a power of attorney document, giving my mother and brother control over all his possessions. It was only after I questioned my mother's will years later and saw what was supposed to have been my father's will that I realized nefarious acts had been committed long before the Alzheimer's diagnosis. I finally received a copy of my father's will after my mother died, six months after his death, and saw that my father's signature was inconsistent on all pages of his will. At the time, however, when I first began taking care of him, I naively told Daddy that my brother knew how mentally ill my mother was. Daddy quietly responded, "I'm not sure about that." I realize now that he knew that the plan had been concocted by the two of them together. He always knew. But he kept quiet out of fear. At that time he had no one in his camp – no advocate.

In the beginning phase of his Alzheimer's, I did not know any of these facts, including this plan to put Daddy away. It was only in a conversation with one of Mother's bridge friends that I learned of her scheme, one that she had already begun. She started by circulating mounds of propaganda about her "horrible plight," and my father's "uncontrollable actions." This power of attorney issue would be used for years to come to control events, even as my father lay dying.

In order to take his car away from him, my mother had to convince others that his eyesight was too bad for him to drive. After I finally persuaded her to allow Daddy to have eye surgery, she had to change the story again. She told friends how he was too confused, how he had found the car keys and had been stopped by the police on the side of the road. Then there was the time he had been found in the church parking lot. Maybe he had gone there to have a quiet place to pray as he looked at the cross outside. Without the Alzheimer's diagnosis, these would not be exceptional incidents.

She spread tales of how he was found by people in the community and brought back home. When family members and friends asked her who these people were, she was evasive. The truth was that my father *had* drifted from the house occasionally before I began to have more time with him, but my mother had avoided telling the whole story. I came to learn that there were two reasons he would leave the house: He was either looking for my mother, who refused to sleep in the same area of the house where he was forced to sleep or he was "going to Cookeville" to escape from her. In response to the first reason, I pleaded with my mother to consider sleeping in one of their several bedrooms near his room, or allow him to sleep in one of them near her bedroom. "What about ME? I would get no rest if I tried to sleep in the bedroom near his room...You don't care about me, just him," she whimpered. I offered to pay someone to sleep in the house. Mother refused. The bed my father was forced to sleep in over the years was a single bed which had been my maternal grandfather's bed when he was a little boy. Though there were other bedrooms with full-size beds, this was the bedroom where he had to sleep. Later, as he spent more time at my house, he often exclaimed, "This bed shore sleeps good. It's good and big." I tried to address the second reason by taking Daddy regularly to Cookeville where he could see his home place and relatives he had grown up with.

In the telephone calls I made to their home shortly after the first diagnosis, my mother would begin with some story of Daddy's aggressiveness about his car keys. While I recognized that it actually might be unsafe for my father to drive by himself, I also recognized that for Daddy, particularly, the car represented his only means of escape. And he had always loved cars. He had taken such good care of theirs and seemed to enjoy seeing about my own car when I visited. He always checked the oil and made certain it was in good working order. He just loved cars. I begged my mother, "Maybe you could go with him and just let him drive around the block?" This prompted her ire. "Don't start. I can't take it from you anymore. You don't know what this is doing to *me!*" She began screaming, her preferred method of responding. Meanwhile she continued to complain to her friends and church members and anyone else who would listen, "My life is over; no one knows what I have to go through." I told Daddy I was giving him my old car which I had used in my business, because now I didn't need two cars and that we would keep it at my house for safekeeping. I don't know if he believed me, or if it made any difference if he did. He said nothing. He seemed to know when the statements made were inauthentic or patronizing. If I made artificial comments, my identity was perceived as artificial and arbitrary. In some ways his insight and senses heightened with the progression of his disease.

My mother's selective reading about this disease combined with her listening to just enough from her friends to select what she wanted and use it as fodder against her husband became a powerful weapon. To develop the case for institutionalizing Daddy, she began making certain she had documentation. When Daddy went outside to try to find my mother, sometimes within yards of their home, rather than looking for him herself, she would telephone 911 to get the police to recover him. This was a way to perpetuate the propaganda about Alzheimer's patients "wandering." She had the "records" if she needed them to put him away. It was years later after the death of both my parents that the local police indicated to me that there had been trouble in the house and how they had found my father sometimes just walking in the rain, or at a nearby church. My mother was unwilling and evidently incapable of changing the home environment to create a calmer and more reassuring environment for my father. I remain amazed that he did not exhibit more agitation than he did and that he was able to hang on to any sanity within that insane house.

She told her friends that her husband had become aggressive and threatened to hit her when she refused to give him his keys. Again, these statements often resulted from propaganda she had gleaned from skimming literature about the disease. Mother had told so many lies that I wasn't certain she actually could even tell the difference any longer between truth and falsehood. Some of her tales about Daddy's wanderings and increased aggressiveness may have been true because of his increased isolation, but many, I later learned from the police, were not. He never once wandered away from my house.

When I asked her if she might at least give my father some house keys, she threw them at Daddy and cursed. "Damn you *and* him." She later said that he had lost them and that he had hidden his driver's license. After he died, I found his little crumpled up social security card he had hidden in one of my dresser drawers. He tried until the very end to hang on to some of his identity. Maybe he wanted me to have something that was truly his.

The pain from knowing all this remains almost unbearable for me. Oh, Lord, how will this ever go away! How can I possibly carry on with these painful memories in my head?

The truth was that my mother took Daddy's automobile immediately following the Alzheimer's diagnosis, then his house keys, and then everything else. She had him cornered. Just so he could have some keys, I had taken a set of their keys to have another set made. I gave them to Daddy, and said, "Daddy, here you are; hide these in your shoe." "Okeydoke," he quietly said as he winked at me. Mother found out that I had done this and had a screaming fit. Once upon returning to their home after I had driven the three of us to the store, she grabbed the keys from me, and hurriedly put them in her purse. She slammed the car door. "Watch her....She always grabs the keys, so I can't get them," Daddy whispered. Even as his Alzheimer's progressed, he still showed far more mental stability and wits about him than she did. He said so much through his eyes. I was really afraid to hear from his mouth what his eyes were entreating.

Many times I tried to tentatively frame a question, realizing that, even though delicate, it would probably infuriate Mother. I sometimes chose to ask it anyway, on the presumption that if there's a response, some of the statement had to have been heard. After a time it became more functional to write my mother notes. There was a greater opportunity she would "hear" the content. On this particular issue, I mentioned to her that a man's property helped define his self-worth. She did, in fact, become irate, but at least, the statement had been made uninterrupted.

The reality was that, yes, Daddy did become extremely upset and depressed and didn't want to get out of bed all day long when he was at her house. He had become more of a prisoner than before since he couldn't escape even for a little while. The car was the toughest loss, for with it went his independence and any chance to get away from her tantrums. From friends I discovered there were times when my mother went to play bridge with her friends and forgot to lock the car. Daddy would take all his clothes out of his closet, put them in the car and just sit in it. Mother had already locked his case knives, collected over many years, in the trunk so that was one less thing my father had to remind himself that he still existed. Besides his clothes, these were the only items my father could still lay claim to. But now they, too, were put out of his sight. Like his clothes, I had purchased so many of those knives for Daddy over the years, and even after he could do little else, he could talk with others about their history and use.

Long before Daddy lost his mental faculties and was displaying only just slight confusion, Mother was complaining so much to her bridge friends about him that one of them encouraged her to make application for Daddy's "residency" in a VA facility in middle Tennessee which took Alzheimer's patients. This same friend inadvertently revealed this suggestion to me over the phone. She told me that she had told my mother, "This facility is close to your daughter, and she will see about him."

The major reason she planned to put him there was money. Because Daddy was a veteran, Mother thought that she would get funding. She would place him there, it would cost her virtually nothing, and she could get on with her life.

Apparently the manipulation by money, coupled with the desire not to be bothered, had prompted my brother, who lived a few miles from my parents, to support his mother in her scheme. My brother's sons, who also lived near my parents, were lured by the same. All this was confirmed after Mother's death, when I discovered their scheme had been in the works long before the Alzheimer's diagnosis. The diagnosis just helped their scheme along. Being the sensing man that he was, Daddy had known about this plan all along, and this was just one more reason he tried to escape. But at the time, I didn't know all this plotting had been going on for a couple of years.

Furthermore, Mother began giving Daddy's possessions to my brother's sons right under Daddy's nose. Even their neighbor had once remarked to me, "It's a shame that she doesn't allow *him* to give them away." I couldn't understand why there was such as rush to take everything away at all, and at least the neighbor had understood the need for a man to have a little control over his own property. Once in a conversation, Mother had made it very clear to me that she planned to leave everything to my brother's sons to make certain that his wife, Marie, wouldn't get anything. When I questioned her ever so slightly about what she was actually saying, she retorted, "Surely you wouldn't resent giving everything to the boys...they would certainly get what you have anyway." I said nothing, as I thought about the antiques and all the paintings in her house that I had bought for her. And about all her clothes I had purchased for her. And the trips. And about how I might indeed need some funds for my own health care before I died. As it later turned out, I did need funds I didn't have, when my osteoporosis worsened, along with my degenerative disk and scoliosis, after both parents died.

But mainly I thought about how my poor little daddy would have no power over who would get what, just as my grandmother had had no control. I thought there could rarely have existed before such a self-absorbed controlling person. Or was she just that mentally ill? I would not know for certain until the day before my father died.

Mother also used flattery about "the boys," my brother's sons. "He is wonderful. He telephones a couple of times a week," she bragged to friends about one of the grandsons, who was married with a child and lived within walking distance of my parents. Actually there were two grandsons, and Mother had given both of them money every month through the years, and had continued giving them money after they were grown and had families of their own. She prepared meals for them when I had Daddy with me. She babysat for their children. She bought them a boat. All these were positive actions, and I was glad at first that she did all this for them because I loved my nephews and wanted the best for them. However, the degree of attention she gave them versus what she gave my father made me sick at my stomach. She mainly cooked when I had Daddy with me; this way she could have *her* family all to herself and wouldn't have to bother with Daddy's confusion. And Daddy loved little children. I could tell that he didn't see the great grandchildren much because when I asked about them, he just usually answered with a word or two, or shrugged his shoulders. Finally I just didn't mention them at all, since it seemed to depress him all the more. All he would usually say was, "I don't get much to eat up there."

Much of the pandering to her son and grandsons was done to seduce the family into her schemes. It worked. Except for Marie, my ex-sister-in-law who saw through a lot of the manipulation, there was no support or defense for Daddy. And Donald, my brother, had made certain that Marie and I had very little contact with each other. After I became an advocate for Daddy, Donald would not talk to me, and I wasn't allowed to speak with Marie. As I repeatedly tried to enter into some sort of telephone dialogue with him, his screaming response resembled my mother's, "Don't start. I don't want to hear it. Leave her and us alone." He had become so much like his mother, evidently resulting partly from the alcohol, partly from his desire for money, partly from his need to control, but mostly from his own fear of her.

Being frustrated that no one in the family had inquired or seemed to care a whit about my father's earlier blindness, I had years before telephoned this grandson who had received Daddy's tools from Mother and who lived nearby to tell him about his grandfather's recovery from eye surgery and how much better he was seeing. Rather than express any interest about him, I was met with the accusatory, "You need to stay out of this.... What are you trying to do? You need to leave Granny alone. This is none of your business." This response had nothing whatsoever to do with the call.

Just as my brother echoed my mother, so my nephew echoed his father. It had always felt like Daddy and I were up against a whole army. I tried to comfort myself with the passage from Luke, *Behold I give you power...over all the power of the enemy; and nothing shall by any means hurt you.* But the reality was that my father's abuse, inflicted by members of the family, *did* hurt. It hurt more than anything I could remember, even more than my pain from what my grandmother had to endure. At least the aunt had fixed meals for my grandmother and allowed her to see some visitors and relatives.

During this time, in the early stages of Alzheimer's, Daddy was fairly self-sufficient in terms of dressing and feeding himself and the dog. He also liked to bring logs in for the fireplace, though he was usually denied this opportunity. He wanted to read his Bible, although with his failing eyesight, this proved to be more difficult. But he became more deeply depressed over losing control of all his assets and his life because until I became more involved with him, there was nothing to fill in the vacuum. My awareness of *his* awareness was probably the thing that tormented me the most, contrasted to my mother's insistence that he was aware of nothing. When he was out of his wife's presence, my father repeatedly told me that she had taken everything from him and expressed fear of her. I never felt I was doing enough to reverse things.

Mother's self absorption seemed to reveal itself in almost every action I took. After I began bringing Daddy more frequently to my home in Nashville, I came to realize that he needed a better small suitcase. The one he was using was held together by some kind of draw string, and it had actually been my mother's week-end bag. I thought that giving him a suitcase would give him something of his own that my mother didn't own. I would put his name on the ID tag, and it would be big enough for all his clothes. But I didn't dare purchase this for him without first checking it out with my mother. "Mother, how about if I get Daddy a small suitcase for Christmas, and this would help you? You wouldn't have to hang his coat on a separate hanger, nor would you have to have a separate bag for his medicines." "He doesn't need a bag; he has one good enough," she responded with exasperation. "I know, but I just thought it might help you to keep everything together." "Well, whatever," she sighed. I took that as an "okay." I knew that if I didn't get agreement, Mother would simply not use the suitcase when she packed his clothes.

"You mean this is for *me?*" Daddy responded, as he opened the case. "This shore is nice." "Daddy, see, you can put your socks here, your shirts here, and see, here's your name already on it." He seemed excited, and I was delighted.

When I took him back the next day so that he would be there to go with my mother to her son's house for Christmas, I took out Daddy's new suitcase. "I told you he didn't need a new suitcase!" Mother screamed. My father looked straight ahead, and I saw tears in his eyes. He understood, and his tears I know now were more for me than for him. With dry mouth and knotted stomach, I quietly but quickly responded. "Mother, remember, I asked you if I might get him this case since it would help you." She turned around and in a bluster walked briskly away. I turned around and prayed, "God WHY won't you kill this evil in my mother?" Way down deep, however, I wondered if my mother's maniacal behavior resulted from already being taken over by Satan. But for whatever reason, God had chosen to not control this evil in her. And my father had become collateral damage. Did God intend for him and me to continue to accommodate her? I wasn't certain.

CHAPTER 7

The wicked worketh a deceitful work: but to him that soweth righteousness shall be a sure reward.

—Proverbs 11:18

WHITE LINEN TABLE CLOTHS

About a year later I telephoned the facility I had suspected was the present target of my mother's plan.

I was able to secure the telephone number from a social worker at the Veterans Administration and a liaison at some of its facilities. During the conversation I learned that my mother had threatened to sue the VA for ineligibility for any funding and call her congressman. So her volatility was starting to seep out to others. The social worker told me what he had finally said in response to her threat. "Look, lady, you go right ahead, but here's the deal...." She had calmed down a bit with this response and backed off her threat. He also informed me that she had become impatient and unwilling to wait at the VA facility where she had the appointment. In a huff she had left, dragging my poor father behind her. Her pathology often prompted volatile irrational responses if her needs were not immediately met, whatever they were and wherever she was.

After the encounter with this facility, my mother had become interested in an assisted living facility with an Alzheimer's unit in East Tennessee, which also had some sort of connection with the VA. At least a year or so earlier at her house I had noticed a brochure ostensibly of this facility, displaying on its cover a beautiful Victorian house, pictures of white linen tablecloths, and pretty furniture, the sort of thing that appealed to her. Later I learned that this picture had nothing to do with the real facility, which was the conversion of an old hospital which had an Alzheimer's unit in the basement.

But there *were* white linen table cloths - at least in the assisted living part of the facility, located on the main floor. Mother had gone to an open house there with one of her friends who encouraged her to have her husband committed there. That would give them more time to go on trips and play bridge. From years of volunteer work in nursing homes, I realized that visitors are not always shown the Alzheimer's unit in facilities. I later learned Mother had not wished to see it.

After I learned of her visit to the facility, my concern increased. But when

I tried to talk with her about the place, she was evasive and said she and my father were getting along fine as they were. These statements took away some of my fear that Daddy would be dumped somewhere to die, but they really were intended to get me off the trail.

Be that as it were, Mother was temporarily stopped from her plan since she wouldn't be able to get the money from the Veterans' Administration she had anticipated. So money, her greatest weapon and the answer to everything, had become her Achilles heel. That actually had become one thing Daddy and I had on our side. But it wasn't enough. I realized I must have more support to get help for him. I had also begun to wonder if Daddy's visits with me might be hurting more than helping since the contrast between the treatments he received from his "two homes" might be too tough to handle and increase his depression.

I therefore wrote my sister-in-law, Marie, and expressed this concern. I was grateful for the letter she sent me. It gave me a sliver of hope that there was at least one person in the family who could see the truth. She was a sensitive person and had written that she had noticed that my father was less depressed and in a more joyful mood after he had visited me. This note came along about Christmas time, and I considered it the most wonderful Christmas gift I could have received. I knew that Marie was in a difficult spot herself since her husband had a strong alliance with his mother, at least in terms of plans being made for Daddy. He didn't dare contradict anything she planned or did, unless it was to talk her into getting something cheaper since he was aware that everything was to be left to "the boys."

In Marie's letter she wrote that she, too, had begun to see some evidences of my mother's rage and changing attitudes, especially regarding anything connected with money. The friendship with my sister-in-law was indeed a blessing, since I was virtually isolated from everyone in the family by this point, due to my expressed concern over my father.

I tried in vain to talk to Mother's friends, whom I had entertained and hosted over the years, about the need for me to have more interaction with my father. They too, would have little to do with me. Mother's propaganda had been too poisonous. She had done such a remarkable job of brainwashing an entire town that anything else complicated the situation. Putting Daddy away would ease everybody's conscience, and they wouldn't have to think about the issue. His depressed frail self would be out of sight and consequently out of mind. Besides, it would make it easier for them to be around my mother.

Again, I tried talking to my brother and again received his usual response, "Stay out of it...it's none of your business." Upon returning from a trip I had taken my parents on in which my mother's behavior had been particularly abusive, I telephoned Donald, hoping to just have a little conversation. The minute I said, "Donald, do you have a minute to talk?" he immediately cut me off and snapped, "Why don't you leave her alone? You always upset her. Don't call here anymore." He hung up on me. At that point, I had just suspected that his drinking had exacerbated his temper and his self-absorption, only later realizing how it had begun to consume his life, as it had impacted my mother's.

A few months following, my suspicions about my brother's alcohol consumption were confirmed. This condition, coupled with his desire to abdicate, gave me no hope for any cooperation from him. Though he lived within a few miles of his parents, I, who lived some 180 miles away, was the one who was always telephoned by friends and neighbors if Mother became ill or any special needs arose. Any, that is, except the plan to institutionalize my father.

Appeal to my mother's minister: that's the answer. After all, ministers are called especially to consider the least of these, to consider even the dead sparrow by the roadside. They hear many family secrets, and surely he might see that Daddy's day-to-day life was just as hallowed as anyone else's in his congregation. Even so, I knew I had to approach him delicately, emphasizing help for both parents. Though I knew I had to be extremely careful about making any evaluative statement about Mother, I hoped my statements might prompt enough questions from him to enable me to just state some events that had happened. Though the minister showed a little willingness to listen, I soon realized that he was not about to intervene. After all, my mother, not I, was his customer. At my mother's funeral about five years later, he began with the statement that my mother's greatest concern was that she was able to leave enough for her grandsons. He then stated that my mother never left my father's side and how hard his illness had been on her. If my mother's casket hadn't been only a few yards from where I was sitting, I would have sworn I had gone to the wrong funeral. Even though someone else had probably written those statements, I was still disgusted because ministers especially are supposed to speak the truth.

My mother was unwilling or incapable of changing the home environment to create a calmer and a reassuring environment. It was therefore amazing that my father was able to retain *any* of his sanity. But he had been a marine and had been through so much after the war that in spite of his disease he must have built up incredible strength and resistance to endure the increasingly stormy life.

Throughout my attempts to make things better, I knew it was important to try to resist bitterness and strive for peace. I reminded myself of the scripture which tells us to *follow peace with all men, and holiness, without which no man shall see the Lord...lest any root of bitterness springing up trouble you, and thereby many be defiled.* But as the family depravity increased, this scripture began to ring hollow to me. When my mother's scheme became clearer and I discovered the degree of neglect and abuse Daddy had suffered, the attempt to maintain peace became more difficult. I knew on the one hand we're supposed to wait on the Lord, but I also knew that God helps those who help themselves. I concluded that more action than just prayer was required. So I telephoned my mother's attorney to try to enlist his support. But the attorney had been a part of the plan for Mother to gain power of attorney in the first place, and consequently, he was in no position to be sympathetic to me (Later I learned that he had also been complicit in wrestling this control over my father's possession years before his Alzheimer's condition). He, like so many others, had been manipulated by my social, gregarious, "victimized" mother and her money. Plus, he, like everyone else, just didn't want to stir the pot.

So here I was, a life-long advocate and rescuer of the elderly, and now feeling more powerless by the day to save my own father. I felt a little like Jesus when the jeering crowds mockingly yelled at him to "Save Yourself." Throughout my adult life, I had taken care of many orphaned people who had no support system or family, not from any virtue or righteousness, but only because their pain created such a pain in me that I couldn't bear it. Other people had continually admonished me, "Kathryn, you can't save the world. You can't take on the world's problems." Or they sometimes declared that this compassion was my spiritual gift. Spiritual gift, maybe. But this "gift" often felt more like a cross. I recognized that if, indeed, this inordinate empathy with others was a spiritual gift, then it was supposed to be desired, according to the scriptures. And when I looked back and reflected on all the unloved alienated persons God had put in my path to love and help, it did appear to be God's will that I possess this ability. All I knew for certain was that I had a highly unusual identity with others' suffering and pain, and that it had produced the greatest pain in me since I was a small child. Maybe it was because I had suffered so many of the pains I saw in others. Maybe it was because I had felt abandoned and estranged by my own family. I didn't know why I took their pain on, but I could never turn it off or run from it.

But now I was helpless to save my own father – and after I had promised my grandmother that I would take care of him. The pain of a broken promise to Mammy was doubled by the degree of awareness I had gained over the previous couple of years about Daddy's tragic life.

CHAPTER 8

For the love of money is the root of all evil: which while some coveted after, they have erred from the faith, and pierced themselves through with many sorrows.

—1 Timothy 6:10

MONEY WHISPERS

Fortunately, there was still the money obstacle. The knowledge I had gained from the social worker at the VA that Mother was ineligible for financial support because of *her* income continued to give me hope that the plan to have Daddy institutionalized would not materialize. The very thing that drove Mother to do what she was doing was the obstacle to doing it. There were so many ironies in this saga.

Money had always been a preoccupation of hers. Several times throughout my life, I was compelled to leave jobs when I was directed to take actions which contradicted God's commands. Obviously this meant a temporary loss of income. While a good ultimately resulted from the decisions, my mother always became furious when she found out because she couldn't imagine why anyone would leave a job because of some integrity issue. "I can't *believe* you would leave a good paying job over a student's grade. Why didn't you just change the grade? I've never known anybody like you." And so it would go. When my sister-in-law had to take a sabbatical for her health, Mother became sniping and angry. Money had become an end in itself, and virtually every action she took was tied to how much money she might gain or lose. When her cousin was burned to death in a senior apartment complex, Mother's immediate reaction was not one of grief or sadness. It was, "I am just about the only relative. Perhaps I need to get a lawyer and sue; I'm sure we could get some money." My brother had replied in the affirmative, with a slight chuckle.

More recently, however, I had become suspicious that she had not given up her plan, and she would somehow figure out a way to promote it. I therefore must figure out other things to do. I always had to anticipate Mother's actions to protect my father. I wrote her, stating that the only way I would support any effort to place my father in a facility was that she did not just dump him there, rarely coming back to visit, as my mother's brother, my uncle, had been left in one East Tennessee facility. The second condition was that I could continue to bring him for visits to his home town, his home church and his relatives. I sent a copy to my brother and his wife.

This letter was an attempt to remind my mother of the circumstances surrounding my uncle's death some years back. I recalled how upset she had been that her Alzheimer's brother was "dumped," in her words, in this facility, his wife returning only rarely to see him. Mother had been so upset and angry that she told me she couldn't stand it. She told me that her blood pressure was so high that she might have a stroke because she couldn't help the situation. She had not once extended a hand to take care of him during the several years preceding his being institutionalized, but the fact that she could feel some pain for her brother showed me that at that point in her life, she still could feel some empathy for others. I remain comforted by that realization. When I look back on her reaction today, I think that perhaps some satanic force really did take her over during the last years of my father's life and before then, she may have been able to distinguish evil from good. Sin tends to breed sin, and once we turn from God and start down that road of rationalizing sin and placing self on the throne, God can withdraw the light from us so we lose all discernment. Perhaps this is what happened with my mother. Either that or her mental illness just became greater. Or maybe in some cases demonic forces and mental illness become one and the same. I'm not certain I can tell the difference.

My mother's method generally was to lay out a problem and express such extreme reaction to it that I felt compelled to try to "fix" it. Afterwards, she always insisted that she never had asked me to do anything.

Even so, after visiting the facility where my uncle was "residing," I was also distraught and determined to take action to ameliorate the situation because my uncle *had* been neglected to the point of abuse. In two months he had gone from eating and dressing himself and recognizing me to a skin and bones virtual vegetable, lying in a fetal position, unable to do anything and as far as I could tell, and unable to recognize anyone. My mother and I visited him together, and she was actually kind to me there and to her brother. It was one of the few times I saw empathy from her, and I believe it was genuine. These moments I must always try to remember. I agreed with her that my uncle's treatment had been horrible and wrote a letter to the administrator about it. I also inadvertently uncovered other cases of neglect and complaints about that particular facility.

But this rare moment of agreement was short-lived. Later, when I sent my mother a copy of the letter to the facility's administrator, she became enraged and screamed, "You are always causing problems!" The threatening response to the letter was not from the facility administrator, but from my mother's nephew, who I had learned was getting kickbacks from the facility and wasn't about to let anything interfere with his deal. It was filled with rage against both my mother and me, and so I never showed it to her, not wishing to upset her further. I just absorbed the rage myself. I knew that Mother's response would be to blame me for the problem anyway. Here again, the love of money was the culprit, the root of so much evil in this family. This same nephew killed himself a couple of years after that. A first cousin of Mother's, who was at the time Secretary of State, also committed suicide over a money deal which involved him and the then Governor. I have always been aware of this propensity toward the love of money and power in this family and therefore must be more on guard than most.

A couple of years earlier when Daddy and I were waiting for Mother to have her eyes examined (which she chose to do the day before Daddy was to have his pace-maker surgery), an older woman who was quite bent over kept approaching the receptionist desk inquiring about her ride. Finally I asked the woman at the desk about the situation, and she told me that this lady was a Medicaid patient from a nursing home about 40 miles away. She said that it was not uncommon for this little lady to wait hours on her ride. Thinking that unacceptable, I quietly telephoned a yellow cab and asked if a taxi might come to the eye center and take this woman to her place of residence. I explained where it was and became satisfied that the cab company knew the place.

Within a few minutes the cab arrived. I quietly asked the folks in the waiting room to keep an eye on Daddy. They were warm and friendly and seemed relieved that I was helping this woman get a ride. I escorted the lady to the cab to ensure the cab driver in fact knew exactly where she lived and paid him the fifty bucks plus a tip. I quickly returned – but not quite quickly enough. Mother had caught me in the act and had a fit. "You mean you spent money on a woman you didn't even *know?*" she loudly accused. I was embarrassed for her. Others had witnessed this behavior, and Daddy was also embarrassed. As I drove my parents to their home, Mother kept complaining about my spending money on this woman. "Surely, Mother, you can find something else to criticize me for," I quietly sighed. That did it. She didn't say another word all the way home, and threatened to jump out of the car as I was driving. She didn't jump but slammed the car door when she got out at her home, a typical scenario of any time she was questioned about any action. Daddy just looked at me and shook his head. I knew she would pout for hours over this, and Daddy and I would have hell to pay.

My mother and I operated from such different core values that it made any understanding between us virtually impossible. She deeply resented my volunteer work for the elderly throughout my life. Whether it was a lonely, dedicated security guard who had no family, or it was an elderly patient at a nursing home, if Mother found out, her response was the same: "You better be helping your own family; I can't believe you spend money on *those* people."

My grandmother had taught me that integrity is the foundation of all that is high in character. She also valued education (though she herself had very little *formal* education) but taught me that knowledge without integrity is weak. She taught me and her son, my father, that capital is not what a man or woman *has*, but what he or she *is*. In her world character and honor were capital. She taught my father and me not to sell our integrity. She was wise. She knew that money, gold, and other man-made treasures perish, but that character was the valued keepsake. I was never as unselfish as my grandmother, but her values made their way into the heads and hearts of both my father and me. Ultimately that would prove to be one common denominator which united us.

I realized that the extent to which I became involved with strangers' lives wasn't conventional, but *much* of what I had done throughout my life wasn't. I had often taken the elderly who had no family home with me from nursing homes over the week-end and thought nothing of it. I had housed various ones in my home for temporary periods of time when they were ill or had no other place to go. I knew but for the grace of God that I could have been like them – no one to care for and love them. Perhaps it was because I could easily imagine myself in that same situation. Ironically, that *is* just about how my life became.

I reflected on that particular time in my life when, as a young graduate student and teaching assistant, I had very little money myself. Yet, I seemed to always have enough to eat and pay my basic bills. Looking back, there seems to be no way I could have made it financially but for God's hand. He alone enabled me not only to survive, but to also find the resources to help others.

It was natural therefore that one of my major concerns regarding my parents revolved around the impact of this obsession with money. I knew that my mother was not properly feeding Daddy. And much of the reason was that she didn't want to spend any money on food. She appeared to have little interest at this point in her husband living, except for his monthly retirement income which she would lose if he died. At a certain point in time she apparently calculated that even though that would be cut if he died, the amount required for an Alzheimer's facility was greater. So her net gain would be reduced to nothing.

Because his immune system was vulnerable and his heart condition deteriorating, it was critical that Daddy eat well. Trying various strategies to enable both of them to eat better, I discovered through some of Mother's friends a very nice woman who would be willing to come to their house a couple of days a week, stay with Daddy, and prepare meals so my mother could get out more often and have less to do. So I telephoned her and asked if she might be available, prepared to pay for her services as long as I was able. Upon hearing this plan from me, my mother quickly rejected it, declaring that having another person in the house would be more trouble than it would be worth, and insisted that my father wouldn't stay with anyone else. Again, her fear of losing total control over her husband overcame even financial help for some care for Daddy, even though she frequently complained to her friends and to me about her lack of opportunity to go places. She snapped, "It is none of your concern; stay out of it."

Nothing much seemed to work. When Daddy was at my home in Nashville, I tried to make up for his lack of food by feeding him heartily, but it was more or less a losing battle. Daddy had become violently ill after one particular visit a couple of years after he began staying more with me, and I suspected it was either because his system wasn't used to real food, or the difference in the amount of food he was fed at my house and hers was too great for his system.

On that particular occasion, I was returning him to his wife's home by way of Cookeville so we might attend the country church Daddy had attended until he joined the service. This was the ritual that had been followed for a couple of years, until my mother decided these visits would end. After exiting the interstate and before driving to the church my father loved so much, I stopped at a fast food restaurant for a restroom break. This was during the time when Daddy could manage going into a restroom alone, as long as I led him to the doorway.

On this morning, when Daddy came out of the men's room, his entire body began shaking, as he slumped onto the floor. He began projectile vomiting, and went into a seizure. With vomit all over my coat and in my hair, I tried to hold his head. His body went limp. He looked gray. I was afraid he was either having a stroke or he was dying. I screamed for someone in the restaurant to bring me a cold rag and to phone an ambulance. The people just stood there. "PLEASE HELP ME," I loudly repeated, and finally someone called 911. He was taken to the ER room at the local hospital, with me closely following the ambulance. He was still vomiting upon arrival, and I was terribly frightened about his condition. I also sensed that I was about to be plummeted once again into the pit of hell.

Horrified about my mother's probable reaction, I tried off and on for hours in the ER to reach her, knowing by this time that I couldn't have him back to her house at the appointed time. She always became irate when something happened which made me just a little late. I had wanted to give her a cell phone so I might telephone her if we encountered something unforeseen, but she insisted she didn't want one. I telephoned my brother Donald to tell him that Daddy had to be hospitalized and to solicit his help in locating Mother. After sarcastically saying maybe I could call the police to locate Mother, he hung up on me. When I finally did reach her, she screamed, "What are you doing to him? You are killing him!" In the meantime, I tried singing "Amazing Grace" in low tones to Daddy. That seemed to bring some calm, although I don't know how since my voice was quivering from fear of what my mother might do.

I must digress to explain why this incident was so threatening to both Daddy and me. After an asylum incident – which is discussed later – my mother told me that *her* plan was that Daddy was not to go to Cookeville any more or to my house. This threat became a recurring one, and later I came to realize it was only a blind one since Mother really didn't want to take care of him. Nor would she release the funds for him to enter a nice facility. But at this time I hadn't come to that realization, and I was still frightened about the threat. Mother knew it.

Daddy was becoming painfully thin. I had suspected that he wasn't getting enough to eat before, and now it was being confirmed. I didn't know which was worse: Daddy being dumped in an institution or being starved to death at my mother's house. As also discussed more in a later chapter, the time came when Mother refused to take needed actions to help my father's deteriorating condition because she didn't want to spend the money. At that time things had become much worse, so I felt compelled to change my approach. This change was prompted by a telephone call to my mother, asking her if I might come to get my father and take him home with me. "Oh, I don't *think* so," she had answered, her voice dripping with sarcasm. This reminded me of the way I became isolated from my grandmother during the last two years of her life when the only way I was allowed to see her was at my aunt's house with no privacy. Then I could do nothing because I was only a granddaughter with no rights. Now although I was the daughter who was never really claimed by my mother, the difference was that I was older, had taken care of my father, and had used my money to do it. Therefore I felt I did have some rights. So I hired an attorney to convince her to allow my continued involvement with him.

The letter chronicled the actions my mother had taken and the actions I had taken to address my father's medical needs, demonstrating the relationship between the lack of attention to Daddy's health needs and his dramatically failing physical health. Though the letter evoked fury from her and she threatened to "fight it," she ultimately agreed to allow me to bring my father back home with me and get him the health care he needed because she wasn't about to shell out any money for legal fees.

This trip which ended up in the ER room was only the second week-end I had had the chance to get Daddy after my mother conceded to allow the visits to resume.

Immediately upon cessation of the vomiting, he was given various tests, including a cat scan to determine if he had had a stroke. He had not, but what he did have was severe anemia. I was not surprised.

One year later he still had the anemia.

I continued to try different ways of encouraging Mother to eat better herself and feed Daddy. She was physically able to cook, but she barely did, maybe because she just didn't want to prolong her husband's life at home; maybe because her increased alcohol intake prompted a craving for junk food and little hunger for real food; but most probably because groceries cost money.

I had taken fish and chicken meals to them; I had bought foods at groceries which were easy to prepare. These were pointless efforts. Knowing that she was rarely cooking any more except for her grandsons and because of her drinking, I got an idea. What if I purchased some food coupons at a local restaurant for Mother and Daddy? That would certainly ameliorate my father's anemia and be a benefit for my mother as well since my mother's neighbor had said that my mother needed the socialization of eating out. I understood.

So I telephoned the neighbor and asked him his opinion of possible local restaurants that my mother might like and which served "real food" since I knew the small town had only a few restaurants which weren't fast food. I was careful to emphasize the benefit to my mother. He told me he thought it was a great unselfish idea, and he mentioned one close restaurant where he himself had eaten. He volunteered to pick up a menu and read it to me over the phone. This might just work. It would at least be one answer. I telephoned him back the next day, he read me the menu, and I decided this restaurant indeed had had some healthy food that both my mother and father liked. I telephoned the restaurant manager, confidentially told him that my parents were not eating healthily enough, and purchased a few hundred dollars of restaurant coupons. I had him put an expiration date on them, thinking this action would ensure that my mother used them right away. My plan was to continue buying them when they expired.

The manager told me he would personally deliver them and would say to my mother that a friend was just interested in helping her out and had purchased the coupons. What seemed like a good idea at the time ended up being a disaster, because after eating there a few times, Mother complained that the restaurant didn't have enough variety and that it was too expensive. So the next month I purchased some coupons from Cracker Barrel, a chain restaurant with a wider menu. Although not quite as close to their house as the first restaurant, it was still within a few minutes' drive from Mother's house, and I knew my mother liked some of the food there. However, I later learned that she had expressed intense anger at receiving this gift, by this time realizing who had sent it and quite concerned about the image it might project of her. So she took a group of her bridge friends out to dinner with the coupons, leaving my father at home alone. She prominently displayed their "thank you" notes throughout their home so I could see she had not taken my father to the restaurant.

THE EASTER GIFT

The focus on money was never ending. One Easter a couple of years after I began trying to rescue Daddy, I purchased a nice leather bag for my mother. I was always very careful to take her a gift when I went to get Daddy, or when I took him back to their house. It was just one attempt to decrease her agitation for a little while and make her feel less of a victim. This was one of those trips when I was getting Daddy. Fortunately for me, one of my mother's neighbors was at the house when she opened it. My mother said very little, but didn't overtly object to the gift. It had been an expensive bag originally, but had been marked down considerably. It had several compartments, and I had often heard Mother say that she liked bags like this. I had left the price tag on the bag, deliberately, if nothing else, to please her.

The neighbor left shortly thereafter, and my father and I also got into the car, preparing to drive away. As we were pulling out of the driveway, my mother yelled, "I don't want this bag; I already have a brown bag." She had evidently not yet looked at the price tag. In my car, I simply telephoned Mother's neighbor who had been at the house and asked her if she could use that bag. I explained that Mother didn't want it, and that I would purchase her something else. "Well, yes, I could use it," replied the neighbor, a little tentatively. I then telephoned Mother and explained what I had done, since I didn't want her to throw the bag away. "You did WHAT?" she screamed. "You told Martha! "Yes, Mother, I told her I would get you something else." "No, I don't want you to get me anything else," she railed. Later in another conversation, she said she wasn't about to give away a bag that cost over a hundred dollars on sale.

On that week-end, with Mother's pouting victimized voice still in my head, I said, "Daddy, let's go find Mother something else for Easter." "Okay," he said. He picked out the skirt, one with colors she liked. I found a matching blouse. Going to a store was always a little tricky. I had to discover an area where Daddy could sit because of his heart condition, but also an area where he would still be in my sight. We found what I thought was the perfect outfit. On that Sunday, when I took him back, I told Mother that we both had gotten the skirt and blouse, and that Daddy had picked it out. "Who paid for it? I know *he* didn't have any money, and *you* don't have a job!" she sniped. This was all said in front of Daddy. Daddy looked at me, shook his head and closed his eyes. I thought to myself at the time that this would be the last time I would try this. But I had bought virtually all her clothes, and though I might tell myself I wasn't going to buy any more, down deep I knew I had made that assertion to myself many times over, and I was still buying.

TRYING TO HOLD ON TO JUST A LITTLE

It was not surprising, then, when Daddy developed the Alzheimer's condition, that he was continuously concerned about loss of his money and possessions. Clearly he had lived a life where the control of both had been wrested from him - first by his sister, then by his wife and her partner, my brother. There were always "money whispers." I would listen carefully when Daddy began talking to himself. He talked about hiding the money at the mountain, about people stealing money from him. This was one reason he wanted to sleep with everything he had left - which was very little.

His sister, the same aunt who had despised me, and from whom I hid when she came to see my grandmother, also was focused on money and possessions. Looking back, I try now to understand her resentment. I know part of it was about Mammy feeding me and washing my clothes. Once, when my father was asked by his mother what in the house he would like, Daddy tentatively responded, "Well, I guess I would like to have the cherry cupboard." This cupboard had been made from the cherry off the farm when some of the cherry trees had been cut down. His sister immediately snapped, "I'll see it smashed to bits before you get it." Those words still ring in my head, as I remembered both Mammy and me trying to choke back the tears at the time these words were spoken. Daddy's sister and brother ended up with most all the land, the house and virtually all the property after Mammy died, that is, all but that cherry cupboard. My grandmother, though frail and arthritic, had hobbled through the house and made certain Daddy got that cupboard. That was only one of the many signs of her courage and inner strength, a strength that didn't come from money. Her strength still gives me strength, as I strive to overcome the pain from my own arthritis.

It was little wonder, then, that Daddy had become so focused on money. He had not been earlier in his life. He was an honest man who always stood for right. He was like his mother, a mild-mannered man who wanted peace and harmony in the family. But because of his mild manner, he allowed the two women in his life, his sister and his wife, both of whom were driven by money, to control him. Mother was always insisting that he work double shifts, week-ends, and holidays to have extra money. And they had both taken all which was rightfully his. In times past my mother was forever talking about the evil Jenny Dillon, this aunt, proclaiming how she had gotten everything which should have been "theirs." Now Mother had gotten control of all her husband's assets and determined that she would not lose any of it. The resultant greed had wrought much damage and was one of the primary roots of her manipulation and evil doings.

After I had finally succeeded in securing physicians in Nashville for Daddy's Alzheimer's condition, his dental care, his eye problems, and his internal health, trying to manage his overall health, my mother still would not give me even shared alternate power of attorney because she was afraid of losing control of the money. It was always the damned money! But the major difficulty was her refusal to give me at least a shared *durable* power of attorney, a legal document which gives someone the right to secure – or not secure – medical attention, because not having this placed me in a very ambiguous position when Daddy was with me. My mother was so insistent about the living will, but she never allowed me the chance to explain that if Daddy's heart stopped while he was with me, I would have no choice but to allow those attending my father to do their job, even if that meant administering CPR. I was never able to get her to hear the fact that a living will is not a legal document.

I had told Mother many times over that I didn't want her money, but I did need at least this alternate durable power of attorney status since by this time Daddy was with me more than he was with her. Even her neighbors tried to convince her of this need. One of the reasons this was so critical was that inevitably when I picked Daddy up from their home, he would be weaker and thinner than the week before when I had taken him back. He was more vulnerable. And time could be critical in saving his life. Both Daddy's neurologist and internal physician had remarked that there was no question that Daddy was alive because of my efforts, and I wondered if this might be part of the reason for my mother's great disdain for me.

Of course my heating, water, automobile, and pharmacy expenses had increased, but I had not asked for any money from my mother. After all, Daddy's mother had taken care of me. But I was hoping that since Mother had been halted from institutionalizing Daddy because of the money, she might volunteer a little financial aid. One minute she would say, "Money is the least of my concerns" and *offer* financial assistance; the next minute, if I dared thank her for offering such help for his various conditions, she would throw out the not-so-veiled threat of "Well, on the other hand, maybe we just need to stop this." She never really followed through on her offers of financial help, instead using this threat to prevent me from seeing Daddy. So I learned pretty quickly to negate any need for such help.

When Daddy had whispering conversations with himself, they were often about money. I was so anguished about *his* anguish, and there seemed to be little I could do about it, beyond strewing some coins over the floor so he could find them and do with them what he wanted. So before I traveled to East Tennessee to get him, I threw pennies and dimes over my floors, knowing Daddy would pick them up and feel some sense of past purpose. It worked, and he always grinned when he came upon a dime or penny and turned it over to me.

Consequently, around my house Daddy was often preoccupied with finding the change. He continually looked for it not just on the floor, but in drawers, in my jewelry boxes. And he generally would show me his find! One of his past "jobs" that he liked to do was clean out my car. I had always told him he could keep any money he found in the car, so I made sure I had left change in the seats or on the floor.

Not wanting him to feel so powerless, I would slip some money into his wallet. Or I would say, "Well, Daddy, I guess we don't need too much money anyway in this world, and in the next, we won't need any!" That seemed to pacify him for the moment.

At church services, I always slipped a couple of dollars to him for him to put in the collection plate. But reflecting on this action, I don't think it was a good idea, since it wasn't real, and Daddy seemed to always know when something was patronizingly done for him. Many people think Alzheimer's victims are like children. They are in one sense, in that they are candid and often unrepressed, but not in other ways that many people assume.

He always wanted to pay for any meals, but since most of his money had been taken from him, he only had, at the most, a few single ones. Inevitably upon sitting down at a table in a restaurant, though, he would pull out his little worn wallet and try to give me what he had. He would do this several times before the end of the meal. I might take a dollar bill, and say, "Since you're buying lunch now, I'll get supper." "Okeydoke," he always responded.

Why oh why, I wondered, had God given me *this* cross of having to endure the abuse of my father when I had hurt so long for elderly folks who were strangers! Was it to punish me for drifting from Him years ago for a short period of time? It had been years back and I had repented over and over for my past sins, but perhaps this was it. Some day in heaven, if I made it there, I would know why God had laid this one on me. Was there a sin I had not asked forgiveness for? I tried to cover all of them, but all I could deduce was that I hadn't atoned enough.

I prayed to God that if Daddy had given money a greater significance in his life than he should have, He would understand why and forgive him for it. I knew that Daddy really knew that one cannot serve God and Mammon, but "money whispers" from controlling people throughout his life had, by osmosis, produced the same concern in him. Surely God knew my father had courage, integrity, and modesty because I came to see that all these attributes ran deeply in him. While the world might say that he should have stood up to his wife, I began to realize that he was trying to protect his children, not knowing what might set his wife off. So he, in turn, found himself being occupied by money, earlier in life to appease her, later because he knew that all of it had been taken from him and he was trying in some way to ensure that I got something. If any moral weakness had taken possession of my father, I trusted God understood the reason and prayed that Daddy's walk with Him, which never failed, even until the last day before he died, would make up for any preoccupation with property.

62

CHAPTER 9

Mortify therefore your members which are upon the earth; fornication, uncleanness, inordinate affection, evil concupiscence, and covetousness, which is idolatry; For which things' sake the wrath of God cometh on the children of disobedience.

–Colossians 3:5-6

NARCISSISM, SCHIZOPHRENIA, OR THE DEVIL?

Such was the realization I had acquired about my father. The understanding I came to have about my mother was equally tormenting and equally poignant, but the effect was quite different. Whereas with my father, my torment was the result of deep pain for his suffering, in the case of my mother, the effect was becoming hatred and resentment of her.

One of my greatest spiritual battles was forgiving my mother's behavior when that behavior continued to destroy others and continued to serve her. I had always had some difficulty with the idea of hating the behavior but not the person. How could one separate the two if the demons had in fact taken over a life?

Maybe I could resist hating my mother if I could see her behavior as insanity, rather than totally evil. There was plenty of evidence which would point psychiatrists to a very serious mental illness. Yes, that's what I must do. If I didn't, then possibly I, too, could be condemned. Consequently, in the first years of my journey, I thought I had to forgive her and keep trying to reach her. But the impact was still destruction of lives. Part of the reason forgiving her was so difficult was that Mother had done such a remarkable job over the years of masking her temper and ire in front of friends who saw her for only brief periods of time. While a person *can* recognize schizophrenic and bi-polar tendencies, when you're the target of the person who possesses them, it's almost impossible to excuse the resulting behavior at the time you're suffering.

THE IMPOSSIBILITY FOR NARCISSISTS TO LOVE ANYONE ELSE

Narcissists have no interest in things that do not help them to have what they want. They are focused on one thing alone, and that is power. They often project a grandiose, but false image of themselves. They draw others to them, in part because they are so overwhelming. As a norm, they lack conscience and can be ruthless. My mother exhibited these traits, but it was the type of narcissism which intertwined fantasy and reality. My father, it appears, was drawn to my mother, and so were other men. Years ago when I was out with my mother, and she was talking with anyone, but especially men, she always stood as if she were posing for a magazine.

Though rare, there *were* a few instances before my father became ill where my mother displayed some interest in someone other than herself. She certainly had shown some interest in her grandsons and her great grandchildren. And there were even a few times when I was a teenager that she showed a little interest in me. She made me a couple of dresses which were very pretty. Made of gingham, they had eyelet on the cuffs of the sleeves. Both of them had cummerbunds. And then when I was a college freshman, she made me a jumper which I loved. She put her name labels on the inside of them. Clearly, she was proud of her creations, but so was I. My grandmother had always made my clothes up until that time, and I told everyone that Mother had made these. People commented on how pretty they were. The compliments seemed to make her happy and helped abate her temper. Her brief periods of happiness also made me extremely happy, not just because she wasn't throwing things at me, but because I wanted more than anything to make her feel less deprived. I often think about those dresses because they help me realize that Mother had not always been entirely self-absorbed. She had also paid for me to take piano lessons when I was a young girl, and I might never have developed a taste for classical music, had I not had those lessons. Though the motive for these actions may have been her guilt from not being able to love me, or just from the compliments she received when I wore those dresses or I played well at my recitals, this was probably all she was capable of. Then there was the time she seemed to listen as I talked to her about a Girl Scout badge I was working on. All these actions occurred a very long time ago, but they *did* occur. I made a conscious effort to remember them, just like those moments with my uncle at the nursing home, because they illustrated that at least in an earlier time, Mother had sometimes demonstrated an interest in someone other than herself.

But in terms of any empathy for me demonstrated by ever holding my hand or listening to me about some setback I had suffered, or offering me encouragement, I cannot recall a single time. I don't remember her ever holding me when I was little. I never remember her looking at my report card or asking me about any school assignment. I made straight A's in school, but I don't remember a single comment on my grades. She just didn't have the capacity.

After I began to realize what sacrifices my father had made for her and especially after I realized that Daddy's mind was changing, I stepped up my effort to take both my parents on trips. One of these was a work trip to Oregon. As always, I ran interference to ensure that everything was the best situation it could possibly be for them. I bought them first class plane tickets, even though I had never in my life ridden first class, because I wanted the entire trip to be special. Daddy had never flown in his 80 plus years, and with his heart condition, I thought this seating would make him less anxious. His doctor had said it would probably be all right for him to fly. I also knew that Mother could feel "superior" and could have a glass of wine when she wanted it. At that point I did not realize she was an alcoholic.

I had made preparations with a company which did customized tours, so Mother particularly would have something to entertain her while I was conducting my training sessions. I knew that Daddy would have been satisfied with just watching television or doing something simple, but this would be an added treat for him as well. I had reserved a suite room with a nice view. All of this cost me more than I could really afford, and it was exhausting, but that beforehand preparation had paid off in past trips. The flight was smooth, and both parents seemed all right.

However, upon arriving at the hotel, the nicer room I had reserved was not quite ready, and so we had to wait a short time in the lobby. It was a nice lobby, with comfortable chairs, and this shouldn't have been a big deal. But with Mother's patience being what it was, she began her usual complaining. "Things never go right for me," she whined. I wanted to slap her, but instead, I pleaded, "Mother, I think the room will be worth waiting for; they are going to upgrade your room." "I don't want an upgrade. I'm just tired of waiting," she whined again. I had negotiated the upgrade and thought overall it would be worth waiting for, since they would be here a week.

A short while later they entered their room. It was indeed a beautiful suite room with a nice view. Whew, I thought, Mother will see that this suite was worth waiting for. Suddenly, however, she fell to the floor. At first frightened, Daddy and I ran to get a cold wet rag, and Mother snapped, "Get that damn cold rag off my head." She started this weird eerie laughter. There seemed to be something about this incident beyond just a mere feigned fainting spell to keep all attention focused on her the rest of the evening and to keep attention off my father's heart condition. I began to wonder if there could possibly be some demonic forces at play. I asked her if I could go down to the restaurant and bring them something to eat. "I will just eat this little pack of crackers," she whimpered. The tone of her voice had changed; it reflected an entirely different personality. "Brian, do you want anything?" Of course, always feeling he had to echo his wife, my father quietly shook his head no. I knew Daddy was hungry, so I brought them a plate of sandwiches and fruit. My mother ate most of it, leaving a little for my father.

I was still a little concerned about any remaining impact on Daddy who had had this first experience of flying and had expressed this concern to Mother. That had been a mistake to shift attention to him. There was no space in this scenario for that concern.

Over recent years, I had come to realize the impact of the lack of affection my father had suffered throughout the years and had come to understand the reasons for my father's actions.

Through the years he had confirmed that he really did love me, when my mother was out of sight. "Shh...don't tell your mother, but I love you," he whispered to me many times after she had gone to bed. The pattern was the same; as soon as she would retire, which was usually quite early in the evening, Daddy would come over to me, kiss me, and say these words. Some form of this statement was made to me from the time I was a young girl throughout my earlier adult life – until the Alzheimer's had taken hold. Before I understood the basis for these kinds of statements, those moments had been uncomfortable. They were in such contrast to the interaction with my father when my mother was present. Therefore I would usually just tell Daddy that I was going to bed.

During later years I came to understand that his "silent approach" to hug or kiss me resulted from his fear of Mother's jealously and her intense competition with me. He had wanted me to know that he really did love me, but he was afraid to express this in front of his wife. I had already come to understand in the first direct interaction we had together how much he was starved for affection.

One evening in the living room many years ago my mother was reading the novel, *Peyton Place*, a sexy book that in its day would have earned at least an R rating. I was twelve at the time, and the three of us were sitting in the living room. Mother was touching herself as she read the book. My father's words echo in my head even now, "You'd better be reading the Bible." He had been raised by a woman who venerated the Bible, and now he had a wife who preferred reading trashy novels. I remembered my mother's sneering laughter at these words. There's was something about that laughter that I have never forgotten.

This behavior was more evidence that she was only able to love herself.

She preferred to touch herself rather than to allow her husband to touch her. She was oblivious of any adverse impact her behavior might have on others, including her daughter who couldn't help but witness her action.

Mother's narcissism was pronounced and explained why she could rarely ever identify or empathize with another person. If Daddy or I ever began a statement with concern over another person, the focus was immediately shifted to her. It was always, "What about me?"

When Mother became anemic some years previous to my father's Alzheimer's diagnosis, she refused to accept the doctor's diagnosis that nutrition can prompt a system to become anemic. And so when my Alzheimer's father also became anemic, Mother's response was "Well, *I'm* anemic...and *my* count is worse than his," a statement reminiscent of a six year old child. With Daddy's Alzheimer's condition, his immune system needed nutrition, and I found myself always trying to make up for the food he didn't get at her house when he was with me, though I recognized that it was a losing battle. His system just couldn't respond well, vacillating back and forth with too little and too much food.

Mother always competed for attention and displayed this competition between me and my father. She competed for it even if she had to feign illness to get it – which was often. Various times after Daddy's Alzheimer's diagnosis, she had called 911 for herself, and each time she was sent home with no known problem – other than nutritional deficiency. Neighbors telephoned me in the middle of the night, urging me to get up to the area right away because Mother had been taken into the hospital.

One of the most difficult spiritual battles for me was the ambivalence about how to respond to my mother and reconcile the Lord's admonition to honor and obey those over us if they have been overtaken by some evil force they cannot control. If I obeyed Mother, then clearly I would be disobeying God. I would be putting my concern for her over my love for Him – which Jesus told us not to do. How could I possibly love that which the devil had in his grasp, or as it appeared to ultimately become, the devil himself? For years I tried rationalizing her behavior as a serious mental illness and later, as the behavior became more bizarre and destructive, rationalizing that she was lost to some demonic force which she couldn't control. In the beginning, I tried telling myself that however much she might be in the folds of Satan, she was still a creation of God. Though I couldn't love her as a mother, maybe I could love her in an agape way. But even with this thinking, I was putting her priorities above God's.

Up until the last year of my father's life, I felt I just couldn't give up on her; there was no one else that would ever dare confront her. Even though I realized that it wouldn't be heaven for me if she were there, I still didn't want her to go to hell.

THE THREE PERSONALITIES

Over the years I had occasionally wondered if my mother had experienced such deprivation that this narcissistic personality was formed as a defense mechanism. But even that didn't explain the schizophrenic symptoms which had become more pronounced during recent years, making it possible for her to switch moods and entire personalities in an instant to get what she wanted.

There was the small, pouting child, who would shake her fists and cry immediately if she didn't get her way and scream over someone she didn't want to hear. If she were questioned about why she might have done something, or someone was saying something she didn't agree with, she would either run away, or fall on the floor, kicking and screaming like a three year old. She exhibited little interest in being a mother or a wife. To me, it often appeared that she simply displayed all the tricks she had learned as a spoiled child, as her brothers were forced into pandering to her; later, as her husband placated his "child"; and finally as I continued to accommodate her. "Who is taking care of her?" continued to be the refrain of my father, long after his Alzheimer's had set in. She could not have a sense of duty for her children since she was a child herself.

Then there was the gregarious socialite who loved a party. She had a way of luring strangers, which was the personality that most of the world saw. She could certainly be a charmer, the beauty queen, with enticements she had learned from her early womanhood. These she used to keep the center of attention - of *this* world. The next world didn't appear to be of any matter to her. Her beauty was her strong suit. My grandmother had taught me that beauty is shallow - only skin deep and fleeting, with only a few years' reign and often leading to sensual pleasure. It was never that my grandmother thought beauty was a bad thing; she just knew it had charms which should be used for good purposes. But my mother's beauty became the source of her vanity, of her ability to lure and manipulate others. It was this trait that had lured my father, a man who had been taught to venerate religion and to pursue women who resolved to follow God.

This personality was often the one that had embarrassed me as a young girl. As a teenager I worked in a drugstore in the small middle Tennessee town where I grew up. This drugstore had a lunch counter and served home-made sandwiches, soups and desserts. My mother had entered the store. I knew it was her, because I could hear her loud, commanding voice from the back of the store. She went up to several of the men present and gave them a hug. My father was with her. "Who in the world is *that?*" one of my co-workers queried. I shrugged my shoulders as if I didn't know and made an excuse to get some stock from the back of the store. Her behavior surely was also embarrassing for Daddy.

But the third personality – the mean-spirited, sadistic personality which enjoyed inflicting pain especially on Daddy and me – this personality was a lot more destructive than either of the other two and a lot harder to figure out its origin. This was the evil manipulator whose smugness and craftiness saw no end when it came to plotting and scheming. This was the personality that most affected my father, since he had always been known as a kind, quiet and religious man who respected good women. I can only imagine the pain of those many years of realizing he had fallen prey to a licentious woman who had compelled him in many cases to defer to her preferences than perhaps to God's. Daddy realized his accountability for his weakness.

DEVIL IN THE DETAILS

I became increasingly frustrated with God. If demonic forces were working on my mother, and as time went on, her behavior seemed to exhibit this influence more and more, why didn't God use His power and destroy them? So many people's lives could be saved! For so many years I had prayed that He would do something to cause her heart to be opened up to Him. I did realize that for God to enter into any heart, the person must be a willing participant, and that He will not force any door open. Well, doesn't this put us in a catch 22? Because, if, in fact, the devil had totally taken over my mother to the point that she could not recognize her evil, maybe it was too late. In the meantime I had no choice but to endure this evil but at the same time not to become a part of it.

I recognized that one role of Christians is to guide non-Christians to Jesus. Though I tried not to impose my thinking on my mother, for so much of my life I did feel a responsibility to encourage her to read the scriptures and search out God's intent. I just knew that if she would just seek the Holy Spirit, God would teach her truth. And then everything would turn around. How naïve I had been.

Any time I brought up the subject of salvation, Mother worked herself into a rage, her diatribe usually beginning with, "I'd be ashamed accusing me of not being a Christian." I never said to her that she wasn't, although I had asked her once if she ever considered what God thought about the way she was treating Daddy. I still feel the chill from that question. I understand there is only one lawgiver who is able to save and destroy. The only thing that I knew for certain, at least during the last 20 years of her and Daddy's life, was that her life did not demonstrate a Christian life, that she did not possess the capacity to love anyone but herself, and that she did not recognize her dependency on the Holy Spirit. Mother thought that her church attendance covered the territory.

Occasionally rationalizing her behavior, I considered that if Mother couldn't see the good or understand selflessness, her actions might not be as sinful for her as they were for me who knew otherwise. The scriptures tell us that the more one has of the Holy Spirit, the more awareness one has of right and wrong, and the stronger the belief, the more God expects of that person. Sin separates us from God. Perhaps she was just too far away from God's presence to have any discernment of her sins.

For many years I had kept the faint hope that Mother might still recognize evil. I remembered how she wouldn't look across the hall to where the patients at the Alzheimer's unit were eating in the basement of that Victorian Center place, the place discussed in a later chapter. Maybe the fact that she didn't stay but a few minutes when she had dumped Daddy there might be a sign of some remnant of a conscience. Indeed, my image of her *potential* kept me believing my entire life – up until the last year of my father's life – that somehow she could change her ways, including her lying, deception, and intent to hurt others.

Daddy and I had been blamed for any and all mishaps in her life. During earlier times when I had been ill or suffered some major loss and she found out about it, the response was always, "You're killing me," or "You're worrying me to death." So many years ago I learned to always put on a happy face to her, to always act as the parent would to her child. After all, we both couldn't be children. When as a child she pressed me to tears, I learned to choke them down and wait until I was alone and I could talk to God. And then I would apologize to her for upsetting her. At the supper table she often needled or ridiculed me to make me cry. Even as an adult, I choked down those tears. I knew there would be more ridicule if I cried – and more satisfaction for her.

As an adult I tried hard to remember what I had done as a youngster to provoke my mother to such rage. I couldn't remember, except occasionally questioning the why of something, or not being interested in going to parties or social events as a twelve year old. When I was forced to live with her at that age, I often overheard my mother's conversations with her friends about how "weird" I was in spending so much time by myself. I vividly remember her exasperated sighs when she talked about me to others after I had retreated to my room. The truth was that by this time I had such a low self-esteem and was so lonely that my only comfort was just being alone with the Lord. Some of the resentment appeared to be about my desire to be with my grandmother who had reared me. The contrast between my grandmother and my mother was so hard for me as a young girl; later I reflected about the contrast my father had in coming home with me and then having to return to his wife. I will always remember how he touched my hand as I pulled out of my mother's driveway, saying, "Thank God, you've come to get me."

In my adult years, my mother's rages had increased. By the time my father was in the third phase of his Alzheimer's condition, I abandoned rationalizing her behavior as the result of severe mental disorders and saw it mainly as an evil force that had taken over her life. My mother appeared to have lost her entire soul to this force. Many times the rages were so great that I just prayed that I could survive her mental instability and evilness until Daddy passed away.

MY FUTILE ATTEMPTS TO TURN MY MOTHER TOWARD GOD

In the beginning of my journey with Daddy, I really believed that I could convince my mother to turn toward God. Therefore, I continued to pray that her heart could be opened up to Him and that by reading the Bible, she might make an effort to really know Him. I thought this would give her and the rest of us more peace. I prayed that she could realize her blessings and that she would be able to love Daddy unconditionally. Had she been able to do this, surely she could have prevented so much pain and suffering in this family. This was my thinking until I learned that she really could *not*.

I tried subtle and not so subtle attempts at talking with her about the Lord, the Bible, and eternity. I thought that it was part of my job description as a Christian to tell her about Jesus, regardless of the reaction.

When I tried mentioning my own struggles with sin and how tough it often is to be a Christian because the world pulls us in a different direction, I was always interrupted before I could complete the thought. Regardless of how much I avoided convicting her, my mother always heard a different message. She was galled at my inference that she might not be a Christian. "I've got more friends than you," she sniped. "You're the one who can't keep jobs and has no husband." Sometimes the response was a hissing, sarcastic, "Yeah, you're so good." She told her friends that I was a "religious fanatic," and I had no right to be.

I could only remember once or twice, outside church, that my mother had actually read more than a verse or two of the Bible at a time. In one of her whimpering episodes when she complained that God never answered her prayers, I tried suggesting that we all have to listen first to God, by reading His word, before we can expect a reply. This suggestion provoked one of her "fits," and she screamed, "Who are you to tell me what to do?" She was right. Who, indeed, was I to suggest this?

Because I couldn't verbally complete a sentence about the subject, I tried writing her. In one letter I wrote, *The only way I've been able to endure the persecutions in my life has been through the Lord. He alone has sustained me.* In that particular letter I never made mention of *her* relationship with God, just my own. I knew that only God knew the complete truth. But even in the writing, Mother heard different words than were written, and they provoked great anger. Shortly after receiving the letter, she hissed at me over the phone, "How *dare* you talk to your mother that way. I'd be ashamed talking to me the way you do. What right do you have to say I'm not a Christian...You're not a preacher." She had some other choice responses, but they were always a variation of the same theme, "Where do you get off telling me I'm not a Christian?"

Once during that five year journey with my father, I had asked her if she might be interested in the text I had written for the Sunday school class I was teaching. "Oh, I don't *think* so," she had sneered. Knowing how much Daddy loved church and missed it when he couldn't go, while visiting their home to stay with Daddy after one of his surgeries, I asked if I might switch the television channel to one where a church service was being broadcast. "That kind of program makes your father nervous," she quickly snapped. Since I had really not known him without her intervention until about this time, when Daddy shook his head and appeared distressed, I thought that maybe she was right. I supposed I *was* the one upsetting him by the suggestion. Never once in those days did I consider it was her. A master of manipulation and control, she often used Daddy to get her own way, always insisting that some action would make him nervous or upset.

I bought various religious books which I thought might be provocative enough to capture her attention, quite a stupid action on my part. I should have known she would never read them.

None of my prayers had altered my mother's lack of interest in spiritual matters, and there was a reason for that. Since she rarely listened to God through the Word, either through conversation or through reading it, there was no one really to confront her and therefore no way for her to be aware of her sin. My social worker thought I served as her conscience, and that was one reason she had such disdain for me. Whether or not that was true, what *was* true was that I was the only one willing to talk with her about what being a Christian means.

At one point, I became so anguished, confused, and physically ill from the constantly changing whims and moods and my mother's continuous lying, I wrote her a letter in which I asked a question similar to one I had posed to her earlier: "Do you ever consider what God thinks of your behavior?" This was a letter driven out of a desperate need for me to have a little authority to make some medical decisions since I then had more responsibility for Daddy's life than she did. It also came on the heels of my brother's increased dependence on alcohol and his own extreme mood swings resulting in verbal abuse toward his wife who had been my only source of encouragement from the family. In that same letter, I was so spent that I also asked, "Also, Mother, have you ever considered the impact of your behavior on your husband and children?"

I told my mother that I was continuing to pray that at least in the matter of my father's health, that she and I could respond as intelligent sane adults and do what was best for Daddy. Though I still feared her, I began to actually sound more like an adult, instead of that quaking, timid ten-year-old voice I had become so disgusted with. Daddy's life was at stake, so I had no choice. In this letter I didn't mention the Bible, or Jesus. I realized there was only a slim chance that my mother would read this, but I sent it anyway.

Though I realized there could be repercussions from this more assertive letter, I also knew that all the catering and pandering through the years had come to naught. So I thought changing my method of persuasion might work. It didn't. Still, despite others' admonitions that I "give it up," I just found it impossible until the last year of my father's life to just let the subject be.

If a person isn't obeying the revealed will of God, it isn't likely that this person will receive further instruction on the specific choices faced. One has to make a concerted effort to know and follow His will, and then he or she can ask Him for directions on the specifics. Maybe Mother simply had not made that commitment to know and follow Him. Or then again, maybe she was just so mentally ill that the part of her brain that distinguished self from others was too scrambled. Or maybe I had committed too many sins myself and though I had repented for them, they might be the reason God didn't answer my prayers about my mother. But Job's friends were wrong, so I can't be certain.

I must make a confession. There eventually came a time when my primary motive for urging my mother to turn toward God was to save my father, rather than her own soul. I had almost gotten to the point of thinking, "To hell with her" after I began to see the degree to which evil had overtaken her life.

Marie told me that even though my brother worked five minutes from my parents, he never went over to their home unless his mother called and was screaming or scheming about something. Yet, Mother often bragged about "how much" Donald did for her. What he did was scheme with her on how to keep both Marie and me from getting any of *their* possessions.

Because I always had felt it was my duty to make my mother happy and because I was never able to feel indifference about her happiness or sorrow, I came to believe that her evil ways were the result of having unknowingly given herself over to the devil. The few people, including physicians, who had witnessed my mother's pathology kept insisting that she was severely mentally ill, but I could see little difference between the behavior being the result of her pathology or of her soul being taken over by some demonic force. The more I tried to turn the other cheek, the more her ire increased.

Regardless of whether her behavior was a personality disorder or pure evil, the result was the same: destruction of a family. Indeed, the wrong person was about to be locked away. But the skill and lifetime practice of the master manipulator made it virtually impossible for me to convince anyone else who had the power at the time to reverse her plan.

CHAPTER 10

For some have already turned aside after Satan.

—*1 Timothy 5:15*

THE MOST DESTRUCTIVE PERSONALITY

The evil that had taken over much of my mother's personality manifested itself in very insidious ways throughout those five "Alzheimer's years." Every act of life is a stone in the building of character. Just as one leak will sink a ship, and one weak link will break a chain, so one mean, untruthful act or word can forever leave its impress and work its influence on our character. There were so many mean, untruthful acts committed and words spoken around my father during those years that it seemed miraculous to me that he was able to keep his character at all. It can only be explained by God's presence in his life, before and during his mental condition.

A couple of years before Daddy landed up in the Alzheimer's unit of Victorian Center, I planned to visit my parents with the major purpose of encouraging my father to get back on the golf course. He had been such a good golfer and had always loved the sport. His neurologist had encouraged him to do something that he had always enjoyed doing, and my mother was a good golfer as well. But over the past year, she had claimed that he didn't play golf anymore because, in her words, "He can't see well enough to play," "His back hurts," and "He has no interest in playing now." I wasn't buying her argument. So over the phone, I asked her, "How about if we *all* play some golf?" She replied, "*I* would love to play, but your father won't." Although I didn't push it in our telephone conversation, being the eternal optimist, I knew once I got to their house, I could convince both of them that we all could play. This was before I learned she had already given his clubs to her grandsons and had no intention of Daddy ever playing again. I just replied, "Let's just see how it goes." On the evening prior to when I still had hopes that we were all going to play, I had encouraged my father to hit a few balls with me in the back yard just to get his confidence back up. He did all right, topping only a couple of balls. The next morning, I casually asked Mother, "How about if I load your and Daddy's clubs onto the cart?" "He doesn't feel like playing," she abruptly replied. Oh no. I knew that if Daddy heard her, he would indeed say, "No, I don't feel like playing." I acted as if I didn't hear her.

The golf course was just a short distance from their house, and they had always ridden their golf cart on the back street to it. Stepping outside the house, I proceeded to load the two sets of clubs in the utility room onto the cart. One looked terribly beaten up to be my father's, but it was the only other set there. Mother screamed, "I TOLD you he can't play golf." That sick feeling swept over me once again, as I said, tentatively, "Mother, he doesn't have to hit every ball perfectly." She started screaming, "I'll not play then...Nobody cares about me...." In predictable fashion, I hurriedly stammered, "Okay, Mother, it's okay." As I was responding, my mother gassed the golf cart and sped down the road, with me trying to run along behind them. My breath becoming short and my head beginning to spin, I stumbled and fell. My mother turned the cart around, let out that same eerie laughter I had heard previously on the Oregon trip, drew her head back and hissed, "I see you fell!" It was at this point that I knew for certain that some evil force had absolutely taken her over. Any doubts about her becoming possessed disappeared from my mind. Her look gave me chills. It was a look that was to recur during the next few years.

As I struggled to get up and dust myself off, I continued to hurry to the course, half limping, having hurt my leg when I fell. Rushing into the club house, I paid for myself; I knew that my mother and father had membership. The lady behind the desk was kind, but she explained that Daddy's membership had been cancelled, at the request of my mother. So *that* was it, the real reason Daddy wasn't playing golf any more. My mouth becoming drier, my stomach more knotted than before, and my leg beginning to really hurt, I was still determined Daddy was going to play golf that day. I wasn't going to allow this evil force to defeat him or me. "Could I just give you a green fee for my father, then?" I asked. "Honey, don't worry about it," the lady replied. "Just let him play all he wants to." I thanked her for her kindness.

My mother had already teed off. As I placed a tee in the ground for Daddy, he reluctantly hit a ball and topped it, the ball landing up in another fairway. After all, he hadn't had the chance to play in a long time, and he knew his wife was just waiting for him to miss it. Also at this point I had figured out that these weren't his clubs, and it's always harder to play with someone else's. "I TOLD you he couldn't hit a ball," screamed Mother. The next thing I knew she was driving the cart as fast as it would go into the other fairway, apologizing to a foursome there about the shot her husband had made.

And thus the day went.

My mother decided when her husband's medicine would and would not be given. She gave him "real food" when it was convenient and junk when it wasn't. If I suggested anything to try to alleviate Daddy's nutrition problem, she became incensed and began screaming, "You don't care about ME." After Daddy's anemia was diagnosed, I begged my mother to allow me to take him full time until his physical health might get stabilized. This set off another tantrum. So, knowing the rejection of anything coming from me, I telephoned one of her friends and asked if she might integrate the idea into the conversation about the need for more nutritious food. It might be that Daddy's immune system was highly vulnerable as a result of the Alzheimer's; it might be that vitamins were often prescribed for Alzheimer's patients. Even though it had been Daddy's neurologist who had prescribed vitamins along with his other medicine, this advice was rejected, since I had secured this doctor.

I was never quite certain how much control my mother had over her personality switching, but it looked as if it was becoming less and less. I finally came to the conclusion that mere self-absorption could not account for the scheming and plotting and sheer joy she seemed to get from hurting pure and good motives. Rather, I became convinced that what I once thought was neurotic, manic behavior was actually some evil force which had overtaken her life. Regardless, neither could be controlled because neither had been acknowledged.

Some years ago, after Daddy had had the Alzheimer's for a few years, his relatives had planned an historical event commemorating his grandfather who had served in the civil war. I had actually done a lot of work on the genealogy myself, which would be given to everyone there. While visiting one of his relatives, she suggested it might be a good idea if Daddy held his grandfather's sword at the ceremony. I thought it was a grand idea and would make him feel special. I noticed, however, that his brow had wrinkled a little and his eyes had that sad look I had seen so many times before. The corners of his mouth turned slightly downward, he quietly responded, "Well, I don't know." He probably didn't even have the sword since it had probably been given away like everything else. Later I learned that was the case. Daddy always had much more realization than anyone recognized he had. He showed it through his eyes and his body language. What he didn't say was more significant than what he did say.

Determined that Daddy could have this opportunity, I telephoned my mother and tried to broach the subject in a benign way, with naiveté. "Mother, in the ceremony, they want Daddy to hold his grandfather's sword." "Well, uh...," she mumbled. Then, "Surely you remember that *we* gave the sword to Donald years ago, and it's mounted on the wall....I don't think it can be taken down...."

Stomach in knots – again – I merely asked my mother to consider asking

Donald if Daddy could *borrow* his grandfather's sword for just the day. I suggested that my mother might invite Donald and Marie to the ceremony. "Oh, I think they're going to Florida on that day," she nonchalantly replied. Not trusting that my mother would bring this up to my brother, I decided myself to telephone him and invite them to the ceremony. He gave permission for Daddy to use *his* sword, and he said that this was the first he had heard about the event.

At the little service, which occurred at the cemetery of the small country church Daddy grew up in and where I had been taking him to church, my mother took the mounted sword out of the trunk. She said she wanted everyone to see how beautiful the *mounting* was! One of the reasons for asking Daddy to bring the sword was so the photographer could take pictures of him holding the sword, as well as some of the children descendents holding it. "Mother, I don't believe the children can handle the huge mounting. Could we just take the sword?" I timidly asked. I was forever disgusted at my diffidence with her. "Damn her," she screamed to my father in the church parking lot. She grabbed the entire sword with mounting and pranced it up to the cemetery. She had to show it off to those gathered. She had her picture made with it for the local paper. Once again, the self-absorption had prevented her from acknowledging the point of the sword.

Self-absorption doesn't enable any empathy for others. My mother's continued response of "You are killing me," when she found out about any mishap which had occurred to me was just one example of her narcissistic behaviors. It was always about her, which was the primary reason I had learned never to reveal any problem or adversity that might have occurred in my life. Once as a young adult, I was hospitalized for stress and dehydration resulting from several traumatic events, including the loss of a job and the loss of my fiancée. After being released from the hospital, I telephoned my parents to see how things were (There had never been a single time in my entire life when my mother had telephoned just to see how *I* was). Evidently, I wasn't able to project my usual "happy, everything's great" personality, and my mother disgustedly asked, "What's wrong with you *now?*" I was on medication and sounded groggy and evidently a little depressed. My defenses down, I proceeded to tell her. Big mistake! About three hours after that, there was a pounding on the door and a screaming, "Let us in."

I stumbled out of bed and opened my apartment door. Without saying a word, both my parents, my mother leading Daddy, barged into my bedroom, ahead of me, where they grabbed my medicine bottles and promptly threw them down the commode. "I need that medicine, Mother," I pleaded, with that ten-year old voice again I despised. Too late. "That's what's wrong with you now; all this medicine," Mother railed. "Get out of that bed!"

It is true that I had had a sleeping disorder throughout my life – from the time I was a very small child. I remember our grandfather's clock striking two and three in the mornings long before I started school. My physicians over the years always believed it was rooted in the relationship with my parents, but though I certainly had had my share of anxiety, I had always explained it away as just not knowing how to quit thinking. I had been to sleep clinics; none had helped me. I had taken prescription sleeping medication since I was a young girl.

Many boyfriends had come and gone, most often gone as a result of my placing my mother's agenda and demands above everybody else, including them. So many times when I might have an event planned with a friend, my mother would take control and make all the decisions. On one particular occasion about 20 years ago, a friend whom I had just started dating, and I made plans for a particular evening. My parents arrived at my house on that same afternoon, unexpectedly. Mother said that my brother, his wife and children would also be coming over. Anxious that all this would be so overwhelming to my new friend and scare him off forever, I mentioned to my mother that I would telephone my friend and we could make it another time. She became enraged, and screamed, "You don't want us here, and I don't want to be here. I'll call Donald and tell him you don't want him to come either." I just stood there, dazed.

Before I could respond, my mother had grabbed her suitcase and said, "Let's go, Brian." She flew out of the house, in less than fifteen minutes after she had arrived. My father turned quietly to me, as he shook his head, sadly, and helplessly responding, "She doesn't treat you right." I just muttered, "Daddy, I'm so sorry." There was nothing else to say. We had both enabled her behavior. Years later I felt such anguish that I had not always realized his pain resulting from her behavior when I had greater strength and possibly could have helped him more. But I can't be certain.

On another occasion, when I had telephoned my mother to inform her of the passing of one of Daddy's relatives, I felt I better confirm the anticipated funeral arrangements of my own parents. I had always been told by my mother they would occur in the town they were from – the same town where I had frequently taken Daddy to church and where we had visited relatives. She laid another bombshell on me. "Well, of course, I'll have his funeral here," she blithely commented. I was sickened. "Mother, how can you mean that? Daddy doesn't have any relatives there. You know how he loves Salem, and he's always told me his funeral would be in Cookeville." "If we had his funeral in Cookeville none of *my* friends would be there...There wouldn't be a handful of people." There it was again, even in Daddy's death, it would still be about my mother. It was always about her and her image. After all, it was in *her* town where she had the pity and where the propaganda had succeeded in painting her as the victim. Cookeville, the town she was originally from, knew better.

For me the great dilemma was always how much I should compromise God's way to appease and accommodate my mother. I knew I had been guilty of trying to get her to be kinder to Daddy by bribing her with gifts and secular opportunities. And they never really worked, except for the moment. But neither had my attempts at talking with her about God and the Bible. My mother always heard those words as accusatory. So ultimately I concluded that my mother was not going to change through any means, so I was less at risk to try to follow God's will – even though it did mean exclusion from my biological family.

CHAPTER 11

Lying lips are abomination to the Lord; but they that deal truly are his delight.

—Proverbs 12:22

ECHOES OF THE PAST

The recurring patterns sent chills down my spine. The devil really is relentless, I mused. So much of the last year had been reminiscent of another time in the not too distant past when I began to realize the lengths to which a family which had been taken over by demonic forces would go to keep control.

I thought back to that wet and dark evening some two years before when once again I had fought back the tears and tried to take deep breaths to control my shaking. On that particular evening, I kept saying to myself, "Stay on the road, just stay on the road." The fog was so thick up on that East Tennessee mountain that I could only see the road immediately in front of me. I thought for a moment that if I drove off the mountain, it would look like an accident and nobody would think differently – except of course, God. He and the hope of being with Him in eternity had been just about the only thing in my life which had kept me from going stark raving mad through the previous four years. He had been my mainstay. I had even thought about faking my own death. But I could not afford to blow it now because I was all my father had in his corner.

I had found myself in the middle of what at that time had become my worst nightmare, one I had repeatedly had for years, ever since my grandmother had died some 23 years earlier. I had been unable to save Mammy from the clutches of jealously and greed, and the same saga was now playing itself out with my father. I had promised this angel of God who had raised me that I would take care of her son. I found myself praying the words from 2 Timothy: *Lord, help me to guard the good deposit that was entrusted to me. I must guard it with the help of the Holy Spirit who lives in me* (1:14). Yet, here I was, forced to leave my dad plopped in the midst of drooling, screaming insanity, a place where he knew no one and where no one knew him. The images of that horrible evening filled my head: Mother's whispering with her new-found friend, the nurse with whom she had conspired, too intent on promoting that alliance to be concerned about my father's difficulty with walking into the facility; their disregard of my request to allow my father time to catch his breath;

the "residents, " some bent-over in wheelchairs, some in fetal positions, some wandering aimlessly, some being fed; the bedside table beside the single bed my father was to occupy, containing pictures of everyone in the family but me; the locked cell-like unit with no windows; the blank expression of confusion in my father's eyes. I felt the trauma my dad was bound to be experiencing.

As darkness settled over the Cumberland Plateau, I began to see the events of the last two days as a continuing battle between the forces of good and evil, between heaven and hell. Little did I realize that in the years to come, there would be more distinct battles between these two forces, culminating in one final climax when God would at last clearly control Satan. But at this time the events were so poignant and graphic that I thought I would never again see such a battle so clearly displayed. I prayed, "Thy will be done. Lead *me* not into Temptation, but deliver *both of us* from evil." My grandmother had taught me the Lord's Prayer when I was very young, and it had been a constant source of strength for me throughout my life.

I was also thinking of John's revelation about heaven. I had it memorized by now: *And God shall wipe away all tears from their eyes; and there shall be no more death, no more sorrow, nor crying, neither shall there be any more pain: for the former things are passed away* (Revelation 21: 4). *And there shall be no light there... for the Lord God giveth them light: and they shall reign for ever and ever* (22: 5).

The clarity of that vision had enabled me to weather my trials in this world so far. It had inspired me to live as an eternalist. Heaven had always been a destination worth sacrificing for, and now was not the time to relinquish it.

Because heaven had always been my reference point, my life had been radically different from many of my friends and family. I had come to believe that people, possessions, career, pain and pleasure all have meaning only when viewed through the lens of heaven. But right then, on that Cumberland Plateau, things were getting pretty murky; even this vision was becoming almost as dim as the fog which had gathered around me. Usually it was compelling and vivid; right then, I just kept repeating the words hoping that God would help me retain some clarity of that vision and help me keep some of my wits about me.

I realized – as I knew God did – that Mother and the rest of the family would prefer having me, their stumbling block to dumping my father, out of the picture. Thus, I had to stay on the road. I simply had to remain focused on my *ultimate* destination and that would enable me to reach this immediate destination.

Though it seemed like a lifetime ago, it was only the day before that my father had been in good spirits as the fluid around his heart had abated, and he was breathing easier. He thought he was going home from the hospital where he had been admitted for congestive heart failure, or at least that's what Mother had said. I had thought so too, up until just a couple of *hours* earlier.

Three days prior to this evening, I had unsuccessfully tried to telephone my parents when I was on a short work assignment in West Virginia. Though by this time I had considerably scaled back my business, I had kept trying to work a little to pay my basic bills. And what work I still had helped me remember who I once was. But I telephoned my parents frequently when I traveled out of town to monitor how things were going, always giving my mother a number where I could be reached. After hours of unsuccessful attempts, I had telephoned one of their neighbors, attempting to discover why no one was answering the phone at my parents' home. With surprise in her voice, Martha responded, "You mean you don't know about your father?" "No, I've been phoning them about every hour to see if anything's wrong." With Martha's response, I knew something was indeed wrong. She told me that my father had been admitted to the hospital the previous day, suffering from heart pains and breathing difficulties and told me which hospital.

His Alzheimer's condition increased my concern. Daddy had always been reluctant to complain about anything, especially in the presence of Mother, and his fear resulting from his confused mind and of being "put away" made this reluctance even more pronounced. Moreover, I knew that his confusion about everything increased when people around him were anxious or agitated. And since the least thing agitated Mother, now she was bound to be angry. As a result of an evil habit in her soul, the propensity to be angry, her mind had become peevish, ulcerated, and wounded by the least occurrence.

Unlike some sins, anger leaves no compensation. It is really a torment. I had watched my mother's anger grow to wrath. I had seen her fury resulting from outrages over the smallest inconvenience. And finally I had seen her anger intend to hurt and therefore turn to malice. I had a sinking feeling that I was about to experience all three of these results of her torment.

So as always, I must direct all energy toward keeping her calm. Therefore I prayed as I always did before I telephoned my mother that I would just agree with whatever she might say, and show concern for *her*. That was the key.

"This is your entire fault that he's in the hospital now. You and your medicine," carped Mother, immediately upon my telephoning Daddy's hospital room. The accusation had little impact since virtually every mishap in the family had been pinned on me in one form or another through the years; however, its implication was more serious now. I had to try to reduce her rage because of Daddy's heart condition. My mother had for some time expressed resentment towards my father's neurologist in Nashville who had been treating him for his Alzheimer's, and she had threatened to disallow me to continue taking him to this doctor. She had also dropped veiled and not so veiled threats that she was going to quit giving Daddy the Alzheimer's medicine this doctor had prescribed. I had secured this Nashville physician in the beginning because Mother was not satisfied with the neurologist in East Tennessee.

I tried to reassure her with my usual, "I'll take care of it Mother..." But she complained, "I can't take this anymore; I've been at the hospital all day." Her pitiful personality was starting to creep in. Soon it would transform itself back into anger. This was the part that drained my saliva and made my stomach queasy. Knowing all too well Mother's impatience and volatility, I hastily said I would hurry home the next day, as soon as I was able to get a flight out. It was snowing in this part of West Virginia, and I just prayed that flight schedules wouldn't be cancelled or delayed because I must quickly get to the hospital. There was no mention of my brother who lived near my parents.

This was a significant partnering session between the Department of the Army and private contractors, which I had been asked to conduct. It involved various parties, including the mayor of the town, several council members, and representatives from various federal agencies which would be affected by the proposed flood control project. A couple of Army colonels would also be present. It was important that I was on my game. I had been grateful to have this opportunity because my skills at leading partnering sessions would really be tested, and it was the sort of assignment where I didn't have to be away from home very long. But of course, because I had so many other concerns in my head, the following day I was split-focused and my work wasn't up to my usual par. However, I couldn't even think about the evaluations, because there was something much more urgent to worry about. So I took the first available flight out and immediately upon arriving in Nashville, I raced to the hospital in East Tennessee.

When I walked into the hospital room, my father was sitting in a chair with his little flat wool hat and his socks and shoes on, all of which I had bought for him. He still had his hospital gown on. I thought he looked like a cute little munchkin. As I walked in, a grin broke out from ear to ear. "Heh, partner, how're you doing?" I wanted to give him a hug, but I didn't dare in front of Mother. "I'm feeling fine," he said happily. He was better, and his cardiologist told me that he might be discharged the next day. My dad was in a good mood because he thought he was going home, and all his family would be together. Later as I reflected back on this moment, it broke my heart to realize my father always hoped that his family could live happily together, that they would accept me as part of it. Later hospital scenes would echo this one: deception, control, power, and unconcern about the impact of their behavior on the patient. It did not matter anymore how they felt about me, except the impact it had on Daddy.

He couldn't stay in the hospital, since his heart condition had improved for the time being. Good news in most families, but not for me, because I had hoped that my dad might stay for awhile in a place where he would be safe and where I might stay with him. However, for his other problem, the Alzheimer's, a continued hospital stay couldn't help. I had an uneasy feeling that something was very wrong and that he wasn't going either to his home or to mine. He couldn't stay, nor was he going home. My father's life and mine were about to be radically altered – *again*.

Mother had come and gone from the hospital that day and the day after, much to my puzzlement, since she had screamed at me over the phone that she had been at the hospital too long and that she had to have some relief. "Mother, why don't you go home now since I'm here now and you can get some rest?" I urged. "There are people I need to talk with," she evasively responded. Even for her usual nervous nature, she seemed particularly furtive and tense that she might miss someone important.

I finally persuaded her to leave for the evening and entreated her not to be concerned about getting to the hospital early the next day. "This will give you a chance to get some rest," I suggested. "I *have* to get back here early," Mother tersely insisted, "There are papers I must sign." She implied these were his discharge papers, and I suggested she leave my father's wallet with his papers so that she wouldn't even have to come at all. "Uh... I left his wallet at home," she mumbled. "I'm sure I can check him out with no problem," I continued. "He doesn't have many things here." "No, no, I'll have to do it," she nervously again insisted, this time her voice rising. Looking back later, I wondered how I could have been so stupid not to realize what she was up to.

My mother mentioned that she had a lot of paper work to do that evening, and I wondered how much paper work could be involved with merely discharging someone from the hospital. "Uh, your father might not be going home," she responded a little tentatively for her. "He'll be able to eat on white linen table cloths, not like this hospital tray," she responded with an artificial saccharine smile at her husband. This was all most curious, and I felt my breath grow shorter and my mouth get drier. I tried to coax her to take a walk down the hall so I could discover what was really going on. "Let's go get a coke," I urged. She quickly responded, "You can go; I don't want one."

Okay, then, I would have to ask her in front of my father. "Where *is* he going?" I managed to whisper. "He may be, um, going to a place so he can recover." "You mean a continuing care facility?" "Yeh, something like that." I breathed a sigh of relief as my worst fears were not coming to pass. Actually I told Mother this was a good idea as I would have the opportunity to stay with him that evening and for as long as he was there. "He'll have his own room?" I queried. "Oh, I don't know; don't start," the standard reply to silence me.

On the day of Daddy's discharge my brother telephoned, and I had asked him if I might telephone him back. I felt I should tell him that I learned that my father wasn't going home. "Don't start," began my brother, the exact same response Mother used, when I had tried repeatedly to talk with him about the family. I was forced to speak candidly next to Daddy's bed. "I just wanted to let you know that I don't think Daddy is going home," I quietly explained. "*I know that*," he smugly responded.

Later that day my nephew called, and he too knew that Daddy wasn't going home. Everybody knew, it appeared, except Daddy and me.

From these two calls and the hints dropped the previous day from Mother, I had begun to piece together that my father would be going *somewhere* else other than home. Shortly afterwards a woman came into my father's room and talked briefly to Mother. At first I naively thought these papers were related to his discharge. But then I noticed that she seemed not to want the woman to go into any detail. When she began asking questions, my mother interrupted her and said, "Everything's fine. It's all worked out."

"What's all worked out, Mother?" I asked after the woman left the room. Teeth clinched together, resentment seeping from my eyes, she snapped, "Don't start, I can't take it now." Here it was again, that same old common refrain she used so successfully to avoid issues and control every situation. "You have created all the mess in this family," continued Mother. Transferring her motives, actions, and behaviors was a technique that had worked successfully through the years to place others on the defensive. Normally I would shrug off a statement like this, but something about this statement seemed different to me. *The mess in this family* seemed to imply more than just my father's heart condition. I mused momentarily about what all that might mean, but I had more urgent matters on my mind right then.

"Where is this place, Mother?" "Rockdale, it's Victorian Center," she sighed on her way out the room to go get a coke. So that was it. All this time I had thought Mother had given up the plan to have Daddy institutionalized. My mouth felt like it was filled with cotton balls; I was almost gasping for breath. "Do they have a continuing care facility," I faintly queried, pretty certain they didn't. I was always silently wishing that things weren't as bad as they seemed, that there was a piece missing that would rationalize Mother's actions and make them less horrible. I tracked down Daddy's cardiologist. Hoping that this was a decent place he would be going to, I broached the subject. "I understand that Daddy is going to Victorian Center." The physician looked me in the eye. "Is this a good place?" I asked. "I really can't speak to this," replied the doctor. What! My father was being discharged to "who knows what kind of facility" and his primary doctor could not verify its credibility. Great.

I reentered Daddy's room. Now realizing what was really going on, I again posed the question, stammering, "Will he have his own room...so I can stay with him...?" Sighing, Mother responded, "Oh, I don't know; don't start...I can't take it now." This recurring response was usually made in Daddy's presence to render me even more powerless to respond since I didn't want to upset him. At that moment I wanted to claw her eyes out.

Mother had always exhibited much resentment toward me, and lately, as I had taken over more of Daddy's care, this resentment had increased to utter disdain and hatred. When I had asked a couple of close friends over the years what they thought could be the reason for such disdain, they both said that for starters, I had served as the family conscience. That was the same thing my social worker had said. Whether or not that was true, I had discovered that any question related to God, the Bible, family, country, or responsibility was off limits and generated only rebuffs. The only statements I could ever remember my mother allowing me to complete involved her needs – for compliments, clothes, freedom, or sympathy. The scriptures tell us that if the telling of a truth shall endanger one's life, the Author of truth will protect that person from the danger or reward him for the damage. That remained some comfort to me and probably was the only thought that enabled me to continue to ask the questions that simply had to be asked.

So the scheme had been well-planned out, and it included neither my father nor me. A cold chill ran down my spine, as I realized the fullness of the evil that had engulfed my family. My father and I were powerless in the middle of a scheming plot to put him away. After years of taking different actions to lessen Mother's intent to do this, I realized I had lost the battle. Joined with my brother and nephews, she had succeeded in pulling this one off, over Daddy and me.

While the few who were around her for any length of time might continue to attribute her behavior to severe mental disorders, in my mind by this time Satan had become a significant player in this drama. He really was the behind-the-scenes plotter who had misled my family through lies and false deceptions which were a little later to become fully apparent. Their foothold was in this world. This world's citizens had encouraged them to act on their self-will. Truth has no place in Satan's world. God is the author of truth; the devil, the father of lies. I learned at a fairly early age that an adorer of truth cannot be bought and therefore is often abused and even sometimes despised. I also learned that it is impossible to love one in whose truthfulness one cannot confide. Chicanery, concealment, disguise: these were some of the hallmarks of Satan and these were becoming apparent in this latest scheme.

CHAPTER 12

A true witness delivereth souls: but a deceitful witness speaks lies.

–Proverbs 14:25

TOO LITTLE ADO ABOUT SOMETHING

Daddy was taken from the hospital in a wheel chair to Mother's car (She had had ownership of all their possessions for some years by then), with me walking beside, carrying his little plastic bag of clothes. By this time, I sensed that my father's earlier positive mood had begun to fade. He always knew more than anyone in the family was willing to admit. But at this point, both he and I just had to follow along, my own breath becoming shorter by the minute and my hands trembling as my fear increased of what lay ahead. Helping him into Mother's car, I was forced to ask where exactly they were going, as I was also going. "You'll just have to follow us," Mother sighed, as she rolled her eyes.

As I followed them, for some reason I thought back to a time about six years earlier and a couple of years before I became aware of the Alzheimer's diagnosis. My mother had a lump on her lung, and the doctor didn't know if it might be cancerous. Mother was convinced she was going to die. Donald was also convinced she was going to die, but mainly was concerned about what the entire ordeal would cost. "We'll have no money left. This will take everything." I tried to console him, but he was just certain Mother was dying, and the process would take all his inheritance. The doctor was objective and wanted to run some more tests. I asked him if there were any possibility that this could be an infection and perhaps antibiotics might reduce the lump if it were. He said there was only a slight chance, but I urged him to prescribe some for Mother. He was totally cooperative, agreeing it was worth a try. So Mother took the antibiotics for three weeks. Meanwhile, I telephoned friends and colleagues in my church and all over the world, asking them to pray that the lump in my mother's lung would decrease. Three weeks later, Daddy and I waited in the lobby, while Mother went in to see the doctor. I was still praying. After a few minutes, the doctor asked Daddy and me to come into his office. "Oh, no, it must be really bad," I thought. Instead, the doctor, smiling, said, "I think we might have gotten a miracle." I held my breath, waiting for him to continue. "It looks like you were right to ask for the antibiotics; there is no evidence of any spot on your mother's lung." I fell to my knees right there in the doctor's office and thanked God. I hugged the doctor. I was crying, and Daddy was crying. I know some of Daddy's tears resulted from his gratitude for the lump having disappeared, but as I looked back later, I realized they were as much for his realization that something wonderful had happened to the family. Mother was happy. She wasn't scolding me. We seemed like a family. But that was then. As I drove along behind my mother on this day, I almost regretted having made all that effort to save her life.

Driving from the hospital to *somewhere*, my mother speeded up as if trying to lose me. However, I knew her driving had become more erratic since there were all kinds of dents and scratches on her car which she attempted to hide with various bumper stickers. I almost chuckled, as I thought about the efforts to which she had gone to cover them up. I have heard that people with many bumper stickers tend to be the most dangerous. Pretty good assumption, I thought. She had insisted that Daddy couldn't drive, but obviously neither could she. Eventually we both drove up to the converted old hospital, hardly a facsimile of the beautiful Victorian house on the cover of the Victorian Center brochure. I helped Daddy out of the car and carried his few things. Mother walked briskly ahead to see the nurse whom she had already seen that day and with whom she had obviously had previous conversations.

I was trying to help Daddy walk into the facility, but he was obviously weak, having walked no farther than a few feet in several days. I was also a little weak from hurrying from West Virginia to Nashville, and then to East Tennessee, and then staying awake all night in my father's room from concern about what really was about to happen. My mother and the head nurse were several yards ahead, whispering and laughing together. I heard Mother say, "Yeh, that's her behind us." I called ahead and asked them both if Daddy and I could sit down for a minute, since he had just come out of the cardiac unit and was weak. I hated the weak pitiable image I must have been projecting of myself.

In earlier times I had wondered what I would do if my mother ultimately insisted on having her husband institutionalized and actually gave me the opportunity to have input into that decision. At one point I had entertained the idea that the "right" facility might actually be better than the conditions he was living in. Of course, this was at a time before I had really come to know my father and had limited first-hand experience with Alzheimer's patients. Even at that time, though, I knew I would have made several unannounced visits, noted any drugged inmates and asked the administrator what the qualifications of the aides and nurses were who took care of patients with dementia.

I would have watched the interaction between staff and residents. I would have walked through the facility and noted if staff members were speaking with residents, holding their hands, hugging them, keeping them company, and responding to residents who might be calling them. I would have looked for side rails on the beds. I would have noted whether the residents appeared lethargic. Having worked in the quality business for years, I might have even asked for the Quality Indicator Report. I would have sought out family members of residents and asked them about their perceptions. I would have tried to speak privately to a couple of staff members and ask them how long they had been working at the facility. I would have come to see for myself the actual "activities" the patients were engaged in. I knew my mother had done none of these things.

Thoughts of my volunteer work at a nursing home in Nashville many years ago flashed through my head. I remembered how the patients were gotten up early in the morning, bolted in their chairs, and then drugged so they wouldn't cause too much trouble the rest of the day. They were treated as if they were all alike. Self had been stripped from them. If they acted differently, rejecting established protocol, then they were punished for it. I also remembered how, if they were "bad," they were locked in the bathroom, and often denied their meals. I shuddered. I had always vowed that when I got to the place where I simply couldn't take care of my father, I would spend the needed funds to have people come into the home and help out.

I realized that many families didn't question the practices. There were so few places then which took dementia patients, and many of those that did were understaffed. Children of these patients were still forced to work themselves since they often had families of their own to take care of. They didn't go back to see their parents much, because if they did, then they had to deal with the images. They often justified to others, "They want them to get adjusted; they don't encourage family members to go frequently. " This was the idea that so infuriated my mother when her brother had been "placed" in a similar facility some eight years earlier. Now she had sold herself on that lie.

Here we were at the locked doors, which signaled that this was some kind of psychiatric unit. The code 1234* to the Alzheimer's cell. There was no evidence of the pretty pictures of the lounge areas and dining room where the "normal" residents ate. My stomach began to churn even more, as I immediately noticed elderly patients who were staring blankly ahead, or wandering aimlessly down the halls, or mumbling to themselves. The nurse walking with my mother led us to my father's semi-private room. As we walked down the hall, I noted that familiar smell of nursing homes, disinfectant and air freshener to mask the smell of urine and decaying flesh. I looked in at the single bed and wondered how Daddy who needed an elevated bed due to his congestive heart failure and breathing difficulties would be able to have any comfort in this bed. I also glanced at the small bedside table with pictures of all the family members, except me, standing neatly on the little bedside table, representing the continuing attempt to delete any thoughts of me from my father's brain.

After I had finally realized Daddy was going to some facility *other* than a continuing care facility, I had tried to put some positive spin on this ordeal. As I had followed in my car behind my mother, I tried to imagine that my father's room might be one where I could stay as long as I wanted. Maybe I could bring him his own TV, and his southern gospel music tapes. His case knives – no, probably not, since I suspected my mother had already given most of those away. Maybe a golf club or two – not those either because they had also been given away. No tools. Same story. At least maybe he could have his diet cokes which he loved. No, those my mother had taken away as well. He cherished his wallet with his few dollars. No, the nurse's station would have to keep that. What was really left of Daddy's to bring over that my father could keep? Well, at least I thought Mother might let him have his lounge chair.

Those thoughts were in my head until I saw the room and Daddy's room-mate. The nurse had explained that this roommate was in the later stages of Alzheimer's. Not only was there no place for my father to have any of his own things, I had no place to even sit that evening.

Things were getting worse. With each step, I had to come face to face with a more depressing view of what this place really was. As I glanced across the hall, I noticed a few people were eating. Most of them were bolted in their chairs; some were being fed like small children. "Mother, that's where Daddy will eat," I pointed across the hall. She refused to look. This was a far cry from the white linen table cloths she had said earlier that day they would be able to eat on, as she cheerily mentioned to my father that he was going to a place so he could recover. "Mother, that's Daddy's roommate," I said as I nodded toward the man in diapers being held up by a woman. Mother refused to look.

Most of them had death in their eyes. Daddy would have nothing in common with these people! Though he had difficulty articulating his thoughts, he at least *had* thoughts! He needed to be around people who could stimulate him. Clearly, this wasn't the place. I couldn't bear the thought of Daddy as one of them sitting in a row.

I thought I was going to suffocate. About this time the nurse appeared and asked us if we were hungry. "You'll get to eat in the *pretty* dining room today," she cheerily offered. Apparently, upon the patients' first entry, they were allowed to eat with family members on a nice dining table in the pretty dining room.

There was no way I could choke down any food. But somehow I had to stay calm and put my best acting foot forward for Daddy. As we sat down at the table, I felt compelled to tentatively ask Mother a question, hoping it wouldn't send her into a rage. "Mother, are you going to stay until bedtime?" "Don't start...I can't take it," her voice rising and her mouth puckering up to cry. "Mother, please don't do this now, not now." She then leaned her head over on my father's shoulder and whimpered, "Brian, make her leave me alone." At that moment, I actually hated my mother. Her own voice seemed to always incite her to some kind of crescendo. First the pitiful tone, then the anger. Here was coming that impetuous passion of anger that the ancients called "short madness." That was the passion that had inflamed my mother's blood and was well on its way to destroying this entire family. At this time, the old tape which had been played so often was played again, as she used my poor little daddy as a pawn. Daddy, shaking his finger at me, complained, "Get out of here and leave us alone." He had been duped again.

And this had been part of the core of my father's tragic life. When I became the common enemy, Daddy had the opportunity to become his wife's protector. This, he always believed, would enable him to gain some leverage or affection from her. But even if she tossed him a crumb, allowing him to hug her, or sleep with her for an hour, it was always short-lived. It was always only for the moment, and then it was gone. The torment I felt at this moment was almost unbearable because I suspected that as soon as I left - and I felt I had to leave in order to avoid upsetting Daddy - my mother would be out of there.

Stumbling out of that God-forsaken place, I mumbled to the receptionist that I had had to leave my father who had just come out of the hospital. I was sobbing uncontrollably by this time and knew that if my mother had spun some propaganda about her daughter being "unstable," as I suspected she had, my own behavior would now verify it. Just as my mother had poisoned her friends - whom I had befriended many times over the years - so she probably had also made insinuations about me to the staff here. Slander seemed to be a spice in her conversations with people, and especially poisonous words about me seemed to give her joy. But all of that was insignificant and irrelevant now. There were greater urgencies. I got in my car and just sat there for a few minutes. What was I to do? The thing in my life I had feared the most after my father was diagnosed with Alzheimer's was happening.

I drove across the street, still in view of the facility and decided I must telephone my sister-in-law, the one person in the family who seemed to have a Christian heart and compassion. I had been warned by my brother not to telephone their house, but that warning flew out the window with the urgency of the moment. Trying to control my sobbing and panic, I managed to tell her, "Marie, I've just had to do the hardest thing ever in my life. I've had to leave Daddy in this place." Marie, who had understood about my mother, tried to calm me, "Look, Kathryn, maybe this is God's way of protecting him. At least he's away from your mother." Under other circumstances I might have been able to rationalize the same, but I had been in the place. "Are you and Donald coming down here this evening?" I pleaded. "If we don't come this evening, I promise you we will in the morning." I knew I could trust her words. After I got off my cell phone, I just sat there for a few minutes, dazed. Then I saw my mother driving away. She had only stayed about ten minutes! Should I go back and hold Daddy's hand and talk to him? No, even I didn't have the nerve to face him at that moment. What in the world could I possibly say to make him feel any better about this abominable scenario? I felt like I was going to pass out, and I was sobbing again so he couldn't see me in this state.

For my brother, Donald, it had always been out of sight, out of mind with regard to issues related to my father, as it was for anything which made him uncomfortable. He had been totally manipulated by his mother with money as the co-conspirator in this whole deal. But I had a hope that if nothing else, maybe the money obsession might actually be helpful here. There was a slight chance he would be bothered about the amount of money going into this place, if he came to actually see it. At that time I was actually unaware that he had been made alternate power of attorney, but I did know that money for everybody in that family, except for Marie, was the driver of most actions. Marie and I were the only ones in that family who had graduated from college, and the only ones who could not be manipulated by it. The love of money really had become the root of evil in this family.

There was one huge irony in this scheme. My mother had perceived that all this planning and striving would result in independence and security. She had not yet learned that any effort which is not directed by God can become misspent and end up in wasted energy. No one can ultimately control things except Him.

Nor had she come to grips with the fact that it's all about motive. And God knows motive.

I considered that sometimes my own motives might not be aligned with God's. I wanted Mother exposed. I wanted justice. Maybe I even wanted her to die. At a deep level, I realized that these desires were not godly and I could be sent to hell for them. But I had been too scorched for these human desires to be gone forever. Maybe eventually they would dissipate. I knew that God was getting me ready for the Kingdom, but as long as I had revengeful thoughts, there was still considerable work to do on my own soul.

CHAPTER 13

I cried by reason of mine affliction unto the Lord, and he heard me; out of the belly of hell cried I, and thou heardest my voice.

–Jonah 2:2

GOD, WHERE ARE YOU?

Somehow I made it over the foggy mountain to my home that evening after I was forced to leave "the cell." Racing to the phone, I immediately telephoned the facility to inquire about my father. By this time it was nearing ten o'clock, so he was bound to be getting agitated or afraid. That is, if he had not been sedated. For over an hour, there was no answer at the facility. Trying not to panic, I finally reached the person who evidently performed simultaneously as switchboard operator, nurse, and sergeant-at-arms.

Thinking that I could manage this situation if I remained calm, I mustered up my most professional, calm voice and identified myself. "This is Dr. Huddleston." Since I wasn't a medical doctor, I rarely ever identified myself by this title, but things were serious now. Daddy's life was at stake, and anything I could leverage to save him, I would use. In as matter-of-factly and non-accusatory tone as possible, I continued, "I have been trying to get an answer here for over an hour." "Yes, um, well, we have our phones on night call...," the woman on the other end of the line stammered. I continued, "I am the daughter of one of your patients who was admitted late this afternoon. I am calling to see how he is, since he didn't know he was coming here and he's bound to be confused." Perhaps she may have become a little disarmed when I mentioned I had been trying to phone for an hour; maybe she was a little intimidated by the doctor part of my name; maybe it was that no one hardly ever telephoned at that hour of the night. I didn't care. My objective was to get frank information from this woman, and she appeared willing to give it to me.

"I am concerned about my father's condition. Have you had a chance to interact with him?" I asked, still trying to sound polite and objective. "When I first came on duty, he was agitated and confused." No kidding, I thought. "What was he doing?" "Well, he was sitting in the hall, repeating over and over, 'Jenny Dillon said she was going to come right back to get me.'" At this statement, I thought I was going to pass out from what felt like a huge boulder thrown on my chest, which I couldn't remove. But I had to continue.

Suddenly, I heard loud screams. "What is *that?*" I almost screamed myself, the calmness leaving my voice. "Oh, that's the man who's in the room with your father," the nurse responded. "How often does this go on?" I tried to again sound calm and collected. She timidly offered, "Well, don't tell anyone I told you, but they go on night and day. He's in the final stages of Alzheimer's." "Can't you give him something to control those screams?" I began pleading, the coolness again leaving my voice. "His family won't let us give him any-thing. We go in there several times a night and try to give him something to eat to calm him. He's reverted to an infantile state."

I had been through a lot of pain, but this was the worst yet. I hung up the phone and dropped to my knees. In utter despair, I cried, "God where *are* you!" While I recognized that surely God hadn't lost my address, I couldn't find *Him.* "Why won't You *do* something? Why are You letting this happen to my innocent father? You *must* do something! You know the need here! I'm imploring You to work this mess out." I was almost demanding that God take this over. All those statements I had made to my Bible class about the Lord al-ways being by your side seemed artificial. "You know that Daddy is one of your children; and You know I've always fought in your camp. Your promises may be real, but they don't seem real now. I am bleeding; Daddy is bleeding. You simply *must* do something! You know I rarely ask anything for myself. Where *are* You?" I just went on and on, not being able to stop. I was so frustrated with God and almost disgusted with Him, since I knew He could change all this if He wanted to. And then, after wearing myself out, I finally relented. "I can't depend on my own understanding in this. I am begging you to help me believe and trust that You will work this out." I was hungering to believe in Him with every part of my being, when I really couldn't believe in much else. I was trying hard to hang onto my belief that He was a God of love and power. But it really took an effort.

I stayed on my knees for about forty-five minutes. I had always realized that true disciples would follow Christ to the cross. It was biblical that they would experience ridicule and rejection from the world. And up until now, I had managed to deal with it. But this was too much, even for me. I simply couldn't bear Daddy's pain.

But as sometimes is the case when we lose all our resources, even our spiritual ones, I came face to face with the reality of God. Maybe it was my helplessness; maybe it was my intensity of will. Maybe He just couldn't resist my honestly admitting how helpless I was. Whatever compelled it, God gave me an idea. I phoned back to the facility, against the advice of two of my clos-est friends who told me to "leave it alone; you've done all you can do." I never believed that I had done all I could do.

Calling forth my best acting ability, I managed to ask the nurse in a non-chalant manner what the procedure was for checking family members out. I had been told months before by a social worker when I suspected a plot was underway to put Daddy away that the facilities encouraged family members to continue interaction and take them out on week-ends. This was contrary to what Mother had said, but she was accustomed to selecting information that benefited her. She had asserted that *her sources* told her that one shouldn't go back to see patients if they were in a facility, that they had to get adjusted.

I knew this was nonsense; as a volunteer for years in nursing homes and a life-long advocate for the elderly, I knew that one of the reasons for the fast deterioration of patients (particularly Alzheimer's patients) in most facilities was abandonment and isolation from those familiar to them. Conversely, one of the reasons President Reagan lived with the disease as long as he did was that his beloved Nancy remained by his side.

The nurse replied, "Oh, nothing much...just sign them out. There's usually no problem."

I knew then what I must do. Get out of my jeans, put on a "Sunday, church suit" and get back over the mountain to that facility. I tried to sound casual. "I think I'll come, then, and take Daddy to Cookeville to the church service we've been used to attending. That way he won't feel abandoned and will be comforted to realize he'll still be able to go to his home church. You know, just continue one of his rituals." The night nurse told me she would get off her shift at seven, so I was determined to get there before then.

So I headed out about 2:00 a.m. and once again met the fog, which by this time had made driving more than a snail's pace impossible. Luckily, there wasn't much traffic on the highway.

It was still dark outside when I had arrived at the facility at 6:30 that morning. But no one inside the locked Alzheimer's unit could tell since there were no windows and all the overhead fluorescent lights were on. Lights often make people feel closer to the light of Christ; these artificial lights reminded me of a blaze coming from the darkness of hell. I noticed that all the "residents" had been awakened and most of them dressed. "We have to get them up this early to get them all dressed," one of the aides told me when I questioned her as to why "the residents" had to be awakened so early on a Sunday morning. These poor people can't even rest on Sunday; they have *no* days off, I cynically reflected. Wonder what they do after they've eaten, since that leaves about 12 hours before bedtime. Some were bolted in "high chairs," waiting to be fed. Others were just mumbling and rambling.

I remembered how well Daddy slept in the early mornings at my home; he usually didn't wake up until about 9:30. I always just let him sleep until he awakened naturally. With that mind of his going 100 miles a minute, I knew how important it was for him to get sleep any time. I had to awaken him a little earlier on Sundays if we were going to church in Cookeville. But Daddy and I were going *somewhere*. These people were going nowhere except into their bolted chairs!

This morning he looked haggard and worn. And he had been there only one night. Of course, he had just been released from the hospital cardiac unit the day before, and I had already figured out there was no special medical treatment here, including no elevated bed, to accommodate his heart condition. That, coupled with the asylum atmosphere, was enough to make anyone look haggard.

I faked a smile. "Good morning, Daddy," I greeted, sickened at the artificial cheeriness I heard in her own voice. "Wanna go to Cookeville?" He said "sure," managing a wan smile himself. Realizing his frailty at being released from the hospital the day before, I knew he was not able to travel far, but I knew I had to get him out of *there*. About that time his "roommate" let out the same bloodcurdling scream I had heard through the receiver the night before when I was speaking to the night nurse. I had not thought far ahead enough to know exactly *where* we would go. Maybe we could just go to a close motel so he could feel safe and get some rest. Anywhere would do.

Just away from this insanity.

Trying to act normally and perform some familiar ritual to reduce Daddy's confusion and fear, I grabbed Daddy's electric razor and began shaving him. I teased him about his two sweaters he had a habit of wearing. These were the clothes he was wearing when I had been forced to leave him the evening before, and they were rumpled now. He had obviously slept in them, or perhaps just lain with them on because I couldn't imagine how he had gotten any sleep with all that screaming next to him and the flat bed which couldn't be elevated. Though it was Sunday, of course there was no neat sport coat, dress shirt and tie I had bought him and helped him into on other Sundays. But this would have to do. There was no time to change clothes. Besides, I had no intention of going to church, just somewhere out of there.

I quickly grabbed a plastic bag and threw a few clothes into it along with his zippered little pouch he kept his comb and toothbrush in, which he always had in his pocket. My heart was pounding so hard I hoped Daddy didn't hear it. I was trying to mask my own rush, and my own nervousness. Just a few more details, and we would be out of there. I had already asked for the night nurse I had made the arrangements with over the phone and was told by the nurse that had just come on duty that she "was busy and it would be a while." I thought this odd, as the night nurse had told me that she would get off her shift at seven so I would need to get there before then. I had raced back across the mountain thinking my intention was clear to the night nurse and there would be no problem.

CHAPTER 14

For God hath not given us the spirit of fear; but of power, and of love, and of a sound mind.

−2 Timothy 1:7

FREEDOM...ALMOST

All I had to do was *find* that night nurse and everything would fall into place.

"What's your russsh?" another nurse, one who had just come on duty, asked, making the word *rush* into three syllables. Oh, no. Stay calm, I told myself. "Oh, we're not in a big rush, but I wanted to take Daddy to breakfast before the church service we've been attending in Cookeville." I tried to sound cavalier. Going out to breakfast...and to church...indeed, I thought, the day after Daddy was released from the hospital's cardiac unit. But I had to say something.

Then the night nurse appeared. There seemed to be a glitch. "Do you have power of attorney?" the night nurse quizzed me. Not that again! "No, I don't." Once again, I could feel my heart beating faster. "Why, is there a problem?"

"The facility administrator is on the phone and would like to speak with you," the nurse replied. I learned that the night nurse whom I had been seeking was at that time telephoning the administrator, obviously from seeing something in Daddy's file that prompted a phone call. There was a little fortune in this because this was the woman I had talked with over the phone several months earlier when I had first noticed brochures with this facility's name on them lying around my mother's house and decided I better telephone the place and find out what the deal was. At that time I had told this administrator that my father had been severely neglected and that if my mother ever managed to place him in their facility, mostly what he needed was care and compassion. Of course, I recognized that now my mother was the "customer," so any previous dialog with this administrator was subordinate to the money paid to this facility. Again money was the major driver in this sordid family affair. Money, power, control. These were the issues that continued to dominate every scenario with this family.

For several years - since the Alzheimer's diagnosis - I had taken on the care of Daddy to a much greater degree mainly to lessen my mother's interest in having him institutionalized. Initially I thought with my intervention and help she would back off the idea of placing him in a facility before he was a candidate. It seemed indeed that she had given up this idea at least for the time being, especially since she had not even mentioned anything related to it in a while.

But I realized that my mother was cunning and manipulative, and I had learned she was not to be trusted. The practice of subterfuge is corroding in its tendency, and it had certainly added to the destruction of this family. I came to learn later that Mother's scheme had never been halted, but had just become covert so I wouldn't find out until it was too late. We read in the scriptures that nothing can enter God's holy place which "loveth or maketh a lie." Through the years I had certainly been guilty myself from time to time of telling "little lies" in order to defuse my mother's anger, or to keep someone's feelings from being hurt, or probably just to save my own skin. We are also reminded from scripture that motive enters into God's accounting of our sins, but not one of us can know for certain until the Judgment Day. In my mother's case, this deception was to hurt, and since it was done knowing this would be the result, I wondered if it would fly back and wound her. I couldn't help but think of their marriage contract when she promised in sickness and in health to love and cherish my father. I only know for myself there is nothing I venerate and admire more than simple truth, exempt from artifice, duplicity, and design. My father, with all his scrambled brain, could still discern deception. It was as if the Holy Spirit kept that part of his being that had to do with right and wrong intact. I was intrigued at how much my father really understood on some very deep level.

"Since I had told the night nurse that I would be coming to take him out for the day and have come all this way and most especially since I have already told my father we are leaving for the day, may I go ahead and sign him out?" I asked the administrator, still trying to sound casual and devoid of *urgency*. The administrator told me that my mother had said I was not to take my father anywhere. But she didn't sound autocratic. Maybe this woman had a conscience. Maybe she remembered the earlier conversation I had had with her when I had told her about the neglect of my father. Maybe she felt some mercy for me, since I had driven some 350 miles since last night, through rain and fog just to try to bring some comfort to my father. Maybe God would compel her to place the patient's welfare over money, for just this one time. Something was going on in her head, because she asked me if I would phone my mother and get her permission. There was a glimmer of trust and hope.

Maybe I might catch Mother in one of those rare moments of an upward mood swing, since I was telephoning with others around. I was told there was no place to privately talk to either the administrator or try to telephone her. Out of one corner of my eye I caught a glimpse of everybody staring at this scene. They were sitting in their row. I hated this scene for the patients' sakes, but it couldn't be helped. Maybe the scene even gave them a little stimulation, since it was definitely something out of the ordinary. The lack of privacy actually might even work to my advantage as one of Mother's overriding priorities was her image as "care giver." So I telephoned my mother. I got a busy signal. Who in the world could she be talking to at this hour on Sunday? After waiting a few minutes, I phoned again and received a busy signal again. After a third try, I concluded my mother must have the phone off the hook. Her phone was off the hook on the first night after Daddy had left the coronary unit at the hospital and the first night in this asylum! I could hardly breathe.

By this time the prospect of getting any okay from her was looking grimmer as the scheme I had begun to suspect earlier continued to unfold, and I knew enough about my mother's ire to have little hope for any reversal.

I had no other option than to telephone the administrator back and tell her that my mother evidently had the phone off the hook. I promised her that I would keep trying to telephone my mother to get her permission.

Then she asked me if I had a cell phone. And with that, I got another flicker of hope. I told her I did and promised her that I would continue trying to reach my mother from my car, if she would permit me to take my father for the day. I also promised her that if I kept getting a busy signal, I would ask my parents' neighbor to go next door and ask her to place the phone back on the hook.

Perhaps the fact that Mother had her phone off the hook prompted the administrator to wonder what kind of "caregiver" does this on the first night her husband is in a new place. Ultimately I gave her my word that if I didn't get an agreement, I would immediately bring Daddy back to the facility. I understood the administrator's concern about the risk if I didn't keep my promise.

As we started up the mountain, I telephoned their neighbor who obliged.

We had almost escaped to freedom, Daddy and I. We had almost gotten loose from my mother's rage and mental conditions. My impulse was to keep driving as far as I could, but I was still too afraid of my mother to do that. As I started back up the East Tennessee mountain, dawn was just breaking. "Daddy, are you warm enough? This heater will take a little time to warm up." Daddy answered quietly that he was okay. I knew he was bound to be exhausted, and maybe cold, but he never complained. I was shivering myself, but wasn't sure if it were the cold or nerves. The left-over fog from the preceding night contributed to the surreal-like feel of the moment. I took my cell phone and as calmly and confidently as I could, said to my father, "Daddy, I'm going to telephone mother now and tell her we're on our way to Cookeville." I hoped I would be able to dial the numbers with my hands trembling so. Daddy stared blankly ahead. He said not a word. Not the usual "Okeydoke." Nothing. He knew better. We both knew better.

I dreaded the call almost as much as anything I had ever done; I could only imagine the response it would provoke. My mouth was so dry I could barely speak. I had always known that the slightest unfortunate word or momentary taciturnity was always taken as an insult by my mother. I shuddered when I thought about the response of my present actions. I knew that the slightest spark historically had set my mother's house on fire. Without any reason at all, the sky could become black, and oftentimes it was hard to tell the origin of my mother's tempest. I had come to believe by this time that she could not control these tempests of her mind. And yet I had taken my father from the facility against her commands! This was probably the worse violation of her orders in my lifetime. Here was my good-natured father, as mentally ill that he was, still in control of his anguish and always in control of his temper, and on the other end of the line, my mother who always had to be approached in the most guarded and cautious way. "Please God, let her hear my words and not be enraged," I silently prayed, but without conviction.

"Mother, I have Daddy," I tried to calmly state. Before I could say another word, she interrupted, screaming, "You WHAT? I'll sue that place for everything they have." "Okay, Mother," I managed to nervously utter. "You bring him HERE right now," Mother demanded before I could complete my sentence. I tried to say that I just wanted to take him away for the day so he could rest, but I was interrupted again. "You bring him back here...NOW...Do you *understand* me," she continued to scream. I thought I had heard rage from her before, but nothing had ever compared with this. I could feel the venom through the receiver. If God had heard my prayer, He didn't oblige.

Still trying hard not to upset Daddy, I responded in as calm a voice as possible, given the fact that I was shaking all over. "Okay, Mother, I'm exiting right now. I'm taking him back to the facility. Please don't get upset." I was shaking so badly that I was having trouble keeping the car in my lane. Mother screamed, "You will *not* take him back there; you will bring him *here*; do you hear me?" Same words and same tone she used with me when I was ten. Why, oh why couldn't I just tell her just once to go to hell! God didn't seem to be paying much attention to me now anyway. Why did I always have to be such a quaking coward? Because of Daddy, it was because of Daddy.

Realizing my mother might kill both of us, I wasn't about to take Daddy to their home. Besides, I had promised the administrator that if and when I did reach my mother by telephone, and she refused to allow me to take Daddy, I would bring him back to the facility. I knew that the facility could be at risk since I now realized Mother had said *I* wasn't to take him anywhere and that even though she frequently made blind threats, she was greedy and enraged enough that she might actually follow through and sue the facility for the administrator's allowing me to take my father. I had to protect her, since she had trusted me to keep my promise.

CHAPTER 15

Help me, Lord, for hope deferred has made my heart sick.

—Proverbs 13:12

DON'T YOU WORRY ABOUT ME

I pulled off on the side of the road in the small East Tennessee town. "Daddy, I'm trying to protect you, but I just don't know how to do that at the moment. You know I love you. I'm going to figure this all out." Daddy looked at me, touched my hand and calmly said, "Don't worry about me....I'll be all right." These were the same exact words my grandmother had said to me 24 years earlier in the driveway of her house. Maybe it was God speaking to me. Maybe it was that special relationship I had always sensed I had with Him but was often reluctant to admit since to fully acknowledge it seemed arrogant or presumptuous. Maybe it was God's way of taking the relationship of Daddy and me to a new level. One thing I did know: it was not that "apathy" often written about in books about patients with dementia. Unlike many who write about a loss of emotional interest in loved ones, in those words and actions, my father demonstrated a greater emotional concern and empathy for me than he ever had. Though there are experts who distinguish between the emotional reactions of those with frontal lobe damage and those with temporal lobe damage, all I really can confirm is what I have personally experienced, and that is that up through his dying hour, my father demonstrated emotional responses to me.

Even so, I felt only defeat. Exhaustion. Waste. Humiliation. Depression because God hadn't responded to my plea. I was too tired to feel my own suppressed rage of the past fifty odd years. Why couldn't I figure out a way to just once stand up to this woman so that I wouldn't have to bring my father back to this hole? We had almost escaped, but "almost" didn't count. As I pulled my car back into the old converted hospital parking lot, I realized that my mother had again succeeded in producing the same cowering, quaking response she had produced in me for all these many years. I hated myself. How could I still have such fear when Daddy's life was at stake? It was because I had gotten so caught up in my fear for *his* life, which had become my life, that none of the usual sources of light for me were working. Hell is where there is no light, except possible infernal blazes, and that is where I felt I had been plunged. Why couldn't I finally just figure out a way to tell my mother what

I *really* thought of her and take Daddy to freedom and never mind the legal consequences? I could not if for no other reason than I had made a promise to the facility's administrator, and I had to keep it. Else the facility might find itself the target of my mother's rage. Plus, I knew that this response wouldn't please God, even though by this time I wasn't certain God cared. Time was not on my side, either. Although normally it dragged a bit when I had Daddy because I had to keep him occupied with something every single minute, this morning time moved on with terrible speed. I did not know but what Mother might be on the way to the facility. I had to get Daddy back to the Alzheimer's unit before Mother's rage manifested itself in an even more drastic way than it had previously. I had to consider the possible risk on the facility.

As I helped my frail father out of the car and back into the ward, I could only say, "Daddy, I am so sorry. I am so sorry." As we walked into the locked unit, the nurse on duty warned me, "Your mother is on the phone demanding you bring your father back to their house. She is on the line with the administrator and said that you MUST bring him to her." Depleted, I quietly told the nurse to just tell Mother that I had gotten confused and thought she had wanted me to bring Daddy back to the facility. "Also tell her something benign to calm her like, 'Daddy's down the hall eating breakfast.'"

By this time everyone on that floor – patients and aides alike – had realized something quite out of their ordinary world had happened that morning. There was really nowhere to say anything that wouldn't be heard by everybody, but at this moment, I didn't care who heard what.

I walked down the hall to the room where the inmates were eating. Some were being fed by the aides; some were eating with their fingers from their bolted-in chairs. Food was all over the floor. Daddy was at a table by himself. I thought of the meticulousness with which my father always took his napkin – even at a fast food restaurant – and laid it under his plate, careful not to spill a drop of food on the table or floor. I looked at his food – oatmeal – which he had never eaten in his life. He looked so weak, so I just said, "Daddy, just drink your coffee." "Okay," he said." I could think of nothing else to say to him. My mother had not allowed Daddy to drink coffee at their house, insisting he did not LIKE coffee, but he would often drink at least two cups of the Starbucks coffee I always served him at my house. "This shore is good coffee," he always remarked. I had purchased bags of it for Mother, hoping she might make it. "You might try this," I had suggested to her. "It might help him be less lethargic during the day, and you might like it too." I had included a French vanilla creamer which Daddy particularly liked. Mother had never used the coffee or the creamer.

When my father and I went out to eat and I asked him what sounded good to him, he always responded, "It don't matter, whatever you want me to have." This was the pattern that had been set by his wife so many years ago. She had dictated everything he did, including what he ate, and it seemed too late to change that pattern now. The only thing she could not dictate was the God he worshipped.

I continued to be very worried about the lack of food Daddy was getting and knew if there were any hope of my mother having healthy or good tasting food of any kind, I must continue bringing it to them myself since buying those food coupons from local restaurants hadn't worked. Whether it was her drinking that took away her appetite and increased her craving for junk food, or whether she knew that not eating enough would weaken my father so he wouldn't want to go anywhere, or whether it was a refusal to spend the money, the bottom line was that she fed Daddy minimally. So I continued to load up my car with easy-to-cook food and the diet caffeine free cokes that he loved, though Mother insisted that he didn't like them either. The anxiety from the Alzheimer's condition, coupled with his medicine, made him thirsty, and the cokes gave him a mood boost on top of quenching his thirst. I could fix a three course meal, and Daddy always enthusiastically exclaimed, "This is the best thing here," as he pointed to the coke.

Daddy had begun hiding his cokes, and he would whisper, "Jenny Dillon won't let me have them." When Mother complained about Daddy not sleeping at night, I suggested she might try the caffeine free, diet cokes, since that would reduce the sugar and caffeine. "I *told* you He doesn't like diet cokes," she snapped. What she really meant is that *she* didn't like diet cokes because with her alcohol intake, she craved the sugar in regular cokes. It was becoming apparent to me that while Mother thought she knew her husband better than anyone else did, she hardly knew him at all. She had made him into what she wanted him to be at any particular moment. No wonder this poor little man's brain was scrambled. But it was not so scrambled that he didn't recognize that something was wrong with her. "She's gotten worse," he said, every time I picked him up.

I had learned that by my suggesting anything, I was ensuring that Mother would never do it. Therefore when it was possible, I would telephone a neighbor and ask her to work it into some conversation. There was a much greater likelihood that she would listen to a third party.

The events of this day had just about made me impotent to act at all. I felt I was in the middle of this nightmare from which I would surely soon awaken. But I was quickly jarred back to reality as I heard mumbles from the table where the other "patients" were being fed, or were trying to feed themselves. I was not dreaming. I still had to try to help Daddy stay peaceful, and make some kind of bridge until someone in the family arrived.

Daddy was in the "dining room," which looked like all the other rooms except there was food all over the floor. He was sitting alone at a table, determined to not let himself be a part of this group. He knew he wasn't like them. Noticing a young man and woman at another table, I went over and introduced myself to them. "I'm Mr. Howard's daughter. He just came in last night." Could it really have been only last evening? Surely it was days ago! So much had happened in so little time.

"Oh, you're the psychologist," one of them replied. "We've heard about you." Yes, I was sure everyone in that ward had heard about me by that point. "I'm not a psychologist, but I've had too much psychology for my own good," I replied, managing a wry smile. Realizing that aides could be a major key to patient comfort, I grabbed this conversational opening. "My father is a wonderful man who enjoys conversation. He's spent a lot of time at my home over the past couple of years, but my mother has now made other decisions." I tried to speak as matter-of-factly as I could without emotion. "He loves music, especially southern gospel music," I explained, trying to get out as much as I could which might encourage them to help him be less depressed.

The Gaithers Gospel singers were on the television in that room, and, with that faked cheeriness in my voice, said, "Daddy, here are the Gaithers you like." Daddy barely glanced at the dim TV picture and then turned away. To acknowledge anything there would be to accept it as part of his life now. He wasn't about to participate in any activity which these other "residents" were doing. "Yes, we let them watch TV on Sunday mornings," the young man said. With every action, every word, my dread became greater. Only on Sundays, I thought. What about the rest of the time? What in the world would they do in this place the rest of the time? Of course, it probably took the slim staff the rest of the day to attend to the patients' needs. But not Daddy! He was not one of them. I realized, however, if he stayed very long here, he would be quickly.

Though I originally thought I should stay with my father until a family member arrived, I changed my mind, fearing that my mother or brother could storm into the facility at any moment and cause a greater trauma on my father if I were present. So I just prayed that God would calm and protect Daddy, that He would rescue him from every evil attack and that He would bring him safely to His kingdom. However, I remained dubious as I recalled Job's lament: *Lord, when I hoped for good, evil came; when I looked for light, then came darkness* (30:26).

CHAPTER 16

Therefore I take pleasure in infirmities, in reproaches, in necessities, in persecutions, in distresses for Christ's sake; for when I am weak, then I am strong.

–2 Corinthians 12:10

THE VICTIMS OF EVIL

Resentment leads to bitterness. It is not the ailment or the condition that causes the bitterness, but the reaction to it. Two people can have the exact same type of cancer. One can accept it and make the best of the situation, understanding that God has a purpose for everything that happens, while the other one can become bitter, lacking this strong faith to lean on. Because my mother had been self-absorbed, my father's condition made her bitter because it led to the disruption of *her* life. Because she didn't have a strong faith in God's will to draw on, there was nothing to take the place of this bitterness. She really didn't have the capacity to listen to God in the dark.

MY MOTHER

My mother could never realize that circumstances may favor happiness, but they don't create it. Consequently, she almost always saw herself as a victim. She seemed to be always railing against someone or something. I recall one time in particular when she was fretting and fuming, and I managed to ask her, "Mother, what would you like me to *do?*" "NOTHING" she screamed. I didn't know what to do with that answer.

The child in her had always blamed someone else for her misfortunes, but this self-pity increased after my father became ill. When I was absent from her, I was more able to be sympathetic, remembering that she *did* have to adjust from having been taken care of by my father. But when I was actually around her, the sympathy was often displaced by fatigue from hearing her continuously attribute her problems to someone else - usually me. If ninety-nine things went perfectly, and the hundredth one didn't, Mother's typical response was, "Nothing ever goes my way" or "I knew I shouldn't have come on this trip." It was wearisome because I never could fix things for very long.

She almost always had an ailment worse than anyone else's. She would call me in emergencies night and day, such that the "wolf cry" became non-believable, and even her grown grandchildren didn't want to hang around her long unless she was feeding them or giving them something. They usually quickly left her house after they had eaten. My mother's bitterness had festered and grown to such a degree that it drove others away, except for my father, who couldn't leave.

My mother had always insisted she got a "bad deal." She had always complained about marrying someone who wasn't as "successful" as other men whom she could have gotten. Nor as "smart," or "charming." Though it was customary in her day for women to willingly leave their former ties and say a graceful adieu to the life of the past, my mother had not been able to do this.

My father had fallen in love with this "prettiest girl in town," and with his kindness and willingness to "take care of her," being eight years her senior, she had agreed to marry him. He was also handsome and well-liked, so those attributes also appealed to my mother. They made for a very attractive couple. I understand how it must have been difficult for an eighteen year old woman, who desperately needed attention, to marry a man eight years her senior and then to be forced to give him up to the marines during World War II, shortly after they were married. Although that scenario was not that uncommon during that war, what was uncommon was my mother's need for attention and excitement at this very difficult time. She was able to conquer some of her boredom by joining the Navy herself and served stateside as a secretary for about a year. This experience gave her some needed notoriety because she was one of only a handful of women from the state who actively served in the military during this war.

After she became pregnant with me, however, her excitement evaporated, and her deprived feelings resurfaced. I had been conceived and born at a bad time, while my father was still in the service, and her pregnancy had put an end to her freedom to go out and to have some fun. Most of my life I had tried hard to make up for her sense of loss by taking her on trips, buying her gifts, and giving her opportunities she would not have had otherwise. But with every increased effort to remedy her victim status, the comfort of her chains seemed to grow. As I grew older, I realized that no worldly goods or opportunities would fill that gap in her, and I would never be forgiven for taking away her freedom and privileges. Likewise, I would also feel a remnant of guilt.

The diagnosis of my father's Alzheimer's condition served to intensify this "victimitis." As she *chose* to continue to mow the grass, or bring in fire wood, she continued to whine in an exasperated, pitiful tone to friends, neighbors, and family, "I have it all to do." Though she had originally said she wouldn't let me hire someone to help around the house, saying that she "would have another person to take care of," about six months later she changed her mind. This person had been employed by various neighbors and was touted to be a gentle and compassionate soul. So Daddy would have someone to talk with, and Mother could go places. What a boon this would be to everyone! She, in fact, *was* kind and gentle, and I felt so much less stress having someone in the house. On Mother's bridge days, when I knew she was there, I telephoned the house, and she would let me talk to my father. Her tone was always cheerful. I could tell that Daddy really liked her, and things went well for a few weeks. But afterwards, something about her presence became too threatening for Mother, and she told me Daddy didn't want her at the house any longer. So that was the end of that.

There were times when I truly did feel sorry for my mother. Over the years, I had taken her several times on short vacation trips to Florida, and on one particular trip, we had visited Cape Canaveral. I was coming out of the restroom when I glanced ahead to see her standing by herself, doing nothing, just staring into space and looking terribly despondent. My heart tore for her because I realized then that she couldn't stand to be alone. Her whole life depended on others to make her feel good, whether it was giving her compliments or just allowing her to talk about herself. Whereas Daddy's Alzheimer's resulted in my need to constantly create activities to stimulate him, Mother's narcissistic traits created pressure to have others around her to provide a degree of happiness, however short-lived it was. Though I had been alone most of my life, without anyone to wipe the sweat from my own brow, I had not really felt totally alone, because I had always had God to communicate with. Often I have rationalized that there must have been someone or something that resulted in mother's pathology; perhaps it was a tendency or genetic trait of some grandparent somewhere lost in mystery, well-hidden away; perhaps it was something that happened to her as a very small child. One thing was for certain: she was never taught nor had she studied the Bible, so she didn't really have that resource to fill in the vacuum.

The irony was that my mother really *was* a victim of what I came to believe was some kind of demonic forces. Because she had her feet firmly planted in this world, with its self-approving and self-centeredness, and because she did not have a strong foothold in God's healing Word, Satan apparently had her in his clutches. She resented and resisted God's disciplining hand and therefore missed a spiritual blessing. The master deceiver had planted lies in her head, had selected information for her to read which reinforced self-centeredness, and ensured that she was forever an embittered personality and a self-made martyr.

MY BROTHER

A narcissistic controller doesn't really have a capacity to think of anyone much but him or herself, and I realized that most of the attention my brother received when he was very young must also have come from my grandmother. A couple of my friends who know a little about my history always ask me where my brother was "during all this." Try as I might to conjure them up, I have very few memories of him as a child. But one does stand out. My grandmother was looking out her window one early morning, saying, sadly, "There's poor little Donald, carrying his blanket and his bottle" as he walked down the garden path that connected my parents' and grandparents' houses. He had to have been very small to still have his bottle, and I was not yet school age. As I peered out the window, I, too, was also apparently saddened, and today I get a lump in my throat to realize he wasn't that attended to either by my mother. Mammy had run out to meet him on that day, as she probably had done every day. My grandfather, who displayed very little interest in me, showed Donald a great deal of attention and always took up for him if I did something Donald didn't like. Maybe it was because he was the only grandson, or maybe he was also trying to make up for what his mother couldn't give him. I also remember how we would quarrel about who had to go home with her and sleep at her house each night. This point alone compels me to conclude that young though he was, there was something about Mother that Donald also preferred to stay away from.

My impression through the years was that Donald wasn't resented as I was by my mother, but just ignored much of the time. When he started school, I remember looking out for him as any big sister might and being concerned about his grades. I went with him to class the first day he entered grammar school. I felt certain that he was bound to have witnessed some of my mother's rage and pathology through the years, although he often went to his best friend's house after my parents moved to East Tennessee when Mother's temper flared and she threw her tantrums. He looked to his friends to fill his empty spaces that God filled in for me. I don't remember my mother ever slapping or ridiculing him, and she did attend his football games when he played in high school. She just didn't have the capacity to pay much attention to him until after he married and had children of his own. That's about all the memories I have of Donald as a young boy. But they are enough to realize that he was also the victim of this hidden, secret malaise that engulfed the entire family.

When Donald was young, his father worked most of the time to appease his wife who constantly urged him to do more double-duty shift work, especially on holidays, so there could be more money. That left little time for activities with his son, and that was part of the reason Donald later held bitterness for his father. One time he mentioned to me that Daddy had not taken him on fishing trips or spent time with him. He was still blaming his father for not paying enough attention to him when he was young and would never listen to me when I tried to explain the reason Daddy worked so much. He had been forced to sacrifice his children for his wife. After my brother was grown, he thought it was great that his father worked so many hours because by this time the money obsession had taken root in him and he figured that he would get all my father's assets – if his mother outlived him. I remember one Christmas years ago when Daddy worked and received double time wages, and he and my mother talked about that amount for hours. He had started even then to develop Mother's values and behaviors.

When his first wife left him, my brother began drinking more heavily. He was so depressed and made statements that hinted of suicide. So distraught over his state of mind and caught up in his despair, I had a hard time focusing on my work. I prayed day and night that if God would send him another woman who might love him then I would never in my entire life ask God for any man for me. Within weeks, God wrought yet another miracle and sent a young woman into his life whom he really liked and grew to love. Through these past thirty years, I have kept that promise to God and prayed that my brother's drinking would never again take over his life.

But the memory of what my father had not been able to do with him when he was young seemed to be the only thing that my brother remembered after the campaign began to get control of my father's assets.

I don't know whether this sense of deprivation was the root of my brother's refusal to support my father in any way, or just that he had caught the family's obsession with money and had become a victim of its evil forces. One thing was clear: by the time my father developed Alzheimer's, he exhibited most of his mother's tendencies: quick temper, refusal to address issues, major denial, greed, need to control, child-like behavior, and propensity to drink. All my attempts to talk with him about helping Daddy were met with total indifference – or wrath, if he had been drinking. When I implored his help on any parental issues, his attitude to me was always, "Leave her alone...Why are you always upsetting her?" The MO of this family was "don't talk, don't trust, and don't feel." It was even passed on to his sons. During the beginning of my mission to save my father, I made a couple of attempts to talk with him about Mother's mental and spiritual state, but always unsuccessfully. At this point in time I had neither discovered how serious my brother's alcoholism had become, nor how much of his mother's behavior he exhibited. But I had begun to see his behavior as an example of the unwritten law in families which have gone out of whack, that law that says family members dare not talk about "it" with each other because any discussion acknowledges that the "it" is real. The "it" in our case was really my *mother's* condition, not my father's. It was not a household that valued truth and openness. The entire family, including me, had lived a life of delusion.

Prior to the Alzheimer's diagnosis, I wanted to ask my brother why he thought Daddy had become angry and depressed, hoping to prompt some reflection. I thought I could do this quietly in a separate part of the house from where my parents were. "I don't want to hear it," he screamed at me. "I'm glad she took his license. He needs to be somewhere." "Donald, I understand... Could we just talk a moment," I pleaded. "Just stay out of our business," he yelled, echoing his mother. He wanted her to hear him and order me away. This kept me as the villain and demonstrated his "siding with" his mother. This garnered him points with her.

Fortunately before Mother and Daddy got to the room, he had slammed the door, and like a teenager, raced out of the driveway, his tires squealing. Later I learned he had not had a drink in several hours, that condition probably contributing to this outrage.

After the Alzheimer's diagnosis, it was easier just to place his father in some facility, and then he wouldn't have to deal with his mother at all. Besides his mother *had* given his sons money over the years, had bought them a boat, had fed them and given them considerable attention; his whole family therefore felt an obligation to go along with her plan. And they must have known that if they kept tolerating her, they would get everything when she died. What a pity they couldn't recognize that it was really their grandfather's money! All my brother could remember was that his father had always only pandered to his mother and not particularly to him.

Until my father's heart condition worsened and he was diagnosed with Alzheimer's, my brother had never felt compelled to cater to his mother at all. In fact, he was never around her for more than a few minutes at a time, and that was seldom, even though he lived within minutes from her home. During the time when he was so concerned about the lump in my mother's lung, convinced that all her assets would be gone, and I was trying to comfort him, I asked him how long it had been since he had been around his mother for a

24-hour period. Half-way grinning, he replied, "twenty years." The larger truth was that he hadn't been with her for more than an hour any time since he was about eighteen. Our mother could usually sustain the charming personality when her son was around, especially if he was accompanied by her grandsons and great grandchildren.

But after he had been made the alternate power of attorney over his father's assets, the money interest became even more significant and outweighed everything else. He therefore began to have more involvement with her on any matter related to that. Once he was in that role, it seemed he couldn't reverse things, even if he had wanted to. On other matters, he pretty much just stayed away after Daddy's mind became worse.

After my father's death, I came to understand the depths to which he had sunk because of this greed.

Naively, I thought maybe there was enough reasoning ability to talk with him, especially after I discovered how mistreated Daddy was. However, any attempt to discuss Mother's increasing instability and rage was met with hostility and accusation. "You call yourself a Christian...You have no right to talk about her that way," *that way* meaning talking about God. Any suggestion that our mother *needed* either counseling to deal with her rage or spiritual guidance to help her open up her heart to God was met with intense anger. I wanted so much to talk about *Mother's* condition, because I thought it was far more dangerous than Daddy's. However, hers was the secret that the entire family had to hide *from each other*.

He always jumped to her defense, and many of his words were the exact words Mother used. I never knew who originated the thoughts, but they certainly echoed each other. Realizing that alcoholics do experience black-out episodes, I thought perhaps mimicking Mother was all he eventually had the capacity to do.

Mother had often accused me of being the only one who upset her. When I had once asked my brother's wife if my mother had ever talked to him the way she talked to me, she answered, "If she ever did, Donald would walk away and never go back." Donald didn't have the reserves to tolerate much pain.

His recurring response, "Just stay out of it. It's not your concern" had finally convinced me after two years that I couldn't attempt any more dialogue with him regarding my mother or father since it was impossible to reach him in that place where there can be hope and healing.

The realization that there must have been some deep-rooted impact on Donald from the family turbulence enabled me for a long time to forgive him for his abdication of Daddy's plight. At least I was able to until after my mother and father's deaths when I at last learned of his complicity in stripping all possessions and assets from my father – long before the Alzheimer's was diagnosed. It was at that time he had also stripped me of my rightful inheritance from my father.

Through the years I have looked at his school pictures in my photo album and cried as I try to reconstruct how he might have been had he been able to resist the alcohol and the love of money and been born to a mother who had *chosen* motherhood.

MY SISTER-IN-LAW

As Donald's alcoholism and his role as co-conspirator increased, he reflected more of his mother's characteristics. The demands, insinuations, and accusations from Mother became his, and he, in turn, passed them on to his wife Marie. He ceased to have independent thoughts and, like his mother, blamed everyone else, including his wife, for everything bad that happened to him. At this point he would not dare attribute any cause to his mother

Evil is contagious, and as Donald began more and more acting with his mother's motives, the situation became more difficult on Marie. When she finally told her husband that she just couldn't sit back and continue to watch the continued abuse inflicted on Daddy and me, Donald became more intolerant. So Marie, like me, was dropped as part of the family. Donald and his mother became careful not to say anything in front of her about any personal matter, especially regarding my father or me.

During the years since I had been trying to ameliorate my parents' problems, Donald had refused to allow me to talk to his wife when I telephoned their home. Unquestionably, I was the enemy. "I don't want to hear this, now," he would stop me as I tried to say, "Donald, could we just have a little talk...?" So I had just managed to send the Christmas gifts and write short notes to my sister-in-law at work until we discovered we could e-mail each other. Donald's discovery of his wife's password, though, put a stop to the only method of communication we had. Marie said he crashed her computer.

Although she wasn't hated and vilified, her husband's obsession with control and money ultimately resulted in grief and stress for Marie, my only friend left in this family, outside of Daddy. And poor Daddy by this time was totally powerless to show his friendship. Ultimately, she was forced to separate from her husband and divorce him. So my brother lost one of the most compassionate and smartest women he could have ever married. Since I have heard nothing from her in seven years, though, she may have reconciled with him.

My Father

Daddy was the most obvious victim of evil forces. By now I had begun to understand his sad and tragic life and the "storms" he had lived through which probably few men could or would have endured. I had come to realize that not only had he been denied affection, but that he had been denied companionship. My realization grew as my intervention with my parents grew. I had not earlier noticed his gap, because I was too focused on trying to meet my mother's needs. I still suffer great remorse for this failure.

He had been lured by the "prettiest girl in town," but this pretty girl was more of a child than a woman, and it was one that *he*, the adult, had chosen. So attracted he was to her in the beginning that he wasn't able to see that this young woman had been pandered to throughout her life and was unable to have much concern or interest for another person's trials. Probably shortly after they were married, Daddy realized that his wife wasn't stable and was childlike and therefore assumed she was his responsibility. Once he had made his bed, he felt he had to lie in it - forever. So he continued throughout his life to give her the same attentions which he gave her in the beginning. He always made his own interests subordinate to hers, contrary to the principles he had believed in about the role of the husband and wife, because he knew how emotionally immature she was and his obligation, therefore, to "take care of her."

In recent years I have often considered the difficult adjustment he was bound to have suffered, moving from the influence of his mother to his wife. My grandmother, his mother, always bore her portion of pain and sorrow and others' pain and sorrow without complaint, and she shone like a star, always grateful for the opportunity to do for her children and grandchildren. And then along came this young, charming, vixen, sometimes stricken by gaudy glitter, who was forever a child herself, not understanding how to lighten the cares of her husband, unless those cares somehow made her life less comfortable.

His wife was never contented with domestic pleasures since they didn't give her enough attention from outsiders; nor was she one to be of good humor if others weren't around. But Daddy *had* adopted those attitudes of his parents, which, though noble, were destined to result in a sad and stressful life for him. Unselfish women accept quiet trust and the loyalty of a husband as a happy condition of marriage. But my mother was never able to appreciate my father's loyalty to her, even after she had strayed from him. During their generation, men were often expected to look pleasant under all circumstances and to say no hasty word at work. They therefore valued that quiet certitude when they arrived at home, resting peacefully knowing their wives love them. What contrast this must have been in my parents' home! My mother translated my father's good nature and willingness to cooperate as boring. On the other hand, she became angry if he dared express any opinion she did not have. So he chose to say nothing and be boring.

To her friends in East Tennessee who had not known my father in his younger days, my mother had framed him out as a weakling who was very hard to live with. She frequently expressed aggravation that he was such an introvert. Because he had such little opportunity to say anything, he began to badly stutter when he tried to speak in her presence. He knew he had to quickly get his statement out, and then he was afraid it wouldn't be something she would approve of. So mainly he got to the point that he didn't talk at all, except to echo her. She often told her friends and me, "He leaves the room when my company comes." Ironically, he loved company, when the company was willing to direct some conversation to him. And when my father was at my house and my mother wasn't around, he talked quite a lot until his health became much worse.

Contrary to the image my mother painted of my father, those who grew up with him perceived him to be generous, interactive, and smart. I myself remembered how many meals he had cooked for my mother during the time I had to live with them. He also helped me clean the house, often after working some 14 hours straight on swing shift. During our journey I came to know that as a young man, he was an excellent athlete, playing virtually all sports, and as he grew older and took up golf, he became an excellent golfer as well. And, though he never mentioned them, I had learned just in the few years prior to his death of the many medals he had earned as a marine in World War II (After I learned of this, I had asked my mother where his medals were, and she told me she didn't know anything about them).

Because of my mother's depiction of him, until my father's last few years, I had imagined that he might be a little academically slow in school. But at Daddy's memorial service, that notion was also corrected when one woman told me he was the valedictorian in his graduating class. I remain pained that he was never encouraged to capitalize on his intellect because of his wife's preoccupation with just making money, regardless of what type of work *he* may have wanted to do, and could do. If he could have been employed in a job which had been more enjoyable and provided more mental stimulation, perhaps his wife's temperament would have been less stressful on him. Once when I made the point to her that shift work was very stressful with the constant changing of schedules and the monotony, she sarcastically responded, "What does he do? He just sits there and watches the boilers." She said that in front of the entire family. So Daddy suffered from at least four major stressors: monotonous job, low esteem of that job, no control over that job and a wife who ridiculed his job.

Sadly absent in my parents' marriage were those wonderful remembrances where the husband and wife might talk with each other about their work, and even if one or both of them don't receive satisfaction from it, they often are endeared to each other by mutual confidence, which can dash almost any unpleasant circumstance to pieces. Or they have joy stemming from interaction with their children to lighten other burdens. Unfortunately, my parents had neither.

Actually, as his marriage became stormier, working a lot of overtime at least provided him some release from the home turbulence, stemming from my mother's rages, tantrums, threats of suicide, and narcissistic ways. When we began our journey, he was forever talking about storms, and I often thought of the storms and tempests in his marriage. But because he was able to work a lot of overtime, he was able to get away from it some and at the same time delight my mother because it gave her more of what she valued – money and freedom to go wherever she pleased and do what she wanted.

My father really was in a no-win situation. He knew he had to always let my mother have the spotlight – and he was contented enough to let her have it. However, when he did go with her to social events, he was ignored as she talked with the men and commanded their attention. He was embarrassed, as I was, when they were out together. Consequently, over the years, he just let her go and have her way. And thus, indeed, he came to be thought of as one who didn't enjoy social activities. The image my mother presented to her friends seemed to become verified. It was only after I began interacting with Daddy directly after the onset of the Alzheimer's that I came to realize how much he longed to have fellowship with others.

There was such a contrast between the image my mother had perpetuated about him and the way my father really was, as I had only discovered in the last few years before his death. Many times she had complained, "You don't know how horrible it is to live with your father." Regarding my first book signing, she told me, when I asked if Daddy might come, "Of *course*, he has no interest in this." Similar statements were made at my graduations and recitals. I figured that she told her husband that he had no interest in any of these activities, and therefore he just went along. How sad it was that we never had the opportunity to experience each other directly until he lost his first mind.

He may actually have enjoyed my piano recitals.

My old assumptions about him had been changed through our five year journey together. Patterns that I had heretofore become accustomed to had changed. Up until the beginning of our journey, he had held a faint, almost non-descript image in my head, and I mostly viewed him as an appendage of my mother. Because of my mother's fear of us being together without her, she had created a major rift between us to ensure there had been very little interaction between us, and none without her. The images I did have from my youth were those of placating, accommodating, and calming my mother, which usually meant picking her up after one of her tantrums and suicide threats and consoling her as one would console a small child.

Before I became his "advocate," my father frequently felt he had to reflect my mother's accusation and anger towards me. Just as she had done, he often also demanded, "Get out and leave us alone," and "This is none of your business." And then there had been the occasional episodes where I would be thrown out of the house for "upsetting your mother," following on the heels of Mother's screams to "Make her leave me alone." Until my intervention, I resented my father for not defending me against my mother's angry fits. I really had difficulty focusing on his needs because of his reactions to me when he was with her. Why in the world could I not have seen what was really going on and done more to protect *him*!

I should have figured it out from those instances when Mother would go to bed and Daddy would come over to me in the den and whisper in my ear, "I love you, but don't tell her" or "She doesn't treat you right." Or those visits to my home when my mother would immediately become enraged over something and order Daddy back into the car, returning to their home 92 miles away. On one such occasion upon entering my house, Mother had immediately become really angry over something; I really can't remember what it was. "Brian, I'm leaving." She ordered: "Get in the car." He lingered for a minute, head bowed, and quietly said, "I'm sorry." And then he repeated the statement he had quietly made so many times during past years: "She doesn't treat you right." It was an acknowledgement, but he had become powerless to do anything about it, not knowing what her temperament could result in. Then I was frustrated that he couldn't stand up to her, but now I grieve for what must have been his anguish. He was a clearly a victim of evil.

But Daddy had *seemed* contented to let Mother go on trips with me or her friends, without him. Even Mother's friends told me *after* Daddy's death how unselfish he always was about Mother going with them wherever they wanted to go - and how he would have meals prepared for them when they returned.

Sometimes he even drove them all himself to wherever they wanted to go. If he weren't satisfied with that, he didn't voice his objections. That was enough for most anyone to see him as a victim, but because he had loved his wife, or at least felt responsible for her, he was given a purpose that no one else could entirely take on. This purpose of having to take care of and protect her prevented him from feeling totally valueless, at least until control over his own life was taken away from him. He had always told his mother that he had to take care of *her*, and even during the last phase of his Alzheimer's, he frequently iterated this responsibility to me. Within weeks of his death, he was still whispering that concern. Though Mother always demeaned him to others, I learned that his understanding was far greater than hers, even during his final days on this earth. So he had managed their marital situation because of some unusual combination of love, fear and parenting and hopefully therefore had been able to have some dignity of purpose through much of their marriage.

However, when his car and other possessions were stripped from him, along with his opportunity to "take care of the house," part of his purpose of taking care of her vanished.

When Mother visited me in earlier years, she said that Daddy didn't want to come with her. Or when I took her on trips and asked if Daddy might want to go, her response was always "No." During open houses that I held and invited friends of my parents, Mother would say, "The crowd will upset Brian; he can stay downstairs and watch TV." The truth was that this would ensure that there would be one less person to take the attention from her. The right thing for me to have done was to have pushed the issue, to urge her more to invite Daddy to go with us on our trips. But instead, I pandered, like Daddy, enabling her behavior, knowing that when she didn't have to share the spotlight, she was happy, and everybody else was so much better off, even if it meant that Daddy had to stay home, or downstairs. This way at least he had some time to have peace and quiet and to make a few decisions for himself. Or was this just my rationalization for not attending more to my *other* parent?

On their home front, if I began any conversation about anything but the weather with Daddy, Mother would intervene and say, "Your father doesn't want to hear that....You are making him nervous." And Daddy would echo that sentiment. I wondered how in the world I could have been so ignorant to the fact that my mother was really talking about herself who didn't want to hear anything that had any real meaning which didn't include her. I recalled the few opportunities over the years when I had driven them on trips and had tried striking up conversations about current events only to be stopped with, "Brian doesn't want to listen to that; you are upsetting him."

Later when I had the opportunity to interact with just Daddy, he always showed appreciation and interest when I talked with him about politics, economics, religious, or social issues. And this was *after* the Alzheimer's had begun! I recall how intently he would look at me and note when I commented on a current event. He was being treated as if he had a mind to think about issues, that it mattered what *he* thought. It was not so important that he might not understand; he was treated as if he did. How could I ever lose the guilt of not trying to free him sooner in his life!

Years after the onset of the Alzheimer's, when Daddy and I were sitting at my kitchen table, I hesitantly asked the question, "Daddy, why didn't you leave?" "I guess I didn't know how to," he quietly replied, with tears in his eyes. "I know she doesn't love me. She doesn't come around me." "Oh, Daddy, she does, but she doesn't know how to show it. You know she's a little child herself," I responded, trying to lessen his pain. And then a little later, when I asked him how he managed her tantrums, he quietly responded, "I just tried to stay away from her." This helped explain why he had often worked out of town in their earlier years and in part why he was okay with working a lot of overtime. After he lost his mind and all his property, of course he had no way to escape her rage, except when I brought him to my home.

Throughout most of my life, there was hardly anything that made me happier than to do something that pleased my mother. So I was always trying to think up ways to create some joy for her, however fleeting it might be. Sometimes it was buying her new outfits, but often it was taking her on trips. I had the idea of a cruise for *both* my parents, just before his Alzheimer's condition was confirmed. Daddy had suffered some min-strokes by this time, and his heart condition was getting worse, but I thought the trip would make Mother happy, and Daddy might enjoy at least having other people around. At a minimum, they could both get rest. So I had worked hard beforehand to ensure that things would go smoothly and both of them would have a good time. I paid extra for an outside cabin, worked to arrange the best flight schedule possible, made certain that the ship's physician could attend to heart issues, and even had checked out meal options.

I was looking forward to both my parents having the opportunity to eat wonderful foods that they rarely – if ever – had had the chance to eat. On the first evening at dinner, mother looked over the menu and sighed, "The only thing Brian will like on this menu is chicken." Not chicken again, I thought. "Mother, how about if he just tries this salmon; I bet he might like it and it would be good for him." "I TOLD you he only likes chicken," she seethed, rolling her eyes and sighing to those on either side of her at our table. As I was just beginning to feel that commotion in my stomach when trying to please my mother, I had a thought. Realizing that you can order anything you want on a cruise, I decided to order two dishes, while Mother was talking about herself to one of the others at the table. Then, when the order came, I took just a bite of one of the dishes, and then said, "Daddy, how about your eating this...I'm just stuffed." "I told you he doesn't like that!" she threatened. But by this time Daddy had already taken several bites and clearly liked the salmon, which was really healthy for his heart. She was forced to be a little constrained by others at the table, and even though I knew I would pay for this later, I thought it was worth it seeing Daddy enjoy something not prescribed by Mother.

My mother complained about virtually everything that was brought except the desserts. The vegetables weren't cooked in the southern style; the names of the entrees didn't appeal to her, unless they were what she was used to eating. But when I gave her a taste of virtually everything I ordered, I could tell she liked it. Her jeering at the menus made others at the table uncomfortable, so I tried to minimize the impact of her complaints by changing the subject so as not to make her look so bad to those around her. Some thought that part of the reason my mother hated me so was that I was often proven right about things. This competitive sense never left her, even if whatever turned out was for her good and pleasure. Ironically she often became the advocate or "teacher" of what she experienced from trips with me.

My father's fear of my mother's rage had rendered him virtually helpless to effect any change, so he just tried to keep his distance or when he was with her, agree with her and go along with anything she wanted to say or do. Yes, I realized later this might have been at the expense of his children, but I came to believe had he asserted himself with her, Mother's behavior would have worsened and his children could have been in more danger.

Though close friends declare that I couldn't have done anything to help him escape from my mother, I remain tormented with the thought that I should have picked up on signals when I was a younger adult and at least tried to prevent him from becoming a victim of evil.

GETTING AND KEEPING THE POWER: SATAN AT HIS BEST

It was just a few years preceding my father's death that I had faced the reality that my mother had been successful in separating me from the rest of the family, but particularly from my father.

Much of her efforts were directed at getting and keeping power and control. And yet much of what seemed to be her victories ended up hollow because her power was self-proclaimed. She had never recognized the great irony that yielding ourselves to God will give us power we never thought we could possess. I had learned many years ago that Christians must give their entire selves to God. At various times in my life I have had difficulty doing that myself, and even after my father's death, many times I have felt abandoned by Him. Still, even through this sense of abandonment, I have recognized that yielding to God is necessary. This idea goes beyond giving up time, or money, or energy for others. While it doesn't imply being a victim, it does mean that we are powerless and helpless if we do not surrender to Him.

Sometimes I thought of the strong dignity of Jesus who responded with meekness and disciplined self-control. He simply rebuked His men for their lack of understanding and compassion and demonstrated the power to control anger and rage. I myself was still struggling to imitate these traits.

In contrast, many times having the control and power over her helpless husband, especially as it adversely affected me, seemed to give my mother the most pleasure. I recalled the numerous times when I needed to telephone her to ask permission to get Daddy an appointment with a physician or a dentist, having discovered that he was anemic or almost blind, or suffering from some ailment that he was reluctant to mention to my mother. After he developed his Alzheimer's, my father never complained about or asked for anything from her – except his tools and his car keys. And after those were gone – the one that helped him have purpose, the other that enabled him to escape – he asked for nothing.

I would pray before the telephone call that Mother might not become angry because of a request for my father, that she might hold her tongue until I could at least get out the entire question. She was forever smugly aware of her power of attorney status, which she thought gave her total control over my father. I can still hear her voice, "No I don't think *you* need to take him to get his blood work done," or "I've decided he doesn't want to come down to your house anymore."

Sometimes she put Daddy on the phone after I had made the request to come and get him, instructing him, "Tell her you don't want to come down there." And sure enough, Daddy, thinking he might gain a small favor from his wife, would say that he didn't want to come down to see me.

Divide and conquer. This was one of the strategies Mother had employed through the years to keep power and control. Just as in a company where the "head buffalo" is able to keep discontent among the ranks and keep everyone at odds with each other, thereby gaining power, such was the case with my mother. She had used every opportunity to tell me negative thoughts and

statements other people had supposedly said about me. Any mere interroga-
tory I made was converted to an affirmative assertion. Likewise she made false
statements to others of something I was supposed to have said about them.

One of the most frequently used ones was "He says that all you do is upset
him." I knew this was a lie since Daddy slept an average of 13 hours a night,
ate three hearty meals a day and laughed and talked with friends – something
he did not do at her house. Mother often attributed her motives to others.

To keep the focus on herself, for years Mother divided other members of
the family. For example, for years she had pitted my brother and me against
each other. Almost a decade before the "Alzheimer's years" when my parents
were visiting me, I was riding in the back seat in their car as my father was
driving. I brought up a recent visit of my brother. Donald, who had been in
Nashville on some work activity, came to see me at my condominium where I
had cooked him dinner. Actually, it was the first time I could remember that
just my brother and I had had such a visit. I had always welcomed him and
his boys to stay with me when they came to the city for a visit, and I had taken
several of his girlfriends and him out to eat. But this was the first time just the
two of us had had a chance to talk. We talked about lots of things, including
the family. It was comforting.

"Donald and I had a good visit..." Before I could complete my sentence,
Mother, with a scoffing laugh, turned to Daddy and said, "God, Brian, did
you hear that...Ha...You ought to hear what he said about *you*." I, feeling again
like I was ten, begged for some confirmation. "We really did, Mother...truly." I
hated the sound of my voice.

This seemed like a little thing, but it cut me to the bone. Why in the
world would you want a division among your children? But there had been
many times she attempted to divide her family. Sometimes it was something
my nephews had theoretically said about me. "Paul Donald doesn't want you
interfering in his life," Mother had insisted, when I wanted to pay for a tutor
or psychologist to help my nephew with his reading difficulties. "You need to
stay out of our affairs." However, years later when this same nephew needed
an apartment and didn't have the funds, the family readily accepted my $500
check. I had known for years that I was primarily considered a commodity, to
be used when needed, and disposed of when I wasn't.

Once when I had purchased a rug for this same nephew, my mother had
told me that he didn't want the rug. Later I discovered that she never showed
it to him. Or it was a negative statement that her friends had theoretically
made. "My friends *told* me I shouldn't come down here to see you" she had
said shortly after she and my father had arrived at my home on one visit.

I remembered the lengths to which I had gone to get my mother's favorite foods in and the special events for which I had gotten tickets. As always, I greeted them with special compliments about how pretty Mother looked, but everything went downhill from there. She became angry when I asked, "What friends?" Only minutes after arriving, she picked up their bag and raced off and got in the car. Poor Daddy had no choice but to go along, just shaking his head. There are so many real images that won't leave my head, but nothing to compare them with in ordinary reality. Probably, only those who have cared for bi-polar schizophrenics or those who seem demon possessed can relate.

I remembered how Satan knows just where and when to strike to bring division between wife and husband. That it is essential for him to bring separation, distrust, fear, and suspicion between male and female. He first used this strategy in the garden where it had worked, and it also worked in my family. After the Alzheimer's diagnosis and until my Daddy's spirit became so completely broken, my mother frequently fostered conflicts between her son, my brother, and her husband. She began telling my brother that his father had become aggressive and hostile.

The action went like this. She provoked Daddy, by taking what was rightfully his – like his case knives, his golf clubs, his driver's license, or especially his keys. Historically, whatever my mother had done, he had just gone along with it. But when he first developed dementia and realized that he was losing everything, he spoke up for his dignity and his property – a rare behavior for him and a behavior my mother was not accustomed to seeing. He tried to defend himself, probably for the first time ever in his life, becoming deeply depressed when he saw what he had worked for so hard all his life slip away. Mother would then telephone my brother, crying over the phone, claiming that her husband had threatened her. Her selective reading and listening about Alzheimer's had given her just enough ammunition to make these claims and make them appear credible. Donald would then speak angrily to his father, provoking Daddy to become angry with him. My brother, having much of his mother's emotional make-up and her propensity to drink, would then become more upset with his father and sympathize with his mother. Apparently he didn't have the empathy or maturity to understand how he himself would respond if everything were suddenly taken from him. Like my mother, he could not allow for any behavioral difference the Alzheimer's made, such as the inability to control behavior. Thus, Mother proved "her case" and successfully drew a division between her husband and her son. This division was helpful in luring Donald to obtain alternate power of attorney over her husband's property. The reality was that my father felt "ganged up against" and backed into a corner. Most people strike back when they feel defenseless, let alone those afflicted with a disease which produces great paranoia anyway.

I did not doubt that my mother believed in God, at least at one time in her life, but as the years had gone by, that belief had not seemed to translate into actions. She had evidently not been willing to put on the whole armor of God to shield herself from the power of the devil and had learned to live with sin in her soul. So many times, out of the blue, she would say to me, "I don't see you going out. I am the one with many friends." Indeed, that statement *was* true. I was rarely intimidated by authority figures and pretty much unfazed by complaints that I should be more focused on what other people thought of me and give more attention to making friends. It's not that I think friends are unimportant; it's just that Christ is more so, and if another person is violating His words, I feel I must withdraw from that person

But in my mother's case, she *did* require others to make her feel good. Unfortunately, those "others" never included me and throughout much of her life, didn't include Daddy either. Some force, and it seemed to be a demonic one, had convinced her that she had gotten a "bad deal," that what was good only for her was the desired end. I kept thinking that an inner healing of her heart might cause her to have an instant liberation from this bitterness, anger, and resentment and feel less of a victim. But I also realized deep down that usually this healing is a slow process and doesn't occur all of a sudden.

Besides, I probably had no right to take God's place and pronounce my mother insane or demon possessed. We are told in Matthew to be ye therefore perfect, even as our Father in heaven is perfect, and in Luke compassion is spoken of in a similar way. Although I probably have always felt more compassion than is normal, I certainly am far from perfect. While my mother couldn't forgive me for just being born, I evidently couldn't forgive her for feeling that way. So, if I had been following Jesus completely, I should have been able to do more good (with good *motives*) to those that hate me, and that included my mother.

MY REFUSAL TO BE A VICTIM

There were enough victims in this family, so I had always resisted thinking of myself as one. Feeling victimized is dangerous to success because it implies there is simply nothing one can do to overcome the obstacles. With the rest of my life - outside the family - I had always posed the question, "What am

I doing or not doing that causes the situation I don't like?" Restating the problem into factors that can be controlled always had lessened the sense of powerlessness.

So many times through the years I had tried to apply that same reasoning to my family situation. If I could only discover what it was that could make them okay or change whatever I myself had done to create the problem, then I could fix it. Therefore I continually found myself trying to fashion some solution to a problem or need my mother had. Mother would lay this "terrible" scenario out before me, and I would place my work, my friends, and the rest of my life on hold to try to make it right, often trying to reverse some action I had taken. But she rejected my various solutions and strategies, responding with, "Nobody asked you to help me," a response which left me merely feeling depleted. My own error for many years was behaving as if my parents were reasoning adults, and the ultimate truth was they behaved as if they weren't.

PART II

LIGHT BEFORE THE DARKNESS

Whether the person has been wealthy or poor, rural or suburban, black or white, communicative or reticent, intelligent or learning disabled, caring or self-absorbed, severe dementia or "Alzheimer's" can be the insidious tyrant that can destroy him or her. In my father's case, it was difficult to tell whether it was due to environmental factors causing emotional and psychological changes or just the deterioration of his brain. In most cases, the differences in behavior that become evident are huge and mean great losses for the spouses or children. But whereas in these situations there is a pretty quick recognition by someone in the family that the person has become someone else, in our family, because my father had been pretty much invisible, no one seemed to notice the emergence of this new person and the death of the other one. Or, when they did begin to notice some changes, they were perceived as him just becoming "meaner" and more annoying. It was actually the close neighbor who noticed some significant changes. Since I had not had an occasion to be around him except on infrequent visits, I only noticed the changes then.

My father had rarely been allowed to have much conversation with my mother. She complained that he was never socially interactive, so that was not something which would be missing. My brother complained that my father was always working, so he didn't have time to take him fishing. So what was really different? The answer is that my father was not now able to take care of my mother, although he still tried. He was not able to cook for them, because my mother stopped buying groceries. He was not able to fix things around the house, because his tools had been given away. He talked aloud in church, because my mother saw church as a social club where she sat a long way from the preacher in order to talk with her friends, while my father was ignored. He disrupted her sleeping because she wouldn't sleep in a room near him, so he was always looking for her at night. But he still just mainly sat in his rocker in the den, feigning sleeping. So in the beginning stages of this disease, he was perceived only as an increasing burden to complain about to neighbors.

However, for me it was different. Whereas the caregiver often grieves for the loss of the person who used to be there, in our case, I had never had a relationship with my father. We had never had a conversation that *used* to be meaningful. We didn't have much of a past at all. So, ironically, I, who had always been shunned in the family, actually *gained* a family member! I didn't suffer the grief of *losing* a loved one. And I discovered this family member was not at all like the person others in the family had painted him out to be. Perhaps in the eyes of my mother, he had become a person who behaved differently than in the past, but for me, those remnants of his old personality that I did recall were negative, and it was great for me that they seemed to be gone. I came to see that this new personality was much like my grandmother's. Though there were significant adjustments I had to make in my life, including exchanging my "regular work" of some 23 years for taking care of my father, taking on much greater responsibility than I had ever had, the loss of income, and the breakdown of my network of friends, God gave me an incredible gift. My father and I had the opportunity to create our own world.

CHAPTER 17

And be not conformed to this world; but be ye transformed by the renewing of your mind. that ye may prove what is that good, and acceptable, and perfect, will of God.
—*Romans 12:1-2*

A NEW LIFE IN MY LIFE

Alzheimer's language. I was learning the "Alzheimer's" language! I had never realized until the last few years that this was a language. It had been over twenty five years ago that I had managed to scrape by required graduate record exams in German and French when I was studying for my doctorate, and for years I had been an English professor before beginning my training business. But I mused how little I had ever used either French or German, and now how standard English was actually getting to be a rarity. This new-found language was the one that commanded the day. Although I had never had children, I thought at first that it might resemble a situation of parents with small children who come to understand what pieces of words or strange syntaxes mean. But, no, it wasn't really that either.

My father had his own language. I had known for many years that there are many different pathways to get a thought into expression, but even as a former English and speech professor, I had not realized the complexities of communication. The brain has different routes that have to be used to get a thought from the brain to the mouth, and when any of these get disrupted, communication becomes impaired. As time went on, my father lost more and more of his ability to translate what was in his head to his mouth. I came to learn that non-verbal language – tone, mood, and gestures – was far more important that any particular word. But there *were* some words and phrases that did seem to hold particular significance for him. He seemed fascinated with mountains, clouds, and high security or electric towers. Daddy often spoke of "the mountain." It made its way into our conversations. It made its way into conversations he had with himself. I began to get some idea of what his frequent references to "the mountain" meant. He often declared that *the money was stolen on the mountain*, which I came to interpret as the family getting control of all his money, since his wife and son lived up over a mountain. He often said, *they're taking it all out*, which I came to believe was about his possessions being given away. But he used to work on *the mountain*, and maybe the word also held another particular significance because his life then had meaning. Sometimes when I tried extending the reference to "the mountain," as in a question such as, "Daddy who stole that money from you on the mountain?" he usually just said, "*They* did." Typical follow-ups were "They were way up on the mountain," "That's where they hid the money," or "That's where we worked." Sometimes he acted as if the mountain had not been mentioned at all. There was a man named "Jimmy Jackson" that he often mentioned when he had conversations with himself. When I interrupted this conversation to inquire about Jimmy Jackson, he invariably said, "Jimmy Jackson? I don't know a Jimmy Jackson." So whatever the situation had been with Jimmy Jackson, it was so well buried that his conscious mind could not recall it, or chose not to share it with anyone else.

He was enthralled by storms. "There's a storm coming," he often declared, as he would point to clouds, almost with excitement, and exclaim, "Look at those boiler heads." High security or electric towers also held some sort of special meaning. Maybe the electric towers reminded him of his work at Tennessee Valley Authority or maybe the phone company where he had also worked. Maybe the storm clouds reminded him of his turbulent, stormy marriage.

I could never be certain whether images of the past were being commingled with the present, or there really existed a real undistorted memory that he just had a hard time verbalizing. Often he would point to a bowl or a comb or another object and see an entire vision of life that had nothing to do with the bowl or comb in normal brains. Daddy had generic statements which could fit into many situations, which made him feel okay and like a participant. That was one way he could fool other people into thinking he was "normal." He was clever enough to know this. "I can see you're a good woman," "He's a good fellow," "Same to ya," and "I feel pretty good today" were a few of them.

When I questioned my father, I learned over a period of several years how to rephrase questions so that they were less difficult for him. But even in our early days together, I found that open-ended questions, such as "What would you like to do today?" were often met with "Whatever you think." The same was pretty much true when I asked him what he would like to eat. I never knew whether the inability to think about the question and formulate a different response was the result of those pathways to the brain becoming strangled, or the result of my mother always deciding what he should do. I discovered that sometimes if I gave him options, as in "Daddy, would you like to have a hamburger or a fish sandwich?" he could choose one or the other. Gradually, though, as the Alzheimer's progressed, the only way I could get a response would be to ask him yes or no questions, as in "Daddy, would you like to go to the mall to see the little children play?"

Over a period of about two and a half years, I had developed a pattern that worked reasonably well. I traveled from my home in Nashville to East Tennessee, picked up my father, and then I drove to Cookeville, the small town in Middle Tennessee where he grew up. We visited relatives there and drove around to places which Daddy remembered, places near his early home, the cemetery where his mother, my grandmother who raised me, was buried, the old town square, and the small church he attended as a young boy. This was the one thing in the vicinity that appeared much the same. None of his relatives lived in the town where he and Mother resided, and when he had left their house at night, he would tell the police and others who had found him that he was going to Cookeville. That was the home he remembered, the one that held good memories, the one that had a reference point for him.

I then began bringing Daddy home with me to Nashville. It was awkward in the beginning, since at that point I had limited understanding about Alzheimer's, compared to what I came to discover. I thought, for example, that since we had not had a relationship of father and daughter in the past, that I would have a tough time knowing what to say or how to interact. I didn't know that this made little difference, because for my father, there was only the immediate present and the long-ago past. Anyway, he had developed his own new version of the world *and* his own language.

At the start of this new phase in my life, before every trip to get my father in East Tennessee, I frantically combed every newspaper and called various theaters to discover possible events or movies that might keep his attention. I nagged my friends to keep a watch out particularly for church events because these were Daddy's favorites and just about the only things on which he could focus for more than a few minutes.

In the first year and a half he did not really know me, much less feel comfortable at my house. So he would become restless and say, "I'm going home," shortly after we arrived. He really had never been around me without the presence of his wife, and so he mainly knew me through her translation of me, which he had always felt compelled to reflect. Since she had stripped him of all his possessions and had deceived him for so many years, and since his sister had also manipulated and controlled certain events throughout their lives, he could have little trust of a third woman either. He would pick up his little suitcase, sometimes right after arriving at my house, and it was nothing else for me to do but say, "Okay, let's go." We would get in the car and just drive. One day I drove around the city for four hours, pointing out various sites along the way, playing gospel music tapes, but driving to nowhere. Minutes seemed like hours. An hour seemed like a day. He and I both lost our sense of time.

During the early visits, Daddy frequently turned aside and conversed with someone whom only he was seeing. "Where are you?" he whispered. "Yeh, we're coming to get you," he might say, as he put his hand half-way over his mouth and turned sideways. After about a year, those conversations diminished. The more time he had with me, the more he seemed to let go of his responsibility for his wife, although it never entirely left him.

Sometimes I would just let him step outside the house and leave him be, to his thoughts, his world, while keeping an eye on him from the window. Many times when he was traveling in that world and seemingly talking to himself, I almost considered it an invasion to ask him a question. If I did, he expressed annoyance or just ignored me completely. This was one of the reasons I thought many of those moments were moments with God. Though the rest of the family ridiculed this action, who was to say he *wasn't* talking with Jesus, especially when he went to bed, and his talking to "someone" was more common?

As I looked back later, I realized the emergent sense of self of both my father and me had become altered. But it was nonetheless real.

Because he spent time at both my house and my mother's house in the first few years of our journey, the paranoia he expressed wasn't unexpected. It usually took a couple of days for him to recover from it and trust me with regard to his medicine, his money and the like. "Daddy, I'm your girl, remember, I am not going to hurt you." "Oh, okay," he would respond. Because he had had virtually everything taken from him, including his self-respect, it was natural that he would feel paranoid, just like anyone else would in a similar situation, with or without Alzheimer's.

I discovered that playing southern gospel music tapes in the car was extremely helpful in decreasing his anxiety. The music seemed to nourish his soul. He would "plug in" to them and sing along on all the verses. Sometimes I thought if I heard "Church in the Wildwood" one more time I would scream, but then I would get over it and be thankful that this was one way to lift his moods.

In the first couple of years I rented a lot of "I Love Lucy" and Andy Griffith video tapes, thinking that the only thing Daddy could relate to were images of his long-ago past. He could sometimes catch the one-liners, and these were tapes which did indeed have a reference point from long ago. Or even if he didn't catch them, he heard the audience's laughter, and then he knew something in them was comical. As with anything on television, however, I discovered that he still couldn't stay entirely focused unless I reinforced whatever was being said, comment on it, paraphrase it, or ask Daddy a question about it. "Daddy, did you have a car like that?" I might ask. Or "Mammy used to love this show." "I know," he would say. Sometimes these were good for thirty minutes at a stretch, since I could fast forward tapes through the commercials.

Later, however, I learned that we could watch the news about the stock market, the war on terror, or the weather. I began assuming that he *could* understand more than I had originally thought, even though he might not have the words to demonstrate his understanding. The key was to talk to him about whatever was on the news. "Daddy, let's turn on the news and see how much I've lost today on my stock...See those red marks...that's my Intel," I would say lightheartedly. He smiled and nodded as if he understood. I could never know for sure. But the fact that I acted as if he did know seemed to calm and satisfy him. I always talked to him as if he understood. If I didn't keep up some type of engagement, he would continually pick at his fingers, his hair, or the chair arm.

Sometimes we would just go to the mall and sit and watch the little children. He liked talking with them. It was as if they could see each other's souls. He knew they were innocent. It was intriguing to hear him make complete sentences with them – something he rarely ever did with adults. Sometimes I thought it might be because the very young weren't judging him. They weren't interrupting him or finishing his sentences for him. Even in his demented state, he was still their elder, their superior.

Because we would be away from my mother, I figured he might enjoy hitting a few balls at the golf course. He had told me in the beginning that he was not allowed to play golf, and I knew this was a fact at my mother's home. Nevertheless, I thought Daddy and I could at least go to the driving range, so I asked Mother if we could take a few of his clubs. She was evasive and declared that he couldn't play golf any more (as she earlier insisted), but finally scrambled about to find some old clubs which I knew weren't Daddy's. He also knew they weren't his because he knew his had been given away to his grandson. It was tough rebuilding any confidence and just to convince him to get out of the car.

In the beginning, I rented a golf cart and paid the green fees for both of us, although I had little intention of playing myself since I didn't want to hold people up behind us. Knowing he needed help selecting the right club, I helped him to discern the relationship between where he was and where he needed to be. I led him to the tee-off place and pointed in the direction of the green. Running a few yards down the fairway, I pointed in the direction of the green. I then ran back and turned Daddy in that direction, since his motor skills had begun declining. More times than not, he was able to hit the ball pretty smoothly, swinging as he had always done. He had always been such a good golfer, and this was just one more thing he had not been allowed to continue. It was time-consuming, and many foursomes played through. But his delight was worth the effort when he did hit a ball that stayed in the fairway.

He became easily discouraged, however, when he topped a ball, and he responded, with some agitation in his voice, "I told you I can't play golf anymore." I then decided the driving range was a better bet and began to take him to just hit a few balls. Armed with water, cookies, and an outside lawn chair so he could sit down if he became tired, we headed out. With his aortic stenosis and arthritis, he had a hard time standing. I would hit and then say, "Daddy, now it's your turn." "I told you I can't hit a ball anymore; I'm not allowed to," he despondently muttered. "Daddy, you're doing great; you can't expect to hit it like you did fifty years ago; look how awful I am." And eventually, he would get up out of the chair and hit a ball, probably more to appease me than anything else. As Daddy's sight and heart conditions worsened and he began topping more balls, I thought it better to just try the putting green. But if in any way I touched the ball with my foot to ensure it went in the cup, he became sullen because he knew the ball had not landed in the cup from his own effort. I was pandering to him. Then, it was the hall, where I had placed one of those fake turf runners with a cup, and we putted there a little. After a time, though, I decided the activity had more of a negative impact on him than positive and gave the whole thing up.

I thought mistakenly that he might enjoy watching golf on television. He did not. I ultimately concluded that it reminded him of something which he could no longer do and that it was not "up close and personal."

Once, Daddy went with me into a nearby hardware store where he purchased a small item. It choked me up to see what a simple thing like making a purchase did for him. This was something he had not had a chance to do for a long time. He promptly and proudly pulled out his little wallet and several dollars. The kind clerk took the amount she needed.

He was always trying to give me something. It could be a piece of paper towel, a penny, his comb, his one pocket knife he had been allowed to keep. It could be anything. Even in the later stages of his disease, Daddy seemed to be conscious that I had been sacrificed in this family, and he in his own way wanted to make it up to me. By this time he had learned that I was "not one of them." "Here, take this," he would say, as he handed me his little case knife. He carried on his person just about everything he had left that hadn't been taken from him. He would often try to give me his wallet. When I would go into his room to check on him through the night, he would always have his little pouch with his change and dollar bills clutched in his hand. It tore me up to realize how little he felt he had left of his life. That's why I just had to make him think about other things and try to keep his mind off what he no longer had.

He continued to struggle for some control over his life. I was racing against time to make up to him his life-long deprivation, and ironically, he seemed to try in his own way to do the same for me.

When he first began staying with me, he wanted to sleep on *top of* his razor, belt and wallet and with a weight of things in his pockets such as change, tooth brush, tooth paste, combs, case knife, and toilet paper. This action was triggered in part because he was used to doing that at my mother's house but in larger part because he realized he had lost all his property, and the paranoia that usually accompanies Alzheimer's patients was intensified. I came to believe that one of the reasons he didn't sleep well at his house was that all that stuff he slept over had to be bumpy. I knew he couldn't be that comfortable. I kidded him that he was just like a boy scout – prepared for any emergency. I continued to suggest to him that it might be a little more comfortable without all that under his head, but I always added, "But it's your decision." He would smile back, but he usually didn't remove them until he came to understand my motives and trust me.

Over a period of time, after I did gain his trust, I was able to convince him to put his items on "his" little bedside table, and I finally got him to agree to sleep in pajamas. "Daddy, I believe you'll be more comfortable in these, but it's your choice, of course," I recommended every night.

I slept on a couch right outside Daddy's room at my home, so I could always hear him when he got up. Eventually, I put bells on his bedroom door and bathroom door, which led from his bedroom, so that if I did drift off, I would still hear him. Although his motor skills decreased at night, he had never stepped outside my house, but as he began losing recognition of most everything, he would mistake parts of the house for the bathroom, heat vents for latrines, or oriental rugs for water closets. This confusion came to be one of the biggest challenges at day or night. Sometimes I didn't wake up until I heard the splatter of water on the floor. I became compelled to frequently ask him if he needed to use the bathroom and show him where it was. He might have just used the restroom a couple of minutes before, but that minute had passed. This was now.

I found all kinds of things in all kinds of places. Often I would spend an hour looking for the garage door opener, or my keys, or my television remote, only finally to ask, "Daddy, I just can't find my keys. Have you seen them? We just can't go until I find them." "No, I haven't seen them." "Just in case you picked them up by accident, would you mind looking in your pants' pocket?" There they would be. I became convinced that much of the reason he tried to take whatever he could was so that he could find them for me and therefore be helpful. It gave him a purpose. I tried to always remember to say, "Daddy, thank you for keeping them safe for me." "That's why I kept them for you," he would respond. Or maybe it was that he was quite conscious that he had lost control of all his possessions, except what he had on him, and this was his way of trying to have just one more something of his own. Maybe it was a combination of both.

Processes for Taking Medicine, Bathing, and Dressing

I usually let my father sleep until he woke up, which was usually late in the morning, and he therefore ended up sleeping about ten hours. He was exhausted. He told me that it was wonderful to be able to sleep so well. Maybe it was because he felt safe and secure at my house. So many things broke my heart, like at meals when he would eat so heartily and tell me that he wasn't used to getting much food. Some might say that with his condition, he just didn't remember. I knew better because every single time I picked him up, he had lost weight from the preceding time when I had taken him back to my mother's house. I sometimes had to awaken him in order to give him his medicine and food before it became too late. Bringing a warm washcloth for him to wash his face and hands, I always greeted him with, "Good morning, Daddy. Did you sleep well? I think you did." He always responded, "Lord, yes, I shore did." He would look at me and grin, almost like a little baby when he's gotten his nap out and wakes up with that beatific smile. I would then bring him some coffee so that the caffeine would get that blood flowing, giving him a little added boost and lift for his spirits before I gave him his medicine.

Because Daddy had two major conditions, Alzheimer's and aortic stenosis, he had to take a lot of medicine. Some were prescribed by his neurologist, some by his cardiologist, and some by his internal physician. He had a pill to help get his brain going, one to help stop it at night; a pill to prevent constipation and one to prevent diarrhea; a pill to increase his mood, and one to decrease his agitation and hallucinations; a pill to reduce the thickness of his blood and a pill to increase his blood pressure. He was supposed to take vitamins, but because Mother refused to give him those, I thought it best on his stomach to leave them off to have some consistency. She had told me more than once that he took too many pills and thought that most were unnecessary. She also said he didn't want to take the pills. I halfway believed this statement because he said more than once, "She's trying to kill me." One reason she didn't give him his pills was that she didn't want to bother with the process; another was that if Daddy didn't want to take them, she became angry and then just him alone for him to take them by himself. Naturally he didn't. So I was never confident that the pills which had been prescribed by his neurologist and cardiologist in Nashville were given when Daddy was not with me. Sometimes I thought she told me this just to worry me. Whatever all the reasons were, I knew he had not taken all his pills because I counted them when he was with me, and the numbers never added up.

It was even tricky for me at first to get him to take his pills because I didn't realize there was a process required. Sometimes I would find them thrown under the table, under his pillow, or in his shoe. Always trying to give him a choice in taking them, I said, "It's your decision, but I think it would be better if you took these pills. What do you think?" I did learn I had to stay right with him while he took them, but I always thanked him for obliging me.

As the Alzheimer's progressed, the process for his taking the medicine became longer. Ultimately it involved about ten steps, and providing one-step directions seemed to help. "Daddy, I've brought you your appetizer," I kidded him, as I brought him the pills while he was still in bed and put them in his hand. I was careful to only bring him his medicine after I had brought him his coffee he loved, which continued to lift his mood a little. "Daddy, here's your pills. I thought we could just go ahead and get this out of the way." "Okey-doke," he would respond. "Here are your first ones," as I placed the pills in his hand. "Now you can put them in your mouth....Here's your juice to take them with. Now, Daddy, you can go ahead if you want to and drink the juice." He would open his mouth wide and show me had taken them. In the final stages I had to cue him in to place the glass to his mouth, and then even to swallow the liquid. Eventually, I had to hold the glass and help him with the straw. I needed to cue him in on how much liquid to take for each "batch," or he would drink all the juice at once and there would be none left for the rest of the pills.

If giving him his medicine was a 10 step process, bathing had to be about a 20-step. Many people with dementia have an aversion to bathing, and no one seems to know why. My father was no exception. Even though he had always been a very clean man, he was never excited about a bath and almost always required some coaxing. It actually became quite stressful at times, especially in the later stages. It could have been related to his getting cold. Since his blood pressure tended to run low, he often was chilly. Also, he had always been a very private and modest man, and this modesty could very well explain part of the stress. Preserving that modesty and dignity was challenging, but I was determined to do it. After our coffee and "appetizers," I asked him, "Daddy, how about sitting up now. Can you put your feet on the floor? We're going to get you ready for your bath, so you will feel better." He was never convinced with that statement. The bathroom was just a few steps from his bed, so after helping him undress down to his underwear, I quickly turned the shower on so the temperature would be just right and made certain there was only a gentle stream before I had him step into the tub. In the final stage of his life, I just gave him "sponge baths" in bed. In the shower he had to be cued about what to do with the wash rag and the soap, and the actual process of washing all his body. When his short-term memory was totally gone, he might wash his feet ten times. All through this I tried hard to leave the shower curtain almost totally closed, with just a small opening so I could peer around the edge of the curtain to ensure he was okay. I also had a bath seat, and when he sat on it, he could use a wash rag to cover parts of his body while I reached around the curtain to wash his hair. I would then move the shower head to rinse it. It was important to move the shower head around his body instead of having him move. Occasionally he preferred to stand rather than sit on the bath seat, and when he did, he seemed less fearful standing with his body away from the shower stream. And such the process went. The shower always ended up with water all over the bathroom floor and all over me, but it was only water. It became more difficult for me during the last year of his life, as my osteoporosis and degenerative discs worsened. But I was determined to help him shower in a way to preserve his dignity.

People tend to take for granted the complex physical and cognitive skills involved in selecting and putting on clothes. It was even more complex for my father because of the difference in attention my mother and I paid to this activity. Sometimes he put the pajama bottoms on *over* his pants, and we had to reverse that action. He also continued to keep on two sweaters – both cardigans – at bedtime. But these actions together were virtually harmless, just taking a little extra time to reverse. Dressing becomes challenging for all Alzheimer's patients, but the different attitudes my mother and I had about what he could and could not do probably made his confusion worse than others with the disease.

In our early interactions, getting him to leave off some of the bulk of his clothes at bedtime and change into his pajamas was a challenge because he was accustomed to sleeping in all his clothes – hat, sweater, jacket, and anything else he may have had on his body. Shifting the rituals was tricky. I often thought it was like joint custody of a child where one parent tries to make up for the gaps when he or she has the child. But then the child always has to go back to the other home.

Once when I asked my mother if she might encourage him to sleep in his pajamas so he would get used to them, reminding her that she would have to cue him, the question triggered one of her tantrums. "You do it your way, and I'll do it mine," she snapped. She didn't have the patience to take the kind of time required to help him in and out of clothes. So I just had to let that alone.

In the early stages of his disease, I learned that when he was at my mother's, he changed his clothes often, perhaps because this was one task he could still do without her permission or help, or perhaps just because it gave him something else to do besides sit all day in his chair. It reminded me of T.S. Eliot's older character Prufrock, who came to measure out his life "with coffee spoons," reflecting on the limited opportunities he now had to prove to himself he was still living. Daddy's clothes were just about the only thing he had left, so he had taken all them out of his closet at my mother's home and put them in the car, just trying to hang on to some of his possessions and a remnant of his independence. Then my mother locked them in the car trunk. How frightening it is to those afflicted with the disease, especially in the beginning stages, to realize that their brain is becoming so scrambled that they lose all control over all aspects of their lives.

When I first began interacting with my father, he could still dress himself pretty well, even tying his tie. I liked for him to decide what he wanted to wear to give him some control over at least one part of his life. However, in the beginning, he tended to respond, "Whatever you want me to wear," as he shrugged his shoulders. As time went on, however, he seemed pleased to be able to do this, and for his daytime wear, he tended to prefer his khaki pants and long-sleeved shirt and cardigan that he had worn for years. But he did not change his clothes often because we were always doing things.

As the disease progressed, choosing clothes became more challenging, especially if there were too many choices. So I began limiting the choice: would he like to wear the khakis or the dark colored pants? By the middle stages of the disease, I temporarily had to hide all clothes except those he was to put on, so he wouldn't try to put them all on. Wanting always to preserve his modesty and dignity, I laid out his clothes to be worn that day on the bed, with the items to be put on first at the top of the bed, the second ones next, and so on, and then I left the room. He then could still fairly effectively dress himself, especially since all others were out of sight. Only by taking them from his sight could the *recollection* cease.

Besides the fact that he was not used to sleeping in pajamas at my mother's house, there were two other challenges in getting him out of his day clothes and into his night ones. When his motor skills began to rapidly decline, he became confused about whether he was getting dressed or undressed. As fast as I would button his pajama shirt, he would unbutton it. Also, with the deterioration of time consciousness, he would forget whether it was morning or night and therefore if he needed pajamas or regular clothes on.

With the progression of his *stormy* disease, he had to be cued more and more about dressing. It got to the point where it took both of us about an hour for him to get dressed. Giving him the opportunity to do what he still could do made the process longer than if I had just dressed him myself, but giving him that opportunity helped preserve a little of his dignity and was worth it.

After his motor skills were pretty much gone, he could not dress himself at all. During the last year, I turned him around toward me and dressed him much as I would a baby. It was so painful to see his pain of losing all of his independence. By this time, when he was at Mother's, I was told he stayed in the same clothes for days. Cleanliness had always been important to Daddy, and having to stay in dirty clothes was one more thing that broke my heart.

If we were going to Cookeville on Sundays, I needed to allow an extra hour and a half to have enough time for helping him take his medicine, bathe, dress, and eat breakfast before we headed 95 miles up the road to his old country church. In the beginning, the preparation time was shorter because he could do more for himself, but after a couple of years, timing exactly became more important. I needed to have breakfast well under way before awakening him and all his morning medicine laid out. Every minute was important, because once Daddy was awake, he had to be moving or doing something. After about three and a half years into our journey, I had to cue him in on most everything, and unlike an infant, I could not contain him if I were not in his presence.

Trying to Reconcile with Our Nemesis

I wanted to take my father to places that held good memories for him and to people who enjoyed being around him, so I was determined to help reconnect him to those whom he remembered from long ago. Therefore, on Sunday mornings I took him to see people who either didn't know he had

Alzheimer's, or if they did, acted as if they didn't. They talked with him, not about him. He loved to visit his relatives he had grown up with. We all could talk about names which were familiar to him. Sometimes he would just sit on the couch in one of his cousins' homes and pat her hand. Sometimes we would have a bowl of ice cream with her and her husband. The visits were always non-threatening. But after about thirty or forty minutes, he would say, "I guess we better go." And then of course, we left.

In the early years we attended church services at the church he grew up in, so he had a history here. He felt valued. Daddy sang every word of every hymn. He repeated the Apostles Creed and the Lord's Prayer. He would tip his hat, the same hat he wore to bed at night and everywhere else, to those who would wave to him. He was seen as a normal human being.

I thought that the house where he grew up in *might* hold some of those good memories. But I wasn't certain because his sister, Jenny Dillon, now owned it. It wouldn't be the same as it was when Mammy lived there, but we might be able to create a new good memory if I could facilitate reconciliation between my aunt and my father who had always wanted a positive relationship with her.

It would be really tough, because this woman had indicated throughout our lives that she despised both of us. Evidently she hated me because my grandmother, her mother, had raised me. And she must have despised my father because he allowed her to. I remembered my grandmother and grand-father's fiftieth wedding anniversary when Mammy begged her to have her picture made with Daddy. And then there was that time already mentioned where she said she would see the cherry cupboard "smashed to bits" before my father got it, after he had reluctantly responded to Mammy's question of what he would like to have from the house. I recalled the many times my aunt had said, "Kathryn, you need to be at home with your mother and daddy; you have no business living here." This home, including the property surrounding it, had been manipulated away from Daddy years earlier, after his mother had become powerless to control *her* own life. All these thoughts rang in my head as I contemplated visiting this house which had been the home of both my father and later me. I didn't know what emotions this experience would evoke from Daddy, my aunt, or me.

Still, I thought it would be worth a try, since in the early years of his Alzheimer's condition, he frequently talked about his home in Cookeville.

It would be painful to see my grandmother's house after all these years. For some twenty-three years since her death I had avoided the road that the house was on, since I didn't think I could stand the memories that it would summon in me. Mammy had asked for so little in my lifetime, but the one thing she pleaded for was the chance to live in her own home. Papa had made provision to hire someone to stay with her after his death when she became disabled, but because her daughter gained the power of attorney (Yes, there it is again) after Mammy became arthritic and had suffered a couple of falls, this daughter made other decisions. She controlled my grandmother's assets and her life. She moved Mammy out of her home and into hers – which was just a mile and a half away – but it may as well as been in another country because Mammy was rarely permitted to set foot in her home again.

So Mammy's independence was totally gone. And her beloved home may as well have been. This was the house she used to beg to go and see just from her driveway. And because Mammy was there, it had also been my beloved home, or at least the only place that had ever seemed like home on this earth.

On the other hand, maybe seeing the house wouldn't be so bad, since it probably bore little resemblance to the house that once was. I had learned that immediately upon securing it, my aunt had torn down the smoke house and the cellar. The barn was also demolished. She had the big oak trees that I used to play house under and climb cut down. As a child, I had dragged Mammy's beautiful quilts out into the yard and had picnics on them, but Mammy never complained. I used them for making tents. Hand-made quilts! I cringe now at that thought. The fireplaces were removed. The little tinned roofed room off the back porch where I slept as a little girl with Mammy in the summer time, falling asleep listening to the summer rain pelt the tin roof, was now a laundry room. Yes, maybe the place would be so changed that it would provoke no memories. Besides, if I could connect Daddy up with his sister, any pain would be worth it.

As I became more determined to discover ways to give my father some comfort during his last days, I thought I would just have to "suck it up" and attempt to take Daddy for visits with his sister, despite her disdain for me.

My mother had often talked about how "mean" this sister was; after my father developed the Alzheimer's and she became more like her, they became best buddies. I always thought that Daddy called my mother "Jenny Dillon" not because of the Alzheimer's, but to make the point of how alike they had become.

The last time I had had any real interaction with my aunt had been many years earlier.

I bought her a mum the first time I took Daddy to visit her. Holding it in one hand, I knocked on her front door with the other, with Daddy at my side. I realized she might throw the mum at me and slam the door in my face. She did neither. Upon seeing this woman, bent over and thin, who had for so many years created such pain and grief for both Daddy and me, I felt most of my own fear dissipate. So this was what the woman who had controlled my grandmother, Daddy, and me, to an extent, had become. "I...er...wondered...if I might bring Daddy in to visit you for just a few minutes." She motioned us to come in! I noticed the old porch swing, where I had spent hours swinging with my dolls. The porch pretty much looked the same. That moment was painful.

The whole scenario seemed surreal. As we sat there in the living room, I gradually made myself glance at the couch on which I had done my homework. I noticed the library table on which my grandmother had always placed fresh flowers she had grown. That moment was also painful. I had wanted so much to purchase some of my grandmother's furniture from her daughter's children, to hang on to something of my happy early childhood, but it was not to be. After those moments, I just determined that I could psyche myself over this time and focus on facilitating some dialog between Daddy and my aunt. "How's our mother," Daddy asked. She scowled at me with that look of long ago and tersely asked, "WHAT are you talking about, Brian? She's dead." "Oh," Daddy quietly responded. I quickly added, "Daddy, she's in heaven." At that moment I would have given my life if my father had just had the opportunity to see his mother. I tried just to focus on how good the house looked, but after a few minutes, I knew we must leave. My comments were artificial, and Daddy and I both knew they were. Daddy again tried to hug his sister, as he had done when he first arrived; again, she resisted.

The visit wasn't as horrible for me as I thought it might be because the house had been remodeled, my aunt wasn't all that rude to us, but mainly because Mammy's presence wasn't there. There was hardly anything familiar, except for some furniture and the front porch. Maybe it wasn't all that horrible for Daddy either, for the same reasons. Strange maybe, but not horrible. I could not be certain whether the visit overall was more negative than positive.

Except for a few more visits, I just drove Daddy into the driveway where we sat for a few minutes and talked about Mammy. That seemed to work better. I shuddered as these moments resembled that time when my aunt allowed me to take Mammy for a drive and Mammy asked me if I would drive her to her house. We had just sat quietly in the driveway, and I didn't have the courage to look at her tears. Both of us were powerless to change things. It was also similar to the time on that morning when I had to take Daddy back to "Victorian Center," and I had pulled off the road. We both realized we were helpless. A couple of times I had gotten up the courage to tentatively ask my aunt if I could take my grandmother home for a few days and stay with her there. "She needs to forget about that place. No, she doesn't need to do that." Unlike my father, my grandmother's mind had been keen. She would not forget about *that place* just because she couldn't see it. There were so many parallels between the situation with my grandmother and Daddy that it was almost like God was giving me a chance after so many years to resolve an issue I had had nightmares about for over 20 years, trying to save my grandmother and not having the opportunity to take care of her after she became crippled with arthritis. I remain even today haunted by the fact that she had fallen in her garden and lay for an entire day and again about a year later had missed her chair in the kitchen and had lain there for almost two days before my aunt came over to find her. At the time I was teaching school in North Carolina, and my aunt lived within a couple of miles from her. It was after these two incidents that my aunt determined that Mammy could no longer live in her house. And after she gained control over my grandmother's life, I only could visit her briefly and infrequently. I am grieved by how much pain Mammy had endured because of her willingness to raise me. Just as I never felt free to hug Daddy or show any affection to him in the presence of my mother, I never felt free to hug Mammy in my aunt's presence. Hopefully if I make it to heaven, I will have the opportunity to openly show love to both of them without any fear.

I took my father for visits to his sister once she entered a nursing home. And with each succeeding trip, as my aunt became frailer, she seemed to be almost glad to see us. I remember the last time, just a few weeks before she and my father died. She had the morphine patch on and was glaring blankly ahead. I told her we would pray for her. There seemed to be a hint of awareness in her eye.

TRYING TO FIND OUR NON-THREATENING "GROOVE"

After a few rough starts, we had begun to find "our groove." Believing more strongly that it was God's will for me to know my father and to spend time with him, I began to believe that he might very well, indeed, be my real father. I almost had a family member now! Really, it wasn't quite like that, but a person who could sense that I cared about him and who needed me – at least a remnant of a family which I had not had since Mammy's death some 25 years earlier.

Beginning to believe we had a plan, I starting scheduling what little work I had left around my father's visits with me since they had become more frequent. But about the time we were both feeling more comfortable, my mother became threatened by them. She was not able to project the "victim" status so easily to her friends, with Daddy with me as much. Thus, sometimes I was forced to turn around in the driveway because my mother had changed her mind and convinced Daddy that he didn't want to come home with me. Or she had transferred her angry and agitated moods to him, and he would be afraid to leave his house. Mother remained conflicted with two incongruent desires: the one to have her freedom, and the one to control. After the Victorian Center incident, Mother began saying he didn't want to see me. She continued the game of getting Daddy on the phone, and much like a child is often used as a pawn in a divorced situation, directed him to say that he didn't want to see me.

After a few years, I felt less frantic about planning "activities" with Daddy, and often we would just talk about the Bible, Jesus, and Mammy, who had raised us both. I would also ask him questions related to his youth, to which I felt assured he could respond. What an irony that I only came to know him after he had lost much of his *other* mind.

CHAPTER 18

The Lord preserveth the simple.

—Psalms 116:6

JUST A DIFFERENT PATH

I knew my father had short term memory loss. I had always known people who had become senile, gone "soft in the head," as some called it, or who had some form of dementia. Many of the Alzheimer's symptoms used to be referred to as "hardening of the arteries." Some years before, I realized that he had some of the characteristics of Alzheimer's, and I had concluded that he was in the early stages. However, I was never totally convinced that he wasn't just exhibiting Alzheimer's *symptoms* because his major artery, the aorta, was blocked. I also knew his carotid artery was an issue; he often would rub the back of his neck when it hurt and say that it was his "old arthritis" acting up. That's what his wife had said it was. But since artery blockage can affect different parts of the brain, I had wondered if the blood, and therefore the oxygen, couldn't get into that part of his brain that holds short-term memory. It that were true, perhaps that part of the brain had become vacant, since it had become famished and starved for oxygen. Regardless of whether he technically had Alzheimer's, I had to deal with the symptoms because my mother had repeatedly refused to allow him to have surgery to open up his aorta.

The one question people frequently asked me sympathetically was, "Does he know you?" I understood why. A common perception is that Alzheimer's patients are drooling, rambling, wandering remnants of their former selves who have entered facilities or some other unfamiliar place where they are indeed lost. What many people don't understand is that as their short-term memory slips away, there is very little new that can enter the brain to fill in the spaces, except memories of long ago, some with attached long-suppressed emotions. And, consequently, there is nothing in their brain wires to connect with the strange. Likewise, there was nothing in Daddy's past which connected to a place like an Alzheimer's unit in a facility. But the playing of the fiddle did. People often mistake the reasons that habit and ritual are important to Alzheimer's patients. They are *only* important if they connect with something that isn't strange or threatening. In the case with Daddy and me, I was finally able to create in him a sense of security about being with me, and this *was* something new. But it took almost two years to develop it because he didn't have positive interactions with women in his past, so he couldn't connect our relationship up with anything.

It's almost like trying to store a Windows 2007 document in a dos based system. Anyone who has ever tried to convert an old dos file to a windows based file ends up with bits and pieces, but mainly gibberish. Alzheimer's patients do lose most of what they were in recent years and recover what they were many years before, but the past cannot always be poured into the present. Many times when the two are juxtaposed, a third reality emerges. This definitely happened with Daddy and me, because for most of his life he had the notion of me that my mother had reflected to him. But as we interacted more and more, he began to finally see the difference between the present reality (what I actually was) and the past reality (my mother's perception of me).

In the case of our own historical relationship, the habits and the expectations of the past thirty or so years didn't necessarily make a lot of sense. Or at least they did not until the very end of his life, when his cognitive skills became strong again.

DO YOU KNOW HIM?

Consequently, instead of "Does he know you?" the more appropriate question should be, "Do you know *him?*" Others have to enter the world of the Alzheimer's patient, not the other way around. The disease often does generate changes in personalities, and the new personalities often resemble those that have been hidden away, sometimes for many years. But the caregiver must still enter their world and accept the present personality and behavior. This willingness facilitates a more peaceful coexistence.

Clearly my mother's self-absorption and her child-like response to life rendered it impossible for her to enter my father's world. Her immaturity disallowed the tolerance or patience needed to deal with these personality changes. She had never been able to love unconditionally, and she certainly wasn't able to accept that the disease renders its victims virtually powerless to change their worlds to accommodate others, although my father certainly tried. On the contrary, she led the campaign about how different and horrible her husband had become and how horrible her life was with him.

"When he's around you, his personality is different than when he's around me," she accused. Though I said nothing, I always thought, "That's because I'm not like you." Though I certainly made mistakes with my father when I got into a big hurry, at least my own personality and nature, which he had come to know over the past three years, was evidently perceived as similar to his and apparently non-threatening. Much of his confusion remained when he was with me, but the depression and anxiety decreased. Likewise, I had much less stress when he was with me than when he wasn't.

From my life-long volunteer work with the elderly, including those afflicted with dementia, I knew that patience, a calming spirit, and love can reduce their anxiety and thus help reduce their confusion. I learned that Daddy, much like a small child, saw the spirit. He recognized evil, he recognized goodness, and he recognized motive. I recognized that he was a candidate for Alzheimer's or dementia, since both diseases tend to be greater in those who have been isolated and have had little interaction with others.

When I took him for his visits to his neurologist who would ask him where he lived, for example, he would say, "I live in Cookeville, Tennessee." And until some forty five years ago, he did, in fact, live in Cookeville. That part of the brain which houses the long-ago was still partly intact, and this fact especially was retained because he had good memories there. That's where his mother and father lived. He had an importance there, an identity. He was not invisible. When I took him for visits with his relatives, he interacted with them, and those who didn't know he had Alzheimer's often didn't think anything was out of the ordinary. Daddy had always been a quiet and unassuming man, so nobody noticed much difference. I made it a point at these visits to introduce subjects or people that I knew he and his relatives remembered and associated with from a long time ago. This gave him a chance to take part in the interaction.

His relatives and my friends in the city where I lived were also always kind and attentive to him. He remarked about what nice people they were and what a good time he had with them. I rarely had the sense he remembered the details of any event - or if he did, he didn't mention them - but his mood stayed positive for some time afterwards. So even though the plaque that builds up in the brain prevents communication between synapses and the neutrons in the brain are gradually strangled to death in the Alzheimer's disease, apparently some part of the brain can remember the sensation. Not the event, but the sensation.

It was almost as if the details went into some part of the brain, a few were dumped into some kind of holding bin - something akin to the trash holding bin in your computer - and others were dumped immediately. Then at the most unexpected times, these details could be juxtaposed with details of the present and a third reality could emerge. The sensations surrounding the event appeared to be transferred to someplace else and held there permanently. So even though I was never certain if Daddy knew me, when I interacted with him without my mother, or if an agitated mood were not lingering, the sensation was a familiar and positive one. It was retrieved from the holding bin.

SPIRITUAL MATTERS

Besides fiddle music, the only thing that seemed to always capture my father's attention for any period of time or from any distance were activities related to God and religion: biblical passages, sermons, hymns, and especially southern gospel music. He was totally focused on any church activity. It was almost as if these things represented absolute truths for him that he was determined to retain. Certain activities and thoughts had been placed in a locked box, never to be emptied. Almost everything else in the present was lost on him. Even in the later stages when he could hardly generate any verbal statement, he recited every single word of the Lord's Prayer, the Twenty Third Psalm, the Apostles' Creed, and could sing every verse of hymns without cues. Some might say this was just very deep programming, but I was convinced there was more to it. During this time when he couldn't recognize a commode, or a comb, he still knew religious truths. Could this be related to the fact that though a major part of the brain was impaired, much of the spirit remained intact?

It was quite incredible to see what effect God and spiritual matters had on him. Many times when Daddy became anxious or fidgety, I would put on a southern gospel music tape, and he would completely change. While deep programming may explain part of it, I came to believe this was not the entire reason. His statements, "You know Jesus comes into my room every night" and "I'm a man of God" gave me the belief that Daddy was in very close touch with God. Perhaps this is what made him say that awful morning when I had to return him to that psychopathic ward, "I'm all right; don't worry about me." At the mention of God, or when he was watching a television evangelist at my house, he would become almost reverent. He never displayed anger or a mood swing during any of these occurrences.

THE IMPORTANCE OF INTERACTION

Paul Tournier, the great Christian doctor, declares that for one to really have life, there must necessarily be dialogue. And it must be authentic dialog. Our identities and sense of self are usually formed from our relationship with others. That implies that no one can find "life" in any real sense of the term in isolation. This was one of the toughest parts of my father having to live with his wife's personality during his Alzheimer's condition. My mother had never developed the capability to dialogue with another person. She talked a great deal, but never developed two-way conversation skills, especially with Daddy, who had always been a rather quiet, tentative man to begin with. If the other person began to say anything, even just a word or two triggered Mother to immediately interrupt and transfer the thought back to herself. This behavior was so persistent that at this point, it may have just been a nervous tic which she couldn't control. It manifested itself even with her friends who were fairly loquacious, so one can imagine the impact it had on my father.

Daddy became extremely depressed and felt abandoned if he found himself a part of anything which had no reference for him, even though he might be surrounded by people. It was worse when he did relate with something but was still ignored. Mother often complained that he would get up and leave the room when her friends came. I happened to be visiting at their home when her neighbor had come over. They were talking about an issue which my father knew something about. Although he was in the next room, he came quietly into the kitchen and tried to interject a comment. He was ignored. He wanted so much to make a contribution, to be heard. On another occasion, when the rest of the family was discussing something at Christmas time, Daddy began several times to try to say something related to the subject under discussion. I finally managed to ask, "Daddy, what do you think about that?" I shudder today when I remember their response. My mother said, "Brian wants to say something." There was dead silence, and everybody looked at Daddy as if waiting for a circus act to begin or a baby to say his first words. I was mortified. Of course, Daddy felt intimidated and couldn't get his words out.

Even though he always knew that the focus had to be on her, I think my presence gave Daddy a little more courage to try to become a part of the activity. But my comments were pretty much ignored as well, so my being around didn't help all that much. Still, the very fact that he was trying to insert himself into conversations showed that this life-long willingness of subordinating himself to my mother, one of his deep programmings, was gradually and very slightly changing. With the progression of the Alzheimer's, a few suppressed reactions began to surface.

THE IMPORTANCE OF "DOING THINGS"

"Doing things" benefits everyone in many ways. Activities can bring us joy and a sense of purpose. They can shape our identity and help structure our days. Engaging in activities can lead to more restful nights. Even though my father had pretty much been ignored for much of his life, it didn't mean he didn't *want* to interact with others. I came to learn that he really *did* enjoy activities and social interaction with others, if conversation included him. When he developed his Alzheimer's, the opportunities to participate in activities decreased even more, and so, conversely, his depression increased. When my father was not with me, he continued to live in virtual isolation, and with the onset of Alzheimer's, he didn't have the opportunity to leave the house and go on his own to seek any fellowship or dialogue with anyone. When he was found by the police at the church, he may have been searching for someone he could trust to talk with who might bring him comfort. I became convinced that when he "talked to himself" he did so primarily because there was no one else to talk *with* him. Since he had difficulty articulating, another person had to be genuinely sensing to understand what he was really saying because he was really talking what was "in" his head.

When he made those statements about Jesus coming into his room every night, he also often said that they (he and Jesus) talked. When others claimed he was seeing visions and talking out of his head, I came to believe that at least some were, in fact, conversations with Jesus. Daddy seemed to know that he had direct access to Him. He didn't need to go through a chain of command. He didn't even have to get permission from his wife. Jesus was "up close and personal." I continually prayed that this would be comforting when he wasn't with me and bring him some peace and even joy.

When Daddy and I attended the church he grew up in, for a couple of hours afterwards, he talked about how much he loved to go there. On one particular Sunday I spoke at the church. When I returned to my seat, he patted my hand and said, "That was good." Because he was either working out of town or his wife told him he wouldn't enjoy my piano recitals, he had never had the opportunity to attend them. Nor had he had the opportunity to come to my school plays, or my high school graduation. And because my mother had told him he shouldn't, he didn't come to any of my book signings or any of my conference speeches. But he had heard my church testimony, and he understood enough to know that I had done something worthy and that he had a relationship to the speaker. The pastor asked if Daddy and I would stand at the door and greet the members as they left. Daddy had a purpose. He was a participant. Also in the last few years he had the opportunity to hear me sing a few solos at church, which seemed to make him happy.

Daddy loved to interact with little children at my church, just as he loved to interact with little children anywhere. One particular church function was a Halloween event, and all the children were dressed up. There were lots of activities including sack races and musical chairs. Daddy and I sat near enough to the activities so that he could distinguish the costumes and the behavior. Some of the children came up to him, and he teased them. Some of their parents who had been praying for him a long time came up and hugged him. The pastor and associate pastor came up and talked to him. His response to all this was the most wonderful reaction I had observed from him in a long, long time. He had a part; he felt their Christian spirit. They were happy. He and I were happy.

Many of us forget that the coming of Jesus is the proof that God is not the hidden and the unknowable God, but that his great desire is to be known by all. This knowledge is not only available to the philosopher, or the theologian, or to those with high intellectual capacity. It is open even to the simplest of us. Daddy could sense love, just as children can.

Since Daddy seemed to enjoy dogs and cats, I thought the zoo would be a terrific idea. Nashville has a very good zoo, with lots of chimpanzees, elephants, zebras, and all kinds of exotic animals. But I knew I would have to rent a wheel chair, since many of the trails were pretty steep, and his increasing heart condition would make it virtually impossible for him to climb them. I packed a picnic lunch and told him that we were going to the zoo. He seemed pleased.

Though Daddy didn't actually get agitated, the zoo animals didn't elicit the interest I had hoped for. He received much more pleasure from the little children who were there. He would speak to one in the stroller, and I would stop his wheel chair and allow the two of them to dialog. The only animals he seemed to really enjoy were the small ones he could get close to. I laughed to myself later as I remembered how I was determined to get up one particularly steep trail so that Daddy could see some elephants and zebras. I was almost parallel with the ground as I was pushing his wheelchair up the trail. Once at the top, he hardly expressed any interest in either animal, and I concluded it was probably because they were so far off. He had no close interaction with them, as he might with a dog and cat. He couldn't pet them either, and this condition decreased his interest. But watching and talking to the children who were looking at the large animals was a different story! I was always thankful at how kind the children's parents were to Daddy and me.

Sometimes I took Daddy to what I called the "Do Nothing Club." This was a group of men - mostly older men - and me, the only woman, who met a few times a week at a local restaurant and talked politics, the stock market, religion, or whatever was happening that day. A conservative group, we were always decrying the state of the country. Everyone had nicknames: Bait who was supposed to bring in the women; Sky King who was the pilot of the ring leader; Terrible Teddy, who was so-called because he was negative about everything; the Godfather, so-called just because he was the eldest; the Gray Fox who was sophisticated, smart and handsome; Slick, the ring-leader's realtor, the ring leader himself, St. James, and me, the Ice Princess who was always reproved for trying to raise the moral conscience of the group. "St. James" was my good friend who died just a few months before Daddy died. We were always bantering with each other.

When I took my father there, they talked to him, not around him, or about him; they looked him in the eye. Even though he might not have a clue as to what they were talking about, he was treated as if he did. No one pandered to him. He loved it. I frequently whispered to Daddy to ask the ring leader – who was wealthy but never flashy – how his Lucent was doing. Upon getting seated on his little bar stool, Daddy asked St. James, "How's your Lucifer doing?" St. James, smiling, accused, "I know who put you up to this." Daddy would wink at him and laugh. Upon advice of this St. James person, I had bought shares of Lucent Technology at $57 a share; it ended up being classified as a junk stock. St. James drew cartoons displaying different characters in "the club" and my father laughed. It was priceless to see him laugh. It made no difference at all if he didn't know what he was laughing about. He caught the spirit.

They repeated corny jokes – one-liners – which Daddy thought were so funny. Or if he didn't, he laughed anyway. They teased me in a good natured way, including him in on the tease. They made Daddy a part of the group. He belonged.

In the Nashville community, there is a program called "Memory Works" for memory challenged people. It is a wonderful concept. "Workers" go there in the daytime and perform work for "wages." The work is simple and routine and is done for corporations which support the program. It may involve slipping compact disks into covers or packing boxes. The initiative is intended to give the participants a sense of purpose. They bring their own lunch. They clock in. I thought it sounded like a great opportunity for Daddy, since it was not like going into some "facility" as a resident; he was just going to work. I told Daddy that there was a labor shortage in the city, and that some companies needed extra help during this time. "Okay, I'll help out," he said.

I had visited the facility beforehand and was a little concerned that the people who had come that day were obviously in a later stage of dementia or Alzheimer's or something than my father was. Several of them were just sitting in a daze; some of them were wandering aimlessly and had to be continuously brought back to the table. But I was hoping that there might be others who could converse with Daddy the first day we were to go. I was especially hoping some men workers would be there.

I met the "supervisor" who is there to keep the workers cued. I found him to be an extraordinarily friendly fellow who joked and kidded with the workers. But obviously some of them needed more attention on their job than others, so his opportunity to dialogue with those who could do the work was limited.

I stayed with Daddy the first day. On that particular day the workers were packing disks for a major insurance company based in the city. The supervisor would give them a short stack, and when they finished with that, he would replenish their pile.

My father finished his first stack very quickly. No problem. He started to get up. The "supervisor" handed him another stack. Then he finished that one just as quickly as the first. Then the third. "Daddy, you don't have to do them all during the first thirty minutes," I kidded. He was getting fidgety, and the supervisor began talking and joking with him specifically. He settled back down and laughed at the tease. I was relieved. I thought I might walk down the hall, after he seemed for the time being to be all right. Wrong move. He immediately began to follow me. Upon trying to coax him back, he responded with his proverbial, "I'm ready to get out of here." His mood had changed. Maybe he was afraid of being left there, or he had begun to think this was some kind of phony manipulation to make him *think* he was useful. I couldn't be certain. All I knew is that we had to leave – and quickly.

As long as the supervisor was kidding with him or talking directly to him, Daddy was satisfied. He considered the supervisor more his equal; the other workers, who were in a more advanced state of dementia or Alzheimer's, weren't. So the minute the coach turned his attention to those who needed much more cueing than my father on the task, he became depressed and anxious. He would not interact with the "workers," only the supervisor – because there was nothing in his long ago to connect up with "strange" people like this. They were not like people he used to work with. By acknowledging them, he might be saying he was like them, and he knew he wasn't. I thought about how long President Reagan had managed to live with his Alzheimer's – longer than any other person I had heard of. I am convinced it was because he was allowed to stay in his home with his beloved Nancy by his side. Daddy's doctors often attributed Daddy's ability to keep going to my willingness to keep him close to me and engage him in all that he could do physically and mentally. I don't know if it did or not, but they thought so.

So we left "Memory Works," but we had managed to stay a couple of hours, and that only left about 12 hours in *that* day. The next day I thought I would try again, but Daddy wouldn't get out of the car at the facility. He seemed to remember the day before! I concluded that the major difficulty was either that those around him were very different from him (He had no reference for them) and made him feel as if he might be deemed to be like them; or he wasn't getting enough one-on-one interaction to offset that concern; or he was simply paranoid that this was an effort to get him away from his home since the recent goings on of his wife's effort to place in a facility were also in his head somewhere. It could have been a combination of all three. In any event, the lasting sensation was negative, so that was the end of that idea. The good news, however, was that he remembered *something* about the place.

Taking Daddy to movies was not usually successful, unless there were little children there to focus on, or there was enough laughter so that he could catch it. Usually we only made it through the previews before he would say, "I'm ready to get out of here." Gradually I learned to go during times where there would be small children there, and take snacks with me for Daddy to eat during the movie. Some of his favorite movies involved some animation. It was more the tone, again, than the characters, which kept his attention. I recognized that plot was difficult for him to get, but amazingly, the movie *Remember the Titans* held his attention through its entirety, and Daddy really seemed to grasp the overall theme. More than one time on the way out he remarked about what a good movie that was. He also enjoyed *The Rookie*. Of course both movies were about sports, and this fact may have been one reason Daddy liked them. Maybe they made him feel like he used to, when he played sports. But I had the sense it was more about the courage and the determination within the themes that somehow connected with something in his brain. Just about the time I thought I had this Alzheimer's deal figured out, something would occur that changed my mind.

Daddy was particularly sensitive to tone. Sarcasm or agitation put him into a depressed mood. On the other hand, people telling one-liners or making a deal over him resulted in a calm and almost happy spirit – especially if he were made a part of it, rather than an outsider. On one particular occasion, about a year and a half after the Alzheimer's diagnosis, I took my parents on a city tour of decorated homes at Christmas time, some of them being the homes of famous stars. Daddy wasn't that attracted to the lights, but his interest was maintained by the van driver. The van was small, and the driver interacted continuously with the folks on the van, frequently cracking jokes.

Whether he caught the jokes or not, Daddy laughed at them, maybe because others were chuckling (Who knows?), and sometimes even joined in with the driver, with his own comeback. My mother was amazed. She was also embarrassed when his response wasn't quite "normal." But others on the van smiled and included my father in the interaction. I was convinced that Daddy's positive reaction was partly because he could be a part of the group, without being singled out as "abnormal," and that he had an "up close and personal" experience with the driver.

Though he loved music, the singer or musician also had to be "up close and personal" to keep his focus; if not, he was in another world. We had at least one musical outing every day and one every night – even if it were just at the public library. He loved many kinds of music, but religious, country, and blue grass music were his favorites, so I tried to take him every night to some kind of musical event which included these. He particularly became animated by the blue grass music. He had played the fiddle in his day, and when I discovered blue grass bands playing around the city, I always took him. It was wonderful to see him clap his hands and tap his foot. I always requested some of the old tunes, and the bands almost always obliged.

In fact, on a couple of nights every week, we went to hear blue grass, and this was the one activity, aside from church, that held Daddy's attention for longer than thirty minutes. When the fiddler began playing – and particularly on a lively number that he remembered – he would wink at me and say enthusiastically, "THERE *it* is!" He looked around and let people there know that he understood this music. He felt significant because he was there to enjoy the music just like they were. Part of the reason was that the same people would be at the places each week so they came to know Daddy, and he seemed to recognize them more by their tone and their spirit than anything else. They called him by name, and as he seemed to become more familiar with them, he became more a part of whatever was happening. He was a participant. And I made certain that the musicians were within his view. After a few times, each musical group always played a song for "Brian." He would wave and tip his hat. He was special.

Sometimes we went downtown to Tootsie's Orchid Lounge, where many famous country singers got their start, and there was almost always some bluegrass music. The trickiest part was finding a parking place close enough that Daddy could walk, with his heart condition. Usually, I double parked, led him inside, found a table, quietly asked someone inside to keep an eye on him, had him hold my purse, ran back to park the car, and then ran back to the Lounge. Everything was always on fast forward. But upon returning and Daddy seeing me, he broke out in a grin which always made all the effort worthwhile. As soon as the fiddle or banjo player would begin, his grin became wider. He evidently remembered his fiddle playing days. Places like this made him feel like he was equal with the other spectators. He could clap his hands as well as the next fellow. Sometimes we even sat at the "bar" and drank our diet cokes. He was a part. He belonged. He almost blended in. And it was good for at least twenty five minutes, on a good day.

On the other hand, if the event were far away, he became lost and restless to leave. A couple of times, I thought he would enjoy hearing some "Big Band Music" outside at a local park. When I mentioned we were going to hear this music, he quickly went into his bedroom and began re-dressing. This occurred in the early stages when he could efficiently dress himself. Before I realized it, he had on his Sunday shirt and tie, his sport coat that I had bought for him, and his Sunday slacks. He had always worn a shirt and tie to special places. This was one of those painful moments for me that I will always remember because it demonstrated how significant going anywhere had become for him. He was going to some place special, and he wanted to look nice! He had always loved going to church, but he didn't even have that opportunity any more when he was at my mother's house. Oh, how little it took to lift his spirits. I felt a huge lump in my throat because he had taken such pains to get dressed, even tying his own tie, and I didn't want to negate his decision about what clothes he thought he should wear. But this was a very casual event when most people would be wearing jeans and t-shirts. No response would feel right, but I managed a limp one. "Daddy you look so handsome, that some people might feel a little underdressed. How about if you just take off your tie?" He obliged, but his mood definitely shifted slightly. I should have let him keep that tie on, but I just knew he would get too hot and he still could sense differences. I didn't want him to be embarrassed. Often I faced a decision between two undesirable alternatives.

I always took two small lawn chairs if we were going to an outside activity, just to ensure Daddy had a place to sit down. This way we could get closer to whatever was happening. Dragging them out of the car, I carried one with each hand and asked him to take my arm. Though I tried to get as close to the band as possible, Daddy had difficulty walking very far, so we were still some distance from the music. I sat the chairs down near some young families with small children, thinking at least Daddy could see *something* close up.

The music itself proved to be a disappointment because it didn't capture Daddy's attention. He was able to engage with it a little, but only when I was commenting on the dancing or the music. Otherwise, the small children and the dogs around us that people had brought with them seemed to the only thing he was interested in. The moment, however, that someone said something to me aside from him, his mood completely changed, and he was "ready to go." Actually, the music seemed to almost depress him - especially the slower songs. Maybe it reminded him of the war. Or maybe it was my mother's activities during the war. I could never be certain.

TIME AND SPACE

Time and space have different meanings for those with Alzheimer's. As far as time goes, there is the minute right now, and the minutes long ago, with nothing much in-between. Occasionally some of the long ago is sprinkled into the present moment. Also, what may be five minutes for the rest of us may be a lifetime for the Alzheimer's victim. I learned not to mention the place we would be going until I had the car in the front of the house and the motor running. If I said, "Daddy, we're going to Cookeville this afternoon," he immediately got up and said, "Okay, I'm ready right now." Or if I said, "Daddy, I'll have breakfast ready in a little while," he immediately started for the kitchen.

The most that one can hope for is that the Alzheimer's victim feels okay for the "right now." For the "right now" the main thing is getting through the *day*, with an ending that's more positive than negative. There really isn't much light at the end of any *tunnel*, because unlike a teenage phase that parents often hope their children will grow out of, each day will be just as or more difficult than the day before. Even some minutes are harder than the previous ones.

Sometimes when my father seemed to be floating around with his thoughts, he would catch one of them and say, "Rosaleigh (his cousin, about his age, with whom he had grown up) has fallen again. They just telephoned me and told me she's in bad shape." I would listen in as he would whisper, "Okay, yeh?" as if he were responding to the message. Perhaps Rosaleigh had fallen when they had played as children. In his brain somewhere resided the very last links with his generation, his past. The distant past flooded back in to fill in the vacuum vacated by the present. But then he said, "They *telephoned* me." So the long ago was placed alongside the present since he said he was telephoned. At that moment, not knowing for sure whether he was conscious that I was physically with him, I responded anyway. "I believe they rescued her, Daddy...I hear she's going to be all right now." "Yes, she's all right," Daddy echoed. He was okay again.

And then it was on to something else. Every minute was different from every other minute.

I became convinced that my father's service during the war had a profound effect on his mind, and that many of his habits which manifested themselves during this time were deeply rooted in his experience as a marine. We all edit our lives to some extent, and the things that have been the most significant remain with us always. I suppose that's one reason why the details of this journey with my father are still so vivid.

He would delicately place his napkin under his plate at meals, as I said, "Daddy, I bet you had to do that as a marine." Usually there was no response about that comment. "If you would like, here's another napkin you can place in your lap." He left the one under his plate. I would hand him another one. "Daddy, here's one you can just use to wipe your hands on, if you like." "Okeydoke," he responded as he placed this next napkin also under his plate. On one occasion when we were eating out, he placed six napkins under his plate.

The olive green towels I had on the shelf in Daddy's bathroom evidently also triggered something from his Marine Corps days. One by one they began to disappear. I found them tucked in his pants' pockets, placed in his little suitcase, or sometimes, when I looked in on him during the night, he had covered himself up with them, on top of the bedspread. Finally I began just putting one on his pillow every night. There was some kind of security in those olive towels.

I was never quite certain, though, how much of this was an Alzheimer's thing, or how much of it was because all in the world he had left of his own was on him. Much of the time when he was talking to himself, his monologue was about how his money had been taken. Learning I just had to "go with the flow," I tried to join him in his world. It was useless to confront him with my reality. When he said "they" were taking his money out of the mountain, I would go to the telephone, dial some made-up number and say, "This is Brian Howard's daughter, and you better put that money back." Daddy was okay then. I had to remind myself that his world was figured differently from mine, and I simply had to try to enter his.

Alzheimer's patients take on the *mood* and *spirit* of those they're around – but not necessarily the *content* of the other brains' "computer disks." If Alzheimer's patients choose to enter the reality of others, well and good. But often that is not possible. If Daddy asked about his mother, my grandmother, who had been dead for over 20 years, I would respond that she was doing fine in heaven with God and that I was certain Mammy was looking after those who needed attending to, probably even cooking for them. Daddy would agree. I couldn't know how depressed that may have made him because much of the time his emotions appeared monotonic. And then the moment would pass.

Before I understood the best response to that issue, I would drive him to the cemetery where his parents were buried, the same grandparents who had raised me. I mistakenly thought we might get out of the car, stand by Mammy's grave and perhaps talk about her, how peaceful the site was, how close it was to her home she had lived in and such. What I discovered, however, is that Daddy never really wanted to get out of the car. It was as if this reality didn't have any wire to connect with in his brain. When I pointed over at her tombstone from the car, he quickly gave an evasive glance more or less to accommodate me, but that was about the extent of his response.

He came to see a growing gap between his reality and anyone else's and trusted his own above theirs, including mine.

Space also has a different meaning for the Alzheimer's patient. Just as they need affection and interaction with others, those afflicted with the disease also need their space. My father had a very difficult time being stationary. He needed space, and he wanted to be moving in it. He loved to be traveling on the road. He certainly would have preferred driving himself, but just riding was better than nothing. Of all the anguish I had over Daddy's losses, the loss of his car was one of the most upsetting to him and me. I knew how important cars were to him. Every single time we were in my car, Daddy said several times during the drive, "This shore is a nice car...It shore rides good." Even though I had told him that since I didn't need two cars, I was giving him my old Buick (He had owned a Buick in the past) and that we would keep it at my house, his other home, I'm not sure he ever bought that idea. Cars enabled him to keep moving, and they were a means of escape for him. I asked him to drive the golf cart when I took him to hit some balls, but we both knew it was a poor substitute.

As with autistic children, they alone must define when and where they need the space. Also, I came to realize that even their space might connect up with something from the long ago.

Something quite intriguing happened when Daddy was in the early stages of Alzheimer's. It was on a Pacific Ocean cruise, which included stops at various land ports. I figured there would be enough diverse entertainments to keep my mother from getting too angry, and I could keep an eye on Daddy. I didn't think he would jump off the boat, so there was a way to contain him to some degree. On one of the land tours my father remarked, "I have been here before...Colin (his brother) and I were here." My mother rolled her eyes, sighed, and made fun of the remark. Thinking as well that he was probably confused, but not wishing to deny him his reality, I simply replied, "Is that right, Daddy?" I later learned that this spot was very near to Guadalcanal where Daddy had been stationed during War II!

Some may think because their sense of time and space changes, those afflicted with the disease might not be able to make distinctions. This was not true in my father's case. He often demonstrated more ability to differentiate than most people thought. On one occasion, when he was at the church I took him to – the same church he attended as a young man – a cousin of his came up to him and asked "Who's that pretty woman with you?" Daddy said, "Oh, she's the good one." I certainly had never considered myself particularly pretty, as opposed to Mother, who had always been beautiful. But the point is that something in his head made a distinction.

Until the very end of his life, my father recognized me not necessarily as his daughter, but as someone who was kind to him and genuinely cared about him

I certainly can't take credit for that before then. But after a couple of years of our interaction, he had begun to recognize me as someone who was in his corner. I was convinced he knew me as *that* – at least until shortly before he died, when he finally, for the first time, acknowledged me as his "baby girl." That was one of the reasons I believed he slept so well at my home. He trusted me not because he particularly recognized me all the time as his daughter, but that I was someone who was not going to take advantage of him. He had made that distinction.

THE IMPORTANCE OF A SENSE OF ACCOMPLISHMENT

It is so important for the dementia patient to complete whatever steps in the grooming process they can so they can feel at least a little independence and a sense of accomplishment. By the middle phase of the disease, however, I had to cue him on just about everything, including brushing his teeth, which he had always done with great regularity. He would pull out his little plastic zippered pouch housing his comb, his toothbrush and his toothpaste. He always carried it in his pants pocket and kept it under his pillow at night. This was one habit he retained. I would put some toothpaste on his brush, lay it on the bathroom sink, and casually mention that it was ready if he would like to brush his teeth now. "While I was brushing my teeth, I went ahead and just put some on your brush." I tried to de-emphasize his dependency. "I've already brushed them," he would respond. "Okay," I would answer. But about five minutes later, I would bring it up again, saying something like, "Daddy, I envy you not having any cavities. How do you do it?" He would reach for his little zippered packet, and I would remind him that I had already put some paste on his brush if he would like to brush his teeth. "Okay," he would say.

I exerted most of my energy trying to replace some of his eroded dignity and self-respect, spending lots of time thinking up things which could give him a sense of purpose. I never had the feeling that I accomplished very much, although a few friends encouraged me. Too much had been lost, but I tried, nonetheless. The tough part was that the disease was progressing so rapidly that by the time I had figured out how to preserve dignity in any given action, either his motor skills or his cognitive skills had decreased again so as to nullify the effort. I felt that both of us were in quick sand, and there was no one to pull either of us out. Without memory, there tends to be chaos. Sometimes I felt my own brain was just as chaotic as his.

During the early stages, I tried to take him to places for which I thought he would have a reference point. It tore at my heart to see him as we went into a hardware store where he had always loved to visit. "Daddy, do you see anything you would like to buy?" This was some time after my mother had taken any buying opportunity away from him. "Well, I might *could* use some of this tape." I noted the duct tape, and said, "Good, go ahead and buy it," as we both grinned. I mused about what he might be proposing to do with that duct tape! It was amazing to watch the pride with which he approached the counter and pulled out his wallet. I cued him in slightly on the dollars needed, but he had done something on his own!

Another time I mentioned I had to run into the supermarket and asked if he needed anything from the Dollar Store while I was in the market. I really had nothing particularly I needed from the market, but I went inside and made certain I had a view of the Dollar Store so that when he left, I could see him. He bought a razor blade on his own. I could feel his satisfaction.

Though my father's short term memory left, the past memories became vivid and unrepressed. Events and circumstances of long ago were explained away by his family and friends as the "Alzheimer's talking," but I became convinced otherwise. My father's covered-up life of pain and suffering, his depression, and his secrets had now begun to come to the surface, at least in my presence. The mechanism which had been used to cover them up was gone.

On one occasion, after Daddy had been coming home with me for a couple of years, we were sitting at the kitchen table. I decided to broach the subject of my mother. I knew he harbored so many thoughts and never had anyone to talk with about them. "Daddy, you realize, don't you, that you will be rewarded in heaven one day for all you've done for Mother? "I hope so," he responded, with slight tears in his eyes. "Don't you doubt for one minute that that is the case," I insisted. "I don't know how you've been able to endure all the years of pain that you have." "I just tried to stay away," he responded quietly. This was breaking my heart, but I had to give him this release. "Why do you think she hated me so?" I tentatively asked. Not really answering that question, he just quietly responded, "She never liked me either." "Daddy, I believe she does care for you, but she has always been so emotionally immature, that she couldn't think of anyone but herself. She has always been a child." I was just trying to give him an excuse for his wife's behavior towards him. "Daddy, you mustn't doubt that you'll be in heaven with Mammy and Jesus. And you'll have a crown for all you've done for Mother. Just think of this world as your marine boot camp; this is training for eternity." "I hope so," he wanly responded. "I bet you'll be one of God's front-line soldiers," I responded affirmatively. "You'll be fixing those gold streets if they need any repair. You'll have your tools back." I probably shouldn't have brought up that depressing subject because my response didn't sound at all reassuring even to me, let alone to Daddy.

Because he had always cleaned out my car, either when I was visiting my parents, or when they were visiting me, I continued to ensure my car was messed up - which wasn't difficult - just enough so that Daddy could pick up chewing gum wrappers, dry cleaning stubs, or any other worthless piece of paper. The activity gave him a purpose which he had always had. And besides, it usually took up about twenty minutes, leaving only about 14 hours for other activities to stimulate him. When he was with me, I tried hard to make up for the time when all he was allowed to do was sit in his chair at my mother's house. My objective came to be to try to give him more good experiences than bad. Not that he would necessarily remember any specific event or detail in the good experience, but that he would have a better mood. He would not be paranoid. He might laugh at a corny joke. He would feel involved.

When Daddy found the coins I had thrown around on the floor, he would come up to me and offer me the money. "Here, take it," he said with such pride. "It's yours." Sometimes I would take it and say, "Thank you Daddy; we'll use this to buy us some ice cream later." He always smiled when he thought he was contributing. He tried to give me things all day long - the television remote, a comb, a rubber band, even up until two days before he died. Somewhere in his psyche he was still trying to make something up to me.

CHRIST'S EXPECTATION OF US TO ENTER INTO OTHERS' WORLDS

It was helpful for me to remember that Jesus entered into the lives of others – the poor, the maimed, and the sick, including those with dementia. Much of his job, in fact, was to identify with the "least" of them. He risked catching their diseases, and He became vulnerable to accidents. Christ knew he had to enter our world to make His influence felt. He knew the process – as well as the result – was important. If He were going to influence and change hearts and lives, he had to associate with those who needed his influence. Part of his mission was to bring God's policies to life for the common man as well as for learned scholars.

The *way* Jesus did his job mattered. He did it with humility, passion, empathy, and vision. He made the lowly feel important, and He gave new meaning to words like "goodness." He would have talked with Daddy; he would not have isolated him, as the Pharisees would have done.

Likewise, we are expected to enter into others' worlds in order for our influence to be felt. We cannot shelter ourselves from death and dying and the pain and loneliness of others. Nor should we remove ourselves from those whose brains don't work exactly like ours, those who have learning disabilities who simply cannot help but think on a different level from us. However, Jesus also interacted with those who rejected Him because He came to save the lost. So if I were to follow Christ, I realized I must continue to interact with *both* my parents, however painful that interaction was.

The big question was how long I was expected to do this with a person who clearly was not following Christ and inflicting serious harm on others. During the five years preceding my father's death, I never saw any evidence that my mother could turn away from the evil that had overtaken her. Even so, until the last few months of my father's life, I continued to pray that something would happen or someone would say something that would pique her interest to turn to Him. Clearly Christ forgave those who persecuted Him. But at the same time on one occasion He said that we might even have to hate our family if it meant they were causing us to support them and not Him. Perhaps the reason that prayer was never answered was that my motive had become not so much for her but for the rest of us. If she turned toward Christ, her anger might be reduced, thereby lessening reprisal on my father and increasing peace for all of us. I had just become so jaded that I could not muster up much empathy for her and concern for her ultimate destiny.

I came to realize that the spiritual struggles during those last years of my father's life might be, in God's book, the most important ones in *my* entire life. The Apostle Paul writes that we are predestinated to be conformed to the image of Christ. That means, we must follow Him and do what he *did*. I knew that during those years I probably did not do everything that Christ would have done, nor were my motives always the motives Christ would have had. But I hope that my overall grade on that mission met His expectations.

CHAPTER 19

Now we have received, not the spirit of the world, but the spirit which is of God; that we might know the things that are freely given to us of God.

—1 Corinthians 2:12

CREATING A NEW WORLD

Gradually increasing the frequency and the duration of Daddy's visits, by the fourth year I had him three-fourths of the time with me at my home. I began cutting back my business during the second year and by the third year, except for a little writing, I stopped it altogether. The pattern of my traveling to East Tennessee to pick up my father, stopping in the small Middle Tennessee town to visit relatives and eat lunch, and then traveling on to my home in Nashville had continued. Until the fourth year, on Sundays I usually drove back to the small town to attend the church service where Daddy and I had both attended as young people, eating lunch afterwards, and then driving him to Mother's home in East Tennessee. This amounted to about 600 miles of driving all together each week, but I had come to believe that the purpose was worth it. Besides there had occurred an almost miraculous change by the third year.

It seemed like only yesterday that I was frantically trying to discover ways to overcome Daddy's paranoia and distrust of being brought home with me. The stop in Cookeville was always welcomed, but for the rest of the trip, in the early part of our journey, I had to expend considerable effort to overcome his angst.

I had finally realized that most of this early anxiety had resulted from his fear of being ousted from his house and institutionalized again, along with his distrust of me, stemming from Mother's portrayal. But the more we interacted, the more this anxiety abated.

It was always intriguing to me that institutionalization seemed to be the answer for most people for their loved ones with Alzheimer's. I recalled "Victorian Center" where the "residents" there appeared to be somewhere between living and dying. They were lethargic and depressed, of course, because they had had to give up any sense of self. There were rules, much like prison, and much like the case with inmates, they were not rules that they themselves made.

Many Alzheimer's facilities emphasize "routine" and "ritual," thinking that the sameness will make patients comfortable. What many institutional administrators miss is that the key ingredient for those with Alzheimer's is the personal contact, and those working in the morning are different from those working in the evening; thus the *place* for the resident is different.

So every day that the "residents" are treated like *things*" is absorbed, then with every succeeding day they become more and more *like* things and less like people. They become more robotical and lifeless. So the *presumptions* about Alzheimer's patients then become the reality. The old self-fulfilling prophecy is at work.

The other problem is that the very characteristic these institutions emphasize is the very worst thing for an Alzheimer's patient. "Ours is a secure environment," administrator after administrator said to me, early on when I knew my mother wouldn't allow me to keep Daddy full-time and I thought perhaps some sort of good facility might be one answer. The last thing that most Alzheimer's patients feel is secure. Of course, in the facility, the "secured" part means that the patients are locked up. Institutions are *closed* places, and "closed" was the least thing Daddy wanted or needed. That is why so many patients wander. What an irony of locking up those who are already paranoid, locked up in their brains, feeling threatened just because of the disease. If I were locked up, my natural instinct would be to try to escape also. When my father stepped outside of my house, he always came back on his own accord.

Things had definitely changed over the past couple of years for Daddy and me. Instead of stressing over how to keep him from wanting to leave as soon as he arrived, I now stressed over having to overcome his depression about returning to my mother's home in East Tennessee. I had always been concerned that the contrast between the different responses he received from me and from others might be too traumatic and have a worse impact than him not being with me at all. However, now having him four or five days every week, I felt he might be able to withstand the rest of it.

"She feeds me good," and "You can't beat her," were examples of statements he often made to my friends about me. "It's not you, Lady," he had once stated rather disgustedly to me when he had gone off to his room to be alone upon hearing we would be traveling back to see my mother the next day. These statements tore at my heart. I could see the pain in his eyes when I mentioned that we would be going back to his home. I didn't want to even hint that it wasn't *his* home any longer. "You mean, back to *her*?" "Yes, Daddy, but remember it's just for a few days." By this time I had explained that he was staying with me because Mother had a mental disorder and needed rest. He said he understood. This explanation was offered to counter his conclusion that she didn't care at all about him, which he had repeatedly voiced. Besides, the statement was true, and my father knew it was true; he still referred to her "fits" and "worse condition."

By this time we had developed our own world. I admitted to myself that it was a world and a relationship which I in large part had created. I had re-invented myself, and the new role had to do more with me than with him. Since I had not really had a relationship with Daddy aside from my mother previously, I could not say with certainty what his earlier personality would have been like when he was apart from his wife. I had only known him through her, and he had only known me through her. Therefore, I had to assume a role more for myself than for him in this newly constructed relationship.

Perhaps it wasn't as difficult as it is for many other caretaker family members who only see vestiges of older personalities. For them, they don't how to relate except in the way they always have – as father/daughter; mother/daughter; sister/brother. For them, their memory of their loved ones is everything. For me, the only memories I had of anyone who had loved me in the family was my grandmother, who had died over 20 years earlier. So maybe the whole thing was in some ways easier.

Of course, the reinvention of *this relationship* was continuously changing. As the Alzheimer's progressed, and as our time together increased, so our roles changed. At first, the relationship had been much like trying to assume the care of a helpless elderly person whom I really didn't know, much as I had done in the past with others. Gradually, it became more like we were "partners" in our newly created world. Then it was *almost* like we were father and daughter.

It was natural that others would be a bit perplexed at our relationship. To some it appeared intriguing. "It's wonderful the way you treat your father," total strangers would say. I didn't think that what I was doing should be so rare or exceptional, but I came to see that taking care of him personally, rather than having him institutionalized, was the exception, rather than the rule. A regular customer at one of the restaurants where Daddy and I frequented expressed to me that she thought I was a hired caregiver, due to the degree of attention I gave my father. This view provoked and saddened me since it assumed that paid caregivers pay more attention than family members do. Some of those at places where we visited thought he was my grandfather. And those who knew me assumed we were beginning a father and daughter relationship. Frankly, until the very last year, even that last assumption was not really the way my father and I perceived our relationship to be.

In the beginning of our journey, Daddy's attention was held by religious or bluegrass music. As our journey continued, however, I discovered that interacting with others overrode the *type* of music. On Tuesday evenings Daddy and I went to a neighborhood upscale restaurant, F. Scott's, which had a jazz band playing in the lounge area. It was light, pleasant, and pretty. This type of music would normally not have interested my father, but the three women in the band made such a fuss over him that he clapped and gave them feedback – aloud – on every song. The drummer waved at him and threw him kisses. He waved back. He had never experienced anything like this. Following every tune, he said, aloud, "That's Good!" We always had a "front row" seat. The lead singer's husband, who was a waiter, talked to Daddy and kept refilling his diet coke glass. Daddy's pleasure again stemmed from the interaction.

NOT THE PLACE, BUT THE ATMOSPHERE

One of the most traumatizing episodes during our five year journey together occurred after I was forced to leave my father in evil hands after a hospital stay brought on by his aortic stenosis and anemia. This event is actually discussed in the next chapter. But it was following this event that I wasn't allowed to visit Daddy for about five weeks. It seemed like an eternity, and I was so worried that he would have become so frail that taking him with me to Nashville would pose yet another risk, that he wouldn't remember me, and that I would have to begin again the journey of building his trust. But, after finally getting permission from my mother to bring him home with me again and secure medical attention if he needed it, I couldn't wait to get him out of the atmosphere in that house. I was nervous about so many things as I entered it, but I was determined to get Daddy's things and both of us out of there quickly. It resembled my frantic mission to get Daddy out of that God-forsaken facility a few years earlier. My mouth was so dry and my breath so short I thought I might pass out myself.

But the minute I set foot in the door and Daddy saw me, a grin broke out across his whole face. "Daddy, are you ready to go to Cookeville?" I managed to smile and say as cheerily as possible. "I'm ready to go with you anywhere," he responded, as he jumped up. I was so relieved – and somewhat shocked. He had never said this so assertively before, or so clearly. It was important that he get this statement right, and he did. It seemed to make no difference that Mother was in the room. He said it any way. I had prayed all the way up to East Tennessee that God would help me handle this endeavor, and clearly He did. God had seen to it that Daddy had not dumped me in the trash bin of his brain. He seemed to know he was going to somewhere that was peaceful and cheerful.

Daddy and I were doing more things together: continuing to attend blue grass and gospel music events, church activities, just about everything. I took him with me to board meetings, Kinko's, political campaign headquarters, the post office, Target, everywhere I had to go. Everyone was always so nice to him at these places and made a point of speaking directly to him. They gave him back his humanity. Going to the supermarket was a little tricky at first, with trying to lead Daddy with one hand (as he had his three-pod cane in the other), pushing the grocery cart with the other, and then stopping to gather the groceries. What worked best ultimately was to leave his little cane in the car and use the shopping cart for balance. We both held it, and I would gently steer it. This way Daddy was helping me. He had a purpose.

Try as I might to hide the degree of required attention when we were in public, it got to the point where Daddy had to be cued on drinking his coke, sitting down when we got to our table, or taking out his silverware from the napkin at a restaurant. "Daddy, don't forget your apples; you know you love apples." I found myself talking to him as I would to an infant, and I was annoyed at my patronizing tone because I knew Daddy recognized it. I always asked for a table near the wall where my attention would not be conspicuous to others, and he could retain his dignity. The best tables for us were near the restrooms. The feedback and comments I received from others, as they spoke to Daddy and me, were tremendously encouraging. I had observed, as he interacted with the same people at these activities,   that he had begun to feel more comfortable and begun participating in his own way.

Once I was diagnosed with osteoporosis and my degenerative discs and scoliosis worsened, I knew I would not be able to continue the long drives so frequently. Although we resumed the visits to our relatives, by this point I didn't feel the pressure of having to drive to Daddy's hometown to attend the church he had grown up in. One of the major reasons that the little church made him happy was that he was spoken to directly there by the members; he was called by his name. I came to realize, though, that it was the spirit of the church as much as it was the place. In fact, by this time Daddy's sense of time and place had deteriorated so much that the spirit and tone appeared *more* important than *where* he was. And there were other places where a similar spirit could be found.

So I began to take Daddy more often to my church in Nashville to see how he would react. Members there were somewhat familiar with his situation, and I knew they would go out of their way to be friendly to him. Still in the beginning, he was shy about going there, and he kept his head down in the subordinate way he was accustomed to doing. He had been so browbeaten for so long – especially during the past several years – that his whole body language displayed this attitude. But after a few months, he began to lift his head up and talk *with* those who came up to him. He anticipated going.

This was the church he later called *that* church in his talk with the hospital chaplain after he had received his blood and was remembering things. He wasn't talking about the little church in Cookeville, but about my church where members and pastors, like those in Cookeville, continued to make him feel special. He even began getting his own newsletter which I would read to him. The pastor's wife made special efforts to send Daddy notes, and while she and her husband were on vacation, she sent him his own beach letter! He was beginning to build himself his own little new history. Much of his past had been ripped from him, and who are any of us without a history? In the process of re-inventing myself, I had actually built myself a new history as well.

On Wednesday evenings, we attended prayer meeting there. People were always friendly to him, and gradually he came to even initiate conversation with them before and after the service. He became a participant, a valued member of the congregation. Both the senior and associate ministers who conducted the Wednesday night services always spoke directly to Daddy and would stand so my father could see their faces. He responded to the ministers' questions and statements – aloud. Those attending merely smiled and thought it was a good thing that he felt comfortable enough to speak – albeit not the same way any of them would. My father appeared to understand the message, and he felt a part of it. When my senior pastor asked who would take a card (addressed for members who had requested prayer), Daddy held up his hand. The pastor gave him one.

Oh, the rapturous charm of music, and particularly church music! What power it had in creating a mood for my father. As a religious devotee, my father was called to worship by it. As a veteran and patriot, it drew him to his country's altar. Music is indeed the universal medium, and I discovered it to be such an antidote for Daddy's lethargy and his occasional depressed mood. Singing enabled Daddy to be a participant in worshiping God. His reverent emotions could pour out, and he would not be singled out for any abnormality of mind. It forever soothed and lifted his spirit. When he and I would be in the emergency rooms at various times, and I began softly singing "Amazing Grace" or "What a Friend We Have in Jesus," Daddy joined softly in, even in his weakened state. Sometimes I thought the songs for him were as good as a prayer. They helped us both to keep out angry feelings. They seemed to lighten the burdens of our lives.

CONFIRMING HIS REALITY

On one occasion, a friend had told me that the Fisk Jubilee Singers were giving a free concert at the new library in Nashville. On the day prior to my getting Daddy, I telephoned the library and informed the security guard that I was eager to have my father hear the singers but was concerned about the logistics of getting him to the area where the show was to be performed. I explained that he had Alzheimer's and heart trouble. So he suggested we come an hour early so as to get a good seat. He offered a wheel chair the library had. Both of these "aids" posed several challenges, as I knew there would be no way to hold Daddy's attention for an hour, with nothing happening (let alone the restroom challenge for that period of time), and I didn't know if he would be willing to ride in a wheel chair.

So I decided I must visit the facility that day myself and walk the distance from the closest parking garage to the show area to determine if Daddy could manage the activity, even with a wheelchair. So I did and decided we would give it a shot. We arrived about 30 minutes early, but fortunately, there was a little girl in front of our seats with whom Daddy engaged for that period of time. The show included various Black spirituals and gospel numbers which totally held his attention. I talked about the show for a couple of hours afterwards to help keep the good feeling in his head.

"I heard them here last week," Daddy declared. He may have heard someone who resembled the group some time, years ago. But since music has been said to be venerable for its age and the voice of God's love, it could be that the songs could in some way transcend time. One response would have been, "Daddy, you have *not* heard these people before," thus negating his reality, resulting in agitation and conflict. The other would be to ignore what was said, as his wife was prone to do, or rolled her eyes and added ridicule if another person were present. The best option, I considered, was to engage him and briefly extend his statement. "Daddy, I had forgotten that you had heard them before...Well, they're just as good as ever, aren't they?" And the moment would pass without distress for either of us.

During the Christmas season I scouted out church Christmas specials which we attended. Some included symphony and chamber music, which I wasn't certain Daddy would enjoy since he had never been exposed to it. However, he was totally focused on all the pieces as they seemed to stir his mental being to activity, to move even within him as a common electrifier. He seemed as soothed and uplifted by the chamber music, as he was by the simple carol solos. He was especially happy when the musical events involved small children.

On Thursday evenings I took Daddy to a bagel and coffee house which had bluegrass music on that evening every week. Until the end of his life, he especially loved this music, particularly the fiddle and banjo. It was thrilling to see him smile and pat his foot to the old tunes he remembered. There were regulars there, and the more often we went, the more familiarity the atmosphere held for him, and thus the more comfortable this activity became for him. The patrons spoke to Daddy, not around him, or behind his back as if he didn't exist. He might not remember the details of the event, but the memory somehow lingered somewhere in his brain and served to keep him in a happier frame of mind for the rest of the evening. When we returned the following week, Daddy appeared to pull out of that holding bin the sensation of the previous week.

On Fridays, we went to a restaurant with a piano bar where a married couple performed. They began to recognize my father each time, and on his birthday sang "Happy Birthday" to him. He got balloons from the waitress! He tipped his cap to them, as he did to other singers at other events. For those few moments Daddy was dignified and treated like a normal human being. The waitresses always hugged him and gave both of us wonderful service.

We often ate there, partially because I became too tired to cook and partially because this took up at least 45 minutes of the day. I ordered boiled shrimp for Daddy because he never got to eat this food except when he was with me. He may have had the chance to eat shrimp years ago, and he loved them. I would subtly peel his shrimp, one at a time, being careful that no one could see me doing it. I would then place a shrimp on a cracker, with a little cocktail sauce, and make sure he had a hold of one end of the cracker. "Now Daddy, you can go ahead and put it in your mouth." Sometimes I would forget to step-out every action, and then the shrimp and the cocktail sauce would land on my or Daddy's lap. Sometimes I would order another dozen if he wanted more.

Once an older man, who had several times in the past given seats up for Daddy and me and who had always been extremely kind to both of us, asked me to dance. The table we were sitting at was right in front of the dance floor. I had always resisted dancing - even though I loved to dance - because Daddy would not be a part of it. Also, I was usually too tired to dance anyway by this time of the day. On this one occasion, though, I quietly asked Daddy if he minded. He shrugged his shoulders, which was not a good sign. Still, I reluctantly said to the man, "I'll try it." After just a couple of minutes, I noticed Daddy was becoming fidgety, and I just excused myself from the floor. "I'm ready to get out of here," Daddy responded, with increasing agitation. "Daddy, what about if you and I dance this one," I asked, with no assurance that he would.

"I'm ready to get out of here," Daddy repeated, a little more aggravation in his voice. "Aw, come on Daddy; we can do this," I urged. I managed to get him to stand up, and I just started dancing a little with him there. I then eased him to the dance floor, and I asked the cute Black waitress who always gave Daddy a hug and brought him diet cokes to come out on the floor. She took one of Daddy's hands, and I had the other one. One could hardly call what he was doing dancing, but the waitress and I were making enough movement so it didn't matter. Daddy laughed. I laughed. Things were okay again.

Saturday afternoons were times when Daddy and I went to the mall to see the small children play in the children's designated play area. Daddy loved these children and would strike up a conversation with any child who would stop and speak to him. I concluded that mainly he enjoyed them so because they didn't judge him, and they were untainted and possessed innocent souls. Sometimes, I wondered if a part of it might be that the small children had people taking care of them (called parents) just as he had had someone for so long telling him what he should and should not do. Once in the early stages of his Alzheimer's when I had taken him to the eye doctor in East Tennessee, he responded to one of the doctor's questions with, "My mother didn't come." Then I clearly knew he was referring to his wife, as he said it a little sarcastically and gave me a wink. This mall "activity" was good for about 45 minutes.

Challenges existed aside from the short attention span. Because Daddy had congestive heart failure, he had difficulty walking. Therefore, I always had to seek places to go which would allow ways to get him into the areas, without having to exert too much strain on his heart. I would get out of the car, take Daddy inside a building and find someone who I would discretely ask to watch him until I could park the car. Car parked, I would run to the area where Daddy was waiting. After his heart condition became worse, the doctor wrote a prescription for a wheel chair, which alleviated some of the difficulty, but not all, since by this time my own physical conditions had worsened and even getting the wheel chair in and out of my trunk wasn't all that easy. But it was better than placing more strain on his heart.

God knew about these challenges of course, and often helped us out. Occasionally I needed to purchase something for him, like gloves or a jacket, in a department store, and there was almost always a chair near the entrance where he could sit. Or the clerks were always kind to accommodate us and find him somewhere to sit. God always seemed to send his angels to help us out.

I always considered my job was to produce more good feelings in my father than bad.

CHAPTER 20

Take my yoke upon you, and learn from me; for I am meek and lowly in heart: and ye shall find rest unto your souls.

—Matthew 11:29

TWO PHYSICAL TYRANTS

After four and a half years, both my father's aortic stenosis and his Alzheimer's had considerably worsened. They could have been the same thing because the closing aorta prevented oxygen from getting to his brain, and therefore the symptoms were the same as those who have Alzheimer's but not a restricted aorta. Life had become more difficult for both of us, although we both tried hard to keep an appearance of being all right. Here was that brave little marine who had fought so hard his entire life to make things right, and things were anything but. With these conditions working on him, the challenges became greater for both of us. So the time had come for Daddy and me to reconstruct each other and our world. The exceptional thing about my situation as opposed to others who go through this disease with their loved ones was that I didn't really have to try to recreate the long-ago past. In my mind, my father had hardly existed prior to these last five years, except as an appendage to my mother. So I didn't miss the other person. Perhaps in the eyes of my mother, he had become a person who behaved differently than in the past, but for me, those vestiges of his old personality that I did recall were negative, and it was great for me that they seemed to be gone. I came to see that this personality was much like my grandmother's, and that was the personality I had loved so much. I suspect it was there all along, but it probably became submerged in an effort to survive his wife's volatility and rage toward anyone who didn't go along with what she did or said. Others whom my father had never known before spoke of his kind and gentle spirit. Some spoke of the light that he brought into a room. Even band members commented on how he brought forth golden treasures. Maybe this disease had been necessary for God to prepare him for the Kingdom.

Daddy's motor skills were almost gone, his sight had gotten worse, and he was losing control of his body functions. His recognition of objects was almost entirely gone. He had to be constantly cued about everything – where the bathroom was and what it looked like, what was food and what was not, how to put on his underwear, what his comb looked like. At each level of deterioration, though, God seemed to help me figure out a way to do what was required.

But until near the very end of his life, Daddy still remembered how to brush his teeth, although by the middle phase of his Alzheimer's I needed to remind him to do it. He still had all of his teeth, and maybe that was why he was proud of them. Also they were something that nobody could take away. Until his last days, he carried his toothbrush and toothpaste with him everywhere in his little zippered pocket pouch.

By the third year I needed to put the toothpaste on his brush, cuing him to brush, but he still remembered to turn the water on and off before and after brushing. By the fourth year, I had to turn it on and off. Eventually even brushing his teeth became, like all the other activities related to bathing, dressing, or taking medicine, just something for him to get over with. It was beginning to be that way for me.

TRYING HARD TO PRESERVE HIS DIGNITY

My father had begun to lose control of his kidneys and bowels. After a certain point, Alzheimer's patients cannot know ahead of time if they need to use the restroom, so one has to remember to ask them regularly if they need to use it. With Daddy, the situation was worse, as he only had half his intestines and with a short colon he had had the challenge of frequent bowel movements for many years. Since he only fully understood the present moment, it got to the point where he could only know at that minute when he needed to use the toilet. This presented various challenges.

About every thirty minutes during the day and evening hours, I asked him if he needed to use the restroom. He usually responded, "I've already been." I knew he became tired of this question, and its very nature took away his pride and privacy. I could usually sense from his brow when he was feeling the urge. As this problem became more pronounced, I realized how the situation must be on those three days when he had to be with my mother who rarely came around him and slept in another part of the house. She often complained about the mess she had to clean up. During the first couple of years, during the night my father successfully used the bathroom adjoining his bedroom because he could see the bathroom nightlight from his bed and had very little problem finding the commode. As the disease progressed, he had more difficulty. Occasionally I drifted off to sleep, only to be awakened after the accident had occurred, or was in the process of happening in and on places other than the bathroom. He appeared to want to get into some semi-private place. At least he seemed to make a distinction because he knew his bedroom wasn't the place to use the bathroom.

This action might have resulted from his disorientation, which increased at night, the deterioration of the recognition of objects, or the memory from early childhood when he didn't have a bathroom. Or it have been a combination of all of these, although he always seemed to remember what the Bible was and scripture from it. Even with bells on the door knobs, sometimes I let myself fall off to sleep more soundly than I intended. I would be so suddenly awakened by the accident that I seemed unable to always restrain my startled reaction and rush to clean up the mess. I later hated myself for this response. Perhaps by reflex, sometimes saving my furniture and floors seemed as significant at the moment as the humiliation Daddy was bound to have experienced. It was almost as if I were responding more to a set of symptoms than to a person. During that first moment after the accident, when I turned on the light, he was defensive and almost hostile. Right afterwards, I felt horribly guilty about my initial reaction. After I got him back into bed, I would say, "Daddy, anyone can have an accident." He always just closed his eyes. He realized the inauthenticity of my remark. I hoped that by the next morning he would have forgotten the entire matter. But I could never be sure. While we were both awake during the day or evening, the very minute I might turn my head or run to the kitchen or bathroom, the accident seemed to happen. Sometimes I thought it was not an accident, but just one way of controlling just one action in his life.

I purchased cheap plastic table cloths to cover most of the floors and told Daddy, "I am so messy that I have put plastic on some of my rugs so as not to mess them up. What do you think of that idea?" "I've done that myself," he said. Pampers didn't seem to help him, because his Alzheimer's prevented his brain from handling them in any other way than his old habits with regard to his regular underwear. He did not remember their purpose. Sadly, I reflected how clean Daddy always was, and I knew how distressed he became when an accident happened in the bed, or when we were out. I realized the hackneyed, "Daddy, accidents can happen to any of us; I have a few of them myself" must have become totally artificial and tiresome even to him, but it was the only way I knew to make him feel less ashamed. He was always so sad afterwards. There were other times when I had to actually help get the residue out of him. These were some of the most stressful moments, since there was no way to preserve his dignity. I would just say, "Daddy, just think of me as your nurse, okay?"

He usually said nothing. There was nothing that could really make either of us feel better. We both felt helpless and hopeless. I just hoped he would forget the incident as soon as possible.

It became really tricky if we were out to eat. But people were always considerate. Scouting out the women's restroom, I would go into it to make certain it was empty. If there were women inside, I would warn them that I needed to bring my father in. They always were kind and accommodating. Then I led him in, and turned him around so that he could see the toilet. I would then close the stall door so he could have privacy and just sneak a peek to see how he was doing.

The issue of not getting warning about bodily urges and the challenge of not recognizing objects created dilemmas at other places, like the time Daddy had to use the restroom when we were in an appliance store. "I need to use the restroom," he whispered to me. "Okay, Daddy, just hang on for a moment. There's a restroom in the back of the store that you can use." Because his brain gave him such little warning, I seemed to always be rushing him to a bathroom to avoid a catastrophe. And this created a problem for his heart conditions. As I hurriedly led him through the store, he was clearly having some discomfort with his heart, and so I thought we better stop for just a moment. "Daddy, you can sit here a moment," I whispered as I pointed to a chair in the store. Unfortunately, my father perceived the chair to be the toilet and began taking his pants down! "Daddy, not yet; we must go on a little ways." I tried not to panic. Of course, by the time we arrived at the restroom, the accident had occurred before we came to the stall. But as was so often the case, God helped us even with this situation. I was able to clean up the restroom and Daddy before anyone else in the store even knew what had happened. And fortunately for Daddy, I had some of his clothes in the car. The thing that always hurt me the most was his painful loss of dignity. Once again, I used what had become that old common refrain, "Daddy, accidents happen to us all," but it had sounded increasingly hollow every time I said it. After this incident was over, I reflected back on our moment in the car before we arrived at the store. He had been unusually quiet and didn't respond to my statements. Since it was night and I was driving, I could not see his facial expression and later realized I should have paid more attention to it when we got out of the car. I knew he tried to hold his urges, not wanting to inconvenience me. It was truly amazing how some parts of his brain, like the sensitivity to others, were still intact, while so much of basic programming had been lost.

Then there was the time I had left my home in Nashville earlier than usual to drive to East Tennessee to get him since his doctor's appointment was in Nashville at 11:00 that morning. About 100 miles away from where I was to pick him up, my oil light came on. This in itself was provoking given the fact that I had just had my car checked out, and it was supposed to be in proper working order. But the car was old, and I was continuously experiencing problems with it. The long drives back and forth to East Tennessee hadn't helped either.

On this particular morning, I stopped on the side of the road and cellphoned my mechanic, who advised me not to drive the car. This condition was stressful for several reasons. I would have to figure out a way to quickly rent a car; I would have to telephone my mother who was always highly irritated when I didn't appear at just the exact time; I would have to phone a towing service to have my car towed, and then I would have to rush back to Nashville to make my father's appointment time. I didn't want to postpone that appointment since it was with his neurologist, and I always timed his appointments around the times Mother allowed his visits with me. If I had dared phone her, she might have made her usual threat, "Well, he doesn't have to come down there now."

Managing to rent a car in Cookeville, I drove 90 miles an hour to Mother's home to get my father. Having quickly fetched him and gotten his things in the car, I then found myself racing back to Nashville. Realizing I could not possibly make it in time for the appointment, I telephoned the doctor's office and apprised them of her situation. They said they would accommodate us.

We were on the interstate, coming down a low mountain, with me driving faster than I should have been, when Daddy quietly asked, "Is there a restroom here? I need to use the restroom." I had just asked him a few minutes prior where there was an exit if he needed to stop, and he had said that he didn't. But he probably had caught my own rather frantic mood which may have prompted this urgent need. He could hardly know even under calm conditions until the exact moment. "Okay, Daddy, can you just hang on for a little while until I get to the next exit?" I accelerated. "I've got to go now," he slightly moaned.

There was nothing to do, but pull off the side of the highway and walk Daddy a little ways from the road. There were no trees, and I just had to try to shield him from the traffic with my body. Fortunately cars were whizzing by so fast that hopefully nobody saw the particulars of our plight, and I was actually thankful that no one stopped because that would have made things worse on him. All the while, I was trying to help him pull his pants down. I was somewhat frightened because this was traumatic on his body and his nerves, since we were standing on a hillside, and I was afraid that both of us could fall. Somehow I managed to contain the damage, and just kept saying, "Daddy, it's okay." I cleaned him up the best that I could and, trying to use a positive tone, said, "Guess what, Daddy...there's a McDonald's a little ways down the road, and since we have all your clothes, you can put on some clean ones." He looked pale, his hands were shaking, but he forced a wan smile and said, "God bless you," a usual refrain now for just about anything I did for him. But he really *did* perceive when any extraordinary effort had been spent to help him. I managed to exit to the fast-food restaurant and led him quietly into the women's restroom. Fortunately there were only a couple of people in the restaurant. An older employee sensed I needed help and offered to bring us some towels. God always seemed to send an angel to help us at just the right time. We were a little late for his doctor's appointment, but we did make it.

I constantly worked to figure out ways to preserve Daddy's privacy and yet ensure that he was clean, clothed and fed. But preserving what dignity he had left was as important as anything, being determined that he would not suffer humiliation when he was with me. It took some doing to avoid it, and I was not always successful. Believing that every person has a mental, physical, psychological, and spiritual potential, I remained determined that I would do what I could to enable Daddy to reach his, even at this late stage of his disease. I was still racing against time to make up huge deficits he had accumulated throughout his life.

CHAPTER 21

And there shall be a tabernacle for a shadow in the daytime from the heat, and for a place of refuge, and for a covert from storm and from rain.

–Isaiah 4:6

THERE'S A STORM COMING

I stumbled out of my father's hospital room, dazed, disoriented, and frightened for him. As on earlier occasions, I had been forced to hand over my helpless dad to the hands of a family which appeared to have almost become demon possessed. The vision of the tears coming out of his eyes and his hands grabbing his heart, as he said, "Oh, Oh," was a vision that I knew would haunt me the rest of my life. I thought for a split second about calling in a medical staff person as a witness, but I knew it would increase my mother's histrionics and Daddy's trauma. So I just backed out of the room.

Only hours before, Daddy was laughing, talking sensibly, and even *remembering*! It was as if a miracle had occurred. He thought he was going home with all his family. He was in a mood that I had rarely seen.

The night before the hospital's chaplain visited him and asked him what he would pray for, if he could pray for anything. This was in itself somewhat unusual for Daddy to be asked directly what he thought about anything. People often talked around him or over him, assuming that because he had Alzheimer's and didn't communicate exactly like they did, that he therefore had *no* mind. And my mother had never really asked him what he thought about any subject; she just told him "his" opinion.

So Daddy hesitated, looked off into the distance, and then thoughtfully said, "Well, there's a storm coming," as he pointed upwards, "and you have to get all your family into this house....the church; then you can protect them, and God will protect you." To many people this might have been gibberish, but not to me, or the chaplain. We both understood this was Daddy's way of expressing his most ardent wish - that there would be unity and harmony within his family and that we would all be united under God's protection. Later that morning he asked, "When are we going back to *that* church?" after my mother and brother had arrived. I believe it was his way of trying to tell them that he wanted to stay with me, but also that this church had come to be a place which held peace and a sweet spirit. It was *our* church. We had built our own little two-member family, and *that* church was an important part of it.

During the course of the week his cardiologist and his internal medicine physician had ordered three units of blood, altered his medication, and placed him on oxygen. Upon finding his red blood cell count good and his blood pressure normal, they had told me, my mother, and my brother that he could be released. This would have been good news in normal families, but in this one, it spelled horror for me and perhaps death for Daddy.

The week had had its mountain tops and its valleys. On my weekly journey to East Tennessee to get Daddy only a little over a week before, he immediately said to me, "I've been very sick" as soon as we got in the car. He remembered that he had. He always revealed more awareness and understanding when he was with me than he apparently did when he was with anyone else. Either that, or no one heard him. Or they assumed he was "talking out of his head." One thing I had known for a long time was that my father had learned long ago to fake sleeping and unawareness to survive his wife's behaviors. I could understand why Mother couldn't really discern when he was feeling more ill than usual, since she pretty much ignored him. Even my parents' neighbor had expressed concern that "sitting in his chair" was pretty much all he did at her house.

I had noticed when we stopped to eat at the restaurant on that day and when we visited his relatives in our weekly ritual that he was much weaker than usual and had a harder time walking. His breath was shorter than I had noticed in earlier times, even though during the past several weeks, I could see that his strength was waning. And he had begun to have more pain at various times during the day. His aortic stenosis was probably getting worse because it was so rare for Daddy to ever complain that when he did, I knew he was really hurting.

Still, he wanted so much to go and do our usual activities, even on that day: to see his cousins, to go to the coffee house that he and I went to on Thursday evenings to hear bluegrass and gospel music. Since he didn't have the chance to go to any events when he wasn't with me, he fought hard to keep the impression up that he was okay. It appeared that he had begun to realize when he first saw me each week that he would get to do some "fun" stuff, like going to hear the bluegrass music. It was this music particularly that had seemed over the past few years to give Daddy the opportunity to feel equal with everyone else. I had no idea if he ever played the fiddle much in his earlier years, or if he were any good, but I capitalized on the fact that he did play, and told the "regulars." He wanted to go hear it on this particular evening, so we went.

During the next two days, he was not feeling even as well as usual, but he continued to eat enough and still wanted to do the things that he and I had been in the habit of doing. There was something about how much he ate this time that gave me the impression that he was eating not just because he was that hungry, but to store up enough so that he could make it until he was with me again. Looking back later, I think he also knew he had to somehow "hang in there" for some reason that neither he nor I quite understood. On this particular Sunday, I decided we would attend my church in Nashville because of his own pain *and* mine. Since we had been attending there occasionally and everyone was so friendly to him, I thought their response might make him feel better. This was only a few weeks after I learned I had osteoporosis, so I figured the less driving I did, the less pain I would have as well. I was quite concerned that I might become crippled and not able to take care of Daddy. What would happen if I died before he did? There would be *nobody* left in his corner.

Attending the service proved to be the right thing to do. Many of the members came up to him, hugged him, and talked to him, as they had done another time when we had gone. They all had prayed for him and me. The minister came up to him, asked him a few specific questions, and shook his hand. My father was happy. People were talking *with* him.

It was communion Sunday, and I whispered to Daddy, asking him if he felt like going to the altar to take communion. "Daddy, we don't have to go up, if you don't feel like it." "I want to go," he insisted. The first time I recognized it would be challenging, and I didn't want him to be embarrassed. He stood up right then, and I whispered, "No yet, Daddy. We'll go in a minute." And so I led him to the altar. He was not able to kneel, so we both stood. I had helped him take communion at the little church in Cookeville, but this was our first time here. It was awkward, but he wanted to participate. My senior pastor was so helpful while we were at the altar minimizing awkwardness for Daddy as I took a piece of bread, gave it to Daddy, cued him to eat it, and then gave him the grape juice which I cued him to drink. Both ministers were always patient and helpful as they waited during this process since his hands were a little shaky. Members were also always patient and seemed to appreciate the effort required for my father to participate. Afterwards Daddy remarked several times about how nice "those church people" were.

It was the following day that he began to feel worse. We had continued our visits to a local mall where he had become accustomed to watching the children and talking with them. But as he got out of the car, he just began shaking and said, "I can't go on."

"Daddy, what about if I take you to the hospital just to let them check you out?" I asked. "No, I don't think so," he frailly responded. "Okay, then, we'll go back home and you can lie down." "Yes, that's what I want to do," he said. I knew by that statement that he was really feeling ill.

He was feeling so bad that I didn't try putting his pajamas on him that evening. I gave him some Tylenol and kept putting cold cloths on his forehead. He was extremely nauseated, and his pain seemed to move from one part of his body to another. He usually had some difficulty defining exactly where any particular pain was, if he even mentioned it at all. But on this particular evening, the pain did seem to be generalized. Daddy had a pacemaker which keeps the rhythm of the heart the same during a heart attack, so the only way one could know if the person is having one is through other symptoms. I became more concerned. Besides having difficulty breathing, he was clammy. I said, "Daddy, I'm going to call the ambulance and let them take you to the hospital so you can feel better." "Okay," he responded weakly. I knew then that he was indeed feeling worse than usual.

My mind was racing in a dozen ways. What would my mother say about bringing him to the hospital? I knew that whatever decision I made she would be enraged, but I just couldn't think about that now. As the ambulance arrived, I threw some of his things into his little bag. I was worried about Daddy's difficulty in understanding what all was going on. I told the woman who would be riding with him in the ambulance that he had Alzheimer's and that he would be very confused. "Don't worry, Ms. Huddleston, I will take good care of him; my father-in-law has Alzheimer's." That comforted me, and I said, "Daddy, I will be right behind you." After I had dialed 911, I had telephoned his internal physician whom Mother had recently given me permission to secure. I was so thankful now that Daddy had a highly reputable doctor who could admit him, if he needed to be admitted.

There was a cold front moving in that evening, and as I started the car, it began to sleet. Many thoughts were swirling in my head. Maybe this would be the end, and Daddy would have someone who could pray with him, talk to him about heaven and help him get to the other side. Maybe this was God's way of allowing me to finally get the help for him he had so long needed but had so long been denied by the one who controlled virtually everything about his life. I knew that in a life or death situation neither the hospital not I could be sued by my mother for saving Daddy's life. I prayed, "God please let me do what You would have me do for my father. Please keep me calm and please, please keep him from suffering too much. If this is his time to leave this world, please let him not be afraid." Maybe there actually could be a "light at the end of the tunnel" for both of us after all.

During the past several months, gradually I had managed to eke out permission from my mother for my father to have more and more care in Nashville. A couple of years earlier she had finally given me permission to take him to a neurologist whom Daddy now adored, and in the past year she had granted me permission to have an ophthalmologist in Nashville see him for his deteriorating vision. I had framed the request to my mother with the usual, "Mother I know you have *so* much to do, and this will be one way I can ease some of your burden." The only way I was able to get permission to have an internal medicine doctor in Nashville see him was that on a recent weekly trip to get Daddy, I had discovered he was very congested and coughing. One of my mother's neighbors had urged my mother to allow me to take him to see a doctor and to keep him for a few days longer than I originally had permission to do.

In any other normal case where there would have been love and interest in a person's life, this would never been an issue. But my mother and I seemed to have two conflicting goals: I wanted Daddy alive; Mother wanted him where she could *control* whether he was dead or alive. She seemed to forget that if he died, her monthly income would be drastically reduced.

Daddy and I spent about half the night in the emergency room where blood was drawn for various tests, an EKG was done, and X-rays were taken. His internal medicine physician admitted Daddy into the hospital later that night. Oh, if I could just take on my father's pain! He had been through so much suffering in his life. Not just from my mother's treatment, but he had so much physically wrong with him. For years he had had clogged arteries, arrhythmia, only half a colon, pain from arthritis, and recurring anemia. But every time a nurse drew blood, or every time any medical personnel poked or jabbed him, Daddy thanked them. What a kind and innocent man! Over the past four years I had come to see how strong he really was, and how little it took for him to be grateful. These last few years had given both of us the chance to experience each other directly, without any negative filter, and overcome the negative images which had been fed to us. During that week, I did not leave the hospital, and only one night, I had paid a young man to sit with Daddy so that I might get a little sleep in a room on the same floor Daddy was on. I had hardly dare blink, since Daddy was on oxygen, was getting a blood transfusion through an IV, and his Alzheimer's condition caused him to forget why these foreign objects were on his arm. Once when I had turned away, Daddy had jerked the blood IV out, resulting in blood all over him, the bed, and the floor. It was a scene I dared not repeat. So I stayed in a chair beside his bed. It was the first time I could ever remember that we had the opportunity to be this close. I was protecting him.

In many ways it was a wonderful week. By Tuesday evening Daddy had seen his internal medicine physician and a cardiologist with whom this physician worked. I was delighted because for so long I had hoped for the opportunity to have a team of doctors addressing his physical and mental conditions. I had known he had had extreme anemia for over two years and extremely low blood pressure. But Mother had continued delivering the response, "He's old; what do you expect?" as I continued various strategies to get her to feed Daddy better. None proved to be successful. The reality was that even if she did offer him nutritious food, the ranting and raving were so unsettling and anxiety provoking even to a normal person – much less to an Alzheimer's patient – that he wasn't digesting enough required nutrients.

After he had gotten this blood, his pain subsided. He was joking and laughing. Daddy, I came to discover, actually *enjoyed* being in the hospital. Perhaps it was because he felt safe, or because he could be an equal with other patients, or that he knew he would be cared for, or knowing he would have interaction with others. Possibly he liked being here for all these reasons.

THE CALM BEFORE THE STORM

Daddy was actually remembering! At one point, he had looked at me and called me by the name of his cousin he adored – a cousin that I had frequently taken him to visit and a cousin he had grown up playing with. As I rose from my chair and stood next to his bed, I smiled and chided him mildly, asking, "Now, who did you say I am?" "Why you're my little girl," he replied as he smiled back. "That's right, and don't you forget it!" This was the first time I could ever remember him acknowledging me as his daughter, and I thought that it might be just some response he pulled out of the air. Over the years I had frequently sensed that he thought I was not his daughter, and he had had good reason for doubting that I was. But this was a precious moment worth remembering.

And then there was the evening when the sleet had turned to snow, and Daddy and I were all snugly settled into a private room. Things were quiet and calm. "Daddy, this is nice here, isn't it?" as I pointed out the snow drifting past the street lights. "Maybe we'll just move in here," he responded, smiling.

I chuckled. It was nice just to be there, the two of us. It was safe. There was no one to control us. We could say to each other what we wanted to without fear. Much of my peacefulness was that my dreaded telephone call to Mother had been made, and she had been halfway cooperative. There was much to be thankful for.

Earlier that day, I realized I had to telephone her. I had that queasiness in my stomach I always got when I had to have any communication with her. But this time, my nervousness was greater. At that moment, my greatest horror was that Mother would come tearing down the interstate and jerk Daddy out of the hospital, screaming that I didn't have the right to make any medical decisions for him. That was why it was so important that the physicians get his blood going before I telephoned. On the previous night, I had the excuse of it being so late when my father was transported to the hospital that I didn't want to frighten my mother needlessly, especially before I had seen his doctor. But on this morning, I knew I must try to telephone. Strategy was in order.

I had hoped that Daddy's physician wouldn't come too early so I would have another excuse to delay phoning Mother. I could tell her then that I didn't want to bother her from her activities that day before I had seen the doctor. Fortunately, Daddy's physician had not come until about the time my mother was usually scheduled to have lunch with her lady friends and play bridge. This helped me with my plan.

As soon as the doctor left and explained that he was going to bring in a cardiologist to collaborate with, I telephoned Mother. Knowing my mother had caller identification, I knew therefore that she would know I had attempted the call. That would give me a little reprieve. I then telephoned my mother's neighbor, a sane and level-headed friend, who had been my parents' neighbor for almost 40 years and surely had experienced some of my mother's volatile behavior. "Martha, I had Daddy brought into the ER last night with chest pains and shortness of breath. I didn't want to telephone Mother to upset her needlessly. When I picked him up last week, he told me he had been very sick." I continued the conversation with her and explained that I had tried phoning Mother until I realized it was her bridge day. I explained that Daddy had a great team of physicians working with him – including his internist and cardiologist who had ordered three units of blood. This explanation was done to inspire confidence about his care. I had also made certain that the neighbor knew the weather was worsening, and it would be dangerous to try to drive in this snow.

I asked her if she would tell Mother as soon as she noticed she was home that I would telephone her that evening and explain everything. I told the neighbor my concern that Mother would become angry about taking Daddy to the hospital and asked her if she might reinforce what a great hospital this was. "Martha, if Mother and Donald come screaming down here, it will be the worst thing that could happen. Daddy is finally getting the care he has needed."

Martha said she understood. It was this neighbor's husband who had quietly told me a year earlier that Daddy was alive today because of me. However, because they were my parents' neighbors and friends, I didn't want to put them in a more difficult spot than they were already in.

I also asked one of my own friends in the health care business, who knew Mother, to telephone her and explain the situation. Historically when I felt a sense of real urgency in getting my mother to at least consider an idea, I tried having another person communicate it first to her. Even Martha had at one time advised me that any suggestion from me would automatically be dismissed and contradicted by my mother. "Don't *you* suggest it to her," she had warned me. Of course, she was right.

Eager to hear about their conversations with my mother before I telephoned her myself, I telephoned both of them. The neighbor said that actually Mother had not become hysterical and had even indicated some acceptance of my actions. My friend had indicated that while he had tried to make some statements that I had asked him to make, the conversation had immediately turned to my mother as she began saying she had had to have blood herself and began talking about her own anemia. He didn't have the sense that she heard much of what he had said, but a couple of times he mentioned the bad weather our city was experiencing. This statement was made to give Mother a legitimate excuse for not being able to come to this city. Both he and Martha had told her that I would telephone her later. The most important thing was that both telephone calls had laid the groundwork for my call.

So, heart pounding and hands shaking, I slipped into my father's bathroom to use my cell phone to telephone my mother. I was trembling so much that I misdialed the number three times. I could still see my father but didn't think he could hear me. "Mother," I began, "I understand that Martha and William talked with you earlier." "Yes, I was playing bridge." "I'm glad you were," I responded. "Do you have a few minutes for me to bring you up to date?" For the first time that I could remember, Mother actually let me get a few sentences out without interrupting. She ended up telling me to do what I needed to do! I thought I was dreaming. This couldn't be. But maybe it was. I expressed my gratitude to her for this cooperative spirit, and asked if this would be a good time to telephone her the next day to keep her posted.

She said that she would write the cardiologist in another town who by this time had treated Daddy on a couple of occasions and tell him that since her husband was staying more at my house now, that he would be treated by a cardiologist in Nashville. This was so much more than I could have hoped for. I again was grateful and explained that I had already written him, but of course, if Mother wanted to telephone or write, this would be fine.

I could not remember when, if ever, I had felt this good about any interaction with my mother. I kept wondering if I had dreamed this call. For a little while I forgot about her schizophrenic behavior. I thanked God off and on all that evening for this cooperation. Now I really had permission to go forward with any treatment the doctors felt Daddy needed. So here Daddy and I were, safely nestled in a private room where we could watch the snow come down. Everything appeared so tranquil. What a blessing the snow was. It gave me a comfortable, safe feeling just to watch it, and it would serve a pragmatic purpose to keep my mother and brother away for at least a couple of days, since warnings were issued not to travel. God again intervened to help Daddy and me out.

That same evening, as I retrieved telephone calls from my voice messages, I had a call from my brother. "When you get in, give me a call and let me know what's going on," was the message in that dogmatic, managerial tone of his. My brother, who lived within minutes from my parents' home but rarely saw them, was forever conscious of his alternate power of attorney status. Neither he nor Mother ever allowed me to forget their control over all Daddy's assets and decisions made about him.

I mused how clueless he was about my father's situation. "When you get in" indeed! With intravenous tubes for glucose and blood, I had not nor could not leave the hospital, since Daddy couldn't remember why they were in his arm. I really didn't dare leave his side, especially since he had pulled the IV out earlier when I had to use the restroom. It was so late by the time I received that call that I didn't return it until the next day because I was determined that Daddy and I would have a peaceful night. Still, there was something in me that sensed this peacefulness could be the "calm before the storm."

THE STORM ARRIVES IN FULL FURY

When I did speak to my brother the next day, I heard the rattling of pots and pans, loud television noise, and shuffling paper. He apparently wanted to give me the impression that he wasn't interested. Not having any sense that he was listening at all, I asked, "Are you still there?" I could hear Marie, his wife, in the background, with some consternation in her voice ask, "Would you please turn that TV down so you can hear her?" There was no feedback at all until I had told him all the details. Then, "Why are they giving him blood?" he asked in an accusatory tone. "Because his blood was that low," I replied, quietly. I knew better than to try to talk in detail with him about Daddy's blood count. I just said that it had been low for a long time.

The next day I discovered from my sister-in-law that following that conversation, my brother had said to her, "She's killing him." He was implying that taking my father to church and engaging him in other activities had somehow altered his red blood cell count. This was another example of the ignorance and insanity Daddy and I were both up against. I came to learn later he made that statement every time I had to take my father to see a physician or to the hospital.

On that same day I telephoned Mother at the time I had said I would, and in less than 24 hours her mood had totally changed. She threatened, "I am coming down to take him back to his doctors at *my* home because you are killing him." Another personality had emerged. My brother had obviously phoned his mother after our conversation and once again successfully played to her mental state. She demanded that I tell her when the doctors at the hospital were going to release him. "Mother, they're taking it one day at a time," I tentatively responded. "They must not be very good if they don't know," she sniped.

And then on the following day the bomb was dropped. When I telephoned Mother after seeing the cardiologist, having promised her that I would telephone every day right after seeing the doctor, and explained that Daddy was much improved and might be released within the next day or two, she began screaming. She hissed that she had never given me permission to take him to the hospital, or to let him receive blood, that she was coming down and take him home. Her neighbor had told me previously that even when my father was released my mother had agreed that Daddy wouldn't be able to travel back to her home right away. My mother had agreed with the neighbor that it would be at least a full day before she would force him to travel.

But I had witnessed this personality shift hundreds of times in the past, and that familiar chill ran down my back. I knew my mother's rage. I knew this personality that emerged when she thought she was losing control of any situation. I tried to explain that I had reserved a room for her right around the corner from Daddy's room in the event he wasn't released. Mother kept screaming. I let her scream for a while and then tried to ask her if she would consider staying at my home for just a couple of days. I told her that I would be willing to get myself a hotel room, or stay at a friend's house and just come to bring them meals. She continued screaming. The sound had that familiar hellish sound to it. The third personality, resembling the devil, had been unleashed.

Later that evening, scrunched down in Daddy's bathroom again with my cell phone, I telephoned Marie. "Kathryn, your mother has really gone over the edge this time...You won't believe the message she left on our recorder. It doesn't sound like a human's voice. It sounds like a voice out of hell." I asked Marie if she knew where my brother was. "No, I've tried calling him at work, but I can't get him. They may be on their way down there, but Donald promised me that he wouldn't take your father directly from the hospital to here." I was horrified that he and my mother might be on their way to Nashville, and Marie had confirmed that this could be happening. She just didn't know, as they never shared anything with her any more once she began defending my father. Marie had been aware of her husband's conspiracy to control everything related to his father, and she had also seen his violent streak. His temper, just as my mother's, was exacerbated by alcohol. She knew they could both be very dangerous. Marie turned the recorder up so I could hear the message. This was the same tone I had heard earlier that day. It didn't sound like a human voice. "Oh, Lord, help me, I prayed," realizing the *storm* could be on its way.

I had the dubious task of trying to assume a positive attitude with Daddy and keep my own anxiety from him. After a few hours, I telephoned Mother again, hoping the mood might have passed, and urged again that she consider allowing my father to stay in the area at least for a little while to recuperate. Mother appeared a little calmer and said that she and my brother would be down early the next morning. I didn't trust this calmness. "Ohhhh," I thought. This meant that I probably wouldn't have the chance to warn the doctors and ask them to urge my mother to leave Daddy in the area.

On the day when Mother had given me permission to do all I needed to do for my father, I had managed to find an oxygen provider in both Nashville and Mother's town and had arranged for the technician to come to my home to hook up the machine. I had arranged for tanks to be at both places. I had filled out all the paper work.

After this latest call to my mother, I telephoned Daddy's primary physician and left the message asking the physician to telephone me, wanting to warn him about my mother's attitude. I also relayed the message requesting that he recommend that my father not be transported yet.

But the "storm" arrived before I was able to directly talk with his primary doctor. Mother and Donald walked into Daddy's hospital room just as the physician telephoned. Of course, I could say nothing to clue him in on the situation, but told him instead, as positively and calmly as possible, that my mother and brother were here and wanted to see him. He explained that he would be by before too long. But he had received the message about urging them to leave my father in the area. I had taken the opportunity earlier in the week to talk a little to the cardiologist about my mother's instability and need to control.

Mother and Donald barely spoke to Daddy. Instead, they talked continuously about money matters. It was about suing this person or that person. It was about how my neighbor's heat bill was too high...that maybe Mother wouldn't have gas put in after all. It was about what her grandson's (Donald's son) increased salary was going to be. At one point I tried to speak to my brother on the side. "Donald, I will be glad to bring both of them back if you will let them stay with me a couple of days if Daddy is released," I pleaded. Donald, shrugging his shoulders, retorted, "No, I will bring them back." He knew then, as did my mother, that neither of them intended to stay at my house. I had been duped again.

In the meantime, Daddy quietly asked, "When are we going back to *that* church?" No one heard him but me, and I said "Soon, Daddy...we're going to go back to church soon." Later, as I reflected on the series of events, I realized Daddy was beginning to sense that things weren't going to come out well after all, and he was beginning to make a stab at turning things around. I helped feed him his lunch, while the three of them continued to talk about money and complain that the doctors hadn't arrived yet. I figured that Donald probably had plans that afternoon, and he was in a hurry to get back to his home. And that he probably needed a drink.

Daddy also asked about how my nephew's feet were. The nephew had broken them in a hunting accident the previous year. With that blood going to his brain and the subsiding of his pain, he was remembering details! My mother sighed disgustingly, "*What* are you talking about?" "Mother, remember, Paul Donald broke his feet last year," I quietly explained. Donald gave me a threatening look. Mother ignored the statement. I helped Daddy finish his lunch, while the three of them continued to talk about money.

The cardiologist, Dr. Brennen, came first. She used the information I had given her to try to persuade my mother. "What a beautiful color that is on you," complimenting my mother's pant suit. This cardiologist was a spunky little woman who I came to learn was extremely quick and perceptive. Mother driveled a while from that compliment and eventually gave the doctor a little time to speak. She explained why she had altered my father's medicine and the positive results it had had. "Coumadin doesn't come in three milligrams," my mother quickly insisted in her know-it-all manner. "Well, yes, it actually does...There are different colors for different milligrams...blue for five, white for ten..." Dr. Brennen replied as politely as possible and without any hint of arrogance. "Well, I've already bought the five milligrams, and I can't buy any more," Mother insisted. "Mother, I will buy them," I tentatively urged. However, seeing that this was a pointless exercise, the cardiologist said, "Okay, whatever you choose. It's your decision." "It certainly is; I have power of attorney," snapped Mother. Another personality had begun to emerge. The doctor explained that the internist would probably release Daddy since his blood pressure was normal, and his red blood cell count was where it should be, but that he should stay in the area throughout the week-end so they could check him out the beginning of the week. "I want him at *my* home," Mother whined. Dr. Brennen stood up, went over to my father, and smiled. "Mr. Howard is lucky in that he has two homes," she replied. "Well, I have power of attorney, and I am taking him back to his real doctors." Mother's whining had stopped. Her tone became dictatorial. And Dr. Brennen left the room, with me following her out.

"You see what I'm up against." She nodded and said, "I'm going right now and telephone Bruce." "I'm so sorry," I apologized. I had spent my lifetime apologizing for my mother. "You warned me," Dr. Brennen responded.

When the internal physician came, he did release my father but, like the cardiologist, urged that Daddy stay in the area until he could recuperate a bit – at least over the week-end until he could see him the following Monday. Daddy had not even been out of his room at that point. Once again my mother threw her power around, and declared, "*I* have power of attorney, and I'm taking him back to *my* home." "Of course, it is your right," replied the physician, not wishing to become embroiled in a legal battle. "I just urge you, however, to follow up with your cardiologist in East Tennessee early next week."

Mother said that of course she would do that. This was utterly unbelievable, since earlier in the week she had asked me to write a letter to this East Tennessee physician who had seen Daddy only a couple of times, explaining that my father would thereafter have a new physician in Nashville. Once again the impact of either the schizophrenia or the devil became obvious; I had begun to wonder if there was a difference.

I was ordered to return to my home and collect Daddy's things and bring them back. Again I felt like I was ten – totally powerless to help Daddy or myself. I was so confused I couldn't remember on which garage level I had parked my car. I kept going around in circles until I finally managed to find it, drive to my house, throw my father's things together, and return to the hospital. All the while, I just kept thinking, as I had so many times previously, that this was too horrible to be real. Maybe I would awaken from what had to be still another nightmare.

But it *was* real. When I reentered Daddy's room to bring all his things back from my house, I found a far different countenance than when I had left about an hour earlier. Then he had been joking, laughing, and remembering! He thought we were all going to be together. But shortly afterwards he had begun to realize what was really going on. Somewhere in his psyche he probably remembered that day in East Tennessee when he thought his family were all going home with him together. And, instead, he was dumped in that asylum-like place. Now he looked drawn, ashen, and weary. As I asked my mother and brother if I could have a couple of minutes with Daddy, tears began streaming from his eyes. I had only rarely seen a tear fall from my father's eyes. Trying to put a positive spin on this dark moment, I gently said, "Daddy, we'll be able to go back to church real soon...They just want you with them for a little while." As I saw the tears continuing, I thought I was going to die right there. That boulder was on my chest again, except this time it was heavier. But, as so often the case when you know there is no possible way to make any sense, I tried making a stab at something light. "Just think, you'll be able to play with that kitten." I remembered that someone in the neighborhood had a kitten. I wanted to purchase my parents another dog, after Mother had theirs been put to sleep, because I wanted my father to have something to touch when he was at her house. My mother said she wouldn't have another dog because they were just trouble and expensive. That was that.

I quietly asked Mother and Donald if I could have a few minutes with Daddy. Refusing to leave the room, Mother turned to my brother and screamed, "What is she trying to do? She's trying to kill him...Let's get him out of here!" Their melodrama sounded like bad acting in a play. My brother echoed the same, sighing all the while. My father grabbed his heart and said, "Oh, Oh"! In the only way he knew, he was trying to reverse things. I had considered calling in one of the nurses to have this scene witnessed, but on second thought I realized that if my mother and brother would pay no attention to Daddy's primary physicians, they certainly wouldn't to a nurse. And it would only heighten the already traumatic scene. So I just acquiesced and backed out of the room. Once again, the devil seemed to have won the battle. I, stunned and in partial shock, still managed to pray, "God forgive me for allowing this helpless child of yours to be placed into the hands of this evil....Please help me get out of here." But even as I prayed, I felt fed up by my own prayers. Daddy and I had both been abandoned by God. What in the world had he or I done to deserve this?

I wandered around the hospital floor in circles again, trying to remember what floor of the hospital I was on, where the elevator was, which car I was in, even which garage I had parked in *this* time, and whether my father had all his things. These last few minutes felt like hell, so maybe I had died and gone there. I was struggling to breathe when some hospital personnel made me realize that I was still alive and helped me into the elevator. "Where can I find the chaplain," I gasped. I thought I was going to faint, but I knew I had to get to a safe place myself. I could not bear to see my father, and I was afraid to see my mother.

This nightmare had occurred before. This time, however, it was different. Finally, Daddy and I had developed a real *relationship*. He had claimed me as his daughter, and I loved him as my father. Or something like that. Before this time, all my battles for him were for a helpless, elderly man who had been verbally abused much of his life by a self-absorbed woman. A good deal of my fight for him was because he was my grandmother's son, my grandmother who had raised me, but a grandmother I had not had the opportunity to rescue from the clutches of evil.

I had not been given the chance to offer my grandmother the peace and love during the past two years of her life since I was not allowed to privately visit this angel who had raised me. Nor was I given permission to take her back to her home which she longed to just visit and which was only a couple of miles from her daughter's home. And certainly I wasn't allowed to take her for a visit to my home in Nashville. For the previous twenty odd years I had had dreams about rescuing her from this imposed control and giving her a sense of peace and happiness, but I had not had the chance to talk with anyone about my grief surrounding her death.

So during the past week I had become convinced that God was enabling me to make up for Daddy what I was not allowed to do for my grandmother. I had become convinced that this was God's way of reconciling the painful past for me. But now it appeared that I had been duped again, and this time by God, not just my mother. Could I have been just pretending all these years that God was really protecting Daddy and me? Why else would He continue to defeat my father and me in this struggle and allow the devil to win? I knew that God can control the devil, so why didn't He? For even though the players had changed, the story hadn't. It was clearly the struggle between God and the devil, and the ultimate result was obsession with money and control. Again,

I remembered the scenario two years earlier when my mother had deceptively left Daddy in that psychopathic institution and had used her power of attorney to try to keep me from rescuing him then.

My thoughts were racing back to all those prior dreadful times when again I was powerless in the face of evil. My depression and anguish about why God didn't seem to be helping too much defeat this evil had increased. My own depression was worsening, and my faith was waning. When I tried to pray, I felt as if the prayers didn't get beyond the ceiling.

CHAPTER 22

I am forgotten as a dead man out of mind: I am like a broken vessel.

—Psalms 31:12

A TIME FOR SALT

I was traumatized throughout the week-end. If so much had not happened previously, I would not have believed that my mother and brother would have taken Daddy directly from the hospital 180 miles away...in an old car...contrary to doctors' urgings. I couldn't get the images out of my head of how cheerful Daddy had been, thinking that there was going to be peace and harmony within the family, that he was going home with me, and that finally Mother was accepting me. And then, how gaunt and gray and depressed he had become, once he figured out that he and I had been manipulated once again.

Though I had begun to believe God wasn't hearing my prayers, I prayed anyway. Almost desperately and angrily, I asked, "Oh, Lord, when is this ever going to end? Why oh why do you let this keep happening? My father is help-less, and the devil has rendered me helpless as well. But *You* are not helpless. Why can't or won't You control this evil?" I asked God if He would at least protect Daddy until I could figure out what to do next. There was always a "next," and it was always an urgent "next." I knew that I could not just pray because I was having trouble believing in my own prayers. What's happening in our lives affects the quality of our faith, and by this time the events of the past four and a half years had taken their toll on it. So I telephoned my social worker and talked with her that next night. I felt I had to confront the enemy, so I began to write out nefarious actions Mother had taken against Daddy over the past several years, but most particularly, during the past few weeks.

Christian friends implored me to wait patiently and just pray. "Take care of yourself, so that you will be able to take care of him," they innocently advised. But they really didn't know how vile my mother could be and how much jeopardy Daddy was in. They could not grasp that he would have no-body to shield him from actions taken by the family. I didn't talk very much about this saga with my acquaintances since it was so different from anything they had ever experienced. They had no reference point for it. I reflected back over the many battles I had fought on Daddy's behalf over the past few years, including trying to discover my legal options. Things had become so horrible for both of us that I sought legal counsel to see what the possibilities might be for gaining custody of him. By this point he had begun to show significantly more depression and now *physical* illness the day I had to take him back to my mother's home.

He continued to verbalize to me that he was fed very little. Though I realized he didn't always remember when he had last eaten, at the same time, he did know when he was hungry! By this time he might not have recalled all the significant negatives of the "other place," but he appeared to retain the memory of minimal food. Marie had told me that my mother had locked him in the house on Thanksgiving while she went out with her friends to eat! I had known for a long time that he wasn't getting the right nutrients because every time I went to get him, he would be thinner than he was when I had taken him home previously, and he would be weaker. When we were with my friends in Nashville, Daddy continued to repeat, as he pointed to me, "She shore feeds me good." Knowing this deficit, I kept trying hard to make it up to him when he was at my house. But just like one can't make up sleep, trying to overload him with food didn't really work either, except to magnify the difference between how much he ate at my house and how little he ate at the other house.

Mother's alcohol consumption continued to decrease her own appetite, and consequently she ate a lot of junk food and little "real food." She fed Daddy pretty much the same. "Peanut butter and crackers are nourishing," she insisted. I felt I had to keep gently mentioning Daddy's anemia, but when I did, she continued to respond, "Well, I have anemia, too." That was, indeed, the case, and after she had been hospitalized for it, I urged her to eat better herself. Even her neighbor Martha again echoed my suggestion that she really needed to eat more nutritiously. She blew up at both of us. "I TOLD you all it is not about food. My problem is much worse. I am eating enough." We both responded that of course, food might not be the total answer, but it could help. On the one hand, Mother always tried to negate her husband's needs and interests, framing them as just a "crazy" person. On the other hand, if the occasion benefited her, she acted as if his responses and needs were equal to hers.

The food coupons I had purchased for her to encourage her to take herself and my father to the restaurants hadn't worked and had only served to make her angrier. Nor had the telephone conversations been that successful with her friends when I softly reminded them of how Alzheimer's is as much of a physical as it is a mental disease, since its victims' immune systems require more food than those without the disease. I had wanted to mention my mother's alcohol consumption which also affected her nutritional needs, but I dared not. Mother had complained about Daddy eating a whole quart of ice cream. He ate the whole thing because he was hungry.

Consequently, I thought perhaps I might have enough documentation to take some legal action on Daddy's behalf. The attorneys were older, respected lawyers who had seen spousal abuse before, although not exactly like this. I showed them a written summary of actions my mother had taken, documenting negligence and abuse. They believed me, but neither was encouraging about getting custody of my father. They told me that it would be an uphill battle, that it could cost a lot of money, and that I must think of consequences on my father and myself in the meantime. So I let go of that idea for the time being, thinking at least for now my father and I just had to endure the situation. The fear of greater harm to my father always drove me to take or not to take action.

Things had gotten much worse. Either my mother's mental disorders had severely increased, or demonic forces had totally taken over her life. Evidently there had been at least an occasional awareness of her mental state even among her friends, because once I had telephoned one of her neighbors, a former nurse, to get her ideas on anything else I might do, and she had responded in a kind tone, "Just realize she is mentally ill." I was fearful of many things, and one of them was that Mother would continue neglecting Daddy, and now, the neglect would have more serious consequences, given the advanced state of his aortic stenosis and his Alzheimer's. I thought about the increased number of bruises I began to notice on his body. I was also deeply frustrated that all the good work that the physicians had done in Nashville would go down the drain, as I had no confidence whatsoever that Mother would take Daddy the following Monday to see the other cardiologist in East Tennessee. Besides, I thought, why hadn't *her* doctor picked up his serious anemia and the progression of his aortic stenosis, and ordered my father a blood transfusion himself, if Mother had been taking him with the regularity she affirmed?

I later discovered that Mother had lied about taking my father to this physician; she was only having his Coumadin checked at the lab. I was concerned more than ever about her refusal to sleep near her husband. And lastly, I was worried that my father would think I had abandoned him.

But I resisted contacting my mother for about a week. It seemed like the longest week in my life. I finally telephoned neighbors to get an idea of how Daddy was. Mainly in the past I tried to rely on emails from Marie for information, since for the past three years she had been my only source of contact to know what was really happening. But Marie had her own problems and had been isolated from "Donald's family" for some time, ever since she had told her husband that she wasn't going to continue to be a part of any conspiracy against Daddy and me. She was then not privy to any conversation that Donald had with his mother about matters involving his father. After Donald had discovered her password and broken into her files, the emails stopped. Donald's drinking had gotten worse, and Marie was virtually helpless to help me, since she could hardly help herself. In fact, she herself was in some jeopardy.

I tried to regain my faith in prayer and prayed for courage before I telephoned my mother about a week later, asking when I might come to get Daddy. Mother smugly responded that *her* plan was that I was not to take him any more to my home, and that if I wished to see him, it would have be in her presence at her house. "From here on out, he will just stay with me," she sniped. She had used various forms of this statement before to frighten and threaten me, but this time the threat appeared more serious. Mother and Donald had been furious that I had allowed blood to be given to Daddy during his hospital stay. Though I had known for years that both of them preferred that he would get out of their lives, I had not realized how passionate Mother was about *controlling* whether he lived or died. The threat compelled me again to seek legal help to save my father.

The situation had become more threatening for Mother because she now realized that others, including physicians, had witnessed her behavior, and if she continued to allow her husband to come to my house, she might lose total control over what happened to him. She figured that his life would probably be prolonged if he continued to be with me, but more significantly, she had begun to see me as more competition than in times past. Having been successful for years at keeping a rift between my father and me, she had retained her power. Now the wall had been torn down.

PENETRATING BEHIND ENEMY LINES

So it had become time for a little salt. Salt has been used for centuries as a preservative to prevent raw meat which is exposed to the natural elements of air and sun from decaying; it is rubbed into the meat until it penetrates and is absorbed. We've all been in situations where people need a little salt rubbed into their psyche when nothing else seems to work. There are times when we must penetrate behind enemy lines, disrupt their communication, and attack strategic targets, especially when the situation is dire and life-threatening. I had come to the conclusion that I needed some authority behind me to get my mother's attention, attack her strategic target, which was power and money, and to stand up for me, since I was getting nowhere standing up for myself. I had tried many strategies on my own, including complete accommodation to my mother. Nothing had worked. Feeling more and more angst about my mother's latest threat, I knew I needed reinforcements. I must try a little salt.

Consequently, I immediately wrote a letter for an attorney, an acquaintance from my church, to send to her, factually outlining the events that had transpired involving Daddy's physical state of health, including his extreme anemia and extremely low blood pressure when he had entered the hospital and his blood count and blood pressure when he left. It chronicled events over the past three and a half years, including how my father had lost control of his property and his life, even though at that time I had no idea that the plot was hatched by my mother and brother to strip Daddy of all his assets years before the onset of his Alzheimer's. It was only after the death of both parents that I discovered this. My report also included specifics about the plan I ultimately foiled to put Daddy away in an asylum. Lastly, the letter included expectations, including that one half of Daddy's assets be restored to him and that I be able to keep Daddy at least half of the time to ensure that he was fed and cared for properly. The letter asked for a telephone call by a certain time.

After my attorney sent the letter, I learned from Marie that upon receipt of it, Mother immediately showed it to her friends, her son, and her grandsons and told all of them that she was going to fight *it* with her attorney. She telephoned my attorney and told him what attorney she would be using. This was the same attorney who had drawn up the *Power of Attorney* document years before, stripping my father of all control of his property and giving it to his wife and son. Though I was aware of the POA action, I did not know until years later that at this same time Daddy lost control of his possessions, years *before* the Alzheimer's diagnosis. The shameful act made me so furious that I could feel my own irregular heartbeat increase. This attorney was supposed to represent both my parents, not just my mother! Of course, since Mother had managed to coerce Daddy into signing the document giving her this power, and because she was the one paying, once again money won over integrity.

After the legal communication began, I had no way to really discern what care – if any – Daddy was receiving during this time. Since both Mother and Donald had blamed me for Daddy's latest hospitalization, I shuddered to think of the negative impact on Daddy of their fury about this action. But I had no choice. I realized that my mother had no interest in having Daddy live, except that she would get less money if he died. It seemed she had temporarily forgotten this fact. If she had put him in a nice facility, she wouldn't have the money either. So she was conflicted and vacillated between trying to maintain her victim status and wanting her freedom, two incongruous desires.

After a week and a half had passed with no response from anyone, I asked my attorney to try contacting the attorney Mother said she would be using. He sent the letter which he had originally sent to her, explaining that my mother indicated she would be using him [this attorney] to represent her and that I wished to resolve this issue expeditiously and amicably. Of course, since this attorney had enabled my mother to take everything from Daddy in the first place, he would probably play hard ball. Or his complicity in this action could manifest itself now in ignoring my attorney all together. A couple of years earlier I telephoned him myself, trying to appeal to some sense of mercy on Daddy's behalf, but he had ignored me then. After a week and a half, my attorney had received no response at all. Later I realized since any activity between Mother's attorney and my mother would be billed to her, there had been virtually no communication between them.

Recognizing that with each passing day, Daddy could be in more danger, I then asked my attorney to telephone Mother's attorney to discover whether he had had the opportunity to read the letter. He did as I requested, but the attorney wasn't in, and he did not return the phone call. Another week and a half passed, and I was frantic. So I asked my attorney if he would send a brief fax, just asking my Mother's attorney for some kind of conversation about the matter. He wasn't comfortable doing this because he realized the strategy this attorney was using was the arrogant one of ignoring the issue. But he did it anyway, realizing how stressed I was.

These weeks were horrible. I could think of nothing else. I tried to rely on God to protect Daddy, but I had no peace of mind. I began to think of God as being extremely hard to please and relentless in seeing how much I could take. Spiritual doubt had definitely set in, but I had to keep going. After about three weeks of fearing answering the phone, I received a bogus letter, theoretically from my mother. It was typed, and neither the language nor tone resembled hers. The letter stated, "My friend and attorney say that we should try to work this out together." The tone was contrived and affected. The address had errors in it, and I figured that either one of her friends or a family member wrote it.

After two more unsuccessful weeks of faxing and telephone calls to my mother's attorney, my attorney received the terse response: *I am not presently handling any matter for Mr. or Mrs. Howard.* So that was it: Mother had lied about employing this attorney, and her attorney didn't want to deal with the matter at all. In the meantime, I had spent a sizable sum of money on legal fees, but I should have known she wouldn't have spent a penny of her own money. I should also have known that pathological liars and alcoholics can't always know when they're lying. But at the time I was just disgusted and depleted.

For years I had known that Daddy had not been receiving proper nutrition or getting the correct medicines, but God only knew what else had happened during those past weeks following this legal action. By this time Mother had learned she could not get veterans funds to have Daddy placed in any facility, so I thought she probably wouldn't discard him in another one. I learned that she had not taken him to *her* doctor as she had promised Daddy's doctor in Nashville. She had bragged many times about her "friends" at the lab where Daddy's Coumadin was checked. She was a master manipulator, and any expenses at the East Tennessee medical center were being covered by "her" insurance. And so I figured that her alliances there would do whatever Mother wanted them to.

By this time, Marie had told me that my mother looked horrible and was definitely tired of being confined. I had figured that eventually her desire for freedom and rest might outweigh her need to control. So I asked my attorney to write a brief letter directly to Mother, stating that I was concerned about her need for rest, and that I would like to come get Daddy to help *her* out. The focus had to be on her well-being. He had included a brief statement for her to sign allowing me to seek medical attention if Daddy needed it. If Mother agreed, then she was to telephone his office. The same day my mother received the letter, she telephoned my attorney, and nonchalantly stated. "Why, of course, she can come get him. I need the rest. She can keep him for a month, for all I care." A month, indeed, I thought! I prayed that Daddy did not hear this statement. A couple of days after that, my attorney received the written permission for me to get Daddy medical care, should he need it.

Merely because she had become exhausted and was unwilling to let go of any funds for a facility, Mother gave me the authorization to *seek* medical attention if Daddy needed it *but only if* his living will were protected. So the situation was a bit ambiguous because the living will is not a legal document. But at least she had signed a statement giving me permission to get him medical help, and that was the main thing. "Thank you God, Oh, thank you," I prayed. So God hadn't abandoned Daddy and me after all, but instead had once again delivered us from the pit of hell.

Once my attorney had received the permission slip, I began scurrying around to make preparations for Daddy. It felt like a huge boulder had been lifted from my chest, and it was only later that I discovered that this piece of paper wasn't as significant as I thought it was. I really thought at the time that I was given the legal authority to make medical decisions, and I thought it would override any legal document my mother might have previously made. I did not know anything at this time about a *durable* power of attorney that was actually needed for medical care. But Mother obviously didn't know about it either, because she only had a *Power of Attorney* document.

I gave myself a few days for my back to become stronger. By this time, the stress of the past month had taken its toll on my degenerative discs and my osteoporosis, and I felt I better see a chiropractor to try to get some relief since I would have to lift Daddy's oxygen tank I had arranged to be placed at my mother's home. This I did, and asked my own internal physician for more pain pills. I could not blow this opportunity to get Daddy again and take care of him.

But on my drive to East Tennessee to get Daddy, I did have concerns to which I have already alluded. Would he remember me or my home? Would be too frightened to even come with me? Had he been able to realize that I had been fighting the entire time to get the opportunity to take care of him again? How frail had he become? What risk would I now have, not knowing what had been denied him in the preceding months? Since Mother had not taken Daddy to any cardiologist in her home town after pulling him out of Nashville contrary to doctors' orders, I was particularly concerned about whether he would have any strength to visit the places he loved to go. I didn't even know if he could walk, since my mother said that he had not been out of the house! Of course, these past few weeks made it even more important that I had gained permission to obtain any needed medical care, and most especially have the opportunity to take him back to the doctors who had addressed his needs three months earlier.

Though I wasn't at all certain God was still hearing me, I prayed anyway, all the way up to my mother's house. "God, please, let Daddy and me get out of that house quickly with the least amount of resistance."

When I entered the house, I was so nervous that I could hardly speak, but fortunately the little great grandchildren were there, and they helped relieve some of the tension. Their father, my brother's son, was also there. This was the grandson, I was later told, who was complicit with my brother in changing Daddy's intended inheritance to me. I only knew at that time that he was always around when Mother was giving Daddy's things away. At this time I mainly just wondered if Daddy would remember me, and if he did, would he want to go home with me.

I also was somewhat concerned that my skeletal conditions might inhibit me from being able to do all I needed to do for him, like bathing and dressing. What I did know from Marie, with whom I resumed exchanging emails after she had her computer up and running again, was that the blood had evidently helped Daddy's strength, and he had been more alert for a time following his previous hospital stay. I tried to dwell on this thought. But I realized that my sister-in-law's contact with Daddy was very limited, and so she couldn't guess how much weight he had lost, or whether he was aware that I was working to get him back. I had asked her if she would whisper to him that I loved him and would come get him soon.

Perhaps if nothing else, the letters from my attorney may have prompted my mother to be a little more careful about doing something to significantly worsen Daddy's condition. By this time, she knew I was on to her, since I had chronicled in the letter for the attorney that Mother ultimately received all actions during the past couple of years which had negatively affected Daddy and had drawn the connection between his declining health and her and my brother's lack of care and attention to his conditions. Their refusal to follow strong recommendations of my father's doctors during his last hospital stay was also included.

As soon as I stepped inside the house, many of my concerns dissipated as I smiled at my father and caught his eye. He beamed at me from ear to ear. He remembered me! My fear about him having no recollection of me and that the work over the past few years might be undone was over. "Daddy, are you ready to go?" "Yes, I am ready to go with you anywhere," he emphatically answered, with no hesitation. I quickly grabbed his little suitcase and his oxygen tank, and we were out of there.

When we were in the car, I quietly said, "Daddy, I hope you didn't think I had forgotten you. I have been working on getting you....I asked Marie to tell you." "She did," he said, in a voice just as clear as a bell. "Oh, thank you God, thank you God," I silently prayed. Maybe God hadn't forgotten Daddy and me after all. "Daddy, we're going to have such a good week; we're going to see your cousins in Cookeville and then we're going to Nashville." "Oh, good. Thank you and God bless you," he said as he touched my hand.

CHAPTER 23

The grass withereth, the flower fadeth: but the word of our God shall stand for ever.
–Isaiah 40:8

WILTED PEONIES

"**D**addy, are you okay?" I asked as I helped my father out of the car. "I guess so," he quietly responded. Not the usual, "I'm all right." Though I had parked very close to the mall entrance in the handicapped parking area, I could tell that Daddy was having difficulty even getting out of the car. By this time I had secured a handicapped parking sticker which helped alleviate his having to walk very far and kept me from always having to load and unload the wheelchair. He seemed frailer than usual, and I thought that maybe the hot, humid day was the reason for his shortness of breath. It had been just a couple of weeks since finally being allowed to bring him home with me, after agonizing weeks of wrangling to get my mother's permission to seek medical attention should he need it.

This particular mall was still his favorite because of the many small children he enjoyed. He continued to have some sort of special communication with them, even in this late state of his disease. I mused how most adults assume that because brains of Alzheimer's patients are a little scrambled, the rest of them is as well. But my father's spirit was not scrambled. It seemed pure, as the child's spirit is. Thus they had a unique interaction.

There was a restaurant very near the mall's entrance where Daddy and I had occasionally eaten. This was the restaurant we were going to eat this evening.

"Oh," Daddy moaned, as he grabbed his heart. "I can't go on," he whispered. "Please, God, don't let this happen all over again!" I prayed as I tried to hold my father up and help him to get inside the mall entrance. "Daddy, the restaurant is just inside those doors....We'll soon be there."

I was aware that his aortic stenosis and arrhythmia were getting worse, and that his pacemaker was probably having to work overtime. Daddy had been unusually quiet most of the day, and we had done nothing much but ride around in the country. Sensing that he was weaker than usual and not feeling well at all, I had asked him several times if he were okay. "I'm all right," he had responded, with little conviction. But he almost always responded this way, regardless of how he really felt because he had been programmed to never complain. But his unusual quietness and wrinkled brow were clues that something was off. Sometimes I didn't know whether it was physical or mental pain.

Prior to the few preceding years, I had thought of my father as weak and passive. But now I knew he was exceedingly brave and enduring. I lightheartedly affirmed that his tours of duty as a marine in Guadalcanal during the war had made him so tough. I had also come to realize within the past four and a half years what he had been through within his family which, undoubtedly, had raised his endurance level for pain and stress.

I had thought about cooking that Saturday evening but had decided against it since I knew I needed to preserve my strength for the following day. It was homecoming at the church where some of Daddy's relatives still attended and Decoration Day at the cemetery where other relatives were buried. Though I had begun frequently taking Daddy to my church in Nashville, I had always attended services there on Mother's Day to put flowers on the graves and to see older relatives and friends from long ago. We were attending the church less than we were in the beginning of our journey, after I discovered that he also enjoyed my church in Nashville. But when we did go, the members continued to talk to Daddy as if he were as he always had been. I loved the church too, and I always felt I had come home when I went there. Mammy took me to church there when I was a very young girl.

The next morning would be busier than usual, getting the peonies arranged so that I would have plenty to place on everyone's grave. I had already cut them, but had just placed them in a jug of water so they would stay fresh until morning. I loved peonies because they reminded me of a happier time when Mammy used to pick them for the graves. I had assured my mother the week before that I would place flowers on the graves of both parents' families, as I had always done.

I would need to get the flowers ready before I awakened Daddy to prepare him for the day because by this time the process of getting him ready required more time than in previous years. I would still begin with my usual question, "Daddy, did you rest well?" And he would probably respond with his usual, "I don't know when I've slept so good," whether or not he had. This was one of those generic acceptable responses that he stored in his head and pulled out at the appropriate time which enabled him to appear okay. The question was redundant because I always knew when he was asleep and when he wasn't. His bathroom accidents during the night had become more frequent, thus interrupting his sleep, and sometimes he just had more trouble falling asleep because his aortic stenosis had worsened. If either of these conditions had occurred, I tried to wait as long as possible before awakening him. And on this Sunday, there would even be more energy required because he was going back to my mother's house after church.

With some slight alterations, our Sunday morning ritual had continued. After waking him up, I would hurry to the kitchen for his medicine and some juice to help give him a little quick energy. Now, however, I needed to cue him on placing his hand around the juice glass, to drink it, and then to take his pills. "Thank you, Daddy, for taking that medicine," I always tried to remember to say after he took his medicine. More recently, Daddy had begun to also thank *me* for the medicine and for every task I had helped him with. He would follow the "thank you" with "God bless you," and it choked me up to realize how little it took for him to be grateful. While he had lost recognition of most everyone else, he still knew God. He had taught me so many lessons about gratitude during the past few years and so much about the importance of knowing God *before* your brain gets scrambled. He confirmed that the Holy Ghost, once with a person, doesn't desert him even though his brain might.

So, though it was tricky to keep up the pace of these rituals, my father's gratitude always made it worth it. Hurrying back to the kitchen to bring Daddy his coffee while he was still in bed to strengthen him a bit more, having a little conversation with him as I sat in a nearby rocker and drank a little coffee with him....these were so insignificant efforts compared with Daddy's resulting uplifted spirits. They had become more so as the Alzheimer's had progressed.

Because of the time now it took for his medicine, bath, and dressing, the more I could have done before he woke up, the better.

All week Daddy had frequently asked when we were going back to Cookeville, and all week I had told him, "Sunday, Daddy, we're going there Sunday." "Good," he had always responded. At this point he trusted me and enjoyed staying with me in Nashville, so I wasn't quite sure why he asked this question so many times that week. Was it because he knew his health was worse and realized somewhere in his scrambled brain that death was near?

On this particular Saturday, the day before we were to go there, I prayed again, "Dear God, please help him be okay," as I tried to help him walk the few steps to the mall entrance. But Daddy again whispered, "I can't go on." He stumbled and fell just inside the mall doors. His hands started trembling. As he fell down on his knees and then onto the floor, he started convulsing. I screamed for help. His eyes rolled back in his head, and his whole body was now shaking. He was having some kind of seizure. Was it a stroke? It looked similar to the seizure he had had a year or so earlier in the restaurant in Cookeville when we were on our way to the church there, but this one looked worse. I felt faint myself but managed to take his sweater off and lay it under his head. He was clammy and was beginning to have what appeared to be dry heaves. I tried to talk to him. I thought, "This really *is* the end. God, help Daddy - and me." By this time there were several people around, and fortunately, one of them immediately stated that she was a nurse and could administer CPR. Another was a fireman. Angels were all around.

So many thoughts whirled through my head. The many weeks of labor I had spent to finally obtain my mother's permission to allow me once again to take care of him. The huge legal effort to convince her that I would respect his living will but just needed permission to obtain medical attention for him, should he need it. My mother's accusations when Daddy had to be hospitalized earlier when he was staying with me. My mother's wrath that was bound to ensue when she found out about this incident.

But mainly I felt the pain of this dear sweet man whom I had only really known for a few years. Would he be better off *not* being resuscitated? Would he want to be, if he had had the choice? Watching the involuntary movements of Daddy biting his tongue, his body growing more rigid and writhing with pain, his breathing halting, I had my dilemma removed. Through these overwhelming thoughts, I faintly heard the by-stander nurse say, "There's no pulse," as she began administering CPR. Later I realized there must have been a pulse, since Daddy had a pacemaker, but perhaps the rigidity of his body made it too difficult to discover it. In any event, the nurse took over and told me to turn away as she worked on Daddy. I did as I was told, forgetting to tell them about his pacemaker.

Everyone was trying to be helpful. People came running out of the restaurant to help. One woman telephoned 911, and another helped take Daddy's clothes off. I heard the nurse say, "He's back...there's a pulse." Another person told me to talk to Daddy, to call him by name, which I did. "Daddy, I'm right here, it's going to be okay," I managed to clumsily utter, without conviction, seeing the gray color Daddy had turned.

The ambulance pulled up, and the medical personnel began the process of getting Daddy ready for the ambulance. Gasping for breath myself, I quickly told them the most critical information: he was a Coumadin patient, he had a pacemaker, and he had Alzheimer's. In the meantime, the medical team with the ambulance ushered me out of the way, and I heard one of them say to the driver to take him to St. Thomas Hospital, which was the closest medical facility. I stood there, almost frozen as they loaded Daddy into the ambulance. Trying to think ahead through all possible consequences, I asked them to take him to Baptist Hospital instead. Although it was a little farther away than the other hospital, that was the location of Daddy's doctors and his medical records. The ambulance personnel warned me that time was not on their side, and from the looks of Daddy, a few minutes could make a lot of difference between life and death. For a moment, I acquiesced, but a minute later, I asked them to take him to Baptist. I knew I was gambling, but given everything that would probably ensue, I must take this chance. My mind had already begun to envision the difficulty of dealing with my mother about this incident even if we were at the hospital where his regular doctors were, much less at a different one.

As I sped to the hospital, I prayed, "God, if this is the end, please let Daddy live until I can get there. Please don't let him be afraid. Please free him of pain, and please let this decision to have him taken to this hospital be the right one." The prayer was fragmented, but I knew God would piece it together. I told Him if He would answer this prayer, I would try never again to pray for anything for myself. When I think back to that moment and my fear of not being there to hold Daddy's hand if this was his time, I still feel that awful pain and guilt of not being with him later that year when he actually did die.

My decision to have him taken to this hospital proved to be the right one. I raced to the hospital to discover that Daddy had made it, and miraculously his primary doctor was actually on call that night. I thanked God for this. By the time I arrived at the ER, Daddy was alert, and the medical staff had notified his doctor. Daddy forced a wan smile back at me, as I smiled at him. He always responded in like expression to tone and expression from the other person. Various medical personnel were attending to Daddy, and one of them gave me his clothes, soiled with urine. Daddy's physician ordered him to the coronary intensive care unit, where a kind and thoughtful head nurse allowed me to stay with him, an action which was most unusual. I knew that with the IVs and the pain that would surely result from the aggressive CPR, Daddy would not understand what had happened and be more confused than ever. I knew that even with the heart monitors on him I needed to be by his side to help keep the tubes in him and to lessen his fear.

The night passed, and except for the pain resulting from the aggressive CPR motions, Daddy appeared to rest fairly well. The doctor decided he had not had a stroke and told him he would see him in the morning.

Throughout the night, I prayed that God would help me know what to do about my mother. I was aggravated with myself because with everything Daddy was going through, this fear of my mother's wrath was occupying the bulk of my concern. But the memories of the past hospitalization were still so vivid in my head that I anticipated an even worse reaction from her this time. I was to have returned Daddy to her home the next day after the church homecoming, and I knew, therefore, that telling her what had happened could not be avoided. So far, I had bought some time and not telephoned her, since the hour was late, and I could always tell her I didn't want to scare her in the middle of the night. But soon it would be morning, and that excuse wouldn't exist.

Around midnight after Daddy was resting fairly comfortably, I retrieved my voice messages from my home phone. Mother had telephoned and said that she would be going out to eat with my brother and his wife the next day, and not to hurry back with my father. An unexpected gift, this phone call gave me a little more time to stall.

That night the doctor thought he would take advantage of the hospital stay and ordered a unit of blood for Daddy, having discovered by this time that his red blood cell count was very low again. I was grateful for this, not only because I knew Daddy needed it, but with the blood going into his arm, my mother could not take my father from the hospital.

His doctor had given him three units some twelve weeks earlier, and it had helped his strength – and his memory. At that time when he had to be hospitalized, two days after I had brought him home with me, the doctors discovered that his red blood cell count was dangerously low and had evidently been low for a long time. It had still not been addressed. After that hospital stay and my subsequent legal struggle documenting the jeopardy my father was in from my mother's actions, I had thought that surely Mother might be a little more attentive to feeding him and to his blood issues. But obviously she hadn't been. On this night since his blood pressure was threateningly low again, the doctor concluded that the seizure was a combination of several factors, including this major dropping of his blood pressure and his resurfacing anemia.

That evening in the intensive care unit I wondered if I had done the right thing by allowing him to be resuscitated. I had not considered the unusual pain from the CPR because of his pacemaker. But I came to realize what the medical staff at the mall meant when they told me I had no choice in the matter. A *durable* power of attorney is needed in order for firemen and medical staff *not* to resuscitate. Even with all the effort and expense to have my mother sign a statement allowing me to get medical attention for Daddy when he needed it, the result was not a *legal* document. So the medical personnel were compelled in their job to follow the law. There were so many ironies throughout this journey to save Daddy. While my mother and brother thought they had all power over him with their power of attorney, all they really had was control over his *assets*, not his *body*. They didn't have the *legal* power to take my father's life. But who would know if Mother starved him, or gave him too much medicine, or performed some other insidious act? Daddy's statement, "She is trying to kill both of us" was always in my head.

Even with the severity of my father's condition, when the doctor came the next morning, I knew we must make a decision of whether or not to keep Daddy in the hospital. Under any other similar circumstance, there would be no question but that he needed to stay. But the doctor remembered the episode three months earlier when my mother and brother had accused me of causing Daddy's hospitalization and jerked him out of the hospital, contrary to his orders, not allowing Daddy to stay in Nashville at least over the weekend. So we discussed the best option since he realized that this time Daddy would not be able to travel some 200 miles directly from the hospital because of his extreme chest pain.

We decided that he would go home with me, and hopefully, by the time I reached my mother, it would be too late for her and my brother to start to Nashville. Maybe my mother would surprise me and be cooperative and tolerant. After all these years, I still found myself hoping and praying that she somehow could get released from whatever demons had possessed her to think of no one but herself.

So Daddy and I went to my home. He was so weak, and by this time the chest pain from the aggressive CPR had increased. I had rarely ever in my whole life heard Daddy complain, and now he had tears in his eyes. Later I wondered if these tears were all the result of the pain in his chest around his pacemaker, or whether somewhere in his psyche he was aware of the trauma which had happened to him. Near death experiences make everyone more emotional than they are at other times, and I was uncertain about how to communicate the event to him of what had happened.

"Daddy, I'm so sorry. I hope I didn't make this happen to you....I wish I could take this pain onto myself." I quietly whispered, as I put my arm around him and tried to make him as comfortable as possible, piling up pillows on the bed so he wouldn't have to lie flat. "It's okay," he quietly whispered. But he also said, with a slight smile, "Maybe you should just have let me go." "Oh, no, Daddy, you're going to be okay," I managed to eke out, not thinking he was going to be okay at all. As I glanced at the drooping peonies on the kitchen table, they seemed to reflect our whole lives at this point. I was trying hard not to cry myself. During my whole life I always had to hold my tears. Someday I knew they would come pouring out. "But not today, God, please not today." It was Mother's Day, and I knew my friends all had family events planned. I had no one to telephone to help me or even to go get medicine if the doctor ordered any for pain. But I knew I just had to stay as calm and unemotional as possible.

I also knew the time was drawing near when I had to telephone my mother, because it was almost three o'clock, the appointed time I was to have had Daddy at her house. And that was increasing my anxiety.

So that Mother would know I had tried to reach her, I did my old trick of telephoning her a couple of times before I thought she would be there. Since she had caller identification, I hoped that this might ameliorate some of her anger. Then a little after three, upon my third call, she answered. In as objective tone as possible, I asked, "Mother, did you have a nice lunch? I got your message about...." I had rehearsed my opening statement to include the message my mother had sent about going out to eat with her son and not to rush home with Daddy. "WHERE ARE YOU!" she demanded in the middle of my sentence. With this common occurrence of my mouth becoming so dry I hardly could speak, I tried to answer calmly. "Mother, everything's okay, but we're still at my house...." "WHAT?" She screamed again. "Mother, Daddy had to go to the hospital last night..." I was cut off. "WHAT!" OH, MY GOD," she screamed again. "You did it again. You will NEVER take him home with you again! I have the money to get an ambulance and take him home from the hospital," she threatened. She had not heard me say that Daddy and I were at my house. At that split second I realized that again I had made the right decision with the doctor to bring him to my house. At least my home shouldn't be as threatening to her as the hospital. I did not think that either she or my brother would come to my house. "Mother, we're not at the hospital; we're at home," I quietly stated. "OH, MY GOD!" she hissed again. When I tried to tell her what had happened, she just demanded to know when I was going to bring Daddy home. This was the same woman who only a couple of weeks before had told my attorney that I could have my father a month, or three months, that she didn't care. And yet, Daddy had only been with me this time for eight days.

"This has been the most depressing day for me" Almost suddenly Mother's voice fell to a slight whimper. Another personality, the child, was starting to surface. "And now you have made it worse, as you always do." "I'm so sorry, Mother." Trying hard to say something benign which might refocus her for a moment, I asked, "Mother, did the clothes I got you for Mother's Day fit?" "Only the long skirt, and it's not my style," she pouted. But pouting was better than screaming. "I can exchange it for something you'd rather have," I tried to sound optimistic. "No, I don't want anything else from *you*." A second personality was coming back, but this reply had no effect on me as I was accustomed to this kind of response. I was just grateful to at least have a subject for a moment that focused on my mother. "Mother, I need to get back to Daddy," I quietly stated. "When are you going to bring him home? If you don't bring him right away, I'm coming down there and get him." She always knew this blind threat usually succeeded in leaving a huge knot in my stomach and continuing concern that she might follow through on the threat.

Dilemmas about what I should do never abated, as I was always trying to envision my mother's reaction to every single statement I needed to make. This time the dilemma was how much I should tell her about what had really happened. On the one hand, I wanted to minimize it, so she wouldn't become so enraged and feel she had to come to Nashville to control things. On the other, I wanted her to know that it was a serious enough situation that Daddy wasn't able to travel, although that hadn't stopped her and Donald before from ignoring doctors' orders. "Mother, his chest is hurting where the medical personnel had to help his breathing..." "YOU MEAN THAT HIS HEART STOPPED!" There it was. I was able to say honestly, "No mother, since Daddy has a pacemaker, the rhythm continues. The doctor doesn't know exactly what happened, but he has ruled out a stroke." I eventually got the sentence out. I tried to say that the doctor didn't want to put my father through unnecessary tests – thinking that this would satisfy her, but again I was interrupted. "How do they know if he didn't have a cat scan?" Normally my mother would have been critical of any tests conducted on Daddy, but I realized I would not be able to say anything she would approve of. It had been a lifetime of no-win situations. I had to just hope that I could get through each moment with minimum rage from her. "Mother, the doctor wants to see him before he travels, so how about if I bring him home Tuesday after he sees the doctor?" I had learned many years ago that there was no such thing as a two-way conversation, with listening involved, and response to the other person's statement. So I was forced into jumping from one sentence to another to disrupt Mother's rage. Mother just hung up on me, leaving me with that usual disruption in my stomach, wondering if indeed she would again talk her son into coming down to Nashville and taking my poor ailing father back with them. Donald, I concluded, wouldn't want to bother with it at least that evening since he had probably started drinking after having spent some time already that day with his mother.

I was feeling so vulnerable and guilty myself this time, because I did not know about a critical blood pressure medicine that Mother had withheld from my father. So the words stung more than usual. I worried that I may have, in fact, overdone it with outings that week, but Daddy, as always, wanted to keep moving and our daily activities were low-key, involving very little walking. Still, I was aware that at my mother's home, he had virtually no interaction with anyone and had not been out of the house, not even to church, his favorite activity. Her excuse was that he talked there. For Mother, church was primarily a social event where she talked and laughed with her friends, excluding Daddy. And she always sat near the back of the sanctuary so she could have her conversations. This way Daddy could not connect to the sermon, and so he just talked with himself. Always when I took him out of her home, he was freed from enforced isolation. So the contrast was bound to make some difference.

A couple of days afterwards, I took Daddy back to East Tennessee, as I promised my mother I would. The ride was extremely uncomfortable for him, but I really had no choice. Once in a while, he would slightly moan. Oh, if only I could take on his pain. When I drove up the driveway, Mother came out and whimpered to Daddy, "You poor thing....What has she done to you this time?"

I said nothing, but carried his bags and other supplies into my mother's home. Because of the air of evil, I found it very hard to look at my mother in the eye, and I always dreaded stepping foot inside that house. So I made as quick a turn-around as possible. I did mention the doctor's report, though Mother talked through my statement. Noticing the low-seated rocker that Daddy usually sat in, I mentioned that since he had a very hard time sitting in a low chair because of the chest pain, I had put quilts in chairs he sat in at my house. I was careful not to advise my mother about what to do, but just told her what I did. She retorted, "That's your business... He likes this chair, don't you Brian?" Of course, Daddy responded that he did. I turned to go.

Just as I drove out of the driveway, I saw my mother out on the porch, hanging the fern I had bought for her. Since she didn't like the skirt I had earlier purchased and had told me that she wanted a fern, on the way to her house, I had stopped and bought her this one. "Mother, could you just go back inside for a few minutes, as Daddy's chest is very sore and he can't get up out of the chair without some help?" She muttered something under her breath, as I drove off.

PART III

PREPARATION FOR THE STORM

I n looking back from the future, perhaps it really *was* my closeness to God and His purpose for my life, manifesting itself long before the journey with my father, which accounted for my involvement with those who had either become abandoned, invisible, or had suffered such great hardships that others ran from them. God had placed many obstacles and circumstances in my own life prior to this journey with my father, including feeling compelled to stand up against major institutions when everyone else was telling me to "leave it alone," to prepare me for traversing the difficult, treacherous, and evil path my father and I had to travel. He also taught me lessons during the journey itself, such as the need to overcome my own anger about my mother, which may help others who may be dealing with mentally ill parents or friends.

I have come to believe He didn't just allow this final journey, but that He ordained it. Maybe it was because He knew that I had unrelenting determination and could survive it because of my ability to navigate through and survive previous encounters and battles. Only recently have I come to fully acknowledge this might be the case, because earlier I always thought to do so would be presumptuous and self-righteous. Of course I cannot know for certain until death if this thinking is correct. But one thing I am certain of: believing in Jesus Christ has to be more than discussing theology. It must be making life-changing decisions and then acting on them. It must be about becoming a beacon of light, even in our own darkness, for those who cannot see through theirs. Daddy and I were hit by what I had come to see as a divine huge lightning storm, dark, but interwoven with jagged bolts of lightning, which lit up our awareness. Previous lesser major storms had helped prepare me for this great one.

Many times when I thought I could not take one more step, I would remember my grandmother's unwavering faith in the midst of her many hardships and the sacrifices she had made for me. Or I would remember various elderly people who had become lost in the city or whose pain no one else seemed to feel, and it appeared that God had put them in my path. It must have been God who enabled me to appear optimistic about their plight because internally I was suffering great pain for their pain and swallowing some concern that everything might *not* come out okay. Or I would recall various times when I resisted money and job security to do the right thing. Though the immediate results were significant losses, every single time I made what I thought was the right decision in God's eyes, the event ultimately brought about a greater good. The following chapters illustrate the infrastructure God had provided for me to withstand the final journey with my father. And there were even building blocks during the journey itself, which helped me cope. Each one gave me one more tool to enable me to survive this greatest "storm" of my own life.

CHAPTER 24

Train up a child in the way he should go; and when he is old, he will not depart from it.

—Proverbs 22:6

TEACHING ME HOW TO LIVE: THE BEDROCK

My grandmother had been my protector, role model, and inspiration. She had enabled me to survive the evil and insanity which had gripped my family for years. She was a godly woman who had taught me to read, my prayers and God's lessons. Though I always knew I could never be as virtuous as she was, I could always hear her voice in my head. She had given me the right values, and none of them incorporated external beauty or the secular world. They have guided me my entire life. She taught me that a life filled with tenderness, compassion, selflessness, and godly wisdom is always attractive. Never did I hear her complain or witness any querulous temper or a fretful spirit.

Though Mammy had only a sixth grade education, she knew how important education was. "No one can ever take your education away from you," she often reminded me. It was as if she could see in the future and know that I might not end up with much else from my family. She was a simple, country woman who never had much money herself and only learned to write a check after her husband died. But the lack of a formal education didn't imply a lack of wisdom. She taught me the importance of keeping God's commandments by living them herself. She got God's point. She knew that the things many crave in this world have no value in God's eyes. She was a paragon of virtue that I have never been, but always aspire to be. "I know you're a good girl"; "Pretty is as pretty does"; "A woman must learn to control my temper"; "Be like Jesus." These admonitions have rung in my head since I was a little girl.

She never strove for prestige or more money or a bigger house. Instead, she taught me all the basic values and precepts required to survive and even succeed.

Unaware of self, realizing that the things that bring this world's glory often keep you out of the kingdom, she knew that God is our glory, not we ourselves. She could not rest as long as there were others with tears in their eyes. Some believe that charity is the brightest star in the Christian's diadem. It often seemed like it was Mammy's mainstream of her action. One of the reasons heaven was so real to me was that this angel bore a balm of such charity into my heart.

One of the greatest regrets of my life is that I didn't tell her how grateful I was that she was willing to take me and suffer consequences for that sacrifice.

Mammy had a very difficult life, but, like her son, she never complained about anything. Or at least I didn't hear it if she did. She was a woman of understanding who held her peace. Maybe it was because there was always work to be done. Labor enables us to laugh at difficulties. It achieves grander victories than fretting over not being invited to a dance, or having a bigger house to live in, or getting a daughter-in-law who is intent on "doing her own thing." Or a husband who has had a heart condition for twenty years. I remember her rough, stained hands, from having worked around the clock, feeding livestock, tendering meat, cooking her husband three meals a day, making all my clothes, cooking Sunday dinner for relatives, always laboring for others. I remember her wiping the dripping sweat from her brow as she helped Papa in the tobacco and corn fields. She was a little woman physically and stooped over with arthritis in her later years. But her size and arthritis belied her strength. She seemed to always maintain a cheerful heart and never let the shadow of discouragement fall on her path. However weary she became, she tried not to let others see the occasional tear in the corner of her eye. I now see her sweaty brow crowned with dignity and peace. Oh, I wish I hadn't been too young to have truly valued all that she was. I found myself wondering a few years ago if she could have held her peace, with the helplessness of her son having increased. But things were pretty bad in much earlier years, and she held her peace then.

She loved her husband and took care of him, through a serious and rare heart condition. When our water pipes froze up, she had to carry buckets of water from the spring while I watched Papa. My grandfather refused to sell any of the hogs after he became ill, so Mammy had to feed all the livestock and tend to them when *they* were sick. I think now of the contrast between the way she cared for her husband and the way my mother didn't care for Daddy, who also had major heart conditions for many years. On the contrary, it was my father who continued to try to take care of my mother.

Papa's heart condition manifested itself in many seizures, not so different from Daddy's, and his heart would actually stop beating for a period of time since he didn't have a pacemaker like Daddy did. During these times I often kept him from swallowing his tongue. Their natural gas well would fill up with water, and there would be no heat. So Mammy carried wood into the house to build a fire. Through it all, she never complained.

She was the greatest teacher I had ever had on this earth. Through all my graduate and postgraduate work, I had never had an instructor with her lucidity. One primary reason was that she "walked her talk." She did as she instructed me to do. She always spoke kindly of others. She gave to those poorer than herself.

She taught me to read when I was about three or four years old, using the ABCs on a little chalk board. She read me the stories of *Cinderella*, the *Three Bears* and *Little Red Riding Hood*. I was transported into those worlds. The images are still so vivid in my head because they were what Matthew Arnold calls moments of "sweetness and light" that I still pull up today when I get really far down emotionally. I can now only imagine how tiring reading those little Golden books every day had been for her.

She taught me my prayers and the Bible by reading stories from the Little Golden Books, including *The Baby Jesus*, beginning when I was about two. I had to have been about this age because I clearly remember sitting on her lap as she read them to me. She knew that religion can heal the wounded spirit and banish darkness from the earth. She took me to church and to Bible school.

I am certain she must have done the same thing for my father because until his dying days, he still acknowledged God, scriptures like the 23rd Psalm, and the hymns he learned so many years ago. She also held up the hope of eternity to me, never allowing the interests of this world to shut out from her soul or mine the view or the hope of a better world. She was one of those people who could see the sun shining long after it is dark in the valley. She gave me the realization that even though one may be destined to live isolated, he/she cannot be alone, for God is always there, in heaven. And on earth. Mammy took me to revivals. We rode on a bus since she never learned to drive and didn't have a car.

She taught me to tie my shoes and to fix my hair. She showed me how to make mud pies.

Most of my happy reflections involve my grandmother. Taking me on walks through the woods as we hunted hickory nuts. Trying a new dress on me she had made. Braiding my hair. Taking me to the county fair. Cooking me turnip greens that I loved so much. Making me quilts out of remnants from my clothes. Making me granny gowns out of feed sacks. Making my doll clothes that matched my clothes. Helping me pick violets near the old springhouse.

I loved plucking wild flowers. Daisies, roses, or just about any flower was special. Why is this activity so much more significant to small children than to adults? Maybe it's because the flowers have the face of God written on them. Or maybe it's just because children are so close to the ground that they see what adults who are too busy and pre-occupied with moving on can't.

I would run breathlessly into the house from the school bus, eager to see what new doll clothes Mammy had made for me on that day. Getting a whiff of her freshly baked sugar cookies as I ran in from the porch, I could hardly wait to get my surprise! She never used a pattern, but there was such intricate detail in those clothes. She lined them, put pearl buttons on the coats, and even made shoes that matched them. She made one of my girl dolls a poodle skirt and a sweater, just like my outfit; she made coveralls for one of my baby dolls with a bunny rabbit on one leg, just like mine. She made them headbands just like mine.

Even today, I maintain a small room in my home, converted from a walk-in closet, with all of my dolls my aunt didn't throw away upon gaining possession of Mammy's house, and racks displaying those doll clothes that Mammy made for me. These were the remnants of long-ago forsaken dreams I had of having lots of my own children. I would swing for hours in the old porch swing, piling up every one of my "babies" in the swing as we waited for the "church service" to begin. I had spent hours dressing them for "church" and spent long hours imagining how it was going to be when I would be able to take my own children there one day. I thought about how I would treat them gently, with kindness and be attentive to their needs, just as my grandmother was to my needs. I would sing the old hymns to them that Mammy had taught me, the same hymns I later sang, not with any children of my own, but with my father in the last phase of his life. Never once do I remember imagining a husband or father to these children. It was just my babies and me. Today sometimes a neighbor's granddaughter will visit and give me an excuse to play house again. Occasionally I just go into the room alone and reflect upon those memories. Sometimes it's comforting; sometimes it's the opposite, as it brings to mind all that was dreamed about, contrasted with what actually came to be.

Yes, Mammy was the angel of my life and served as my mother. She loved me unconditionally in spite of the fact that she had little choice in raising me. I always realized that if I had amounted to anything good, she was responsible.

I felt such love from her that most everything she did with me was good and positive and edifying. Because she had a good heart, she only did good things. She counseled me to seize opportunities of contributing to the good of others. Sometimes she just gave me a gentle admonition. I remember how she would take food to the sick and how she would always made certain everyone else ate at meals before she did – lest *they* would not get the piece of fried chicken they wanted. "Mammy, why do you like the *back* of the chicken?" I asked. Grinning, she said, "Well, I guess that's what was left."

I was pretty much tossed to her while my father was still in World War II, and my mother decided to go up north for a while. From what I've pieced together, Mother really couldn't handle a baby maybe because it took the spotlight away from her, or because she just wanted to do her own thing, or because she was pretty much a child herself. At least she *recognized* she couldn't handle me, and that was a good thing. So Mammy took me. That more than anything highlights what compassion and caring my grandmother was capable of, since that action was behind so much of the resentment her daughter, my aunt, had for her. During her lifetime I was never able to realize the tremendous sacrifices she made on my account. Even after I had received my master's degree and was teaching in North Carolina, it was Mammy who came to take care of me during a lingering illness.

The activities I enjoyed with her followed the seasons. In the early spring there was the cherry picking. I loved to "help" with this because there were no briars, and I usually ate more cherries than ended up in my pail. In the early summer, she taught me how to make kraut from the fresh cabbages in the garden. I can even now visualize the wooden bowl and the chopping which seemed endless. Occasionally she would let me try my hand. She gave me the stalk to eat.

In the middle of the summer I watched Mammy can the other vegetables she had grown, thinking that one day I would can for my own family. I can see her even now peeling the ripe tomatoes from the garden to make tomato juice. Sweat dropping from her forehead, apron covering her calico dress, spotted with tomato juice, she sat peeling those tomatoes. She always gave me a taste.

One of the things that fascinated me as a child was the skill involved with my grandmother's preparation of corn for frying and freezing. I would be perched on the cabinet, watching her take her butcher knife, go around the cob once, just barely slivering it, then going around again and again, until finally she would scrape the cob, releasing the "milk." The bacon grease, the old black iron skillet, a little salt, a little sugar...um, there was no finer food on the face of the earth! I remember that corn every time I microwave the Trader Joe's frozen corn for myself, being too tired to cook from scratch and having too many pains of my own to bother with it. I think my tolerance for pain is high until I remember how much my grandmother was able to do and bear, with all her pain.

After I got to be about the age of eight or nine, every summer night Mammy and I would sit on the front porch, breaking and stringing green beans for her to cook the next day. There was no such thing at Mammy's as eating leftovers. I had usually helped her pick those beans, so I felt "ownership" in them.

Later in the summer Mammy and I went blackberry picking. I recall her stained, scratched hands from that activity. She taught me how to push the briars back and step so as to minimize the scratches. She taught me how to keep the cows at bay and not make them angry. Mammy gave me fifty cents for picking a gallon. That was good money then for a gallon of berries. She taught me how to make cobbler pies from the berries. I remember sitting on the cabinet as she made extra strips of pastry for me because she knew I loved them.

She let me help beat the egg whites for the meringue on her coconut pies. She let me help cut out cookie dough for those fine sugar cookies.

In the fall of the year, peeling and eating wine sap apples around the fireplace was a favorite fall activity with the neighbors as we listened to the "The Grand Ole Opry" on Saturday night radio. I remember how excited I was when I ran into the house and the smell of fried apple pies greeted me. Mammy knew how I loved fried apple pies.

Once the weather turned cold enough, my grandfather killed hogs. That is, before he got too sick to do it. My, what an event that was. I can still see Mammy stirring the lard, grinding the sausage, and sacking it in the cloth sacks she had made. I remembered the cracklings that she allowed me to eat on that day.

And then came Christmas. Mammy and I would go into the woods looking for just the right cedar tree to chop down. Sometimes we couldn't find just exactly the right shape, so Mammy cut one down and shaved it until it was perfect. She let me help make the "snow" for it out of ivory flakes. We never really had lights on the tree, but it didn't matter. The smell of the cedar more than made up for the absence of lights.

All these activities I realized later gave me absolute proof of God. They verified His existence: finding beautiful violets by the stream, watching the growth of vegetables, noticing the turning of the leaves in the fall, discovering just the right Christmas tree in the woods. God's language is too plain to be misapprehended. Even toddlers can get it.

Throughout the seasons Mammy sang hymns every day as she worked in the garden or labored with the meals, or cleaned the house. And she always made time to teach me lessons about Jesus.

Papa required three freshly cooked meals a day beginning with fresh biscuits, gravy, and home-made sausage or pork tenderloin for breakfast. Mammy never used a recipe but made everything from scratch. Fresh vegetables, fried chicken, corn bread or yeast rolls – most people think of this as a Sunday meal; at Mammy's, it was every day. No sooner would she get the kitchen mopped from breakfast than she would start on "dinner" (lunch) and then after that, "supper."

I watched her carefully, knowing that one day I would get to cook like this for my own family, my own children, never thinking that the only family I would ever really cook much for would be the elderly orphans I picked up along the way and my elderly father.

She taught me the "art" of making mud pies, which I did on the smoke house steps. I played for hours, making pies for all my "babies." I could not have been over three or four years old, because I remembered getting so muddy that Mammy had to bathe me outside in a wash "tub" and put clean clothes on me on the smoke house porch.

Stars shine brightest in the darkest night. Kites rise against the wind, not with the wind. Acorns must go through long summers and fierce winters; they have to endure snow and rain storms. Maybe Mammy had so much strength because she had so many trials. Could that be part of the answer as to why I'm still here on this earth? Am I stronger because of seeing what my grandmother endured and having myself to pass through so many trials? Possibly.

One thing I do know: my grandmother's patience and compassion were the strongest in my head when my pain was the greatest. They struck such a sharp contrast to the impatience and quick temper of my mother. Mammy took things calmly and endeavored to be contented with her lot. Someone once said that difficulties are God's errands. Mammy kept on climbing the hill when the hill became steeper. Her whole way of looking at things and making choices was shaped by her profound faith in Jesus and His return. She clearly illustrated the scriptural passage, *I can do all things through Christ which strengthened me.* After I began teaching and would come home to visit her, she hobbled through her arthritis and scoliosis, determined to still cook those biscuits, turnip greens, and country ham for me. Praise God for that angel.

Her faith, in turn, helped shape my view of this world and the next. She had helped me to keep my own eyes focused on Jesus. She had helped me overcome the influences of the evil kingdom for so many years. Unlike Mammy, I had strayed from the straight and narrow path that leads to eternity from time to time in my earlier life, but I always knew when I did, and I always returned. I probably wouldn't have had it not been for Mammy's example. Her view of this world had carried me through the turbulences of the past years, and they gave me preparation for the final battles to come.

CHAPTER 25

The wicked is snared by the transgression of his lips: but the just shall come out of trouble.

–Proverbs 12:13

SURVIVING THE RAGE

My mother was the antithesis of my grandmother. She was a woman filled with anger and rage who resented me for some reason that I probably will never fully understand. I do know that Daddy and I were blamed for just about all her mishaps. It was only after I became an adult that I came to understand that those who have the fewest resources within themselves naturally seek the food of their self-love elsewhere, that the propensity to ridicule or make fun of what another person happens to approve grows with the decline of common sense and decency. I also came to realize that true worth doesn't exult in the deficiencies of others. But as a child, I did not understand these truths. I believed I was deficient because my mother said I was. When I was ridiculed, I did not have the maturity to realize that maybe it was *her* own deficiency which had produced the ridicule. Even after I was an adult, her slings and arrows she tossed at me still managed to result in a feeling of great inadequacy and guilt from thinking that somehow I had made her life miserable. I can only now imagine with deep pain the impact of her constant ridicule on a pure, sensitive and affectionate mind such as Daddy's.

Even so, it was when this misery of my mother's escalated into rage that both Daddy and I had to run for cover, or grit our teeth and swallow hard until the eye of the storm passed. We both had learned survival techniques to cope with the rage, although the rage had certainly taken its toll on both of us.

Psychologists tell us that fear lies underneath all anger. Only in the years after beginning the journey with my father did I come to understand the possible source of Mother's rage, her fear of losing control. When I was a young girl, all I was made to believe was that Daddy or I - or both of us - had somehow caused it, not understanding that the rage was rooted deep within my mother's own psyche.

Later I came to understand that peace and calm often come from the arrival of someone who is trusted, loved, and respected. This was one of the reasons I had such a deep concern about my mother's spiritual health. If she had a closer relationship with Jesus, then this should have resulted in more peace – regardless of what was going on in this world. Or if she had read the Bible, maybe some of her fear and resultant anger could be replaced with ethereal light and life. I wondered if she shunned the Bible because of its admonition for a woman's true mission and the responsibilities of the parent. Whatever the reasons, this book was not a part of her life; therefore, her marriage was just viewed as something she had to endure and then only through sullen resistance.

Through the years I never really knew just how real my mother's suicidal threats were, since her brother, nephew, and first cousin had all killed themselves. All of them had terrific tempers, and her nephew and cousin were extremely controlling and heavy drinkers. My uncle had been kind, though, and I never knew how much he drank. I finally concluded that most of my mother's suicide threats were staged for control and manipulation, since she could be quite the drama queen. I had often hurt for my father's powerlessness as I had to stand by over the years and watch him try to respond to her rage. Throughout my childhood and teenage years, I witnessed the same scene. Mother would become enraged about something, threaten to kill herself, and then lock herself up in the bath or bedroom. Daddy would pick her up, apologize, kiss and comfort her as one would a small child. Since so much of this happened when I was a very young girl, I really didn't know what to do except run to Mammy's house, which was separated from my parents' home only by a garden.

My father was not the only one who got blamed. I thought back to all those times when Mother became enraged about something I had done or said. And so I grew up really believing that I indeed was the reason for her unhappiness and her sense of deprivation, that I had done something horrible to result in this kind of behavior. As I became older, a similar scene continued to be played out.... screams, threats of suicide, blaming me for her misfortunes, the only difference being that in my case, if Daddy were around, he would join in his wife's blame. I came to understand as an adult that at least I was able to deflect some of this anger, all of which would otherwise have been heaped entirely on him. So maybe I had at least served a little good purpose for him earlier in his life.

Later in life I realized this alliance against me was an attempt to gain some favor with his wife, and a common enemy gave them both support. "Get out of here and leave us alone," my father echoed Mother's scream. This drama still played until the last three years of his life, even after he became ill with

Alzheimer's. Many times I reflected on how horribly tragic this was, because the pandering never really gained Daddy any access, leverage or affection, except for the moment. But he had had so little affection that even a brief moment was better than none at all.

Through the years, I had learned the way to manage Mother's rage was either to stay out of her path, buy her gifts and trips, allow her to dominate every conversation, and control every decision. This was also Daddy's way of surviving her anger and self-absorption. It was not necessarily the best thing we could have done, because we enabled her behavior. But the goal at the time was just to contain her anger as much as possible. Accommodating and placating her and allowing myself to be the scapegoat worked some of the time to defuse it, and so that is what I did. The ultimate goal was to reduce her feeling of deprivation she had just because she had gotten stuck with Daddy and me.

Her inability to control her temper many times resulted in slaps across my face, leaving it numb and red for hours. I tried to recall the reasons. Once she hit me when I accidentally dropped a salt map for school on the floor. Another time I begged to go see my maternal grandmother, whom I loved very much. For the most part, though, the reasons for the slaps were never very clear. What was clear was that if I shed any tears from any of the slaps, I was at risk of being hit again.

My primary care physician and social worker always were convinced that my life-long insomnia had something to do with this negative relationship. Though I try not to, I do still think about the frequent put-downs, Mother's continuing volatility, and her ever-changing demands. When I was forced as a very small child to stay with her, I would rarely sleep, hearing the old grandfather clock strike two and three in the morning. I remembered how ashamed I was for wetting the bed and how ridiculed I had been for it. Later I wondered if I was afraid to go to sleep, or if my mother's unstable personality kept me so keyed up even as a child that I just couldn't relax. But I still have insomnia, and my mother is dead. So she wasn't to blame for all of it.

Once when I was quite young Mother said she was sorry after I had first apologized for getting her upset. I always had to be the parent. As embarrassed as I was to admit it, my mother had been quite successful in convincing me that I was the reason for all her misfortunes and problems.

When I was in the seventh grade, my parents rented their house, which was next to Mammy's house, and moved to East Tennessee where Daddy had been working for several years. I was forced to go with them. I can still feel the horrible homesickness I had on having to leave my precious grandmother. But

I had not imagined the hell I found myself in when there was nowhere to run from my mother's rage.

The contrast between the two women was enough to make any child sick. As I look back now, it probably resembled the contrast my father had to absorb between living with me and living with my mother.

During that time, my mother may have still been able to feel slight empathy, or she may have just become embarrassed at my depression. Regardless of the reason, she allowed me to return to my grandmother's for my eighth grade year. I must remember that this was a kind action on her part. At the beginning of my freshman year, however, I was again forced to return to my parents' home because the social embarrassment of trying to explain to her friends why her daughter didn't live with them overcame her discomfort of living with me. As long as we were in Cookeville, I could say to my friends who wondered why I stayed at my grandmother's, "I live with Mammy because my mother works." Older people who had known mother there had figured out the reason. But this was East Tennessee where folks didn't know Mother's past. So when her friends inadvertently found out she had a daughter, they were curious as to why I wasn't with her. Some people *never* learned she had a daughter.

Only in recent years had I learned from Marie, my then sister-in-law, that a friend of her husband, my brother, for over 23 years never knew that he had a sister. Marie had sung my praises, but was in disbelief that her husband had not acknowledged his sister. My mother had also been embarrassed many times to claim me. Often she had said to me, "Forget about us; you are not a part of us." Indeed, I would probably have been so much better off had I in fact been able to do this. My social worker remarked that it was quite amazing how one young girl could have been so threatening to an entire family. Close friends have thought that my fear in recent years of not being claimed by God has resulted from not being claimed by family members. I don't know if it does or not.

Those years were traumatic, and some of the most horrible years of my life. As a young girl, when I withdrew to my room at night, I held the covers over my head in bed, trying not to hear the exasperated sighs of my mother as she talked to her friends over the phone. "I can't do a thing with her; she doesn't want to go to parties...All she wants to do is stay in her room and read her Bible and study....I don't know what I'm going to do with her. She's killing me."

It *was* true that I stayed in my room unless I was made to come out. That was the only place I felt free to express my feelings and pray. At the dinner table I recalled the numerous times when I was ridiculed for a question or made fun of for not thinking like Mother, or scoffed at for an independent thought which didn't reflect the rest of the family's thinking. "Listen to her Brian; she's just like Uncle Grady." Daddy would shake his head, sigh and nod in agreement. I don't know how many times she said this, but it seemed like thousands. Uncle Grady was considered crazy. So I, too, came to believe I must also be crazy.

I could feel the tears welling up, but I was always determined not to let Mother see me cry. There must have been a streak of independence somewhere within me even then because I didn't want to give her the satisfaction of thinking she had made me cry. But some of my determination resulted from knowing that if I cried, she would scream at or ridicule me. So I would choke down a little food and just hope God would keep me from crying right then until I could leave the table. That's why I was so skinny. I remember when I was *very small* and cried about something which had hurt me, she mockingly called me a "cry baby." I was never given the opportunity to act like a child, to have a child's voice. Now I understand that if I did, it took the focus off Mother as the child. This could not be allowed. Mother enjoyed making me cry *throughout my life*. Maybe it gave her a sense of power that she had been able to evoke this response. But I never really knew the reason for certain.

I *did* manage to survive those years by going to my room, praying and reading my Bible every night. I read it from cover to cover. Half the time I didn't understand what I was reading, but I read it anyway. Maybe I read it just because my mother didn't want me to. But I do remember gaining strength from some Biblical characters who had suffered for God. I prayed every night that if I couldn't be with Mammy, that God might take me to heaven so that my family would be happy and I would be in a place where I wouldn't be made fun of. I was too young to realize that one of the main reasons family members were uncomfortable around me was that my core was different from theirs. I didn't understand anything then but that I was an embarrassment to my mother, and that I was crazy like Uncle Grady.

When I asked if I might watch the gospel quartets on television, Mother would respond that my father didn't want to see them, that they made him nervous. The truth I later discovered was that Daddy loved gospel music, and this was one of the primary ways of keeping his focus and attention after the onset of his Alzheimer's. It was my mother who didn't want to hear it.

LEARNING TO KEEP THE WORLD'S FOCUS ON MOTHER

One particular event illustrates why I usually ended up *not* taking the action with my mother that psychologists and sociologists would have recommended, but instead the one at the time that was the most expedient and would produce the less injury. I often faced a choice between two bad alternatives. On this occasion I actually tried to use assertive communication, and it didn't work.

After I had lost a long-term relationship with a man whom I deeply loved, I thought that a short vacation might be something I could use. Because I had often taken my mother on trips, forever trying to make up something to her that I really never understood, I thought Mother would also like to go. So I arranged for us to take a four day trip to Mexico. My mother was pleased, and this thrilled me. Nothing made me happier in those days than to see Mother happy – even if it were for just a little while. It was one of those American Express tour packages, where some, but not all, activities are planned. I had worked hard to run my usual interference ahead of time to ensure that things went as smoothly as possible for my mother.

On the second evening after arriving in Mexico City, our small group of eight went together to eat at a very nice restaurant, one that had been converted from an old convent. There was beautiful music, and the food was top quality. The group members were all friendly and quite conversant. One of the men asked me about my work. My quick reply of "I'm in the training business" prompted another question about what type of training it was and to whom. Knowing that I would pay for any prolonged attention away from my mother, I gave another quick answer and then hurriedly said, "Mother is in the banking business." That brought the focus to her, so she spent the rest of the meal time talking about her banking work. Because she never asked any of them a single question, I became embarrassed for her in that no one else in the conversation had had the chance to say anything. So I tried a time or two to redirect it to one of the other members, with no success. But Mother had noticed my effort.

Upon arriving back at our hotel room, she immediately accosted me. "You think you're so smart!" The accusation seemed to come out of nowhere. Fearing this had resulted from the group's interest in my work, but hoping this would not escalate into a major encounter, I responded naively as if I didn't know why she had made this statement. "Why are you saying this?" She pouted, "Because you think you're so much better than me, or anyone in the family." A form of this statement had been frequently made in the past, but it was so disappointing now after such a wonderful dinner and such nice company.

This was one time that I mistakenly expressed my feelings. "Mother, I don't think I'm very smart, but I'm smart enough to know that it's important to listen to other people." What possibly possessed me to dare say something this risky, I don't know. I knew better. Mother went into a rage, and as was so characteristic of her, said she knew she shouldn't have come on this trip and that she would just go back tomorrow. This was a familiar trick, and usually the manipulation worked. Normally I would have said, "Oh, Mother, I'm so sorry I said that. You know you're the one who is so much smarter than me." Whatever the reason was, however, this time I sat down and quietly replied, "Mother, if you really want to go back, I'll help you find a flight."

I couldn't believe I had said that. It was the first time I had ever spoken up to my mother like that, speaking to her as an adult. But I knew she didn't have the capacity to operate in that mode. As soon as the words were out, I knew I should not have said them, and that I would pay for them.

Sure enough, the rage escalated into a tantrum, with Mother crying, then screaming, and then ordering me out of the room. When she began a tantrum, it always appeared that she somehow got herself more worked up and spun out of control - from her own words rather than from anyone else's. I obediently left the room and went to the lobby, staying there for over an hour, hoping that the rage would subside. I left in such a hurry that I forgot to take my room key, and when I returned, Mother wouldn't let me in. It was not that late, and I knew she heard the knocking. But she didn't let me in. So I spent most of the rest of the night drinking diet cokes in the bar. I found myself praying that God would forgive me for speaking up to my mother and making her this upset. "Help me to hold my tongue." And at this time I was 36 years old and still feeling entirely responsible for her happiness or unhappiness.

I tried knocking on my hotel door again several hours later, and this time Mother let me into the room. "Mother, are you okay?" No answer. This was a common way to punish me - by not talking to me at all. By this time I had begun to feel nauseated. Not knowing if it were Montezuma's Revenge or Mother's revenge, I just lay down and tried to be very still. The next morning I was quite ill; not only was I vomiting but I had horrible pain in my lower back. We were scheduled to leave on a bus to Taxco that afternoon, and I just prayed that God would heal me enough so she could make the bus ride. Otherwise, Mother would blame me for disrupting *that* trip. Again I tried making a statement or two to her, getting no response. I hated myself for ruining any portion of my mother's trip and knew I was paying for my words the previous night. I prayed again, "Lord, please let your power demolish this argument and enable me to know what to say which will please my mother."

Sometime that afternoon Mother decided she had punished me long enough and began answering me. After that, she complained about various things, from the bumpy bus ride to the food, but she did not throw another tantrum. I was grateful. This was only one of many times which gave me strength to survive the rage that would result from becoming my father's advocate.

Had I not been forced to endure this type of rage earlier in my life, I would probably have killed myself before my father passed away. I would have had nothing to sustain me for the evil mine fields my father and I had to tiptoe through. I would not have had the strength that had come previously from heavy, dark clouds. I would not have been able to see any light because the path my father and I were on became very, very dark. But never during this time with my father did the light go out completely, and I believe it was in part due to my having survived such dark periods in which my mother's bi-polar behaviors ruled the hour. God preserved enough of my reason and senses for me to have just enough left over for our journey. Also knowing that the focus must always be kept on my mother enabled me to frame certain situations where she could see at least some benefit for herself.

CHAPTER 26

But now ye also put off all these: anger, wrath, malice, blasphemy, filthy communication out of your mouth.

–Colossians 3:8

OVERCOMING ANGER

Many of my battles related to my mother were ignited by anger. However, I came to learn that anger in and of itself would not accomplish the ultimate good, whatever actions it might spur. Mother had verified that. Her resentment had led to bitterness, which frequently manifested itself in anger. It had turned her into a complaining, self-pitying person who eventually drove not only me, but other people away. Whenever any other person in her presence might mention an ailment, Mother's was always worse, more debilitating. Upon telling my mother about my father's increasing headaches and difficulty with swallowing, she immediately began a diatribe about her own head and back aches. She blithely responded to the swallowing difficulty with, "That goes with it."

When her husband could no longer cater to and take care of her, she became more resentful and bitter than ever. Much of the cause of this bitterness, I believe, resulted from not having spiritual reserves with which to cope.

But my mother was not the only angry person in this saga. Though she displayed hers to get what she wanted, I hid mine to enable Daddy and me to survive. My anger was exhausting, but suppressing it was more so. I became tired of trying to put on that happy and cheery face that Christians are supposed to display even in the darkest times when the tunnel seemed to just get longer and longer. My heavenly view was becoming dimmer. My anger toward my mother seemed to be overcoming it.

TRYING TO HANG ON TO MY OWN FAITH

As I became weaker and more worn out from confusion, frustration and eventual anger, I found my own faith starting to wane and depression setting in. This had been the faith that had enabled me to survive so many obstacles. After several years of this journey with Daddy, I found myself challenging beliefs I had held my entire life which had kept me afloat. Wondering if God were playing some kind of mystery game with me, I had become frustrated with Him for what seemed to be "keeping what I should do as a secret" or making it too puzzling. Once, after I was just about totally spent toward the end of Daddy's life, I even dared say to my mother that I probably would only be able to understand after my own death why God had placed such burdens on me. At various times when I had received what I thought was a sign from Him that I was on the right track, I would then get a contradictory signal afterwards, which of course, led to more ambiguity. Though not always successful, I nevertheless tried to remind myself that this very sense of frustration might be the work of the devil wanting to create this confusion. Or that God's ways are not our ways, and we cannot really ever understand His motives until after we leave this earth.

Part of my fatigue and waning faith resulted from continually receiving a negative result from trying to emulate Christ. The more I tried to give up for Mother – the greater tolerance, the more turning of the other cheek, the more material goods I provided, the more responsibility I took on for both my parents' health and well being – the greater my mother's rage seemed to grow. Perhaps it was because it was unsettling. This business of repaying evil with good had not resulted in any warming of my mother's heart. It just seemed to increase her ire.

Delegating Mother to God

The result I had so long prayed for – that my mother would come to know the Lord and recognize that He was in control – had not become verified. All the prompting and effort I had spent on her about this matter had resulted in mostly anger from her, which in turn, resulted in ridicule, rejection, and a loss of freedom and property for me. Generally non-Christians don't want to hear admonitions from Christians, especially from those they despise, and if they hate the person who is trying to emulate Christ, even just their actions can have a negative impact as well.

Maybe she was either incapable or unwilling to open up her heart to God. While most Christians remember the scripture which says that God desires that no one shall perish, they are often unaware of another scripture which refers to those created for destruction. Or if they do know it, the latter is so antithetical to most Christians' beliefs that they merely delete it from their minds. But the reality is that all will not come to the Lord, and the Lord, being omniscient, knows this before any of us are created.

I began to see my mother more and more as being overcome with demonic forces and found myself silently struggling with the idea of trying to obey the scripture which admonishes us to honor our mothers but at the same time to "resist the devil." I had to reconcile this ambiguity.

When there has been no confirmation about one's prayer, maybe the person isn't praying the *right* prayer. So I ended up changing it, asking God to protect my father when he was not with me. I prayed that He would help Daddy build up some immunity to Mother's hateful screaming and ridicule and bring forth some encouragement and care from others when he wasn't with me. If, according to Paul, "the called" are predestined to be conformed to the image of Christ, then the only thing we mortals can do is just focus on trying to imitate Him with our own actions. Maybe my mother would get a miracle one day and something would kill the demons in her. But if not, there was nothing else I could do. Obviously, *my* praying for her to turn to God wasn't going to make it happen. If God's will was for her to turn to Him, He would make that happen. If not, she would not. Her soul and well-being were *His* territory.

My anger subsided some when I finally realized that all I could do was just *walk* my *own* faith and not worry about my mother's spiritual health. Even though I was the only one who would ever confront her about it, and Daddy and I would still have to deal with her demonic actions, still I felt a little liberated. I was reminded by Solomon in Proverbs 17:15 that those who justify sin are an abomination to the Lord. My rationalization of Mother's behavior could in itself be sinful.

DISCOVERING THE GOOD

In order to keep my sanity, I had to discover some good even in the midst of my anger and pain since God was allowing all this to happen. I had to look beyond the obstacles and immediate pain. Consequently, in almost every instance, I was able to discover some good results.

God works in unexpected ways to bring us strength in the midst of suffering. During the trials with my father I found fellowship and empathy from people whom I had only casually known before. One example was those folks who were descended from my grandparents' relatives and friends in both Cookeville and Nashville. Another was the church family I became reconnected with at the small church where I was taken as a child by Mammy and where Daddy also learned about the Lord. I found myself testifying to the congregation there about how the Lord had enabled me to survive many ordeals – both personal and professional. I began to be asked to sing solos at the church, some of the old hymns I learned there as a child. Throughout our entire journey, the members treated Daddy as a human being, rather than a non-person, used his name, and spoke directly to him. Daddy responded with some degree of normalcy himself and a peaceful mood.

There were other times I became convinced that God sent his angels to help me out. Like the times when there would almost magically appear a parking place close to where I needed to park because of Daddy's difficulty with walking. Or the time when I had looked in the same spot in the kitchen cabinet for my house keys a dozen times, only to find them immediately in that same spot after calling to God to please help me. Or the times when we would attend church services and someone would offer to stay close to Daddy while I parked the car. Then there was the time that an acquaintance with whom I had not spoken in over four years left me a telephone voice mail that she was returning my call. Puzzled, I telephoned the woman who informed me that her ID recorder had recorded my telephone number and she was simply returning my call. I had *not* called her initially, but during the conversation, I discovered that the woman's husband had Alzheimer's, and she gave me various helpful ideas on various institutions and day care centers. Things like this cannot be explained away by this world's logic.

On one occasion, I had been trying to find some new frames for Daddy's glasses. He sometimes wanted to keep them on when he slept, so he had evidently bent them when he turned over. Since the manufacturer of his original frames had gone out of business, I needed to use the lenses which he already had. On that day I traveled to several optical stores. On my visit to the first, I struck up a conversation with a young woman who began telling me about some of the trials of her life. She eventually got around to asking me about my need for the frames, which led into the story of my own family situation. The young woman, seemingly somewhat amazed at this saga, queried, "How is it that you're able to handle all this?" "Only though Christ," I replied. "Do you go to church?" the young woman asked. What an opening! "Yes, I go to St. Paul, right up there on the hill and we have a lot of young people about your age," I answered. "I believe I waited on your pastor the other day," the young woman responded. She also sheepishly revealed that she hadn't been inside a church in years.

Before the end of the visit, I had given all the particulars about the church, and the young woman assured me she was going to give it a try. So many important things take place in the "asides" of life. I was not able to find frames that would fit the lenses, but there was some good still that came from that interchange. I left thinking, "We must just keep thinking about the higher agenda," and perhaps the "frames" issues will be resolved from somewhere else.

Sure enough, later that day, as I traveled to another optical place and explained my need, the young woman waiting on me noticed the cross around my neck. This led to a conversation where I once again had the opportunity to testify about how the Lord had held me up through ordeal after ordeal. After trying different frames, the young woman said, "Just a moment. I've got an idea." She went into another room and came out with frames into which she had placed Daddy's lenses. "These were sent back because they weren't right, and you may have them if you like. They're not new, but they fit." It was a small miracle.

Every cause has an effect – though it is not always an immediate effect. Nor does it have to be an effect which seems directly related to the cause at hand. Although my first trip didn't end up with a solution, the solution (result) came later from the seed sown.

At the malls, folks smiled at my father, and he responded. He engaged the children in conversation, and almost always the parents were willing and kind to allow the exchange. This was a gift from God.

FOLLOWING JESUS TO THE CROSS

Words from the Apostle James gave me a little comfort in these most difficult times and sometimes helped me overcome my own anger and continue to navigate through all this evil: *Consider it poor joy, my brothers, whenever you face trials of many kinds, because you know that the testing of your faith develops perseverance.* Surely God was still paying some attention and some day might release me from this hell on earth.

One of the elements in a Christian's job description is to follow Christ not just into the peaceful valleys but into the valley of tears, into the thorny desert, and if one must, to the cross itself where humanity is in agony. Christians almost always stress the importance of prayer to accomplish what appears to be the impossible, but they often shy away from the need to take action. Why? Because it's easier; it's more passive, less demanding. "Just hand this over to God" is a common admonition from well-meaning Christians to those in deep despair or oppression. Sometimes I want to hit people who say this. Often, they have no idea of what the other person is really experiencing. But James insisted that one can only show faith through good deeds. He reminded us that the demons believe, but they tremble with fear. Jesus also insisted that belief was not enough; he demanded action that demonstrated that belief. He himself was believed more for His actions, including his miracles, than His words. He stressed that the test of true discipleship lies not in words, but in actions. The test on Judgment Day will be what out actions reveal about our relationship with Him. What did we do and not do for Him?

Perhaps much of the cause of my suffering was the intensity of my will. The less it is, the less we suffer, which explained why circumstances of other people might precipitate such suffering on my part.

Prayer by itself without action often ends up in mere piety, and sometimes it takes both for the seemingly impossible to be made possible. Some have said that prayer is supposed to be the result of a quiet mind and untroubled thoughts and that one should never pray when he is angry. I was frequently admonished by well-meaning Christians to try to remain peaceful and just wait on God. However, that was a challenge I never quite succeeded in conquering – until the end of Daddy's life, when there was nothing else I could do *except* pray. In those times when I had the most difficulty in believing that prayer alone could accomplish the impossible, particularly with those family issues which I had spent years praying about, I would take concrete actions I imagined that Christ might take. Although He is often pictured by Christians as meek and mild, the Gospels actually show Him to be an assertive man of action who could use confrontation to compel a right conclusion. My challenge for the anger I had over some evil action adversely affecting Daddy was waiting for the signals to come, taking patient action led by God, rather than impatient activism led by the earthly enemy.

When those signals do come, confrontation is often necessary. Evil has become so blatant that it often takes strong and unambiguous confrontation to right wrongs. It requires taking unpopular stands. It requires not being that concerned about what others will think or how they will judge us.

I encountered struggles which appeared to be unlike those which most others faced because there was dichotomy in these struggles. Thus my reaction often did not resemble actions which other Christians might have taken.

Many of these struggles resulted in a loss of immediate income or prestige or the world's definition of success, which prompted my family to scoff and severely criticize me. Others involved taking on the pain of total strangers, which man's world could not understand or accept. All of them, however, conditioned me for the final alienation, the final battle with Satan which was to come.

NEEDING APPROVAL ONLY FROM GOD

Something else helped me to overcome anger. I really had been programmed not to *require* approval and acceptance from anyone on earth. I had what some had called a fearless immunity to pleasing others. God never intended that strong independent beings should be reared by clinging to others. Though I haven't always been successful, I have tried to view the difficulties, hardships and trials of my life as having made me more self-reliant, only needing God. Though it's tough to see perils as positive blessings while we're in their midst, once we subdue them or overcome them, we can feel more power and strength. The toughest plants are not grown in the sheltered garden or in the hot-house, but on the rugged mountains.

For the most part, neither had I required love from any*one* on this earth. There were times when, as a young adult, its absence had made me look for it in all the wrong places. But after my grandmother died, I had finally come to know that it was only God's love that could be counted on.

Though I could never come close to the degree of sacrifice that Jesus demonstrated, I did change my agenda to accommodate my mother and give up goods and jobs to help both my parents. Finally recognizing that I couldn't do all that had to be done for my parents, and still write and conduct professional training, I put my life, including my work, and my needs on hold, in spite of getting chastised by others for doing it. Admittedly, much of my motive was to ameliorate my mother's anger, and thus reduce the danger Daddy would be in if I didn't make these changes. Some of it, though, was truly to help her because I knew she just didn't have the emotional or mental strength that I did.

I missed my work, which had given me respect and dignity, and a nice income. And it had helped define me. But I knew I had a far more urgent mission and a new identity. I felt – or maybe rationalized – that God would take care of my *needs*. It was the only choice I could make, given all the circumstances. Jesus died, sacrificing Himself for all of us. Surely, if I aspired to be like Him, I must try to do the same.

CHAPTER 27

If ye were of the world, the world would love his own: but because ye are not of the world, but I have chosen you out of the world, therefore the world hateth you.
—*John 15:19*

UNCLAIMED BAGGAGE

The *Book of Genesis* says that we come from a place farther away than space and that those who belong to God will never feel totally at home in this world. But I have always felt more alienated than anyone else I know, and I have often wondered if I would develop Alzheimer's myself because of this alienated life. Actually there *have been* times when I thought I was already in the beginning stages, but my doctor assured me that it was just stress. It was not just separation from my immediate family; it was also estrangement from my aunts and uncles who bought my mother's propaganda. There was even some alienation when I lived with Mammy because my father's sister hated my living with her mother, and because of this deep bitterness, I had to minimize my love for my grandmother when my aunt was around.

My aunt was the antithesis of my grandmother – just as my grandmother was the antithesis of my mother. She was driven by secular values, particularly money, similar to my mother's values. Outside of her immediate family, she had a sharp tongue for just about everyone, and when she struck, she struck to kill. That seething retort to my father, "I'll see it [the cherry cupboard] gets smashed to bits before you [my father] get it" pretty much summarized her values she had demonstrated to me.

Mammy was deeply anguished over this remark, and I remember the tears in her eyes when her daughter had made it. But she knew the remark had been typical of her daughter. She often explained those statements as "It's just her way; she doesn't mean it." But as was the case when her daughter initially refused to have her picture made with Daddy at Mammy and Papa's fiftieth anniversary, she really *did* mean it. Perhaps near the end of her life when I attempted to reconcile the two together, she may have slightly changed her attitude because only months before her death, she told Daddy and me that she was glad we had visited her in the nursing home and asked us to come back. That itself was an amazing victory. I don't know if Daddy's brain was so far gone by this time that he realized the contrast between her past feelings about him and these more recent, but it didn't matter. Her present statement was what counted with Daddy anyway. It is just so much of a pity that it takes death's door to change a person's heart. All those years when Daddy wanted a relationship with his sister were gone, and there was no retrieving them.

Since this aunt ended up getting most of my grandmother's possessions, it was little wonder that Daddy called my mother by the name of his sister after the onset of Alzheimer's. I often wondered how much of it was really Alzheimer's or just releasing so much that had been suppressed for so long.

When my aunt came over to my grandmother's house when I lived there, her initial greeting to me was usually the same, "Why don't you go live with your mother and father where you belong?" Of course, I didn't belong there either. I often tried complimenting her in some way or making some small talk, much as I did with my mother. But with my aunt, it really fell flat. All I received in return was some ridiculing remark about my hair or the way I looked, or, later in life, ridicule of my education. As she did with my father, she went to some lengths to hurt me. Once when I was about ten, she took me to her hairdresser to get my hair cut. I had thought it was only going to be trimmed, but she had evidently told the hairdresser to cut off all my long hair, which I loved and which others had frequently complimented. I don't know whether she resented my grandmother braiding it or the compliments I had received, but all I knew for sure was that I was left with an ugly short do. I will always remember this aunt's laughter as she sat there and watched my locks drop to the floor, as I tried to stifle my tears. And I will also always remember one Christmas "present" she gave me when I was about 13, a pair of bright red panties, which I had to open up in front of everyone. Again, she laughed because she knew how my modesty would terrifically embarrass me. The attitude towards me appeared to resemble my mother's. But even this treatment probably helped fortify me against later evil actions taken on the journey with my father.

Throughout my teenage years and into young adult life, my aunt's hatred for me never abated. So, as a young teenager, I just retreated to my room and studied or prayed until she left – just like I retreated to my room when I was at my parents' home. At least with my aunt, there was consistency; she didn't feign friendliness or caring when others were around, as my mother's schizophrenic tendencies prompted her to do.

When I purchased a new dress for Mammy, she could only feel free to wear it when my aunt was out of town. Or when I managed to get some new arthritic medicine for her from a Nashville doctor, Mammy and I had to hide it for years in the bottom of her sewing machine, for fear of my aunt seeing it. I never felt I could show affection for Mammy in her presence. I remained afraid of her throughout my adult life until I saw her frail and needy in her last years.

In recent years I have tried to understand her disdain for me, and I have forgiven her for it. But the difficulty has been with how she spoke to and treated Mammy. The worst part is that I feel so responsible for Mammy having to bear the brunt of her daughter's disdain for me. What a job poor little Mammy had of trying to make up for everyone's feeling about me.

Even though I had God to lean on, and though I want to believe I didn't need anyone other than God, I have to admit that the slander particularly when I was quite young did make a long-lasting impression that continued into my adult life. Sometimes I felt like David when he wrote, *For I have heard the slander of many: fear was on every side: while they took counsel together against me, they devised to take away my life* (Psalms 31:13). But David had the strength to resist it. Maybe I was too young or too beaten down psychologically to not let others' words sting me.

Years later I realized how strong and courageous Mammy was to defend keeping me, in light of her daughter's attitude about it. She said, "I want her here...She helps me...." What a pity I never really told Mammy how much I realized she had sacrificed for me. Of course, at the time, I was a young girl, unaware of what all had gone on behind the scenes. But still, I should have acknowledged more of what she was doing for me. Over the past fifteen years or so, every night I have asked God to tell Mammy how grateful I am for all she did and sacrificed for me and how sorry I am that I didn't tell her during my life how she had rescued *me*.

I was never able to overcome my aunt's resentment because she could never swallow my grandmother's love for me. During the last two years of my grandmother's life, I had the opportunity to see her only occasionally. During that time, I timidly asked my aunt's permission to take Mammy for just a week or two to her home and stay with her there, which was only a couple of miles away from this aunt's house. "No, Kathryn, she doesn't need to go back there. If you want to see her for a few minutes, you can come here." This was eerily similar to the statement my mother had made about me seeing my father after she and my brother had dragged him out of the hospital contrary to doctor's urgings. One time I actually went to my aunt's house when she was not there and got the opportunity to visit Mammy alone for a few minutes. It was so wonderful to get to hold her hand and tell her how much I loved her, even though I had a hard time choking back the tears as I tried to say something encouraging. I knew she was pretty much held captive, and what can one really say to make that situation any better? But not one time did Mammy complain.

She just said how much she missed her home and me. One other time my aunt reluctantly gave me the opportunity to take her out for a drive, and Mammy quietly whispered, "Could we just go and see the house?" "Oh Mammy, I wish with all my heart we could move back here and I could take care of you." "I know you do, but don't you worry about me," she had responded, with a tear in the corner of her eye. These were the very same words my father had used when I pulled off the side of the road before I had to take him back to the asylum-like facility.

One thing that really hurt was my aunt's movement into the house after Mammy's death. Oh why could she not have moved there when Mammy was alive so that she might have some happiness and peace in her final days? How can one's conscience allow such action? Until I finally mustered up enough courage to take my father there, I couldn't bear to go near the house after that. The pain was just too great. For over 20 years I had nightmares about trying to save Mammy and taking care of her in her own home. Trying to save my grandmother from another person's control was remarkably similar to trying to save Daddy from Mother. I was totally helpless and unsuccessful in the earlier scenario.

I recognized that a big part of my passion – at least in the beginning – about "saving" Daddy was rooted in my inability to free my grandmother and take care of her.

I could only barely imagine the pleasure of belonging to a family who valued me and where I could feel I belonged. I knew that all of us are pulled toward persons we trust and who accept us as we are. Mammy had loved me unconditionally, but without knowing when my aunt was going to show up and express hostility towards her for raising me, there was always tension on me as a young girl. Later I imagined there must always have been constant tension on Mammy as well. I hated the fact that she had to suffer in any way because of her willingness to raise me – just as I had hated the fact that Daddy had to suffer for any expression of disposition towards me in front of Mother.

The role my aunt had with her mother resembled the role my mother had with my father. Both gained control over their possessions, both told them what to do, and both denied them access to me.

Once when I visited my grandmother before she lost control of her life, Mammy asked me what I would like to have of hers. She had asked me this before. And as before, I quickly responded, "Mammy I only want you to be with me. I don't need anything of yours." I vividly remember as a very young girl in my nightly prayers begging God to take me home before he took Mammy. Mammy asked again. This time, I said, "Mammy, I would treasure your wedding band." She wrote out a note that day on a piece of scratch paper which stated her desire: "I want K to have my rings becuz I luv her so much."

It was when my grandmother had a heart attack near the end of her life and had to be hospitalized, that I had the chance to see her for more than a few minutes without my aunt's presence. Three different times, I got up about 4:30 in the morning and drove some 92 miles to in order to get to the hospital before my aunt arrived. Shortly afterwards, my aunt discovered that I had been given her mother's ring, and therefore denied me access to her mother. This aunt scolded Mammy in the intensive care unit for giving her ring to me. Shortly afterwards, Mammy had another heart attack and died.

At my grandmother's death, my aunt demanded that I bring the ring so she could put it on my grandmother's finger. She used my father as a pawn and had him telephone me to demand that I bring the ring. This action reminded me of the times my mother would put him on the phone and direct him to tell me that he didn't want to come to my house. I did not bring the ring, and for that I wasn't welcome to sit with the rest of the family at the funeral. My father's brother – the one who had never done anything for his mother, not even as much as sending her a Christmas card – scowled at me during the entire service. This was the same uncle who wandered in drunk to Daddy's memorial service, but quickly staggered out, cursing, once he realized that I was delivering the eulogy.

It seemed like everyone in this family was always emphasizing to me that I didn't have a place. The same refrain continued, "Why don't you just pretend we don't exist?" I found myself many times wishing that I could do this. I sometimes imagined what it would have been like to have been born into a family who had wanted me from the beginning, instead of being an unwanted pregnancy who was resented and seen as competition from the outset. Undoubtedly the conditions under which I was born were at the root of much of the alienation.

The alienation was particularly painful when it involved an emergency, especially related to my father, whom I came to realize had lived such a powerless and alienated life himself. One incident previously written about sent the very clear message that I had no place in this family. I mention it again, just to iterate the degree to which I was considered an outsider, one with no place. This was the time I was visiting my parents' home before I began an active intervention into my father's life when Daddy developed chest pains and needed to go to the hospital. Since the hospital was some distance away, I thought surely my mother would allow me to drive them, but she wouldn't hear of it. I should have known that any parent who would not be willing to allow her 50 year old daughter to drive her and her husband to the hospital under such conditions would not allow that same daughter to help *at* the hospital. But somehow I still refused to accept that message. When I tried to facilitate getting Daddy into the emergency room by defining the problem to the attendant, my mother commanded, "I'll handle this; this is none of your business" and physically shoved me aside. A few minutes later, when Daddy was taken to a room with his wife beside him and I was following behind, Mother slammed the door in my face, preventing me from entering. I was again the invisible, voiceless, in-the-way, impotent child, feeling foolish as I sat in the lobby, waiting for my orders.

My brother constantly asked me, "Why can't you just leave us alone?" Years ago when his son was having a very tough time with reading, I wanted to help. My brother's first wife had left him and his sons, and my brother was so devastated that he couldn't really feel the degree of pain which was wrought on his sons. I could. During this time one of the sons had visited me and had talked candidly about his realization that his father had had to marry his mother, and that he knew he wasn't wanted. Denying that this was the case, I nevertheless was aware of the impact of a child not feeling wanted.

I wanted desperately to help him. As an English professor and having a considerable amount of psychology in my graduate work, I suspected the reading difficulty was related to his lack of self-esteem and his depression. He had also become extremely nervous and more defensive than ever. When I tried to mention my concern about his mood and lack of self-esteem to Donald, he snapped at me. "Stay out of it. It's none of your business." I let it go for the time, but being a teacher myself, I couldn't endure the thought that nothing was being done to help my nephew read. I knew the impact that his reading difficulty would have on him throughout life, and I had already seen some results of it. I prayed that the Lord might show me a way to help him. A while later I wrote my brother to ask if I might hire a psychologist or a reading specialist to help him with his reading. "Why can't you stay out of our affairs?" he snapped again. I realized there was little I could do but pray that someone else might show my brother the importance of my nephew learning to read better. Knowing my nephew to be interested in hunting and fishing, I did order a subscription to *Field and Stream Magazine*, thinking this might pique his interest in improving his reading skills. I never knew whether it did or not, because my action was never acknowledged.

After my nephews' mother left my brother, I made stabs at bringing satisfaction to the entire family, particularly at Christmas. Spending much more money on them than my budget allowed, I still enjoyed buying nice things for them – sport coats for my nephews that I knew they wouldn't get otherwise and the same for my brother. Inevitably, though, the gifts were derided with remarks such as, "WHAT do I need *this* for!" I still remember the sneers and the sniping remarks about those gifts. Finally I just began giving them money. That worked better. What worked *even* better was just *sending* the money and staying away.

I was painfully aware of the sources of stress on my older nephew. I deeply loved both nephews and wanted so much to help them reach their potential. Shortly after my brother remarried, the nephew with the reading difficulty became strapped for money and needed help on his apartment rent. Without blinking, I wrote a $500 check and quickly sent it to him and his brother. He was in a monotonous, low-esteemed job, and I was grateful he accepted my help. I was painfully aware that it was no substitute for his reading difficulty, which was partially at the heart of his inability to get a better job, but it was something. A few months later, with a baby on the way, he married, and needed money again. Again, I sent it, and it was accepted.

In fact, money was just about the only thing that *was* always accepted, besides helping him get a better job. My nephew gladly accepted my help on writing his resume and setting up and taking him on job interviews, as well as helping his girlfriends out with the same. Even though I did recognize these requests were only related to money, I was grateful to have these opportunities.

When I expressed concern to my mother and brother about all the sources of stress on my nephew, they screamed "STRESS! He has no stress on this job. He doesn't have to make any decisions." This was the same statement my mother said about Daddy's work. Having conducted stress management training for years, I knew that one of the primary stressors is a lack of job importance and the lack of opportunity to make decisions. Actually a major source of stress in my own life was not being allowed to use my training to help *my* family.

Long ago I had realized I was a commodity to be used and then discarded if my labor and money weren't needed. But for years I lived denying that to myself, surrounding myself with pictures of my family throughout my house. They still hang in my house today. This alone illustrates that I, too, am also somewhat delusional. At some level, I still pretend I had a family although intellectually I know better. Emotionally, I just haven't been successful deleting them from my mind, as I have been deleted from theirs.

The alienation was not just within my family. I attended graduate school during the seventies when the "hippie movement" was in its heyday. Hungry for friends, I found myself accepting invitations to parties which involved activities I knew were contrary to God's word: smoking marijuana, ridiculing moral values, and loose conduct among them. I found myself trying to defend my principles, but I was outnumbered. I was ridiculed and considered a "prude." So I usually just made an excuse of not feeling well and left.

I was often the recipient of sniping sarcasm, "Well of course it won't be good enough for Kathryn" or "Kathryn will be along, so we'll have to watch what we say." People often say what they really mean under the guise of teasing.

Scripture tells us that God even hears the young ravens when they cry. Throughout my life I had usually been able to repress my tears in front of others, especially my parents, because I had been jeered as a small child for letting them out. I had been convinced that they were a sign of babyish behavior. As a young teenager, many nights I cried into my bed pillow, praying to God that Mother wouldn't hear my tears. It was comforting when I was just alone with God; then I could cry without reproach. I had held them in check if they welled up for some unfortunate person if I were in front of my mother or aunt. And as a young adult, many times I made the excuse that I had some work to do, and was able to escape stinging barbs by retreating to my bedroom. Or I would go to the bathroom and flush the toilet several times so no one could hear my crying.

So I came to realize a long time before Daddy's last years that I was running on my own track and that my forced solitude gave me more opportunity than most to discover who God really is and what He wants done. The alienation compelled me to have a growing communion with Him.

I frequently told myself that if I belonged to the world, it would not love me as God did. I justified my alienation from it by thinking that maybe I had been chosen by Him to be set apart from this world and that was why I was "unclaimed baggage." I hoped that God considered what was on the inside of a person more important than a person's dialogue and acceptance in the outside world. Particularly during those last five painful years of my father's life, I had prayed that this was the case.

Though Isaiah was referring to the children of Israel when he spoke of rejection, I was still comforted by his words, especially during the journey with my father: *You are my servants; I have chosen you and not rejected you. So do not fear, for I am with you.... Those who wage war against me will be as nothing at all* (41:10 – 11). I was equally sustained by what Paul told the Christians in Rome: *Our present sufferings are not worth comparing with the glory that will be revealed in us* (Romans 8:18).

But for several years after the storm passed, I had to put forth more effort to keep the quality of my faith as strong as it was *through* the storm. Following my parents' deaths and my continuing losses, for several years I seemed to lose some of that communion with God, as I remained alienated from all family members and fairly isolated. I prayed hard that my earlier beliefs were correct and that I was not rationalizing the reason for my alienation. I have struggled to not yield to the blighting power of rejection and to hang on firmly to that faith that sustained me through the storm. Though I had taught my Bible students many times over that God will never abandon them if they obey Him and feed on His word, I began to silently wonder if it were all an illusion. I fought despair by trying to believe that God would someday bring even me a brighter tomorrow, that sailors' *red sky at night* which is their *delight*.

At long last, God has finally given me some slivers of hope that those earlier beliefs which enabled me to navigate through those troubled waters were based on truth and were not an illusion. My alienation has been justified to me.

TRYING TO FIND SOMETHING TO BELONG TO

The Apostle James helped give me courage from time to time. He wrote, *Blessed is the man that endureth temptation: for when he is tried, he shall receive the crown of life, which the Lord promised to them that love him.* Sometimes, though, I thought I might be just rationalizing my unusual and lonely life and trying to find some basis of scripture which gave it meaning. The evil in my family became so great that my own faith began to wane, and scripture sometimes didn't give me much encouragement.

There were times when I believed the uniqueness of my alienated situations was rooted in programming I had received from my parents while growing up. Because I had such a low self-image of myself as a woman, I had difficulty believing that any man would think me attractive enough to want me for any long-term basis. Besides, all those statements comparing me to crazy Uncle Grady were still in my head. Thus I often forced a confrontation so the guy I was dating would leave me, prompting the old self-fulfilling prophesy, and that no man would ever really want me for long. I remembered my father saying to me as a young girl, as I combed my hair before going out the door, "Nobody will be looking at you. Come on." Later I realized he felt he had to say this because Mother was in the room, and there could never be any doubt as to who would have the attention or who would be thought pretty in this family.

Try as I might, I was never able to dilute my awareness of my sins. However, for a time I let the isolation from family and friends overwhelm me and lead me into thinking that this emptiness could be filled by someone on this earth. I knew I had been rightly punished many times over for that lapse and falling short of the standards that my grandmother had imparted to me. If I had been unaware of the sin, it would have been different, but I was acutely aware of it.

Way down, I never really lost sight of Jesus' teaching that the world would reject and ridicule His disciples, and that made my alienation more endurable. Deep in my soul, I knew that the desires of the flesh are antithetical to God's way and that they really can't compare to the constancy of God's love. But for a time I searched for some perfect, unfailing love on *this* earth. Unable to find it, I soon reverted to my earlier belief that no love but God's could be lasting.

My life-long exile was valuable because it prepared me for the last phase of life with Daddy. Once I was absolutely "fired" from the family, with no hope of any probation, I discovered that being totally alone meant that I did not have those interferences so many have which keep them from interacting frequently with God. For me prayer was not a thing of custom, especially, but it came to be that God was just my only companion. Thus, I spoke with Him often, albeit sometimes in anger and frustration, rather than in the evenness of recollection which is how we are supposed to communicate with Him.

I read His word more in the hopes of understanding what He would have me do. I read it to try to keep hearing the whisper of His voice, hoping it would calm my torment. I realized if there is a moral sublimity to be found on earth, it is in God's Book. At times I have been soothed by the contemplative well-balanced James; at other times I have been calmed by the affectionate and loving John. Still other times I have been assured from the idea presented in Genesis that we actually should *not* feel at home in this world, if we belong to God. Throughout most of my life, the Bible has been my most faithful attendant. It ultimately became a common denominator for Daddy and me, as more and more other ways of communicating with my father disappeared. I came to appreciate that God's word suited the living and the dying, the intellectual, and the one whose brain has become scrambled. Throughout much of my life, it had been the lamp through the dark valleys of trials. It became even more so in the final battle to save my father and help him on his journey from this world to the next.

The alienation I had experienced throughout my life enabled me to withstand my increased alienation in my journey with my father.

CHAPTER 28

For the Lord God will help me; therefore shall I not be confounded: therefore have I set my face like a flint, and I know that I shall not be ashamed. He is near that justifieth me; who will contend with me?

–Isaiah 50:7-8

RESPONDING TO A HIGHER AGENDA

I came to believe that my entire life had been a preparation and conditioning ground for the last eight years of my life. I came to realize, as first my family, then my career, and then my opportunity to socialize with others were taken away, that this deprivation and alienation could only be endured because of the events that had transpired in my life previously. My friends were a bit confounded and vexed that I had spent so much of my energy focused on the family situation at the expense of my own life. I constantly had to remind them that evidently what my life was about *was* others' lives.

I appreciated that they had what they thought was my best interest at heart, and I knew they could never understand why I responded the way I did to others, since I myself hardly understood. But every time I tried to do it God's way, *ultimately* – sometimes years later – there was a greater good which resulted.

TRYING TO FOLLOW GOD IN ACADEMIA

Two instances occurred while I was a young college English teacher which resulted in being penalized for responding to a higher agenda. The first one occurred in a community college in East Tennessee, only my second full-time teaching job after receiving my master's degree. I taught freshman English, and the academic dean was constantly challenging my "rigid" standards for acceptable work. This community college was one where most of the students transferred to a four-year school after graduation, and thus I saw my primary responsibility was to get the students ready to succeed at their next college or university.

I had one student who rarely came to class and consequently did not turn in the required compositions. This particular student had clout in the school since his parents had financially supported the college, and he himself was one of a few minority students at the college. He was charming and self-confident, and he leveraged this charm among students and teachers alike. He remains vivid in my imagination since he was continually asking me out. I always politely responded, "I don't date students." He always called me by my first name, and I always called him, "Mr. Gaines."

It was the end of the spring semester. The grades were turned in to the dean. This student failed, since he hadn't turned in his required work. The dean's secretary called me to his office. I took a deep breath and prayed to God that I wouldn't say anything stupid and that whatever was said to me, I would keep my cool. I had the sense it may have been something to do with my grades being lower than most of the teachers in my department, so I had taken along all my students' folders to show their work, if the need arose.

The dean and the chairman of the English Department were present. They were initially cordial, in fact, unusually friendly. "Ms. Huddleston, thank you for meeting with us today," the dean greeted, with his chin slightly shifted upward. His usual haughtiness was belied by his polyester three-piece suit, pale blue socks and his black slicked-back hair. Although he was a deacon in a church, which was headquartered there in the town, many of the faculty distrusted him and thought he was quite cunning. After some small talk, he brought up the issue at hand. "Ms. Huddleston, it appears you have several low grades in this class. This is really a number which exceeds most of the other instructors. We are particularly concerned about Mr. Gaines' grade." I took a deep breath and responded, "Yes sir, this student failed because he didn't turn in the required work. Would you like to see his folder?" This folder contained the student's theme papers. "Oh, no, that won't be necessary," he replied, still somewhat politely. "Do you realize this student's family has been very supportive of this college?" he continued. Here it comes, I thought. "I have heard this," I responded, trying to stay objective and non-defensive in my tone. I continued, "May I ask you what this has to do with this meeting?" I knew I had hit a hot button, but I couldn't take the question back.

At this moment he turned on a recording device. I, half bluffing, since I didn't know for certain if it were true, responded, "Sir I don't believe you can record me without my permission." He turned off the recorder. But I then knew that they were going to try to manipulate me in some way and get me to make statements which I would later regret. "Ms. Huddleston, as you know, your standards have been criticized for being too high." His tone had changed slightly from that artificial cheeriness to matter-of-fact, which

I actually preferred. I said nothing. He continued, "Therefore I suggest you rethink Mr. Gaines' grade, and we will give you the opportunity right now to change his grade."

I immediately responded – probably a little too quickly – but I was frustrated at the suggestion. "Sir, if you wish to change his grade, that is your privilege, but since I didn't fail this student, I cannot therefore now pass him." His look entirely changed. Wrinkling his brow, he replied, "I don't understand," a slight hint of consternation creeping into his voice. I had my standards for all the grades with me and offered them to him. "Dean, this student *made* this grade; I don't *give* grades. It was his choice to refuse to do the assignments. I counseled with him many times, but he chose to disregard my words." "Are you sure you are refusing to change this grade?" queried the dean, with that tone like "If you don't, you'll probably regret it." I responded in the affirmative. "Well, then, rather than terminating you, we will give you the chance to resign," he coldly replied.

Could this really be true? Teaching had always been my career goal. It was the one thing that brought me confirmation. I had received so many letters from former students giving me credit for their *careers*. So many things went through my mind: why couldn't I just have changed that grade and kept my job? That's probably what most people would have done and rationalized their actions. Who would hire me if the college didn't give me a good reference? What would I tell my mother, who would go ballistic when she found out that I had given up a job because of a principle? I could just hear her sighing and blaming, "What are you going to do? You are killing me," that common response I was accustomed to.

Although I didn't have time to have much of a conversation with God about the moment, I had talked with Him previously enough to know what He would have me do. I responded, "Sir, if you will give me an honest letter about the credibility of my teaching and other work here at the college, I will resign." The dean agreed. It was done.

Now what? Though I felt I had done the right thing for the Lord, what about for me? As I left that school, the first reactions that overcame me were anger, fear, and self-pity. But at least I wouldn't have to face that bunch again who had done me in and whose values obviously conflicted with my own.

It was nearing the end of the spring semester, so I had the summer anyway to discover what else I could do. Since I would not now have the chance to teach that summer, I had to do something. I had bills to pay, so I didn't have that long to wallow in pity. So the next week I went straight to a neighborhood donut shop, filled out an application and found myself donning a uniform and hair net and frying and selling donuts for $2.00 an hour. There is no way to describe my mother's embarrassment and outrage at my actions, so I won't.

Since this job required absolutely no brain power, I had time to think, to ponder my next move. I continued to pray that God would somehow give me some direction. One of the reasons I had returned from a teaching job in North Carolina to Tennessee was to have an opportunity to work on my doctorate at the University of Tennessee. But one day after I had just fried and sold one too many donuts, I got an idea. Why not try Vanderbilt or Peabody? This would get me out of the proximity of my parents, and it might open up doors for me that a state university might not. I really didn't think I had much of a shot, because even though I had had high marks from my undergraduate and graduate work, they were from a state university and I knew the stereotypes private universities often held about state colleges and universities. Still, the thought grabbed my attention. Was it generated by God? Maybe.

So I wrote the English Department chairman at Vanderbilt who actually granted me an interview! The professor was as I had imagined: feet propped on desk (never rising even to greet me), smoking a pipe, wearing a wool jacket with suede patches on the elbows, glasses on the end of his nose, talking to me without ever directly looking at me in the eye. He asked me in a loud, condescending tone why I thought I wanted to come here and why I thought I could make the grade. I found myself looking down at my plain dress, wondering what indeed I *was* doing here. I wasn't at all "hippified" and contemporary looking enough to match the other students I saw out of the professor's office window. Nor did I look particularly academic either. The professor probably thought I was a country bumpkin who would not make it here, and that he was probably doing me a favor by forcing an answer. Rather sheepishly I replied that I wanted to gain depth in my teaching skills both in content and technique and I believed that my undergraduate and graduate work had been demanding enough to lay a solid base. After hearing some spiel about how different private colleges were from state colleges, I thanked the professor for his time and left, believing that this would be the last time I would see him or the school.

Three weeks later I got a shock when I went to my mailbox. A letter came offering me a teaching assistantship at the university. There must be some mistake. Not only did I get accepted, but my tuition would be paid for! I knew right away that God had a hand in this. I didn't know whether the action had resulted from another faculty member hearing about my situation with the dean and recommending me for a fellowship, or whether this was one of a number of charity cases the university was required to hand out, or something else. It didn't matter. All I knew was that it was a miracle and that there appeared to be a direct relationship between my doing the right thing and this event.

The second test for me occurred at a church-affiliated college in Nashville, where I began teaching immediately after receiving my doctorate. Again I was an assistant professor of English where I coordinated the freshman writing program and taught Milton and survey British literature courses. I had been teaching there four years, had served two terms on the President's Council and had been a member of the Accreditation Board. Although along the way some remarked that I expected too much from students, I was determined to not let the increasing slide of standards nationwide infect *this* college. And my students' evaluations remained high, despite my so-called rigorous expectations. So in spite of the fact that I didn't quite fit the mold of the other female teachers, almost all of them married with families, and I was often the gadfly on committees, I had garnered respect from both faculty and students.

In those days, after four years of full time teaching, a professor would generally be eligible for tenure, barring any malfeasance. One event occurred, however, which kept me from getting it. The chairman of the English Department was an attractive soft-spoken married man with two small girls and a deacon in a local church of the same denomination as the college. He was known to be the "fair-haired" son of the administration. With his office right across the hall from mine, I couldn't help but notice frequent closed door sessions with his female students, and though there had been a few rumors, I tried to ignore them. One day, however, I came to know that the rumors were true.

I was working late in my office, and because I was so intently focused on finishing an exam I was giving the following day, I hadn't realized the chairman was still in his office. He came to the entrance to my door, and I stood up and greeted him. After a little idle chit-chat, I told him I was about ready to leave just as soon as I finished this exam, thinking this might motivate him to leave my office. He was always a little disarming to me, partly because of these closed-door sessions with his students, partly because once or twice he had made what most would probably have viewed in those days as an innocent remark or gesture. But they had been personal questions I wasn't comfortable with and once or twice he had put his arm around my shoulders as we walked down the hall to meetings, in what he wanted me to think of as a "friendly," supportive way. While occasionally I had also observed him also putting his arm around a couple of my female colleagues, they were at least 30 years my senior, married, grandparents, and tenured, so it didn't seem like the same thing.

After this small talk, there was this pregnant pause. He moved around to my side of the desk, and I quickly began talking about nothing really, just talking, and shuffling my papers. He took my arm, and I squirmed a little, but I didn't really know what to do because he was my boss. I didn't want to say I had to go, for fear he would offer to walk me out, and then I would really be more vulnerable. So I just stood there. Suddenly, he put his hands on my shoulders and tried to kiss me. I tried to fake a cough to detract from my resistance, but it was clear that he had been rebuffed.

Well, no harm done, I tried to think. But deep down inside, I knew he felt he had been rejected, and I would have to pay for that one way or the other. After all, he was a favorite son and in league with the administration. Sure enough, my performance appraisals (which were always subjective) began to be lower, with each succeeding semester, from no apparent reason. This gave the chairman the documentation he needed to avoid recommending me for tenure, and so I didn't get it. In those days, failure to get tenure usually ended up in some sort of termination. While I wasn't "fired," my contract wasn't renewed, the reason being "over staffing." This of course was not the reason because the nephew of one of the influential teachers in the school needed a job, and having only a master's degree and no previous college teaching experience, he was hired in the fall semester to replace me.

I was devastated once again. It appeared that I was forever being punished for doing the right thing. I hired an attorney, who later became a United States Senator, but even he didn't succeed in getting them to reverse their decision, so he and I decided it would be better just to move on, if the administration would be honest about my teaching and work. They were, and I did. After all, I did have four degrees and years of experience, so I felt I wouldn't have a problem getting other employment. I was wrong. Virtually every company I interviewed with either perceived that teaching was not working in the "real world," or that I was "over qualified." So here I was, in a bit of a fix, and the only thing I knew to do after considerable number of these rejections was to do some consulting, at least long enough until I could again discover some "real work," which, hopefully, would be soon. I began conducting writing seminars for accountants, engineers and other adults who had not been prepared to write for "after college" assignments. In those days I had virtually no competition, and so I soon expanded the scope of the work to include training on other communication skills, performance management, creating a high quality culture and selecting employees for such a culture. Though I had intended this work to be temporary, I obtained work in both the government and corporate world. Not including a brief hiatus with a major corporation, the work lasted until I began to intervene for my father, some 23 years after I began the small business. So a greater opportunity resulted from a wrong that was done to me. God had to have had a hand in this.

Maybe it was partly because my mother had been continuously fearful of losing money, jobs, and possessions that I was almost indifferent about them. And this indifference and failure to give these issues their proper weight vexed and even angered my family. But a bigger reason for their relative unimportance was that I believed that if you walked with God and used His standards, you really didn't have to live in fear. *You will walk...securely, and your foot will not stumble. When you lie down, you will not be afraid* (Proverbs 3:23 - 4).

Citizens of the Kingdom cherish what is old and still valuable in God's Covenant Kingdom, while they spread the good news of the new Kingdom way of life. Solomon was a great temporal ruler of Israel, which for a while prospered under his leadership in material wealth and political power, but then with Solomon's gradual move toward apostasy and immoral living, disaster and division came to his people. Eventually then there were 300 years of conflict. He had lost his moral authority.

I knew that it is only through living the values we espouse and in-the-field leadership that we can hope to have the right influence on others. Paul told us to do one thing he knew he must do: *forgetting those things which are behind, and reaching forth unto those things which are before, I press toward the mark for the prize of the high calling of God in Christ Jesus....*(Philippians 4:13).

TRYING TO FOLLOW GOD IN CORPORATE AMERICA

I knew that Christians have to choose who will control their lives. Will the *big* boss be the "earthly" boss, or will the master be God? By setting the love of God and the pursuit of wealth at opposite ends, Jesus set the stage for a stark decision.

After beginning my new business, one of the first clients I called on to "sell" my services to was a major component of General Electric, which included plants in California, New Jersey, Kentucky, and Tennessee. While I was talking with the Employee Relations manager about the benefits of communications and leadership training, I became gradually aware that the focus had shifted. The manager began talking about the merits of *this* particular component and how there might be more of an opportunity for me than just conducting a few seminars. Ultimately he convinced me to work there full-time as a subsection manager whose primary job would be to conduct management training. The benefits were good, and the job sounded right down my alley.

As of that date, there were no women managers in this component of GE, but that didn't concern me, and I found myself becoming excited about the possibility of making a difference at a time when the bureaucracy and "cubicle" functionality of American corporations had produced a serious negative impact on the quality of products. By the early 1980s, managers had pretty much removed themselves from the product and were managing by charts and graphs, not "walking the floor." Workers in the plants saw them as uninvolved and disinterested in both them and the products. Add to that the short-term numbers orientation of Wall Street, too many layers between the front line and senior management, and finally the segmentation of the employees, and you come up with a formula for low quality products. I became convinced that the organizational structure, the habits, the leadership, in effect, the overall culture, had a significant effect on the overall quality. I just knew I could effect a change in this, so I took the job and put my consulting on hold.

Up until this point, the ER Department had mostly been about "ice cream socials" and benefits meetings. If there was training at all, it was done at the corporate level, and it was primarily product training. Consequently, for several months I did little more than run after donuts for "birthday meetings" and line up the cream and sugar when the VIPs came to town. These activities were fillers and required no brain power. But I had once sold donuts, so I could wait on significant assignments. One finally came along. I was given the responsibility for assimilating data from the *Employee Attitude Survey* which employees throughout the component responded to each year and then making recommendations for training based on their responses. This survey had to do with questions regarding management practices, including communication, appraisal of work, getting enough information to do their jobs, and trust development.

Typical statements which were to be rated were: "I feel free to differ with my manager," "I feel there is sufficient effort to get the thinking and opinions of the people who work here," "I feel I get enough information from management on what's going on in the company," and "How do you feel promotions are handled in the company?" These surveys can do one of two things: give employees the opportunity to candidly express their feelings about their jobs or test their willingness, when confronted with leading questions, to supply the answers management wants to see.

Since I had come to GE from the outside (and from academia at that) I had worked hard during the past several months to gain the trust of employees, particularly those at the plants, and disprove their stereotype many had about PhDs. Already discovering some overall distrust of management, I was determined that I could prove myself to them as trustworthy. The survey gave me a chance to do this.

I was shocked to see the results. The percentage of employees who felt that managers were candid with them and cared about their work was extremely low. Most felt they only found out about things after the fact and indicated they had to operate mostly with grapevine information. Many also felt that the managers didn't care about their ideas on how things should go, and virtually none of the employees ever felt free to differ with their managers! The rest of the questions revealed similar results. The communication was hampered from bureaucracy and functionality, similar to stovepipes today within many government agencies and some corporations which prevent horizontal communication.

I was concerned about how to write up the results so as not to inflame my boss, having learned that he was insecure in his position because he had been "booted up" from manufacturing for failing to perform his job there and was distrusted by virtually everyone in the component. It was also rumored that he was a "foot soldier" for the component's manager and that's how he kept his job in Employee Relations. Thus I did not relish the prospect of informing him of the results, but I knew I must be candid. So I grouped the questions under specific categories such as communication practices, trust, and concern about product, made my recommendations, and hoped for the best. At least, I thought this might provide me an opportunity and a basis for writing and conducting some management training, creating more value for the ER department in the eyes of both employees and managers.

When I took the report in to the manager, he scanned it, shaking his head from side to side. Maybe he, too, was shocked about the results, although I couldn't imagine how they could have changed dramatically in one year.

Anyway, I sat there while he perused it. He looked up at me and hissed, "You will not go to print with that!" Taken aback, I suggested that I might rewrite the recommendations. "You don't seem to get it, do you?" He showed me a corporate blueprint and demanded that I imitate it. "But sir, what about *these* data? I don't believe that I can do a responsible job and keep our trust with the employees if I merely copy last year's report." Last year's report, I learned, was sugar coated, and the real data had been obscured. "Then, if you can't, I'll have to do your work for you."

I was stunned. I knew he had triggered various complaints from employees about forced early retirement issues. When an employee came to be about 55 years old, his performance appraisal scores tended to go down, and then this ER manager used them as a basis for "encouraging" that employee to take early retirement. I also knew that the plants had no use for him. I was not in that age group, but I myself had experienced some of his ire when I had spoken up about a couple of issues which I felt compromised the integrity of the Employee Relations Department. But never anything this drastic. I immediately thought back to the situation at the community college when the student had failed because he hadn't done the work, and the dean forced me into resigning. Was my manager considering my response insubordination and was resigning what he was expecting me to do? Was I being set up?

This time I thought it best to at least think about this scenario and consult an attorney. After all, I was recruited from my consulting business to this job, I had no other work, and I had no trust that this man would give me an honest evaluation of my performance should I resign. So I responded, "Mr. Stump, I'll try again tonight to turn in an acceptable report." I knew I wasn't going to change the data, but maybe I could bring myself to use the corporate blueprint.

The next day he ordered me into his office. I gave him the report. "Sir, I've tried to do what you told me to." A little later, he told his secretary to have me come to his office. Though he was just across the hall and I could hear him, he always sent the message through his secretary. "You have not done a responsible job, so I had to do your work for you," he sniped. Sarcastically he asked me if I thought I could fill in the blanks. I asked him what he meant, and he gave me ambiguous instructions. "I don't know if I can do that, since I don't exactly understand what you mean." "If you can't, then I won't need your services," he snapped as he jerked the material from me. Thinking he was finished, I rose to go, whereupon he instructed me to sit. "I'm not finished with you," he snarled. My heart was pounding, and my mouth was dry, but I silently prayed that God would keep me calm. I also prayed that I would be willing follow God's orders even if I wasn't sure where I was heading. By this time I knew the manager wanted me to change the data, and I also knew I simply couldn't do that.

Surprising myself with my assertiveness, I responded, "I feel there's something bigger here than a difference about an attitude survey, and maybe a third party would be helpful for us to resolve the issue." I was also amazed at how I could be so assertive with others and so totally intimidated by my own family. I watched the veins in his neck surface and his face turn red as he mocked my suggestion and declared that we didn't need anyone else. That smug insecurity of his was resurfacing.

I then asked if we could have the conversation later, since emotions were getting in the way, and again I rose to go. "SIT," he screamed as I stood there in disbelief. I was watching him turn into some sort of maniacal madman. I managed to shakily whisper that I wasn't accustomed to being talked to that way (Actually I had been talked to that way throughout my life by my mother, but not on a job) and could he please use a more civil tone and be less sarcastic. "PLEEASE sit," he sneered. I prayed that God would restrain my tears and show me a way to get through this. After all, I had a life-time of experience suppressing tears. I managed to by placing myself outside the moment and tuning out the whole incident. I responded in a numb monotone, saying that I would try one more time to write a report that he could accept. Experiences with my mother had helped me to be able to do this.

That evening my attorney recommended that I turn something in, however scant and shallow it might be, so as not to be labeled non-responsive, but not to lie about the data. This I did and was careful not to give any analysis as I had earlier done.

I turned in the report the following day to Mr. Stump, who declared that it wasn't a responsible report and that he again would have to do my job for me. Be that as it were, at least I couldn't be fired for insubordination and I had not lied about the employees' responses. By this time, however, my earlier notion that I was being set up had been confirmed.

Some difficult, awkward three weeks later, he and his associate called me into the office whereupon his associate informed me that my job had been restructured and that I would be placed on lack of work.

That was the trick for getting rid of employees who were deemed threatening. Those in charge would begin calling them "boat rockers" or non "team players." They knew they had no grounds which would stand up in court for getting rid of me, and this action would accomplish the same purpose.

I didn't know where I was going, but I was peaceful. Paul's statement in Philippians helped give me that peace: *whatsoever things are true, whatsoever things are honest, whatsoever things are just, whatsoever things are pure, whatsoever things are lovely, whatsoever things are of good report; if there be any virtue, and if there by any praise, think on these things* (4:8). Two years after this occurrence, this component was absorbed into another GE component.

I recognized that this real-life in-house experience within a large corporation added to my credibility with my training participants, and I ultimately gained considerable work as a result of remaining steadfast to my values. I knew that when Jesus told people to give up their possessions before they could follow him, He was doing more than just humbling the proud. God calls us away from our illusions about happiness and toward a radical dependence on Him.

By this time in my life I had received much confirmation that if you do the right thing, things will ultimately come out right. However, it has only been in the last two years that I have realized that the "right" end may not have been what I was seeking. Up until recently, I have questioned my earlier thinking, almost coming to the conclusion that it was only illusive hope.

At the least, the entire experience of fighting evil in a corporate giant would later give me the courage to go up against the evil in my own family. *I will seek that which was lost, and bring again that which was driven away, and will bind up that which was broken, and will strengthen that which was sick* (Ezekiekel 34:16).

CHAPTER 29

He that hath pity upon the poor lendeth unto the Lord; and that which he hath given will he pay him again.

—*Proverbs 19:17*

BATTLING FOR THE HELPLESS

D uring the times I struggled and battled for others throughout my life, naturally I had no way of knowing how they would eventually help me in the journey with my father. But I came to discover how they had indeed prepared me for this last battle of my life. My greatest pain was always others' pain, and this was what often confounded me in terms of responding to a higher agenda. Why was I destined to suffer so much for others? Obviously nothing touched my life without God's permission, and knowing this and believing that surely I would one day be free of others' pains in eternity helped me to endure them on this earth. In the meantime I realized I just couldn't resign myself to a life of depression. I had to continuously distinguish between constructive and destructive forces and always be on the lookout for where God was calling me to go. For some reason, it has been God's will for me to feel greater pain for others than was "normal." So be it. I came to accept the "rightness" of my unordinary journeys.

JUST A PATCH FOR THIS EYE, MS KATHRYN

Living on a teaching assistantship from Vanderbilt University during the early 1970s, I had to make do on $190 a month, plus a little savings I had stored away for graduate work. Somehow, though, I seemed to always manage to have enough to take care of my basic needs and even some for some elderly orphans.

One of these I met at a launderette one evening when I was waiting for my clothes to dry. He was an elderly, stooped-over man who was obviously having difficulty seeing. So I asked him if I could help. Not looking up, he shook his head and quietly said, "No thank you." When he dropped one of his towels on the floor, I picked it up and laid it on the table beside the rest of his clothes. He looked at me, and I could see that one eye was completely extracted. But he managed a thankful look out of the other one. "My name is Kathryn Huddleston." "I'm John Felts," he shyly responded. "I live just a couple of blocks away from here in a small efficiency apartment. Do you live nearby?" He nodded that he did. We ended up talking a little, and I discovered that he had walked to the launderette. "How about if I give you a lift home? I just live a block away from you." "Oh, no; I don't want to put you out; I walk here all the time." "Oh, I insist; it's no problem at all."

Here I was again, forever feeling compelled to become involved with the lives of total strangers who seemed helpless and who sometimes at first distrusted me since they weren't used to this kind of response. My friends were always asking me how I managed to *find these people.* To them it was a troublesome habit that I had, and I had never been able to convince them that it was something that I couldn't exactly help. I never considered it a virtue, or something I was doing for any kind of reward. At times, *I* even wondered why I just couldn't leave people to their own devices.

In any event, once I drove him to his apartment, I discovered why he hadn't wanted to accept my invitation to take him home. He was living in a basement one room apartment with a dirt floor and one exposed light bulb. The house was four-storied, and though old, it looked okay from the outside. I also came to discover later that his nephew, who was a deacon in one of the local churches, owned the house and was charging him sixty five dollars a month to live there. That was quite a lot of money in 1972.

Knowing where he lived was enough for me to become involved with his life. I discovered that his wife had died many years before and that he had no children. He received no food stamps and no welfare check.

As I began visiting him, I discovered a gentle, kind spirit, great humility and almost immunity to long suffering. It seemed that almost nobody recognized his existence. He was almost invisible. Ah, there's the key. Since I had always felt invisible myself to my family, I was drawn to others who were alienated and lost in space – or basements.

I became determined that he would no longer be alone. I must become his warrior.

Trying to get him into better housing was the first issue. We spent many hours sitting in the local welfare office, watching people drive up in fancy cars, asking the welfare counselors for second telephones and television sets. I managed to get him on several waiting lists for senior housing, but they were very long lists. In the meantime, I would just have to do what I could to make his life more comfortable.

There was a "meat and three" restaurant nearby, and every day I went there and purchased Mr. Felts and me a dinner meal. Many years later I wondered how in the world I managed to live on the meager money I was getting for my assistantship, but somehow I did. It was a little like Christ feeding the thousands with a few fish. It was also like trying to live on no income while taking care of my father many years later. Though I didn't have much money, I was determined that Mr. Felts would have a Christmas present. So I asked him what he would like to have. "Oh, nothing, Ms. Kathryn." With my usual persistence, I continued, "Mr. Felts, there's got to be something." "Well, I *would* like to have a patch for this eye." I could not believe my ears. No one had ever bothered to get him a patch for this eye, let alone glasses!

At night I lay awake and wondered how in the world anyone could be this rejected and alienated from the world's concern. There are no insignificant people in the eyes of God, but there are certainly insignificant ones in man's world. Mr. Felts got those glasses for Christmas. He also expressed a wish to go to the stock car races. And so it was off to the races we went. This had not exactly been a dream of mine, but there we were. Known to others by this time as the old man and the young girl, I found myself cheering on some stock car driver I had hardly heard of. Mr. Felts loved it, though, and I loved his joy.

All was going somewhat better for Mr. Felts, and then he became very ill with herpes rostra, the virus of the nerve.

I knew he couldn't stay in that horrible place where he lived; he needed a clean bed and a place to bathe. Since I had not been able to get him into senior housing for low-income people, there was only one choice: I must move him in with me. There wasn't time to worry about what my parents would think, or my friends. He must have some care. So I gave him my bedroom and I took the couch. Desperate situations demand drastic actions. It was a little awkward, but it was a dire situation because he was very ill. At least he had a clean bed, a bathroom where he could bathe, and food. He was resting better, and we were managing okay until I received a telephone call.

"This is John Felts. I understand you have my uncle at your house," came a threatening tone. Oh, dear, what in heaven's name would I say to this man? "Yes, sir...ah...he's here, but just for a little while until he's well enough to care for himself." I wanted to say, "You hypocrite, if you would give him some decent housing and some care, this phone call wouldn't be happening." But I didn't. "Well, he needs to get back to his own home." "Yes sir, but he's really not strong enough yet to do that. I'll take him back as soon as he's able." What could a deacon in a church say to that? He sputtered something, but I knew that I would soon have to get Mr. Felts back to his "home." It slightly resembled the phone calls many years later from my mother, demanding that I bring Daddy back home, even if he weren't well enough to travel.

He did go back, but shortly afterwards he had to have some surgery to correct some abdominal problem. In those days this particular teaching hospital had a reputation for treating the indigent as guinea pigs, and Mr. Felts' case was no exception. Mistakes were made during the surgical procedure which later became the culprit for a more serious illness.

After being dismissed from the hospital, I drove him home, only to discover that what little money he had lying on his dresser had been stolen. This was the last straw! I called the local newspaper and explained the situation. "We've got to have some help!" The editor was sympathetic and asked me if he could write a human interest story on this case. At first I said no, but then I agreed, if my name could be left out of it. The editor explained that I was a big part of the story, and that he felt I had to be a part of it for reader appeal. "Anything" I thought – just to get some help for this man. I was desperate to get him help.

The story ran, and immediately calls started coming in, people asking where they could make a donation. I was thrilled, and one of the businessmen who called offered to help me set up a trust for him at a nearby bank. One of the best calls came from an older man, Mr. Donnelly, who offered to share his modest home with Mr. Felts for a small fee. This was the miracle I had hoped for.

It was a wonderful situation for both Mr. Felts and Mr. Donnelly. Mr. Felts had a friend, besides me. I often visited the two men and realized that this was the best possible scenario. At least it was for a little while. A couple of months afterwards, Mr. Felts developed peritonitis from more medical mistakes. He became very ill and never recovered. I watched him deteriorate in the hospital, and was with him the night he died. Here was this frail little man, tubes coming in and going out of his thin, bony body, lying in a fetal position. But he knew me. "Mr. Felts, I love you." He winked at me with his good eye. And then he died. I seemed to always discover "these people" a little too late.

I had a tough time not becoming bitter with God. It seemed so unfair. Finally Mr. Felts had people in his life; he finally had some dignity; he finally knew he was loved. And then he died, before most of the trust fund could be used for his comfort. There were many parallels here of the final scenario with my father.

The great irony in all this was that most of the trust fund was used for his funeral, from which I was barred. Little did I know at the time that years later I wouldn't be allowed to sit with my own family at my grandmother's funeral or be able to attend my father's funeral because of similar circumstances. I slipped into the quiet grave side service anyway but had to hide from Mr. Felts' nephew and his nephew's wife. Of course, now it didn't matter. Only two people had signed the guest book supplied by the funeral home: the man who had helped me with the trust fund and the banker. But I knew *he* knew he was loved before he died. It was just too bad that I had not gotten to know him through most of his life. Maybe his resistance to disease would have been stronger. This was still yet another parallel and preparation for what I was to face years later during my father's last years and particularly his last days. The trials I had with Mr. Felts and his nephew gave me additional strength to navigate through the many struggles I somehow managed to get through with both parents.

ALECE AND TIMMY

While I was living in the small efficiency apartment, about the same time that I came to know Mr. Felts, I also became acquainted with a neighbor who was deaf. This young woman knocked on my door one day in tears. Little did I realize at the time that it was the beginning of a long saga which would become another preparation for my many trials with my mother and father.

I had only waved at the woman before, or had very brief conversations with her. On this day, tears streamed down her face, as I opened the storm door to her. "What in the world is the matter?" I asked, forgetting for the moment that she couldn't hear me. Alece began some gestures implying some sort of travail, and I invited her in. The young woman told me that she was pregnant, and that she had lost her key punch job at the Sunday School Board of a major denomination because of that pregnancy. During our "talk," I discovered that she had known the father of her unborn child but had not seen him again after her baby had been conceived. In typical fashion, I grabbed her hand and said, "Don't you worry; I'll fix this." Fix, indeed! Here I was again ready to save the world, when at times I could hardly save myself. But this appeared to be a double whammy.

I made an appointment with the Sunday School Board and pleaded Alece's case. Surely this Christian organization wouldn't *fire* this woman who had been employed there for years! As I looked at the polyester suited board members, with their lips pursed firmly together and giving a patronizing response to me, though, I began to wonder. They reminded me of the dean at the community college a few years earlier who forced me into resigning. "Surely if Christ had one quality that outshone all others, it was His compassion," I pleaded. "If she had been a 'bad' woman, she would have aborted this child," I continued. In spite of my appeal, the members ultimately did not relent and merely repeated that they had to let Alece go because her pregnancy was "bad for their image." "You can understand our position, Ms. Huddleston." No, I really couldn't understand it and said so. Neither did they allow Alece to have any maternity benefits since she was unmarried.

So that was that. I would just have to develop another plan.

Leaving the meeting disgusted, I was reminded of many churches which often seem to pander and cater to the comfortable members, those customers with more money and power. Many are far from the squalor and misery of the maimed and helpless. One difference between true Christian churches and nominal Christian ones is that those filled with true believers don't run from those whose plight might make them uncomfortable.

I discovered a family who had enough room that they were willing to take Alece into their home until the baby was born. What a wonderful blessing God had delivered for her and me! I helped her secure a job at the bank where I was a customer, and things seemed to be looking up.

I was with her when her son, Timmy, was born and helped them move into another apartment in the complex so she would have a little more room for her baby. She and I put a light on Timmy's crib so she could respond when he cried.

Things started to go downhill soon after that, however, because after the baby was born Alece was required to perform shift work that conflicted with her day-care hours. Things became rockier still when her elderly father died while Timmy was still just a baby. Alece's mother had died many years before that time of breast cancer, and there were no grandparents or any supportive relatives to help her. That left me to pick up the slack. I muttered aloud, "Why, Lord, do I always have to get involved with people who shouldn't concern me? Why can't I push them out of my head like normal people do?"

It was at this time that I came to know Alece's aunt, a mean-spirited, greedy controlling woman who had earlier insisted that Alece abort her baby and then, using the "incompetence" argument, tried to have the baby taken away from her *after* he was born. "She has no business having this baby," she had insisted to me over the phone. Her cruel words reminded me of my aunt's resentment of me. I supported her decision to keep her baby and thus became the aunt's enemy. Since her father didn't leave a will, the aunt used the "incompetence" argument again to try to get control of the small house of Alece's father's and what little money he had in savings. I ended up getting an attorney who had known her father, and he helped her retain possession of her father's few assets at no legal cost. God always seemed to send angels to help my victims out. But of course my actions produced an eternal hatred from this aunt for me, as well as for Alece and Timmy. The aunt continued to be a thorn to all of us throughout her life. This battle with this greedy, controlling aunt was a preparation to help me later deal with my controlling greedy family.

I helped Alece get an interview for another key punch job with the U.S. Army Corps of Engineers, to which I myself had become a supplier. I knew the personnel officer, and I knew the Corps wanted to hire the disabled. It was a good-paying job. She was hired, and finally I could relax a little over the Alece-Timmy situation. Or so I thought.

However, the various stressful situations, including the battle with her aunt, the demands of a baby, and the loss of her father soon began to take their toll on Alece who became less able mentally and more paranoid. The paranoia and stress compelled her to want to move farther away from the downtown area, and I couldn't talk her out of it. She seemed to always think that being physically farther away from business and people would somehow decrease their impact on her. And she wanted to live in a duplex, which I didn't think would be as safe as an apartment. But Alece was stubborn, and a duplex it was, located some 15 miles from downtown Nashville, her place of employment.

Because she had wrecked her car and had to take the bus now to work, and because she had continuing challenges with day-care for her son, things actually became more difficult for her overall. Her attendance at work began dropping, and this was frustrating and embarrassing for me since I had persuaded the personnel officer that Alece was a fine conscientious worker who would always be at work and on time. She started exhibiting more signs of paranoia and insisted that a city policeman wanted to give her "dirty money," as she called it, and was leaving notes in her mail box, suggesting she perform certain favors for him. Thinking it could possibly be true, knowing the reputation of some of the police in the city, I made an appointment with the Police Chief and told him of the incident. I identified the officer Alece had mentioned. The Police Chief listened but of course denied that this could possibly be true, as this particular officer was married and was a "fine, upstanding" officer. Once again, I had not succeeded in accomplishing much, but at least I had addressed the issue. And if it were true, the officer might be more reluctant to harass her in the future.

Noticing the increasing aggression in little Timmy, I knew I had to do something to ameliorate it. It suddenly hit me that this child didn't have anyone to talk with when he was upset nor could he develop language skills since one mainly learns to talk by imitating others. So I had a phone put in for them and taught him to dial my number. This was the way I taught him to talk. And after he learned to talk, he could phone me when he was upset and needed something. Today he is a successful radio announcer.

It was about this time that Alece began to communicate to me that the "government was bad" and that she didn't want to work there. Her mind was going downhill fast, and I didn't know what to do. Eventually she was released from her job at the Corps for poor attendance, and after drawing some unemployment, went to work for the State in the Department of Human Services at a salary considerably less than she was making at the Corps. By this time what little savings her father had were gone, and she had gotten so far behind on her rent that she was evicted from the duplex. I sent a couple of months' rent in but hadn't realized that there was so much more due. I simply couldn't come up with any more money because I was still a graduate student, working only part-time.

Once again I enlisted the support of my friends to help move Alece from the duplex to an apartment closer into town. The day of the move was cold and rainy. Her dining table got loose from my friends' truck and went flying off across the interstate. Oh help us Lord, I prayed. The "caravan" had to stop on the interstate, and we tried to load it back on, causing a traffic snarl, with cars and trucks blowing and drivers screaming at us. This was one of the few good pieces of furniture Alece had from her mother. It wasn't good any more, but maybe it could be repaired. In any event, there was nothing that could be done now except to get it back on the truck. Timmy and Alece were in the car with me, and Timmy was crying. My heater wasn't working. The whole scenario reminded me of migrant workers in John Steinbeck's *Grapes of Wrath*. But the difficulty of this day gave me just more block of strength which I would need much later in having to deal with illogical and mentally ill people.

Finding other places to live became more difficult for a couple of reasons. When landlords checked with previous landlords, they found out that Alece was almost always late with her rent. Also, she had a baby, and she was deaf. These conditions didn't add up to her being an attractive tenant, so once again I found myself trying to sell my friend's benefits. "She's very smart and ethical, but she has just had a hard time since her father died," I told this new apartment manager. The manager rented her the apartment, probably more from thinking I was there to help if she needed help with rent money, than from compassion.

But the trends continued. Alece was always playing "catch up" financially since she almost always seemed to have spent her month's check by the *middle* of every month. There simply wasn't enough money to meet her basic bills. When she had a little extra money, she bought trinkets. I understood why; they made her feel better for a little while. Just about every other year she was moving to a different place, since she would become so far behind on her rent and would think that another place would be the answer. I tried to convince her that each time she moved she lost money, since deposits had to be paid. But that point didn't sink in because I was usually the one who paid them. I also helped all I could with other bills, but I often had to ask the utility companies for adjustments on her bills. Still it was never enough. I tried to make frequent visits to see her and her son, and I always brought them food because they didn't seem to ever have much in the refrigerator. Alece was very proud, and I couldn't talk her into applying for food stamps, although she was eligible. Sometimes I wondered what she would do if I weren't around. Ironically, as in often the case when someone grows more and more dependent on someone else, with each additional help from me, her resentment of me seemed to increase. She had become jealous of Timmy's relationship with me. At one point she had written me, "Take Tim. I can't help him. He can live with you."

There were other problems and challenges as time went along. Timmy was now seven, and he had never had a male figure in his life. I determined that he needed some adult male companionship, and so I sought out the "Buddies" organization. The social worker was kind and compassionate and put Timmy as a priority on their list, once she heard the story about him and his mother. The "buddy" was a wonderful young man, named Russell, and married to an equally fine young woman, both of whom were terrific to Timmy. He and his wife lived in a nice, safe part of the city, were religious, and the young man's parents treated Timmy as well as their son did. Timmy said their house "looked like the White House." He took Timmy to ball games, movies, and restaurants. Timmy loved him. And then, one rainy New Years Eve, about a year and a half later, I received a horrible telephone call. Russell had been killed by a drunken driver! His wife Amy had to watch him burn up in the car. No, please God, no. I had to go to tell Timmy that his buddy was dead.

But there was actually a good result that came to Timmy from Russell's parents. They asked that their friends donate money to a trust fund for Timmy instead of flowers so that he might attend a private elementary school which had a reputation as a caring and academically sound school, a school where Timmy could get more individual attention. The school which he had been attending just wasn't adequately addressing his emotional and mental issues. Among other things, Timmy had an attention deficit disorder. This new school had a marvelous staff trained to provide better support for this challenge, and it would also provide him a place where he could feel valued. It would give him a way to rise above his circumstance. God had provided another marvelous blessing for Timmy, Alece, and me.

Once Timmy graduated from this school, he had to attend a public middle school, which proved to be a disaster. He was placed in "Special Ed" because he "talked in class," and wasn't allowed to mainstream any of his courses, despite my numerous phone calls to the school. Of course he talked in class; who else was he going to talk with? This action had produced such depression in him that he stopped going to class all together. Clearly, this behavior was resulting in part from the contrast between this "preppy" monochromatic school and the one which he loved so much during his elementary years where his teachers had been caring and attentive to his special needs.

Having received no positive response from my phone calls, I asked for a meeting with school personnel, thinking I could better persuade them in person. I met with the principal, Timmy's special education teacher, and the school psychologist to urge "the team" just to give the boy the chance to be "normal." I had taken a folder of Timmy's work to show them. I was convinced that this would give him the encouragement to improve both his attendance and his work.

Just as I had pleaded his mother's case at the Sunday School Board years before, and my pleas had fallen on deaf ears because of political pressure, the same thing happened with Timmy's case. They refused to look at the folder, and they continued to disallow him to mainstream any of his courses. It reminded me slightly of the time in the dean's office when the dean wouldn't look at my students' folders because the decision had already been made. In fact, I probably insulted Timmy's "team," since "special education" was their livelihood and, I came to learn, a "political hot potato." This was my first awareness of what a political racket it had become and that to drop any student was risky to the program's security. The psychological impact on the student didn't seem to matter at all. I wondered if my meeting did more harm than good because after this Timmy frequently had to stay in the "mobile units" because he had been "disruptive." Or he was being disciplined in some other way. He was accused of stealing another student's jacket. I realized he in fact may have done this since the conditions at school coupled with his home situation had produced such hostility and aggressiveness that Timmy was becoming destructive to himself and to his mother. Now *he* had wrecked their car. Something again had to change for Timmy to have an acceptable outlet to release much of the suppressed rage.

So I made an appointment with the principal of a private church-supported high school, which was touted to be caring and to demonstrate compassion for emotionally challenged students. Many of the students' emotional difficulties stemmed from various difficult home situations. Ultimately, I was able to get Timmy a partial scholarship, and I paid the rest of his tuition. God had provided yet another blessing for us.

The school turned out to be a wonderful experience for a couple of years. It stressed empowerment of students, and the teachers made Timmy feel valuable again. In that way it was similar to the elementary school he had earlier attended. He had a starring role in one of the school's plays, and I drove from a work assignment in Cincinnati to Nashville that night in order to watch his performance. I had raced to his mother's and picked her up so she could also go. We made it just in time. Timmy grinned from ear to ear when we walked into the auditorium. That was when he began introducing me as his godmother. Actually I wasn't, but that was okay. To him I was someone he perceived as "normal" (which was ironic since almost no one else did) whom he could claim around his friends. I was always quick though to introduce them to his real mom.

After several years, stresses on the home front resulted in yet another downslide for Timmy, and he dropped out of high school. Determined to become more assertive with him, if he were ever going to develop emotionally and mentally, I knew I must move him into my place on a temporary basis. But this time I set standards and rules. If he weren't going back to school, he was going to get his G.E.D. This was not negotiable. Giving him the basement floor of my condo where I had had my office, I made him study and monitored him as much as possible. He ended up getting it.

Things improved for a while, but eventually his mom once again fell behind on her rent, and before I knew what was happening, Alece had moved into a slummy duplex, run by a slummy landlord. I later discovered that she had declared Chapter 11 in order to get some of her back bills forgiven, and this consequently was one of the few places which she could get into. It was one of those places which accepted people who had bad credit, so the tenants had to pay for the consideration by having to endure poor construction, broken window panes, loud noises from tenants and an outrageous price for a junky place to live. Old broken down cars, towels hanging from the doors, and aluminum foil taped over the windows told the story.

Alece and Timmy had lived there about a year when I discovered that Timmy did not have a bed. He had been sleeping on the floor since they had moved into this place! How could I possibly have overlooked this? Though I had less opportunity to visit them with my work's travel demands and had mainly focused on helping them have enough food and rent money, there was still no excuse for this oversight. I quickly bought him a bed.

Then a couple of years after they moved there, Alece discovered she had breast cancer. "Oh, God, why oh why can't these people get a break? Is this saga never going to end? They are tired, and I am tired. Please help us," I prayed. It seemed like only yesterday that she had to have her thyroid removed and then had developed a terrible case of carpel tunnel syndrome. She had just received the diagnosis when I received a voice message from Alece's landlord about her being two months behind on her rent. He was going to evict her. Not again! This threw me since for the past several years, I had frequently asked Timmy how they were doing with their rent, and he would say fine, as far as he knew. I concluded that Timmy's past had resulted in him being very good at denial and having an almost cavalier attitude. He was not going to stay in that quick sand with his mother any longer. He had learned to distance himself from her problems in order to survive himself. I couldn't blame him.

I was on a work assignment in Dallas at the time, but quickly telephoned the landlord and said that I would send him a check for a month and would get help for the other one if he would give her a little time. He agreed.

When I returned home, I telephoned the minister of a church in the city which had a large deaf congregation to talk with him about Alece's plight. The minister was cooperative and offered to help. As it turned out, he discovered that Alece *had*, in fact, been paying her rent because when he visited her, she showed him her cancelled checks for the rent. So the landlord was double dipping! I confronted the landlord with my discovery. He mumbled something about a "mix up" and quickly forgave any "outstanding" bills.

All of this resulted in a final good because the incident prompted me to telephone my friend who owned various duplexes in the city, telling him that I just had to have his help. This was the St. James of the "Do Nothing Club" who later interacted with Daddy. He had met Timmy and had been impressed with his manners and countenance, and he told me that he would help them. He had a vacant duplex in a safe part of the city, and we rented it. Helping them move this time, I had more peace because it was my friend who would be their landlord. He didn't require a deposit and assured them he wouldn't go up on the rent for at least a couple of years. Timmy would now have a respectable address, and I hoped that with a little new furniture, he would feel more encouraged to have friends over. Though he was in some denial about his mother's cancer, he was actually scared to death and inwardly distraught. Both the place and the new furniture seemed to make him feel better.

Though I was able to take Alece to some of her cancer treatments, my travel schedule prevented me from being able to drive her to all of them. So I was blessed to discover the "Road to Recovery" program, which provided transportation when I was out of town. During this same period, I was finally able to secure the needed documentation for disability from her state government job, even though she was reluctant about sharing any of her medical information with me. She often said that I was being "nosey" when I tried to explain that the Social Security Office would not qualify her for this early retirement without it. The more hours I put in, the greater her resentment of me seemed to grow.

Throughout our long relationship, Alece's pride and resentment of Timmy's dependence on me kept her from disclosing their needs to me. So I usually managed to discover them from others, like school officials or medical personnel. Alece wrote, "I not ask you to help me," a response similar to that from my mother when I attempted to meet her many needs. I knew that Alece was mentally challenged, and I respected her pride, but I just couldn't allow her and Timmy to go hungry, homeless and without healthcare they needed. Ironically, her resentment of my help actually helped prepare me for the resentment my mother had of me many years later when I stepped up my efforts to help her and my father. Things really did *finally* improve for Alece and Timmy, and that was what really mattered, just as taking care of my father actually did help my mother. I certainly never expected any credit and I had come to realize that resentment just naturally comes with helping those who are extremely defensive about their neediness.

WATCHING OVER ONE WHO HAD WATCHED OVER ME

For fourteen years I lived in a townhouse in a nice section of Nashville. It was not a fancy place, but it was a secure place, thanks to its faithful security guard. Mr. Thomas Carter had been there before any of the residents. He had actually guarded the materials before the condominiums were built, and that was 27 years before. He was loyal, kind, and always willing to go beyond his job to help "his folks" out. He was territorial about his job, and this was a wonderful thing. He did extra favors for the eighty residents, like watching after their places when they were on vacation, taking their mail in, and in my case, actually saving my life at one point when I had a date with a man who became aggressive. He had worked seven days a week, and had never asked for a single night off. The board finally had to make him take a short vacation.

His job was monotonous and confining, and he had little opportunity for interaction. Thus when anyone came by the guard house window, he appreciated any conversation that person might have with him. Most of the residents were loyal to him as well.

But as is often the case with communal living, there are from time to time power battles going on for one reason or another, and they often are instigated by a handful of people. There was a certain middle-aged resident who had attended law school and at one time had been a local television celebrity. But since that time, he had suffered several business failures and had a much higher opinion of himself than most people had of him outside the condo community. Because he was charming and charismatic with the older women, he gained their support. He had for some time wanted to be rid of Mr. Carter.

The condominium community gave him a place where he could wield the power he never seemed to garner in his business life. He managed to get himself on the board by volunteering to fill in for a member who had to resign. And before the condominium community could turn around, he had volunteered himself for president of the board.

From that time forward, I had to stay one step ahead of him since most of the community didn't see plans underway to get rid of our faithful security guard.

As soon as he became president, he came to Mr. Carter and asked him to get his resume together, telling him that our community was having money problems and "we" were just going to have to let him go. Most of the residents were unaware of this, and the by-laws at that time gave the board extremely broad discretionary powers with regard to most financial matters.

The truth was that the community *was* in financial trouble, but it was not because of Mr. Carter. This board president began making unilateral decisions which were very costly, and before the residents realized what was going on, the reserves dwindled to a risky level.

Thus, the president had an excuse to begin pushing to get rid of Mr. Carter. I knew the only way to save this complex from bankruptcy and from losing its most valued asset was to change the by-laws such that major financial decisions, including security, had to have a majority of the homeowners' approval and could only be *proposed* by the board. I believed that once the board's power was reduced in this way, the president – and possibly others on the board – would resign. I put together an ad hoc committee to gain support for changing the by-laws, and at the next annual association meeting, the residents overwhelmingly approved this change. The meeting went as I anticipated; once the president saw his power reduced, he resigned, and the rest of the board followed suit. It had taken almost a year to accomplish the committee's purpose, but it was worth it. The people gained control of their homes, and Mr. Carter's job was saved.

From time to time, I still found myself advocating more money for him. After 27 years, his hourly wage was actually less than the temporary guards that were hired after Mr. Carter became terminally ill. Responses sometimes took the form of, "What does he do?" "He only sits in the guard house." These sounded remarkably like my mother's statements about my father in earlier times. Precisely, I thought, as I reiterated to some of the residents that monotonous, routine jobs – especially those spent in isolation – are some of the most difficult jobs on the nerves. I wondered how many of them would be willing to work seven days a week in that environment.

Occasionally rumblings occurred from time to time to again get rid of him, but nothing came of them. Although eventually the original ring leader who had wanted him removed made his way back to the board, he seemed to have mellowed about Mr. Carter, finally having been convinced that this "home" and "family" were just about all he had.

I moved from the complex after I began seeing some compassion from this board president. I had wanted to move before but was fearful that if I did, Mr. Carter would have no advocate. Finally I felt compelled to shift residences because I thought I might have the care of one or both of my parents, and the condo I lived in had two flights of stairs which my father couldn't navigate because of his heart condition.

Before I left, I knew that Mr. Carter wasn't well. He told me he had some kind of virus and said the doctors thought it was hepatitis. He was looking frail, and I was concerned, but I had already purchased a house by the time I realized what the real story was. Mr. Carter had pancreatic cancer. He told me the day before I left that with me gone, he would be gone soon too. I assumed he meant because he was losing his "champion." He did mean that, but he was also referring to his pancreatic cancer, which I didn't know about when I moved.

The body deteriorates very fast with this type of cancer, and his was inoperable. Since the doctors had first missed the true diagnosis, it quickly became so wide-spread that there was little that could be done. Although my new home was just a short distance away, I felt guilty about leaving him, particularly with his illness. Therefore, at least twice a week, I took him supper and visited with him in his little guard house. I spent Christmas Eve with him there, and we shared many stories about the community over the years he had been there. Some I knew already; some I didn't. It reminds me now of that night my father and I had later spent at the hospital, feeling safe under the blanket of falling snow, with no one telling us what to do or be, just he and I together, like Mr. Carter and me.

I determined that my interest in him would not subside, and as I observed his health rapidly deteriorate, I began to go see him every evening. He had lost so much weight and had become so frail. After his chemotherapy sessions began, he continued to come to work after every treatment. He didn't miss a day of work, but he was barely there. Sometimes I would get to his little guard house, only to find him slumped in his chair asleep. Because none of the boards had ever provided him benefits (medical insurance, retirements, or disability), I helped put together a surprise party for his 27th anniversary at the complex. Collecting a goodly sum for his money tree, I telephoned people to come who had since moved away but who I knew would want to be there. Even the man who had worked to remove him years before asked me to make the presentation. Perhaps because he knew Mr. Carter was not long for this world, that board president began to act kindly towards him, urging him not to feel he had to stay all night on his job, and to go home and rest. He also began to respond kindly to me.

I didn't know a great deal about Mr. Carter's personal life, except that he had a brother whom he hadn't seen in five years (who lived within 150 miles of him) and a daughter in Florida whom he hadn't seen in many more. He had grandchildren he had never seen. I thought this was so tragic and couldn't imagine how a family could estrange themselves from this gentle and wonderful man. I tried not to pry since my own family situation wasn't too dissimilar even at this point. After a while I figured out that the relationship or lack of relationship between him and his family must have had something to do with his present wife whom he had married after his first wife's death. Years later I would see great parallels between this man's estrangement and manipulation and my own father's life, yet another preparation for my final battle to rescue Daddy.

His wife was considerably younger than him and emotionally unstable – or this was his excuse for her behavior. She had left him from time to time during her "mood swings." Rumor was that she left because she had a man friend with whom she stayed off and on and used the "mood swings" as an excuse, though she was not very bright or attractive. I had seen her a few times at the guard house, a heavy woman, with tight polyester pants, tank top, and a cigarette hanging from her mouth. When I lived there, I could always tell from Mr. Carter's countenance when she had left him, and I always tried to have a little extra conversation with him during those times. As I look back now, I find it truly amazing about the similarities between Mr. Carter's situation with his wife and my own family.

It was only during the past two years of Mr. Carter's life that I came to learn a good deal more about his wife. She had spent about everything Mr. Carter made on herself. Although he always made excuses for her (just as my father earlier in my life had made excuses for my mother), I came to discover she either didn't know how to or wouldn't cook for him. So that was when I began more frequently taking him meals.

He told me his wife wanted to move out to the country, some distance from the place where they lived and about 30 miles from his work. I was concerned about this move because he would be farther away from his medical treatments and he would have to drive farther to work. I came to understand differently, however. He was preparing to die, and he wanted his wife to have a new beginning. He always felt he had to take care of her, just like Daddy felt he had to take care of Mother. He *seemed* at first to want to move there too, as he said it was peaceful there. But later I came to believe that he was mainly echoing his wife's desire, much as my father echoed my mother's desires. In any event, I rented a U-Haul truck and asked Timmy, the young man to whom I had played "mom" over the years, and his friend to help me move Mr. Carter.

That was a sad and frustrating day. Arriving there early, my "cavalry" and I expected his wife to have everything ready to go. Nothing was ready. Bed linens were still on the bed; dishes were not packed. Nothing had been done.

At this point Mr. Carter was so weak that he really couldn't lift anything himself, though he tried. He had always been so proud of his physical prowess, bench pressing hundreds of pounds even at 70 years old. He continued to tell me about working out and that he knew he was going to beat this cancer. He told me that people at a church he had attended had laid hands on him. These words mocked his frail image. Later the courage of my little frail father would remind me of Mr. Carter.

Eventually "Kathryn and Company" got the junky furniture into the U-Haul and into my car, and off we went to the country. The "country cottage" ended up being a single-sided mobile home which had little room for this old furniture since his wife had purchased new dining room furniture and a new television set with money from the money tree at his anniversary party. It all hit me at once. This was *her* scheme to begin "chapter two" of *her* life.

Shortly after the move, Mr. Carter had a car accident and totaled his car. I knew then that the end was near. Not so much because of physical injuries sustained, but he had been so proud of his car. I wondered if the accident were deliberate to get insurance money so his wife would have burial funds.

I visited Mr. Carter the afternoon of his death. He lay there, non-complaining as always, but looking almost lifeless, like a little skeleton. I knew I had to talk to him and tell him how important he had been to our community, and how brave he was now. I read the 23rd Psalm to him and prayed for him. I choked on the words. He thanked me, and he died at midnight that night. As I looked back on that sequence of events with Mr. Carter, I realized it was one more preparation God was giving me to deal with the events surrounding the death of my father.

Even then I had begun to realize it was a part of my calling to love the unloved, to try to heal the bruised, and to feed the hungry. I seemed to find myself always taking up the cause of the helpless because they lacked the ability and power to take it up themselves. Perhaps this was far more important than any training business or political involvement.

A UNIQUE LIFE

My mother often expressed outrage, my friends stayed bewildered, and my church associates admonished me for trying to get to heaven on good deeds. I never saw them as such and was provoked when others called them that. I couldn't help my compulsion, so I just obliquely smiled at my friends. I have just been unable to ignore the plights of helpless and unloved people. Perhaps it was an unconditional love, which might account for my later effort and involvement with a father whom I had hardly known growing up.

For much of my early adult life, I could never exactly understand why I was born into the family I was or why circumstances which happened to me rarely ever happened to others, at least not in the same volume or intensity. I had to constantly counter questions and exasperated sighs from others, such as: "When are you going to get on with your life?" "You can't save the world," and "Why bother? They didn't raise you." I had learned in the last few years that my life was as it was meant to be, maybe not like anybody else's, but like God had meant it to be. Had I been dealt a different hand and had had my own family, I would not have had the time and energy to take care of those who had no one else.

Learning fairly early on that you must continuously respond to a higher agenda, I knew that you can't wait for the crisis to erupt to start praying and preparing. You must make every day as if it's the last day you have on this earth. You have to be discerning and watchful for those signs which tell you that you are either off or on God's track. I had to continually remind myself that what came first in *my* life determined the God I would serve and believed that I couldn't totally love God and respond to Him except at the cost of myself.

Knowing that the Kingdom of God is beyond price enabled me to recon-cile competing dilemmas. I knew I could not allow anything to come between God and me, if I wanted to be a true disciple of Christ. I had to stand up for Jesus – not just in personal situations, but in jobs as well.

For years following my father's death, I had to make more of an effort to cling to this admonition because of continuing personal struggles. As my faith in God's caring for me waned, I prayed hard that God wouldn't label me as "unclaimed baggage" when I got to heaven's door, as I was so labeled by my family. Only during the past two years, He has given me a glimmer of hope that He may indeed claim me by placing others again in my path who have had no one else to help them climb their mountains or push through their storms.

PART IV

STORM ENDS...RED SKY BEGINS

I had fought for years to keep my father out of a facility and to try to take care of him at my home because I was convinced I could give him a higher quality of life. In the beginning, I was mainly concerned about assisting a helpless elderly person recover a little of his dignity and make up for what he had been denied throughout most of his life. By the beginning of the fifth year, though, I felt I was actually taking care of my *father*. The path had become rockier because my father's aorta had become more constricted, and consequently, the oxygen was having a more difficult time getting to his brain. During that year there were several incidents when I thought he was dying, and I actually half-way hoped he was because I wanted so much for him to be free of physical pain and confusion. I wanted him to be in heaven where he would not ever again have to worry about anyone. But he did not die, because God had more to reveal to me, and Daddy had more to tell me. Yes, that's right; he had more to *tell* me.

But there did come a time when death *was* near, although no one realized it, including me. There has been much written about the role of social workers, in-home health aides, and companion services in the final phase of an Alzheimer's patient's life. I didn't have the luxury of any of these, but only a couple of people to help me during the last weeks of Daddy's life. It was no one's fault. I really had not comprehended until then that his life was actually coming to an end. It was as if Daddy and I refused to end our story we had created almost out of nothing. So we continued trying to do what we had always done. In fact, it was only three weeks prior to Daddy's death that he wanted to go to prayer meeting even though he wasn't feeling that well. And so we went. As it turned out, that was the last place he went, except to the Hospice facility the day before he died.

After I finally became convinced that my father was dying, I was partially relieved that his pain and suffering would soon be over, but I was also frustrated because we had unfinished business, unfulfilled wishes, and unexpressed love. In some way, I truly believe my father had these same feelings. He couldn't articulate them, but what few words he said and the way he looked at me suggested that these feelings were gnawing at him. He appeared to know his life was ending at last, and issues that had never been expressed seemed to come to the forefront of what mind he had left. As he moaned, half sleeping, half awake, I believe he may have been trying to reconcile unresolved feelings about me and my mother. And some of these feelings could have been quite frightening or disturbing. Was he regretting that he had not supported me earlier in his life? I did not want him to feel any regret, but the few words he uttered demonstrated that he wished he had resolved old hurts. I, too, was frustrated that just as I finally gained a father, he would soon be gone. It was too late for me to tell him how much I loved him and that I really now understood that he had done for me all that he was capable of. I wanted him to know that I forgave him for dismissing me, for echoing my mother through much of my life. I could only hope my actions during the past five years had assured him that I understood why he had done what he had.

But after he died, my pain did not end, as I thought it would. Clear images of the agonizing stages of my father's disease, especially those last days, surfaced daily. I still felt the anxiety, fears, helplessness, and even horror I had felt when my father was alive. Seven and a half years have now passed since his death, and finally the darkness is giving away to some passages of light because of other helpless and victimized people whom God has placed in my path, people who evidently have had no one else to help them through their own "storms."

CHAPTER 30

Therefore, my beloved brethren, be ye steadfast, unmovable, always abounding in the work of the Lord, forasmuch as ye know that your labor is not in vain in the Lord.
—2 Corinthians 4:18

WORSENING MIND, GROWING SPIRIT

It had been five years since I began intervening for my father to save what life he had left. I had finally become convinced during these years that my entire life had been a preparation for this saga with him. They had become the most significant ones in my life, and I had no doubt that God sent them to help enable my father to reconnect with Him and with me. I had come to realize that an unfair loss of work, resulting in a pre-determined contract decision, had actually rendered it possible for me to have this interaction with my father. Had I continued that work, there would have been no way I could have had this time with him. I could not have fought the battles, nor attended to his physical, psychological, and spiritual health.

In the beginning I had intervened for my father, not because he was my father, but because he was a helpless elderly person who had been victimized. During those days he had distrusted me, because all the other women in his life had controlled and taken advantage of him. As I reflected on those last five years prior to his death, I thought of the difference in the relationship I had with him at the end of those years and the relationship I had with him in the beginning. Then he had only known me through my mother's lenses. Since I had never had the opportunity to interact with him directly, he had naturally been suspicious of me.

It was only through time and caring for him directly that he came to see *what* I was. It didn't matter so much that he knew *who* I was; he came to see that I was not going to take advantage of him. It wasn't that he always recognized me as his daughter, but he did *recognize* me. During the last year and a half of his life, when he would first see me upon my arrival at my Mother's home, a big grin would break out. At the beginning of our journey, I felt I had to entreat him a little, by mentioning Cookeville, for him to come with me. After several years of interaction, as soon as I was in the house, when I asked him if he were ready to go, he quickly responded solidly, "Yes." He didn't seem to care where he was going – just that he was going with me. He didn't appear nearly as afraid of his wife. Whether this lessening of his fear was the result of realizing he was nearing the end of his life and he couldn't be hurt much more than he already had been, or whether he had learned that I would always fight for him, I couldn't know.

I, on the other hand, had come to see my father *as* my father, not just as a helpless victim whose property had been taken from him, and who had had his dignity stripped away. I had come to believe that God had planned this so I could give Daddy some value and self-worth that he had not received in his life since he was a young man, and in turn, I could finally have some family! Those in Cookeville and Nashville had viewed us as "father and daughter," and we went everywhere together.

I knew I had to develop trust between us, and it was only through direct interaction for extended periods of time and God's affirmation that I was able to do this.

The struggle to interact with Daddy for these longer times and take care of him never ended, because anything could set Mother off and change her mind about him staying with me. I came to believe that the only reason she began allowing me to keep Daddy at my home for longer periods was that I was the cheapest labor she could find. And saving money had become as important as having power and control over his life.

For the six months after Daddy was resuscitated, I had the opportunity to have him with me most of the time. Each time I drove to get him, he emphatically declared, "God bless you for coming after me" after we were in the car. Sometimes he thanked me all the way to Cookeville. While that was in a way gratifying, it was heart wrenching as well. He was still careful not to say anything negative about his wife, knowing he always had to return to her at some point, but it was what he didn't say and his tears that tore me apart. Inevitably, on the day I was to take him back to my mother's, he would become deeply depressed. Sometimes he just wouldn't get out of bed, and I had to telephone my mother, begging for permission to allow him to stay with me just a couple more days. I was careful not to give the real reason, but to fabricate some other excuse which would look like a benefit to her. Otherwise, I would receive the screaming response, "You have made him sick again" and the threat of my never getting the chance to take care of Daddy again.

Though I couldn't pinpoint exactly when or why it happened, slowly my father began to really enjoy coming to my home. Maybe it was because he began to feel safe and free.

By the fourth year into our journey, my skeletal conditions had worsened, so I had to begin driving less. During the first three years I had felt compelled to drive Daddy back to the town and country church he had grown up in, because I thought he would be more comfortable there. While he *had* continued to love going there because the people knew him and talked to him and thus there remained historical references, I came to discover that the actual place was less important than other elements in our journey.

THE IMPORTANCE OF TONE AND SPIRIT

By the fifth year of the Alzheimer's, it was the tone and spirit more than the place that was most important to Daddy. By this time I had been taking my father to my church in Nashville for over a year. It was here that members had been praying for us for a couple of years, and so they knew my father through me for longer than he had been attending. During the first times I took him there, he had entered the sanctuary of "that church," reticent, with his head down, since he was in an unfamiliar place and his self-esteem had become eroded. But by the beginning of the fifth year, he felt more comfortable. He had become an important participant.

So we continued our trips to Wednesday night prayer service. This seemed to be the event that made the most difference. It was a much smaller group, less formal, and my father by this time had begun interacting – in his own way – with the members. As various ones came up to him and spoke directly to him, he patted their arm and said, "I can see you're a good woman," or "You're a good fellow." The ministers spoke to him directly, as they would speak to any other man. And so did the senior minister's wife; she was outgoing, laughed easily, and was especially sensing. Regardless of what Daddy said, she just flowed with it and made it into some king of dialog. The service wasn't patronizing; it wasn't loud. It just had a friendly tone. By this time, the senior minister had begun making it a point to mention his presence to the others and how glad he was to see him.

After Daddy became more compatible with the group, he walked into the sanctuary with his head held up, and he would actually initiate some dialog with one or two of those present. He orally confirmed statements made by the minister. "That's right," he often declared, as the minister might make some application of the scripture. My father had become a part of the service. He belonged. During a taping of a Christian singer's CD there, my father had openly and enthusiastically said, "That's good!" This was the same CD I had played at Daddy's memorial service.

For some time his verbal responses had not been coming out the same way as his thoughts; he had considerable difficulty getting out orally what was in his head. But even within weeks of his death, he appeared to understand far more than he could articulate.

Though it must have been frustrating to Daddy, it didn't matter to the others present. They just went along with him and continued to treat him with respect and dignity.

By this time I had become totally convinced that one of the main reasons God had brought my father and me together during those years was so that my father could participate with God openly, not having to hide his relationship with Him. Previously, if he showed interest in *any* person or being above my mother, he had to suffer the consequences. There were so many unusual things which happened that couldn't be explained in any other way other than God residing in my father and helping us to stay connected.

On one particular Sunday morning service, I had occasion to speak about the interaction I had come to have with my father over the previous four years and my resultant blessings. Though my close friends in the congregation knew that my father had Alzheimer's, others didn't. So in order for my message about God residing in a person even after the brain becomes scrambled to make sense, I felt I needed to fill them in a bit on my father's "different" mind. Because I didn't want my father to be uncomfortable about any of my words, I thought it best to ask a friend of mine to keep him occupied in the nursery for a few minutes. I figured he would stay without me because he loved being with small children, and she was going to bring him up to the sanctuary afterwards. I was about half way through my message – and just about to the point where I was about to talk a little about this "different" mind – when I saw the door to the sanctuary slowly open. In walked my father – alone! I was so startled and my heart so affected that I just stopped speaking. I never mentioned how my father responded differently from other people to the same event. This moment was far more important than anything I could possibly have said. I stepped down from the pulpit, hugged him, took his hand, and led him to our seat. I discovered later that my friend could not convince him to stay with her, but she couldn't leave the children. So my father left on his own and evidently knew exactly where the sanctuary was in relationship to the nursery (which was even on a different floor), because he had come by himself. I thought what a demonstration of my message: God resides within a person and gives him direction on something really important even when the rational brain has ceased functioning. It reminded me of the time Daddy recognized me after many weeks of being away from him. I knew that God had directed that entire event. He dictated exactly how much I should say, and he led my father to me!

Even in the last phases of his Alzheimer's, where knowledge of place and time seem to disappear completely in most situations, it was different with church. He almost never took off his little flat wool cap anywhere else, but as soon as he and I were seated in the pew, he took it off and hung it on his little three-pronged cane I had purchased for him. He kept his reference for church and God until the end of his life. His spiritual self didn't diminish with the deterioration of his mind and body.

It was on a Wednesday night when my father and I were heading for prayer service that he stopped as we were getting out of the car. He seemed to gasp slightly, and I asked if he were okay. "I think so," he faintly replied. He rarely ever complained, and one just had to sense his discomfort. Because the church was undergoing renovation and the workmen's equipment was at the door closest to the sanctuary, my father and I had been forced to walk a little distance. As we got off the elevator, Daddy winced. "Oh," he groaned. "Daddy, Let's just stop here for a minute," I replied, trying to hide the anxiety in my voice. "Can you go on now? We're just a little ways from the sanctuary." "Okay," he replied weakly. Since the hall was one of the areas of our church being remodeled, there was no place to sit. "Daddy, we're almost at the sanctuary; just a little more distance and we'll be there." I tried to respond calmly, but I could hear tension creep into my voice, as I had heard these responses before. "Daddy, I guess we just overdid it a little this week." "I guess so," he whispered.

I was often conflicted between knowing whether to continue on with what we were doing, or reverse it and take him by the hospital to have him checked out. On this particular prayer meeting night, I chose to stay the course we were on. Later I was glad we did, because it was the last place Daddy went before he died.

We made it to the sanctuary, and I helped Daddy sit down near the entrance. He was clearly still quite uncomfortable. "Daddy, I'm going to go get you a cold rag for your head, okay? I'll be right back." There were already a few members there who knew my father. "Would you watch Daddy?" I whispered. They nodded that they would.

I raced to the closest restroom and wet a paper towel. I hurried back to the pew and held it to my father's head. By this time other members were coming into the sanctuary and were speaking to him. He tried hard to respond, but clearly he wasn't feeling well at all. I prayed, as I had so many times over the previous four years, "God, help me know what to do next." Remarkably, after a few minutes, when the pastor began the service, my father's heart seemed to settle down a bit. I noticed that his brow was not as wrinkled, and his overall discomfort had seemed to lessen. He appeared all right through the rest of the service, and remarkably, even tried to respond when the pastor gave the message.

Although I was breathing a small sigh of relief by the end of the service, as we walked back to the car, I realized that things *were* different. Daddy wasn't feeling well at all. His discomfort continued throughout the night. The next day, he was clearly weaker and didn't want to get out of bed. As the day wore on, he became more uncomfortable, and I felt I needed to take him to the ER.

Shortly after he was admitted, I checked my voice mail and my father's cousin had left word that Jenny Dillon, his sister, had died. Under other circumstances, this news would have been dramatic for me since this was the woman who had despised me throughout my life and who had so negatively impacted it. Her love of money and power had also made her appear to hate my father. But after taking Daddy to see her for a couple of years by this time, the effect wasn't what it might otherwise have been. In fact, the last time we saw her in the nursing home, I only pitied her, since she clearly was close to death, and I was concerned she had not accepted the Lord. How tragic and frightening it must be for people who have refused to accept and obey the Lord their whole lives and then to lose their minds so they are not then able to. Conversely, the Bible teaches us that the spirit can intercede for the mind, and since Daddy had always known the Lord, his spiritual self remained intact until the end of his life, in spite of his mental loss.

I decided not to tell my father this news, until the medical staff had assessed his heart condition.

My own heart was racing. I was to have returned my father to my mother's home the following day. Why did my father always become sicker when I was to drive him back to my mother's home? I couldn't help but believe that knowing he had to go back to her added stress to his heart. There were continuous dilemmas about how to keep him with me when he was too ill to travel.

The ER doctor said it was a judgment call as to whether he should be discharged or admitted, as he explained that the major artery had further constricted. I asked the doctor about a possible blood transfusion, which had helped my father in the past, but the ER doctor didn't encourage it. Though my preference was to have Daddy admitted, the images of last winter when my mother and brother had jerked him out of the hospital and transported him to her home, contrary to his internal physician and cardiologist's recommendations, were still so vivid in my head. If he *were* discharged, I would probably have a couple of days to help him recover a little strength, at least so he could travel to attend his sister's funeral. That would probably turn out to be the day I was supposed to take him back to my mother. Later that day I discovered from telephoning the funeral home that my aunt's funeral would, indeed, be held on Saturday, giving Daddy and me a two-day reprieve.

I immediately thought that we would need to attend the funeral, or else my mother would have a similar response as she had in the past when Daddy had become sicker than usual. She would become enraged and demand that I bring him back. I would again be blamed for his illness. So I made the decision to bring Daddy back home with me and just hope that he would, as in the past, bounce back and be able to attend his sister's funeral. Again, it was the fear of my mother that drove my decision. And again, I felt disgusted at myself that the fear of her volatility dominated my mind almost as much as what might be in Daddy's best interest.

Since the doctor had not recommended a blood transfusion, I then began to realize that my father's condition was overall worse than usual. Still, however, I clung to the notion that he would feel better, as he always did.

So considering everything, the doctor and I decided he should be released. After returning home, I told Daddy about his sister. "You remember we saw your sister Jenny Dillon a couple of weeks ago, and she was very bad? Well, she passed away today." "She did?" he responded almost robotically, without emotion. I wasn't quite certain my father comprehended who exactly had died, because he had called my mother by his sister's name for years, I believe because of the similarity he saw between them. Up until I began intervening on his behalf, my mother had always accused Daddy's sister of greed and coercing my grandparents out of their property and assets. But in recent years, her attitude appeared to have drastically changed, and they frequently communicated.

Throughout that day and the next, Daddy continued to have increasing discomfort. He didn't want to get out of bed. He pointed to his chest, with his brow signifying pain. "Daddy, are you hurting?" "Here," he said. I figured that the pace maker was running overtime. But I could never know for certain what the major culprit was. I decided to telephone his internal physician, who had treated him for his heart condition and other issues and was told by the nurse that his doctor would be out of town until the following Tuesday. The nurse suggested that I monitor my father through the day and if he weren't feeling any better, I might want to take him again to the ER, especially if his breathing had become more labored and if he were having more chest pain.

I knew Daddy would not be able to attend his sister's funeral and knew I had to telephone my mother before that day since I might not be able to get her then. Furthermore, she would become irate if we didn't show up at the funeral, which was being held in Cookeville. "Please God, help me know what to say so Mother won't become angry and will allow me to keep Daddy for a little while longer," I prayed. Therefore, on the day before his sister's funeral, I telephoned her. "Mother, I, ah, wonder, since Daddy hasn't been feeling well, if you think it might be a bad idea for us to try to attend the service." "Well, I had been thinking that he might have to go to the bathroom a lot, so maybe you all shouldn't come." God had worked another miracle. Her social image had come to the rescue! "Mother, what about if I just keep Daddy here until late Tuesday afternoon when he's feeling better?" I was aware that Tuesdays were my mother's bridge days, and this might do the trick. "Okay, then," she sighed. God again had helped me. This gave me several more days to help get Daddy to feeling better, and since he had recovered so many times before, I thought he just might this time. This was a wonderful blessing to have a few more days to take care of him!

On Saturday, the day of his sister's funeral, my father's discomfort had increased to the point that I felt I better get him back to the hospital. I was concerned that because this was a Saturday, my father's regular doctor was out of town, and the ER staff would more than likely not be the ones who had seen my father on that preceding Thursday. But I felt I had no choice; my father clearly needed care I couldn't give him.

A Great Blessing for Both of Us

God performed another miracle for Daddy and me. My father's cardiologist, who had been witness to my mother's behavior in the winter, was on duty! What a blessing! Upon seeing my dad and assessing the situation, including the realization about what I was up against with the family situation, she mentioned that she might help me get my father hooked up with Hospice. What a wonderful boon this would be! Praise God.

The preceding week I had asked my father's neurologist, who treated him for his Alzheimer's, if any home health aide might be possible, and I didn't get a lot of encouragement since home health assistance implied that the patient required skilled nursing, and my father was still able to walk and had not seemed to be in that state of health, at least up until the preceding week. But his heart condition was a different matter. I had been told by his cardiologist at the hospital during the winter that Daddy's constrictor had worsened, and that there was nothing that could be done when it got to the point that it was hardly open at all, beyond giving him morphine to ease the pain. This action of providing me with Hospice would give me the opportunity to get some badly needed help to bathe my father, would give me a social worker to talk with, and a skilled nurse who would come to my home a couple of times a week to check my father's vital signs. She could even do his Coumadin checks. The cardiologist explained to me that there was really nothing that the hospital could do now, but she wrote a prescription for oral morphine. She indicated that Daddy had only a few months to live at the most. This was a little shocking, but I had other matters to think about then and couldn't really absorb that statement.

The cardiologist managed to facilitate this connection even though it was on a Saturday. The oxygen was to be brought that evening to my home and a nurse would visit there as well. Again, God had wrought another miracle.

Of course, always there was the matter of my mother, but I thought since this service would be covered by my father's insurance and would be virtually free for her, this would make a difference. I proved to be right, or at least I was for the time being.

CHAPTER 31

To everything there is a season, and a time to every purpose under heaven.
—Ecclesiastes 3:1

DADDY, THAT TRAIN'S COMING

This time the trip from the hospital wasn't as threatening for me, as it had been two days before. I was going to have some help! This would be such a blessing to have someone who could help bathe Daddy, stay with him while I ran quick errands, and test his blood at home. I was so thankful for this miracle.

Still, while I was driving Daddy home, I began to realize, perhaps for the first time, that he didn't have long to live. And that realization produced ambivalence. Of course on a rational level I had known for a long time that with all his physical problems he couldn't live too long, and I had actually prayed often that God would take him out of his mental and physical misery. It had been so amazing to everyone, including his doctors, that he had been able to go on for this long. What a tough little marine he was! Now, though, I just couldn't think about that notion for very long because Daddy and I had finally succeeded in creating our own world, with its own language, its own inhabitants, and its own meaning. It didn't matter that outsiders would not be able to enter it, or understand it. In some ways it was not as limiting as other people's worlds. It was built around the spiritual and the unconscious, more than the conscious. Against major odds, I had finally succeeded in providing care for my father and had figured out how I could enter his world.

As I thought about it rationally, I knew that Hospice couldn't be secured unless Daddy's condition was terminal. But I would have a few months, and during this time he and I would have help. Perhaps this situation would prompt my mother into giving me permission to keep Daddy permanently without the stress of never knowing when she was going to change her mind. I realized that the cardiologist had helped facilitate this Hospice connection partly because she realized much of the situation Daddy and I were up against. I knew my father would be cared for, and this hookup would give my mother a valid excuse for not having him with her. It would help preserve her image to her friends; she would not be viewed as abandoning her husband since I would now have some support in caring for him.

The cardiologist had actually linked me up with the nurse who was going to visit our home that evening! It was again miraculous how everything was being worked out, so efficiently. The oxygen and bedside commode were also going to be brought that very evening.

While I was still at the hospital, the medical staff helped me find a pharmacy which had the exact type and strength of morphine Daddy would need. So, with all these reinforcements, I was feeling better about everything. And Daddy had caught the mood as well.

Shortly after we arrived at what had become *our* home, the nurse came to officially enroll Daddy in Hospice. He was in such good spirits; he was talking to the nurse and joking with her. He was more upbeat than usual. He seemed to sense he was going to get to stay with me for longer than he had anticipated. Something had put him in an almost gleeful mood.

While the nurse was there, my mother telephoned. This was a rarity. My mother hardly ever telephoned unless it was a demand of some sort. She sighed, "Well, I called to tell you about Jenny Dillon's funeral." After listening for a few minutes to this, I jumped in and said, half-way holding my breath, "Mother, we have been given another wonderful blessing." There was silence on the other end, so I continued. "It's a miracle. Daddy's cardiologist helped get him hooked up with the Hospice organization." Rushing on, before my mother could respond, I quickly added, "Mother this is a wonderful service that won't cost you any money....Can you believe it? Daddy will have his own nurse who will come to the house, and I will have someone to help bathe him....Do you remember telling me that your friends had told you that I could get some home health care if I tried?" I always felt I had to hurry on so I wouldn't be cut off in the middle of an important sentence. All this time, Daddy continued to talk and joke with the Hospice nurse, such that at one point, I touched his arm lightly, smiled, and put my finger to my mouth to lightly shush him just a little. This moment was too important to blow, and I had to totally focus on it.

"Oh, I know all about Hospice. Ellen has used it, and so has Martha....." She continued on about ten minutes discussing how her neighbors had utilized the service, and she was very well acquainted with it. I was starting to feel so much relief, that it was worth holding the phone and listening to her tell all her knowledge about it. When she finally took a breath, I jumped into the pause. "Mother, guess who's sitting right now in my living room? The nurse herself. Can you believe that she came on a Saturday night to enroll Daddy? And they are going to bring the oxygen tonight. Everything has been so efficient....Here, I'll let you speak to her." Before my mother had a chance to respond, I handed the nurse the phone. This was such a great opportunity because I would have documentation that I was given permission to have this service. This nurse had obviously been filled in a little by the cardiologist, because when she first came into my house that evening, she said that Dr. Brennan had told her what great care I had given him. I understood that this statement might have been made just to be nice, but I did have the sense that the cardiologist had given her a little of the family history, including my mother's behaviors.

"Hello Mrs. Howard, this is Betty...." I realized the nurse had been cut off in the middle of her sentence too and that my mother again had the floor. She was "informing" this nurse about Hospice and confirming its value from the use by her neighbors. Still, that was okay, since it would be worth it for my mother to give the go ahead to get this service. "I'm so glad you agree. I believe the service will help all of you," the nurse said. Finally the conversation ended, and I dropped to the floor and said "Thank you God. Oh, thank you God." I couldn't contain my excitement from Daddy and the nurse. "She agreed!" By this point Daddy had caught this happiness and had again become even more spirited, and began offering the nurse a dime he picked up from the floor. "You're a good woman...here take this," he told her. This was one of the phrases he retained in his brain for people who were kind and compassionate. He sensed there was harmony between his daughter and wife, something he had always so desired. I believe he realized on some level that he was not going to have to go back up to Mother's house. So that part was done. God had answered another prayer: Mother had agreed to the service, and Daddy and I would have more time together. Of course, she had agreed to this before discussing it with my brother.

Daddy had a fairly easy night, but by the next morning, he wasn't feeling so well; he didn't want to get out of bed, and I determined that we would not go to church. It was rare indeed that he didn't want to go to church, so I knew he was feeling considerably worse. I brought him breakfast in bed, but he didn't eat heartily the way he had been eating. He ate just a little egg and drank a little coffee. I fed him. There had evidently been some kind of major drop off during the past two days in his physical condition which was masked by his high spirits the night before.

I sponge bathed him around noon, and dressed him into his regular clothes, thinking this might make him feel better. But still he was obviously very uncomfortable.

It was shortly after noon that I received a call from my mother. "I want him to come home," she began in that commonly used pitiful tone. My mouth went dry; I felt that horrible commotion in my stomach. How many times had this scenario been repeated in the past? My mother would finally agree to something; I would be so relieved, and then she would telephone and thwart the entire situation by changing her mind. "But Mother, last night, remember," I rushed to get the sentence out, "you told the nurse this was good and you agreed to..." "I... DON'T... CARE! The pitiful whining voice was gone, and the controller had taken over. "If he has Hospice, then he needs to be *here*." Either she had talked to my brother, or just another mood or personality had come to the surface. "Mother, could we just try this, since the Hospice has gone to all this trouble and has done all the paper work? Everything is set up, and I will have some help. Besides don't you have some tests you are having on your stomach this week?" Hearing the desperateness in my own voice, I was going for the possibility that since this wouldn't be as hard on me because I would have this help, she might not have to justify anything to her friends or her son. She wouldn't have to lose her "caregiver" status. "Well, maybe I can postpone them." I noted a slight shift from the angry and commanding tone.

"Oh, Mother, you don't need to reschedule those tests...Your own health is too important." "You are right about that....I have to take care of myself," she whimpered. That statement did the trick, at least for the time being. The focus was back on her. Then I thought I would allow her to save face even more. "After the tests, you can come down and stay as long as you like. Daddy is actually feeling okay right now; we're watching television, the Titans' game. Here, why don't you talk to him?" I handed my father the phone so they could talk. Though Daddy's voice was weak, he did respond to her with a couple of words of agreement, which was all that was ever needed with Mother. When I took the phone again, my mother said, "Well, I do hate to postpone these tests." And thus my father and I had made it through another day without any additional trauma.

"Thank you Lord; again, You have given me another reprieve to keep her away." I recalled Daddy's hospital stay the previous year when the bad weather had prevented my mother and brother from coming down sooner to jerk Daddy out of the hospital. God always seemed to give me fragments of hope to grab onto when there appeared to be nothing.

Daddy spent most of the afternoon dozing in his chair. I hooked him up to the oxygen, but he was clearly having more pain with his heart. Beginning to give him a little morphine orally, I was tentative with it, fearing an overdose. At this point, I was walking on uncertain ground. I was afraid that if I gave him too much, he could develop some tolerance to it and then it might not help him when he really needed it. At this point, I thought he had months, or at least weeks, to live. But his whole mood seemed to be shifting. He was not watching television; his eyes were closed. Something different was definitely happening.

FROM HELPING HIM LIVE TO HELPING HIM DIE

The day seemed interminably long. He slept most of it, and I realized that this would probably mean he would not sleep that night, but he was simply too weak to go out of the house. I had not processed even yet in my mind that my father had begun his dying journey, and that he would now be naturally sleeping a lot more than before. I continued to think how horrible this must be for him, since the Alzheimer's condition would make him want to go somewhere, but the heart problems wouldn't allow it. I simply still had not grasped how much worse he actually was.

While he dozed, I read a little book the Hospice nurse had given me, entitled *Gone from My Sight*, that defined the various stages of death and behaviors that went with them. Goodness, Daddy appears to be exhibiting behaviors characteristic of a much later stage than he is actually in, I reflected. Closing his eyes, withdrawing, processing information: all this seemed to be happening. I tried to accept this was where he needed to be, with some kind of ease, but when I looked at his face, I saw only misery. Although some of that had occurred because of the Alzheimer's, there appeared to be some kind of difference now. Maybe some of his quiet moaning was an attempt to resolve issues which had sabotaged his life. I didn't know how much of the normal dying process Alzheimer's patients would exhibit, or how one told the difference between the way they were when they weren't dying. I couldn't help but wonder if he was in some mental anguish regretting that he had sacrificed his life for a woman who couldn't love him and who had enticed him to follow her rejection of their daughter who *could* love him. Sometimes when he looked at me, his eyes seemed to tell me he was sorry. I had the sense that even in his scrambled brain Daddy was questioning the decisions he had made in his life, how he had set his priorities. I hoped that this was not the case. He had suffered enough mental pain. I knew now that he did what he felt he had to do to survive and help his children survive. But the hour was too late now for any kind of statement which might bring on an emotion his body or mind couldn't endure.

Wondering if somewhere in his brain his life had appeared as an empty, delusive cheat, I tried to comfort myself with remembering that there is supposed to be some difference between the sufferings of the saints and those of the ungodly.

I could have used some help that week in getting needed items from the pharmacy and a few groceries, but I didn't want to bother my few close friends, since they worked and had families of their own. So many times sickness brings with it spates of affection and love from friends and a wealth of human sympathy. But such was not our case. I really didn't have reserves to draw on. I wondered if, when I came to the point of my own death, there would be any ripple, if my absence would be noticed at all. I realized no one really could understand my situation and therefore couldn't really provide the comfort I needed. So it was just mainly God, Daddy, and me.

That night Daddy ate hardly any supper. His disorientation appeared to increase, as did his difficulty with bodily movements. The Hospice nurse had ordered some medication to help with this physical challenge, and so far they had helped his bowels move. The morphine, however, was creating some difficulties with his urination, so by the time Monday rolled around, I was very glad to have the chance to visit with his skilled nurse, for the first time.

She was a spunky young woman who was touted to be very quick to assess situations. I talked with her about my mother's volatility and need to control, and she seemed to grasp the situation very quickly. She and I thought it might be helpful if the two of them talked directly together and that we use the nurse's cell phone; this way my mother could better imagine that she was still in control of things. My mother answered, but since she didn't know I was present when the call was made, her image of control was preserved. They had a friendly conversation, with Mother doing most of the talking, and the nurse primarily agreeing with her.

After Daddy was resting, later that day I telephoned my mother, and she told me that she had had a telephone call from Sarah. "Oh, good," I replied. "What did you think of her?" "Oh, she sounded very nice and knowledgeable." "Thank you God," I silently prayed.

That evening I had a thirty minute commitment at my church, which was only five minutes from my house, so I asked one of my friends whom I had known for over 25 years, if he would come to stay with Daddy. He had visited my father for a few minutes a couple of times each week and had bought me a new washer and dryer when my old one broke, so I didn't have to keep dragging Daddy with me to the launderette. I was reluctant to go at all, but this engagement had been planned for months, and the audience was counting on me. I did go, and Daddy and my friend sat in the den. He told me that Daddy had slept off and on, but things appeared to be all right. Thus that day again had passed without additional trauma.

On Tuesday morning, however, there appeared to be another drop-off in

Daddy's physical health. He didn't want to take his medicine, and he didn't want to get out of bed. He was complaining about his chest, and since he rarely ever complained, I concluded that he must be really uncomfortable. I continued the small doses of morphine. Not knowing how much morphine to give him, I probably erred on the slight side, which I later regretted. He was sleeping more now, and in a fetal position. "Daddy, what about some breakfast?" I was trying hard to sound cheery. "I'm not hungry; I don't want anything," he weakly responded. "What if I just get you a little coffee then?" My father still responded to that Starbucks coffee. "Okay, I'll take a little." I fixed his usual coffee just the way he loved it. "Here you are, Daddy." I noticed that he was much weaker than usual, and could hardly drink it. I ran to the kitchen and got a straw, and as I held the cup to his mouth, he managed to take just a few sips. "Daddy, how about a little scrambled egg?" "Okay," he replied so weakly. Actually, he only ate a few bites, which I fed to him, and then he said, "That's enough."

It was about this point that I realized that somewhere in his psyche Daddy knew what was about right for him to eat. He seemed to know what he should do more than I knew. The Hospice nurse had told me not to force either food or liquid on him, but just to give him what he wanted. Looking back to that time, I realized he must have realized his life was finally drawing to a close. I wondered when I should stop helping him to *live* and begin helping him to *die*. I pondered death. One short event closes the biography of every man and woman. But it seemed Daddy had been dying for so long, and yet so short a time. Time became very confusing for me.

I didn't try bathing him, because his aide was to come that day and bathe him. Though Daddy was resistant to the aide at first, after a little conversation, he allowed him to have his way with him. But Daddy's discourse and interaction with the living world was definitely ending.

The aide was pleasant with Daddy, and helped him to use the bedside commode. By this time I had begun to realize things were getting physically tougher on me too, and I really did need a man's help to lift my father.

Thankfully, Daddy spent most of the rest of the day sleeping, but his breathing became more labored. Still, I was grateful for what seemed to be relatively peaceful rest, considering how very sick he was.

Daddy was declining more rapidly than my brain could process. That night, when I gave him a little bit of apple juice, he quietly whispered, "God bless you." He was so sweet and so vulnerable and so helpless. He had transitioned in my mind from being a helpless victim to being my father, and now it was almost as if he were my baby. I knew The Holy Spirit was still within him because he was still mentioning God! It tore me up, but also comforted me to know that the least little acts of kindness prompted "Thank yous" from him...even as he was dying.

By the next day, my father had such discomfort and his breathing had become so labored, that I thought that I should telephone his nurse, who wasn't scheduled to make her next visit until the next day. However, she came over and saw my father, and stated that his blood pressure was holding steady. I explained that he was having still more difficulty urinating, and the nurse suggested a catheter. I asked how painful it was. I knew that Daddy's skin and body had become so weak by this point, and I didn't want him to suffer any more than he had to. "Not very painful," she responded. That in itself turned out not to be true, partly because she couldn't get it in right, and had to reinsert it a couple of times. Daddy was almost screaming in pain by this point, and I pleaded, "Stop, please stop." If only I hadn't said anything about his difficulty with urinating, I thought. If only. If only. I had horrible feelings of guilt all through the rest of the day and that evening, as the failed attempts at catheterizing had created horrible burning when Daddy tried to urinate. I still shudder when I think of those horrible moments. There was also a significant amount of blood. "Why did I have to mention this; why didn't I stop her from doing this the first time?" I remorsefully asked myself. One of the most painful memories to this day is that experience. I did not stop to think he might have had an enlarged prostate gland, or that he was probably so tender. Since I had been blocked out of so much of my father's earlier life, I really didn't know much about his other problems, other than his heart condition and his Alzheimer's. I did remember that a portion of his colon was removed some 20 years previously, but I wasn't thinking clearly and felt I had to rely on the nurse to do what was required. I should have thought more about it! I was walking on unfamiliar territory, and I wasn't doing a good job.

Every minute my father hurt, I hurt. "Daddy, I'm so sorry," I said repeatedly throughout the evening to him. "I wish I could take the pain onto myself," I quietly told him as I put my arms around him. He said, "Oh, no." He was still aware. That night, I lay down next to him just for a few minutes and touched his hand. He held mine back. It tore me apart to realize how desperately he had always needed touching, but more so during the onset of the Alzheimer's and how he had received none of it except from me. I recalled how once when I had tried to gently ask Mother to be around my father a little bit more. "Do you think I should sit and hold his hand?" she had snapped.

For the past year or so, I had made it a point to put lotion on Daddy's hands and arms and rub them at night. He was just like a little puppy which responds when its tummy is rubbed. "Thank you and God bless you," he would say when I had done this. Such a little thing, I thought. He was so needy when it came to affection and touching. In the beginning of our interaction, though I knew this was the reality, I felt awkward doing it, given the estrangement through the past years. So I took him for pedicures, primarily just for the massages to his feet and legs. During the first ones, he was reluctant and somewhat distrustful, since he had never had anything like this before. Then he came to enjoy them, and he would use the same phrase of his pedicurist, "She shore knows what she's doing." It was for reasons like this that I knew that my father processed and retained far more than anyone in the family was willing to acknowledge.

I was now having two brand new experiences, and one not so new, which were increasing the overall tension. By this time, I had come to realize Daddy was indeed dying, and though I had often visited elderly friends of mine in their last days, I had never actually gone completely alone with them through the dying process spread out over days. I was groping my way along. I really didn't know how much I should try talking to him, or how much I needed to just leave him alone to transition to the next world. I was uncertain about the potential dangers of his medicine. This was part of the reason I didn't know exactly what dose of morphine to give Daddy. Later I blamed myself for not giving him more to decrease his suffering, but then I knew that the morphine had some bad effects on his bodily functions. And giving him too much could kill him. If I had known at the time how close Daddy was to death, I would have increased the dosage. This first-time issue of walking through the death process with a loved one also accounted for my uncertainty about other steps to be taken, like catheterization. The nurse never made me feel guilty; for a time afterwards, she reminded me that it was her decision to catheterize Daddy, not mine. But I just couldn't rid myself of the needless suffering I felt we had both put Daddy through, only because I thought this action would lessen his difficulty with urinating.

The second issue was how much I should direct or dictate what should be done with him, since I didn't know what might ameliorate his sick condition. I certainly didn't want in any way to alienate the Hospice folks because they were the only help I had. But I had the notion, later confirmed, that even my father's skilled nurse didn't know how sick Daddy actually was, and I felt she thought I was overreacting. As it turned out later in the week, I was right, and she was wrong. The nurse had *not* realized how sick he was. Because Daddy was such a tough little guy who rarely complained, especially when the nurse came to visit him that week, she had not really seen him enough to make an accurate assessment. Nor did I know exactly when to telephone the nurse.

Last, I wasn't certain as to whether I should minimize or maximize Daddy's condition to Mother. On the one hand, I was determined to only telephone her when Daddy was resting, so she would be calmer, and she could tell her neighbors and friends that her husband was doing okay. She wouldn't lose her image that she had taken care of him. The main reason for minimizing Daddy's condition was that I could keep my mother at bay and away from the scene. At one time, when my mother said she was planning on coming down the following Monday, I replied, "Mother, that will be just fine. You can have the whole upstairs since I'm used to sleeping on the couch anyway. That will give me a chance to do a few errands....Daddy can see that we're both taking care of him and that will make him happy." That really was a dumb response because I had realized by this point that my mother, in no shape or form, desired any collaboration or partnership with me. But at that particular moment she seemed placated. On the other hand, I knew that if she didn't realize how ill Daddy really was, she could demand that he be brought back to East Tennessee immediately, a thought which caused shivers down my spine. By Wednesday night, I knew he was far too ill to travel anywhere.

It was on that night that Daddy's terminal agitations began increasing. Though he was extremely weak, he tried getting out of bed, highly agitated. "I've got to get out; I've got to go...Let me go," he insisted. I had no choice but to try to help him up out of bed, and try to move with him. I grabbed the morphine, but he resisted it. "I don't want any more medicine; I want to die....I won't take any more," he clearly demanded. "Daddy, I know you want to go...and the train is coming...It's just not here yet. God is driving that train. We just have to wait on God." That would make him pause for just a few minutes, but then he would begin again. We just stumbled around until finally he wore out and sat down on the bed. I managed to get him calm, and finally he fell off to sleep as I lay down beside him for a little while. I went into his room several times through the night, touched him, just to let him know I was there.

Later I came to understand he was preparing himself to die. The first time he said, "I've got to get out," however, I thought he was talking about leaving the house. He did want to get out of the house, but I learned that he wanted to get out of the house in order to get out of this world. Just as I had been a part of his Alzheimer's world for the past five years, I now felt I was going into this other world with him.

The next day, Thursday, when the aide came to give him a bath, another agitation began. It was utterly amazing how much his determination to "get out" pumped up that adrenalin during these times, when he otherwise was too weak to raise his head from the pillow. It was on this afternoon, when he began to stumble from his room, with me on one arm and the male aide on the other, that he said, "I've lost my eyes." Oh no! I knew then that he had gone blind. From the best I could figure, he had dropped two levels of Alzheimer's in four days. This was one of the most horrid moments yet, which torments me to this day. After seven years, I continue to have nightmares about it. I have dreamed many times since of Daddy, strong and seeing, with us walking together, but unlike the years I led him, he is leading me.

Sensing the seriousness of Daddy's condition, the aide telephoned the nurse who had come the day before. Since she had only seen him once, she really was not fully acquainted with everything that was wrong with my father. "Just go into the living room, and he will follow you," she had told the aide. Go into the living room indeed! Daddy had gone blind, and he wouldn't and couldn't follow anyone anywhere. No one but the aide and I really knew that Daddy was dying. So much for getting any other help.

But, though Daddy was determined to walk – to get out of there – there was no strength, no focus in this reality, as he stumbled from this room to that room, the aide and I having no choice but to stumble around with him. Daddy pulled at his clothing, saying "Get these off me." "Daddy, please rest here just for a little while," I begged. And my father, with me trying to steer him and yet keep him from falling, finally plopped down on the chair in the dining room, more from sheer exhaustion than anything else. At this point, he had only his pajama top on.

He was so sick. He actually stated, "I am so sick. I'm ready to die." He spoke the statement again very clearly. He was trying to vomit, but there were only dry heaves. I was holding his head. He wasn't able to control his kidneys. Everything was coming out from everywhere! I thought this was too horrible not to be another nightmare. Finally in the living room, the aide and I persuaded Daddy to rest for just a moment. But he almost immediately got up again, and began staggering toward the kitchen, with me and the aide on either side of him. In the kitchen the aide tried to convince him to take a morphine pill as he fell into a kitchen chair. "Yes, Daddy, you're going to get out, but you need to rest here first." I asked, "Daddy, honey, can you see me?" He tried to focus his eyes and looked all around. It was clear to me that Daddy at this point couldn't see at all. With each ghastly moment, the pain seemed to be greater than any of the previous pain I had experienced. How could things be worse? At that point in time, his inability to understand why he couldn't see felt like the most horrific pain I had faced yet. There is no word bad enough to describe these images. He was gray and gaunt. He had huge bags under his eyes. He had the look and smell of death. "Lord, please help me stay calm and be able to calm Daddy," I prayed. I had to react so quickly to his deterioration that I really didn't have time to process what was going on. The true horror and mental pain of it really didn't come until later, when I had the chance to think. I was only reacting at this point.

Though his body had deteriorated, and his eyesight was evidently gone, his awareness of everything seemed to be growing. At the prayer meeting, just a little over two weeks previous to this day, when a friend of mine asked him, "Who's that pretty girl with you," Daddy had answered, "That's my daughter." Evidently, he had finally started to see his mother, who had raised me, and himself in me! What a moment this had been, since for as long as I could remember, he appeared never to be quite certain, although he had said something similar in the hospital earlier in the year. The relief for me was great because I wanted Daddy to believe this. He would feel more peaceful.

When the nurse was with him toward the end of the week, he again said that he wanted to go home. He wanted to get out. "Who's there at home?" I asked. My father replied, "No one is there. There's no one there waiting for me." Oh, no! Could this mean he really thought no one was awaiting him? Was he thinking that everyone had abandoned him? He had often said that his wife cared nothing for him. But at this point he knew I did. Surely this couldn't mean what I feared. I knew Daddy was going to heaven. But could he have had a glimpse of hell? Was the blackness the result of his loss of sight, or something much worse? If it were heaven, why didn't he see Mammy and Papa there? Or any of God's angels? I thought my heart was literally going to break into pieces. "Oh, God, please help him see someone in heaven waiting for him. Please."

Eventually the aide and I managed to get him to take some more morphine, and just from mere exhaustion, Daddy fell asleep, and stayed asleep for most of the evening and night. I didn't sleep any of these nights but rested some on the couch, where I was used to catnapping. I had purchased a baby monitor and placed it on the table next to the couch, so that any shift in his breathing was quickly apparent. I crept in and touched Daddy from time to time, covering him up. At one point, I asked him if he would just take a little tablespoon of his apple juice. "God bless you," he said as always when the smallest benefit was given to him. His spirit was *still* intact. "Thank you God for letting me know that my daddy is going home to you."

Each day my mother changed her plan on when she was planning to come down and what she was planning to do when she got here. First, she was coming on Monday; then it was Sunday. Then it became Saturday. The tension of having to deal with her was an added pressure that exacerbated the entire situation. She continually threatened that my father better be alert when she got to my house. This was one reason I was a little reluctant to give him too much morphine.

On Friday, the social worker was present when Daddy had another agitation, and she did all she could to assist me to calm him. He was still having difficulty using the bathroom, and the social worker was helpful with that ordeal. It was such a miracle from God that almost every time Daddy experienced one of these there was someone at my home. However, I realized I would need help at a longer stretch and through the night now because I could not physically contain my father during these terminal agitations. The social worker referred me to a sitting service, and I was able to get a Nigerian woman for the night. She was to arrive at 11:00. I knew I simply had to get some rest, as my own strength was failing from a lack of sleep, and my bronchitis was worsening. I had waited to give him his morphine until shortly before the woman was to arrive because I wanted to make the evening as easy as possible on her since she had never seen Daddy or me.

About half an hour before she was to arrive, one of the agitations began. "I've got to go...Let me out....I want to go home," he insisted, growing more restless. I later learned from the social worker that Alzheimer's patients frequently refer to heaven as their "home" in their final stage. He seemed to want to use the bathroom, and I tried to lift him to the bedside commode. I managed to somehow get him over it, and he used the bathroom a little. Of course, by this point, he had taken such little liquid that I knew there wasn't much to come out of him. And his organs probably were shutting down. He was pulling at his pajamas, and wanted his socks and pajama bottoms off. He was in such a state that I really didn't know what he wanted or what I should do. It was a very cold night, and I knew we simply couldn't go outside. Daddy, with only his pajama top on, began to try to walk. "I want to go outside...I want to go home, I've got to go home," Daddy begged again. "Daddy, please take this medicine," I urged. He resisted it, because he thought the medicine would prolong his life. But I finally got some more morphine in him.

What will I do if the woman is late? I shuddered at the thought. I knew I couldn't hold him up and help him walk. We would both probably fall. My degenerative discs were hurting badly, and if I fell with my osteoporosis, then I could break my own bones.

Fortunately the sitter arrived shortly after that, and she tried to help me contain Daddy. Though she was physically much larger and stronger than me, she knew she couldn't force him down, since she might break one of *his* bones. We both just kept talking to Daddy. In her deep, melodious voice, the woman responded to Daddy, "Okay, we will go; I will drive you, but we can't go now. It's too cold. We have to wait a little while." "I have to go *now*," Daddy insisted. Together, the sitter and I had no choice but to walk with him. He stumbled into the den, his eyes unfocused and glazed. He fell onto a chair. I was stunned at his physical appearance. His color had become grayer; the black circles around his eyes and the huge bags under them had gotten bigger. I could hardly look at him. Feeling his enormous pain, I thought I was going to pass out. He looked up and then sideways. I knew he couldn't see me, but he was trying to find my voice. I will never get that image out of my head. Oh, God, please, please, release my Daddy from this pain," I begged. With each step of dying, the images grew more ghastly. "God, I can't bear this; please help us both." I was totally operating on adrenalin from a sense of urgency. The sitter at that point signaled to me that she could change the bed since he was out of it. "Good idea," I quietly whispered. Together we changed his pajamas, so he had a dry bed and dry pajamas, even though his bottoms didn't match his top. I mention this because later this was to be a big issue for Mother.

Finally, Daddy, as in the previous times, just from mere exhaustion, drifted off to sleep. By this point, it was after 1:00 a.m., and the sitter and I thought I might go upstairs and try to catch a couple of hours of sleep. "If his breathing changes at all or his moaning increases, please come up and get me." The sitter promised she would. I hated to go upstairs, but I knew I would need my strength the following day when my mother and brother arrived. My cough had gotten worse, and I knew I must try to treat it. It had been so long since I had slept in a bed and several nights since I had slept at all that I didn't know if I *could* sleep. I set the alarm for 4:00 a.m.

Sheer exhaustion had evidently set in, as I took some cough medicine, and I fell asleep. I awakened right at 4:00 without the alarm. I slipped down the stairs to find the sitter dozing. "Good grief, great help she is," I thought, as I glanced at the breathing monitor. His breathing had become more irregular, and sometimes it would stop for 10 or 12 seconds or longer before resuming. Besides that, though, Daddy appeared to be still sleeping. I crept in and gave him a little drop of liquid. "Don't ever leave me," he begged, quietly, but clearly. "Daddy, I won't ever leave you; I'm just like a piece of old chewing gum; you can't get rid of me." "No, you're not; you're my baby girl." There it was, again, after all these years. Daddy had come to believe I was, after all, his baby girl. And he had repeated this response just the day before. It was almost as if this thought was one he determined to hold on to. It was not just something that he thought he should say. He was too sick. "Thank you, Lord," I quietly prayed. I realized we would never be able to capitalize on his awareness, but it didn't matter. Daddy believed it. I was certain of it now. I had long ago accepted that we probably would never really feel like father and daughter, but to come to this point! It was miraculous. After awakening the aide and realizing my father had drifted back to sleep, I went upstairs to take a shower.

There was so much going on physically, mentally, and emotionally that neither Daddy nor I could process it all. After so many years of being made to feel that I never belonged in this family, here was someone who was acknowledging me on his deathbed. Why, Lord, did this all have to come so late?

There was really no time to grieve though. I had to think about what I must do *next*, as my mother and brother - the "storm" - were due to arrive about noon, and they clearly wouldn't be able to acknowledge or handle the condition of my father. There was always an urgent "next." Think, Kathryn, think. The sitter was due to leave at 7:00, and I knew I couldn't handle Daddy by himself. The sitter called her service, but they weren't able to find anyone on this short notice.

I decided then to telephone Hospice to see if the nurse who enrolled my father just one week ago might come to see him. I was panicked at the thought of being there by myself when my mother and brother arrived. I talked with this nurse and decided to ask her about the prospect of getting Daddy into the Hospice facility, a facility for patients who often don't have over 72 hours to live. She discovered there was indeed a vacancy for a male. Another miracle! "Thank you, Lord. Oh, thank you." Even though I had been listed as the primary care giver on the Hospice papers, I knew that in order not to send my mother into a rage which could end up killing both my father and me, I needed to get her permission before trying to get the Hospice nurse to facilitate Daddy being moved there. My poor little father had become almost like a FedEx cargo, being moved first to one place and then another. I was really nervous about telephoning her, but I was always nervous when I had to ask her permission for something Daddy needed. I knew my mother and brother would not have left home yet, and so I decided to telephone Mother while the sitter was still present, to ask her if I might transport Daddy to the Hospice facility.

"Mother, I wanted to telephone you and ask you something." I hurried on, fearing my mother would not allow me to get out the question. "Hospice has a wonderful facility...." I was cut off, as my mother sarcastically carped, "*I* have something to tell *you*. We are coming to take him home." That smugness was all too familiar. My mouth became so dry that I didn't know if I could even whisper. "But mother, Daddy is too sick to go anywhere...." Again, she cut me off and hung up the phone on me. I tried phoning my brother. At first his line was busy; then there was no answer. This told me that my mother had telephoned my brother immediately and told him to get over there so they could leave right then. In something of a desperate and panicked move, I telephoned my mother's next-door neighbors. These were the neighbors who had been helpful at various times in the past. Several years earlier Mr. Bonner had encouraged me when he quietly told me in my parents' yard one day that I was the only one doing anything to help my father. I had telephoned Mrs. Bonner earlier in the year, when Daddy was so anemic that he needed to be hospitalized and he needed blood, to enlist her help in getting cooperation and agreement from my mother about having him hospitalized. She was a sensible woman who had experienced considerable illness in her own family, and she would understand why I had to take the action I did. She also knew my mother was much more apt to listen to her than to me. She had told me, "Don't you suggest anything to her. Let me do it." A close friend of my mother's and years ago a friend of mine as well, she knew that anything coming from me would be rejected. At that time because she had talked to my mother first before I did, my mother, at least for that moment, had been cooperative. And there were other times when I had telephoned them to ask if they would talk to my mother and urge her to allow me to keep Daddy when he would be too ill to travel.

Of course since that time, my mother had spread much poisoned propaganda about me, after I had been forced to seek legal help to get my father medical attention, and I realized those neighbors probably wouldn't be so ready to help me now. Besides, usually friends and neighbors don't want to be in the middle of any conflict, let alone one of this magnitude, and I understood this. So I hated to ask them again, but I had no choice. "Martha, I hate to ask you for yet another favor, and I promise this will be the last time. But Daddy is much worse, and with his terminal agitations, neither Mother nor I will be able to handle him by ourselves. There is a room at the Hospice Residence here, and they can take Daddy today." I deliberately used medical terms because of health issues in her family, and I thought she might appreciate my recognition of that experience. "No, you're right; your mother can't handle that," she responded. She knew how little things upset my mother, and somewhere in her mind she surely must have become aware of Mother's pathology. But there was something in the way she said that which sounded different than ever before. "I have just telephoned Mother, and she said she and Donald are coming to take Daddy home...Could you, just this one last time, go over there and perhaps talk to her and mention the facility?" I could tell she wasn't eager to do this, but she said she would. However, her tone had definitely changed from the last time I had spoken with her.

A few minutes passed, and I telephoned the neighbors back, since they hadn't telephoned me. Mr. Bonner answered and said that when his wife got over there, Donald was already there. "She didn't stay long, and they left shortly after she got there," he replied. He was a little terse, which was quite unlike him, and I realized that my mother probably expressed her outrage to Mrs. Bonner and cut her short, and Mrs. Bonner realized there was nothing she could say or do. And after all, the Bonners were my mother's neighbors, not mine. So I knew I only had at the most about two and a half hours before they would arrive.

CHAPTER 32

Wherefore take unto you the whole armour of God, that ye may be able to withstand in –the evil day, and having done all, to stand.

–Ephesians 6:13

GOD'S PERFECT TIMING

After the sitter had to leave, I was really afraid of being alone when my mother and brother arrived, so I asked my next door neighbor, who was somewhat acquainted with the situation, to come over and pray with me. She asked God to intervene and stop this wickedness and that His will would be done with minimal interference from anyone. I prayed that God would protect my father and would bind the devil in my mother. I prayed that I would know what to do *next*. I knew that what we *say*, according to the Bible, can preserve our lives, or destroy them.

Then the Hospice nurse arrived. So far, God had provided someone to be with me so I wouldn't face the "next" storm wave alone.

This was the nurse who was with me at my home on the previous Saturday and who had spoken on the telephone to my mother about enrolling Daddy in Hospice. She had not seen Daddy since then and was really unacquainted with how sick he really was. After all when she visited my house just one week earlier, he was in such good spirits, demonstrating that cheerfulness to her. She and I discussed the dilemma of having Daddy moved to the Hospice Residence. I explained that I had telephoned my mother and that she had hung up on me, but the minutes were passing quickly, and both of us agreed that my mother and brother would be much less apt to drag my dying father out of the facility than out of my home. So with that issue settled, the nurse contacted the facility and made the final arrangements. I knew what a blessing it was to get anyone into this facility, and had my father not already been enrolled in Hospice, it would have been impossible. Then to have a vacant room was miraculous! Now, the only challenge was to get an ambulance, but the clock was ticking. From my calculations, we had an hour at most to get my father moved out of my home. I had determined to leave a note on my door, defining where exactly my father had been transported.

Getting an ambulance proved to be tough on this Saturday morning since 911 city ambulances, which respond quickly, only transport patients to the hospital, and not to any other type of facility. The nurse kept getting recordings of ambulance companies, and she knew that time was not on our side. Finally, she was able to reach one, and its dispatcher returned her call, saying they could come in about 30 minutes. I nodded to the nurse, and she scheduled it.

The nurse, with growing awareness of how frightened I was to face my mother and brother alone, told me that she would stay until the ambulance arrived just in case they were to arrive before the ambulance. This was another work of the Lord. "Oh, Lord, please get that ambulance here before Mother and Donald get here," I pleaded. It was one of those prayers people say when they are in such fear that they feel like zombies and the statements sound mechanical. It seemed that I was always begging Him from a sense of urgency, and later I wondered why I had to keep doing this because He was quite aware of how dire this situation was. While waiting, the nurse had gone in to try to talk to Daddy, and found him mostly non-responsive. He was just moaning a little, but couldn't really answer the nurse. I had still been careful not to give him too much morphine, and later regretted I had not given him more to decrease the full impact of the approaching storm.

The nurse then telephoned the Hospice chaplain who at this point had not had the opportunity to meet either Daddy or me, but who had spoken briefly on the phone to me a couple of days prior. I heard her tell him directions to my home, so I knew that the chaplain was coming over. Here was another blessing the Lord had delivered. "Oh, where is that ambulance?" the nurse rhetorically stated, beginning herself to catch my tension about having to face my mother. She realized that it had been about an hour since she had telephoned the ambulance company.

As the nurse and I were sitting in the den, more or less just watching the clock, she looked out the door. "Looks like your mother is here," she quietly said. "Oh no. God, please just help me," was all I could pray. My mouth was so dry and my laryngitis had worsened to the point that I didn't know if I could even speak. My brain was just about gone. My mother and brother came in through the door, and I tried to sound cheery when I met them. "Mother, this is Betty, the nurse from Hospice who you talked with last Saturday night," I almost whispered as quickly as I could. I was disgusted by my own effort to put some kind of cheery spin on this very dark, depressing, and frightening moment. My voice seemed to be coming from someone else.

In that instant, I felt again like I did when I was ten, possessing no power, no importance, no nothing. I felt transparent. Everything came flooding back. The hospital doors being slammed in my face time after time when Daddy had been taken to the ER; all the times Mother had said, "Forget about us...this is none of your business"; being locked out of their home on dark late nights and forced to go next door to telephone my mother and ask her to let me in so I could get my car keys to drive home to Nashville; my father being jerked out of the hospital earlier in the year over the pleadings of his doctors to allow him to stay at my home just for a few days. All this added up to my feeling of total and complete impotence. I knew I should have assertively said, "Mother, Daddy is gravely ill, and the Hospice nurse is here to make arrangements to get him to the Hospice facility." But instead, here I was, half cowering, artificially polite, mainly fearing the impact of my mother's reaction on Daddy, which kept me from speaking boldly as I should have. "No, I didn't talk to a nurse last Saturday," Mother denied. Ohhh, my, the schizophrenia again. The nurse politely greeted both my mother and brother, and I left Mother and Donald alone with my father and went into the den, next to Daddy's bedroom. The nurse, however, stayed in my father's bedroom for a few moments.

My mother went over to her husband and said in an affected sympathetic and unaffected accusatory tone, "You don't have any socks on, you poor thing...What has she done to you! Your pajama top and bottoms don't even match!" I remembered Mother coming into Daddy's hospital room back in the winter and using almost the identical phraseology. It was the same artificially caring tone which she only used in front of others. Unconscious and unconcerned about her husband's labored breathing and his overall physical state, my mother kissed him on his mouth, an action which she had historically done only in the presence of others. In this case, it was in front of the nurse. "Did that taste good to you?" Mother asked, effecting some surreal and ludicrous image of an old woman trying to be sexy. Oh, the depths of this woman's insanity, I thought. In any other situation, this display would have been sickening, but there were more urgent matters to think about, and I couldn't waste any emotion on this one. My father was trying, but was unable to respond. "You want to go home, don't you?"she continued in a whiny, "you poor little thing" voice.

I shuddered as I feared Daddy might repeat his plea made earlier in the week when he refused his medicine and insisted he wanted to go home, that he was ready to leave this world. Instead, thankfully, I heard no response from him. He clearly had dropped to another phase of the dying process. During this time, he still seemed to feel an urge to use the bathroom and the nurse helped him with that process. I chose not to enter Daddy's room during any of this time, thinking it best to just let the Hospice nurse be in the room with this insane scenario. I sat in the den in a virtual comatose state.

The nurse then came into the den, and my mother followed her. The whiny voice left and a confrontational tone moved into its place. "I have come to take him to *my* home," she stated affirmatively. The nurse, trying to demonstrate empathy and sensitivity, patiently replied, "I know Mrs. Howard, this is bound to be a shock to see how much your husband has deteriorated, but he really isn't able to travel very far..." Mother cut her off. "*I* have power of attorney, and we ARE taking him home." She spoke with increasing aggressiveness and agitation. There was that weapon again, that POWER of attorney, which she so conveniently had used before to maintain control of her husband's life.

At that time, the chaplain was at the door. I sighed, partly in relief, partly in agitation as I wondered why everybody always arrived just a few minutes too late (The ambulance still hadn't come). Or so it seemed at that moment. I had never even gotten the chance to personally meet the minister and consequently had not had the chance to explain the situation and how I had come to have my father with me. I had not talked with him about how my mother had abused him and how I had had to spend thousands of dollars just to have the opportunity to get Daddy medical attention. Nevertheless, it was good to have at least another person here. I just had to rely on God to give this minister enough understanding to piece the situation together.

I introduced him to my brother, just as Donald came into the den from his father's bedroom. "What seems to be the problem here?" Donald asked, standing with feet apart and arms folded, chin upturned and in just about the same commanding tone that his mother had used. The chaplain and the nurse were again polite and tried to show compassion. "Mr. Howard, we know how hard this must be to see your father....." the nurse began before she was cut off. "WE have power of attorney and we are taking him to our home," my brother autocratically stated. The chaplain echoed the nurse's sentiment of how difficult this must be to see his father so much declined, but he added something. "Donald, your father is really too ill to travel." Donald, with arms still folded, threateningly asked, "What are you trying to say?" Things could get real ugly, I thought. Surely he wouldn't threaten the chaplain! "Donald, your father is very sick; he is not able to travel to East Tennessee." I weakly added, "Daddy is very ill, and he has gone blind." As I began my sentence, Donald turned around and walked out of the room. Every time I attempted any word, the reaction was the same. Marie, Donald's wife, had told me years before that this was the same response he gave her when he didn't want to hear whatever she was saying. It was my brother's way of denying the value and worth of the other person.

My mother continued. "*I* have the money to hire an ambulance. *I* have the money to put him in a home, and *I* have the money to hire a sitter." I thought if I could just focus on something, I could keep some of my wits about me and not go into shock, so I counted the number of times my mother mentioned money. After seven times, I quit counting.

Donald repeated what was getting to be a refrain. "*We* have power of attorney and we're taking him home. That's the way it is...We'll get him Hospice in our town." I then began to count the number of times "power" was said. Just anything to keep from passing out.

At this point the chaplain became a little more assertive, without being impolite. He began to ask Donald questions in an attempt to establish some dialogue with him. He tried to explain that his father needed more care than the in-home care that Hospice provided. "But does your town have a Hospice facility?" He asked Donald. He told my brother that the facility in Nashville, called the Residence, had a vacancy for a male. He stated that that this was very fortunate as there was usually a waiting list.

Paying no heed to this last part of the chaplain's statement, Donald declared, "Well, we'll get him into one of these facilities where we live." I realized that my brother hardly understood what Hospice was, much less where Hospice facilities were located. Donald was trying to maintain his authoritarian tone, but it was belied by his uncertainty of what the chaplain was really asking. Realizing Donald didn't know what he was talking about, the chaplain helped him out. "Where do you live?" he asked my brother. "Kingston," Donald curtly replied. "Donald, the closest residence is in Knoxville. I know that one is the closest because I used to live in Knoxville." "Well, can't we get him into the Knoxville facility then?" The commanding tone returned. "I don't know Donald; we here in Nashville have the largest Hospice facility in the state, and it's very difficult to get a room even here, especially on very short notice. There is almost always a waiting list."

At this point Donald began directing the Hospice people who tried to oblige, and the nurse began trying to telephone the Knoxville Hospice facility to ascertain if there was a room. I, who had hardly said anything up until now, meekly whispered, "Mother, the Hospice facility here has a bed..." I was trying to complete the statement when my mother turned to me, and gave me a look that chilled me to the bone. My whole body was shaking. Her eyes were squinted and piercing; the look reminded me of something between a wolf and a snake. It was unquestionably the devil. I had seen some of that look a few times in the past, but it was a little mollified in previous encounters. This time there was no subtlety. Never in my worst nightmares or in the most horrifying picture shows had I seen anything resembling this look. This image was real, but there was nothing in a normal world to compare it with. I was rendered totally speechless.

This whole scene was becoming more surreal by the moment. Surely this was just some bad movie. Here was my brother commanding the Hospice chaplain, of whom he had been so disrespectful, to find a room or bed in the Knoxville facility! I had felt so grateful to have had the help of this organization, and these crazy people were treating their representatives as if they were their servants. "God, please don't let me go into shock...not yet," I prayed again. The nurse obliged my brother's directive to her and telephoned the Knoxville facility on her cell phone. I prayed that there wouldn't be a bed there. The ambulance still hadn't arrived. The nurse determined that while there wasn't a bed in that facility, there might be one on Monday. In the meantime, I was fiddling with my father's little bag that was going to go with him *somewhere*. I had put it together earlier in the morning, packing only the medicine he was taking at this point, along with some pampers and pajamas.

Then Donald's behavior slightly shifted. He began to *think* a little, rather than just react. He stopped throwing his weight around. All this business was clearly out of his league. Also, he had begun to realize that some of his activities might have to be curtailed if his father were transported to East Tennessee. He might have to take his mother to Knoxville. He might miss some hunting opportunities. It was only later that I learned why he had to get back that afternoon: he had, in fact, planned a hunting trip. Of course, I also realized later he probably needed to get back to have a drink. This was not going well for him. So he decided to return to his father's room to actually consider his father's condition. Up to this point, he hadn't spoken to him, much less assessed his physical or mental state. It was all about his and his mother's power and their control. It was the clearest battle between the forces of good and evil that I had ever seen or read about.

He came back out, a little shaken, more vulnerable sounding than before, and said to the Hospice folks that his father was, indeed, sicker than he had realized and he knew his mother couldn't handle his condition herself.

There was a slight opening. God was working one of His miracles. I thought I saw a hint of a tear in my brother's eye as he spoke, and thought that maybe, just maybe, he might have considered his father's need, just for a moment. Maybe he realized that Daddy was indeed blind now. Maybe he had actually *looked* at him! Or maybe his sobriety at that moment provoked some hint of his guilty secret of his complicity in this evil saga. Whatever caused the slight shift in his demeanor, I thought this might be the time to try to say something to Donald again to encourage him about this facility in Nashville. "Donald, this is a wonderful...." Again he turned around and walked out of the room, refusing to look me in the eye or listen to anything I had to say, once again denying my existence.

He came back in, sighed and stated exasperatedly, "We can't stay; she didn't bring any clothes." There it was. There had never been any intention to stay. It was only later confirmed that my brother's sense of urgency had indeed come from his planned hunting trip that afternoon, and the intent was to get Daddy in the car and get back to East Tennessee in time to make that outing. Again, they had deceived me into thinking my mother would stay a few days just as they had deceived me the previous year when my father was hospitalized and my mother had at one point agreed to allow my father to stay in the area until he was well enough to travel to East Tennessee. On that day my brother also had had something he had to do that evening, so they had taken my father in my mother's car to East Tennessee directly from the hospital. "Donald, I've lost seven pounds this week, and Mother can have any of my clothes she wants. I can't wear most of them anyway right now," I barely responded, in a wry monotone. The laryngitis had worsened just in the past hour, probably from the tension. Donald was already in the next room as I finished my sentence. This was sounding more and more like an Edward Albee play, even as I said the words. It was as if I had placed myself somewhere out of the scene and was watching some bizarre drama, maybe even too unreal for fiction.

But the chaplain had also seen there might be a sliver of hope to convince my brother, so he followed him and asked, "What about going ahead, since there is a room available here, and letting him stay at our facility through the week-end, until Monday?" But he began obliging Donald anyway by writing down the name of the facility in Knoxville, the exact location and the telephone number. I observed that my brother was really starting to realize now that *he* would have some responsibility from this point on, if they chose to try to move his father to East Tennessee. I could see his wheels turning; he might be seeing things differently. He had never had to actually *do* anything for his father, except to make decisions, but this might entail some *action*, like driving his mother to Knoxville. This indeed would be a drastic difference. What about his hunting trips with his sons? His other activities? He was clearly conflicted.

Donald then returned to his father's bedroom, and tried to speak to his mother about just allowing Daddy to stay through the week-end. I could hear the loud "I TOLD YOU ALL I'm taking him home," just before she fell to the floor, starting to throw one of her fits. For a brief moment, she forgot there were others present besides her family. It was almost unbelievable the extent to which hanging on to her control had affected this woman. Donald returned to the dining room and sighed, "Now she's mad at *me*," as he shook his head and actually sounded a little embarrassed and like a small boy. For a moment, I actually felt sorry for him. I had known that he had sold his soul to the devil a long time ago for money and power, and this was only one of probably hundreds of ways he had to pay for it. He would not, of course, contradict his mother, since he had – in his mind – every*thing* to lose. I at that moment was actually grateful to God that I didn't have to be concerned about losing anything, since I figured that the opportunity to have much of the family property had been removed long ago. I was aware that God was about to liberate Daddy and me from ever having again to be around this evil. The only reason I had had to endure them up until now was because of the impact on Daddy if I bucked them. Things, though, were reaching a crescendo.

Somehow, even with my mother's whining and carrying on, Donald finally got her to agree to allow Daddy to go to the facility for the week-end. But she was still insisting on "giving it through tomorrow," which was Sunday. In other words, I thought, Daddy has exactly one and a half days to die! But I somehow knew in my heart that God would take him before Monday, and for the first time, I began to feel a little relief from the tremendous evil and stress which had surrounded me since my mother and brother had walked into my home. There were still some *nexts* to accomplish, but the list was getting smaller.

The nurse was in my father's room and gave him some morphine as the ambulance pulled up. I hoped that this medicine would block out some of the histrionics my mother was exhibiting. I thought it best not to reenter Daddy's room, remembering what had happened when I had asked for a few minutes with Daddy in the last winter at the hospital and my mother and brother refused my wish and accused me of trying to kill him. That image of him with tears in his eyes was so vivid that I didn't want anything to increase whatever tension and conflict he might be experiencing now, however much I longed to speak to him. I just prayed that the morphine would prevent him from being aware that I would not say good-bye to him. On the other hand, I knew he could be hearing all this commotion about his plight, and I just prayed to God that if he were, then Daddy might think that there were people intervening on his behalf.

Actually I was trusting *God* to intervene against this devil and just get Daddy to an intermediate safe place until he could get on to heaven. So I was retrieving Daddy's little bag I had quickly put together earlier with basic necessities he would need for a couple of days until he died.

Up until this point, neither my mother nor my brother had actually realized that I had made the decision without them to transport Daddy to the Hospice facility. When they saw the ambulance, they both looked at each other and then at me as if they could not believe I had made such a decision without their permission. I only thought with horror about what they would have done, had the Hospice folks not been present. I took a deep breath, and as the ambulance personnel came into the house to get Daddy, I followed my brother outside and handed him the little bag I had prepared. "What's this? Aren't you going to follow us?" his voice rising. "No," I managed to whisper. "What do you mean, you're NOT going?" He was just about screaming at this point, but his awareness of close neighbors forced him to try to control himself a bit. "All you ever do is cause conflict!" He spat out the words. What an irony. Here I was handing over the precious control he and Mother demanded, and this was his response.

I merely quietly stated in a hoarse monotone, between coughs, "This one contains the only medicine he's now taking; the rest of his medicine is in the other bag. He is only taking a few sips of liquid." My voice sounded to me like a hoarse zombie's. My cough continued to worsen, and I didn't know I could say what was needed. But these words simply had to be said. They were important. My brother was looking at me in disbelief. "She will have to stay here with you!" he snapped. "No, actually, the facility provides beds for family members," I responded, feeling like a "dead woman walking." For a moment my voice actually returned. Later I realized that my brother's anger must have been at capacity since he then realized he would have to drive back to Nashville the next day after his hunting trip. I then walked around to the side of my house, as the medical personnel loaded Daddy into the ambulance and my mother climbed in the back seat.

"Lord, just as I have prayed before, I must just trust you to take care of Daddy from here on to eternity. You know why I can't go. Thank you, Lord." Several reasons drove my decision not to go to the facility. My presence would have increased the conflict in the atmosphere; I knew I was in no state to even have to be around the two of them since at this point I was in some kind of trauma and shock myself; I knew Daddy was going to a safe facility and he would be able to die in as little pain as possible; this way my mother could be perceived to her friends as the final caregiver, and my mother and brother could think they were in the final control of things.

The chaplain followed me, and I told him why I wasn't going to the facility.

He said I was doing the right thing. As we came back into the house, I was trying to tell him and the nurse through that hoarse, coughing voice a little something about the years of abuse my father had endured. I was aggravated that the stress had increased my bronchitis and laryngitis. I had so much I wanted to say to them. After a few words, I realized it was impossible, not only because of my lost voice, but because my mouth had gotten so dry there was no saliva, and I was having difficulty thinking at all. I figured that he couldn't possibly have believed me anyway, since it was all too bizarre even for those who had witnessed it throughout my life. He had no history of this family, and he probably would think I was crazy as well if I tried to give him sordid details. I just stopped, and with my hand gestures I asked them for a minute to regain her ability to speak. I thought if I mentioned two facts then perhaps the chaplain could figure out the rest. I told him the money and effort I had spent these past two years just to have the opportunity to get Daddy needed medical attention, and I mentioned that I had chosen to give up my work to try to intervene on his behalf some years ago. That was it, though. My voice was gone. I hoped that he had been able to see for himself some of the rest of the story.

Trained to perceive trauma and grief, the chaplain gave me a hug, and seemed to grasp at least some of what I was trying to tell him. Later, as he met with me, he offered that he had vividly seen the control and power my mother had over *me*, and he could catch a glimpse of the years of abuse. I had not really wanted to convince him of any abuse to *me*. But later I learned that this was what he primarily saw, a small girl about ten again, cowering with fright. He could only speculate as to the why.

The worst was over. God had interceded after all! He had chosen to control the devil. He had begun the liberation of both my father and myself. Praise Him!

My neighbor asked me to come in, and she talked about God's perfect timing as she had observed some of the morning's events. I really couldn't talk myself, and she perceived that I was in some sort of shock. I had earlier thought that God was late with everything. But it turned out that He wasn't. Had the ambulance arrived earlier, the Hospice chaplain would not have had the opportunity to see for himself what I was up against. At least now, there were other witnesses to my mother's behavior. A few years earlier there had also been witnesses at the Veteran's Administration when my mother realized she wasn't going to get money from them, so her plan to dump my father there had been foiled. They were not nearly as polite and gracious as the Hospice folks were. Secondly, the chaplain would not have had the opportunity to talk my brother into at least allowing Daddy to go to the Residence for the week-end. This way, my brother could appear to still have control of that decision. Had Daddy been transported before they had arrived, the rage that would have resulted could have been dangerous for both Daddy and me. Neither the chaplain nor the nurse would have been at the Residence, so anything could have happened. This way I knew Daddy was going to be safe, because I somehow knew that he would not live until Monday. I was the only one who knew that he had been dying for days. Even though the Hospice staff wouldn't know any history of the past few weeks, I did know they understood pain and would ensure that my father would have as little as possible as he traveled to the next world. Lastly, this gave my mother and brother the control they were seeking.

I knew Daddy was finally going home. I knew that God would take him before Monday. Though I had not said good-bye, I hoped that God would tell him why.

CHAPTER 33

Come unto me all ye that labour and are heavy laden, and I will give you rest.
—*Matthew 11:28*

CLIMB ON BOARD, DADDY

Although I wanted desperately to be with my father, I didn't go that day to the facility because I feared that my presence would make it worse on Daddy and he was in enough horrible circumstance already. It was a decision over which I still agonize. I was determined to do what I could to keep the conflict out of his presence and was uncertain of my mother and brother's reaction if I tried to talk to him there. At least at the house there had been the chaplain and the nurse, but if we were at the facility, the hospital staff could not always be around. I was still traumatized and exhausted, so I knew that I would be easily upset myself. I was also coughing and wheezing, so I shouldn't be around any really sick person.

So I just decided all I could do was pray. I began, but my prayers were just more or less mumbled fragments. My whole body was shaking, more from nervousness than from being cold. Realizing I needed someone to pray with me, I telephoned my pastor who had been aware of much of my situation. Unable to reach him, I phoned the church and talked to one woman on staff and asked her if she could see me. I had to do something to keep from going to the facility and to be with someone who could give more coherence to my prayers.

Fortunately the church was within a couple of miles of my house, and so I was able to drive there, even though dazed and disoriented. The weight of the past few days had really started to catch up with me. God had enabled me to do the next urgent thing time after time, and now that the urgency seemed to be removed, I could actually let out some release. Since I could hardly speak, I just mentioned a little about what had happened and asked her if she would pray for my father to be safe and free of pain. As she did, I shed tears which had been welling up for so long.

Afterwards, I began questioning my decision not to go to the Hospice facility. Would the nurses there know the exact amount of morphine I had been giving my father? How could they have the complete information about Daddy's Alzheimer's as well as his heart conditions? I knew that the Hospice nurse who had spoken to them had not had the chance to know the deteriorating condition of my father during the week. I knew that my mother had not comprehended her husband's illness, nor did she have the ability to focus on him. I knew the medical staff couldn't possibly know about the pathology of my mother and brother. To this day I am still anguished that I had not gone sooner to the facility, but at that point in time, there were just too many unknowns, and I was so concerned about any rage my mother was apt to exhibit. Only God knows whether I did the right thing.

I just kept telling myself that these folks were trained to know and piece together information about dying patients, and I just kept praying that God would give them the insight to know what might not have been communicated to them.

Later on that day, I began to think more clearly, and I telephoned one close friend and one of my father's close relatives and asked them to pray that God would especially guard Daddy now. I was unable to reach Marie or my closest friend, who was on a fishing trip in a remote place where cell phones didn't work. So it was just mainly God again with whom I communicated.

Telephoning the facility that evening after I had taken some more medicine and hot tea for my throat, I talked to the charge nurse, in order to get an update on my father. I knew that on the Hospice paper work I had been defined as the primary care giver, and I knew they would be perplexed about why I wasn't there. "Do you know how very sick your father is?" he asked. Do *I* know how sick he is! At the moment, I was frustrated and annoyed at the question, forgetting that they had no real history about Daddy's care. This nurse probably didn't know that I had been the one who had taken care of Daddy all week – and over the past several years for that matter. "Yes sir, I do, as he was transported from my home at noon today." I wanted so desperately to warn him about my mother, but I knew I had to be very careful. I could be perceived as the crazy one. "My mother is somewhat unstable and doesn't understand how sick he really is. Because I didn't want to increase any conflict in the room for my father, I thought it best not to come to the facility. But I'm very concerned and would you please telephone me if there is any change in his condition? Would you also convey to the nurse who comes in on the next shift about the situation? I will be very grateful." I tried to sound professional through my hoarse voice. I realized that I was taking too much of his time, but I just had to convey my sense of urgency somehow. The nurse said he had to go because he had patients in a lot of pain who needed him. Afraid to ask if one of them was my father, I just said that, of course, I understood.

326 • STORM ENDS...RED SKY BEGINS

I wondered how much the charge nurse believed me. I just hoped that either the Hospice nurse or chaplain might have filled the staff in a little on Daddy's health problems, but they didn't know much about the family situation either. Even if they did, they had to maintain objectivity. My major concern was that the facility didn't have the medical records on my father, since it was on a Saturday and probably no one would be able to contact his cardiologist. In my mother's mind, this was just Alzheimer's, and she had never even acknowledged his aortic stenosis, the major reason he was dying and in such great pain.

Telephoning several times during the night to inquire about his condition, each time I was told that he was non-responsive and gravely ill. I was told he had a morphine pain patch on, and I thought that he probably should have had one on all week. I felt so guilty. How much pain had he suffered at my uncertain hands?

I expected any moment to receive a telephone call that he had passed away. Daddy miraculously made it through the night, but the nurse on duty at 5:30 the next morning said she was amazed that he was still alive. She didn't see how he might make it another hour. I telephoned the charge nurse on duty up in the morning and asked if someone might bring Mother a plate of food, since I was afraid she hadn't eaten. Earlier I had telephoned to discover there wasn't a restaurant in the facility, but I knew there would be a kitchen. I asked her to not tell my mother that I had asked for the food.

Surely God would take Daddy to heaven that morning. He didn't. Toward noon, my mother phoned me. "Are you coming here today? You kept his charger for his razor and I want him to look nice today. Also I need his clothes." The charger for his shaver! Want him to look nice today! Again my mother's reality was so far removed from the events that were unfolding. I didn't know whether she meant she wanted him to look nice when he finally passed away, or whether somewhere in her brain, she was fearful that her image as care giver would be questioned. In either case, my mother's words reinforced her mental state. I quickly put Daddy's clothes together in a garment bag, along with the charger to his razor and took them to the facility. It was pouring down rain, and I left them at the front desk with the receptionist. I asked her to inform my mother that they were there after I had left.

I established some dialog with a young nurse at the facility late in the afternoon. There was something about this young woman which made me feel that I could be more open with her than with any of the others with whom I had previously spoken. I broached the subject of my mother cautiously. "Ms. Reed, I know you don't know me, but I have been taking care of my father.

I am very concerned about my mother's mental condition and its impact on my father. She needs to be watched carefully." The nurse responded, "I'm glad you told me this. Today I realized her reality was different from ours, when she was talking with her friends on the phone. She was threatening to take your father out of here if he didn't improve in a short time. But then she began talking about his funeral, her bridge club, and she was fussing at her son for cutting his hunting trip short."

Oh, no, I thought. I realized then what I had feared was true. Daddy, even in death, had no one from the family really showing him any attention. It was all about the rest of them. If this had been any other person, it would have been impossible to imagine this conversation going on when your husband is dying. But was this so different than everything that had transpired so far? I learned from that conversation that my brother had been there, probably to bring his mother some clothes. I was frightened at how much of this Daddy might have heard. I knew that the last sense to go is the hearing. Again, I tried to trust God that He would block out some of this for my father.

I berated myself for not going to the facility, realizing that Daddy had no one there to hold his hand. But I still realized that had I been there, my mother wouldn't have wanted me near him, and I would have been constrained in what I wanted to say to him. I was deeply conflicted.

Throughout the day I continuously prayed. "Why, Lord, oh why, won't you take my father, so he can be at peace from this madness and in your protective custody?" Suddenly, around seven o'clock in the evening, I had a thought. I later learned that it was at this very time that a prayer group, which included my associate pastor, was praying for Daddy and me at my church. The conversation late Friday night rang in my head. My father had asked me never to leave him, declaring that I was his "baby girl." He had also quietly, but clearly, stated that he had always loved me and didn't care what the "rest of them" said about me. He wanted me to know he still knew the difference between them and me. And yet here I was, at my home, instead of at the facility holding his hand. A friend tried to comfort me by saying what I had already thought could have happened: that I would not have felt free to say anything to Daddy or hold his hand without my mother's scoffing, or worse, if my brother were there.

I telephoned the young nurse I had spoken to earlier and learned that Donald had gone back to East Tennessee. "Ms. Reed, I have been thinking that the last words I spoke to my father were about 30 hours ago. I had told him that I would never leave him. What if he's afraid to die thinking that something has happened to me? He often said that *she* could kill us both. Or what if he thinks I have abandoned him? I believe I *do* need to see my father. Do you think, if I come over there, that you could get my mother out of the room, maybe to a coffee shop or just somewhere?" She replied, "I think you may be right; it's worth a try."

I sped to the facility. Upon arriving at the front desk, the receptionist told me that Ms. Reed wanted to see me. Oh, my, was I too late? At that moment, Ms. Effie Reed immediately came out and hugged me. She was one of those naturally pretty young women who seemed to radiate warmth and compassion. "Guess what," she said in low tones. "Your mother is fast asleep." God had delivered me yet another miracle! Although it was early evening, God had put her to sleep. Effie wouldn't have to get her out of the room. "Thank you God."

As we walked down the corridor, Ms. Reed quietly said to me, "I want to try to prepare you for the physical condition of your father. He's in what we call the death gurgle." I just nodded and took a deep breath. As we arrived at his door, I asked Effie if she would go in with me. I wanted her to hear what I said, and I wanted her to observe my father. We tiptoed in the room; I just barely glanced in the direction of my mother, and saw that she had her head covered up. "Thank you Lord." I tried really hard not to be affected emotionally because I knew I had one more mission to accomplish.

I went over to Daddy, trying hard to ignore as much as humanly possible the image of this poor little marine, lying there in a fetal position and eliciting sounds of what sounded like deep congestion and labored breathing. This must be what they call the death gurgle, I thought. Perhaps they were the faint faltering accents struggling in death to give more one assurance of affection for me. I talked gently but distinctly in his ear, trying to almost smile with my voice. It seemed as if every mission for my father got a little harder to accomplish. But I knew I just had to psyche myself over the difficulty and imagine that I was in a play with a few important lines to deliver. "Daddy, this is your baby girl, and I am just fine. And Mother is fine and Donald is fine. Daddy, that train is here and God is telling you to get on it." About this instant, I noted a slight shift in his gurgle, but I didn't know what it meant or how to measure it. I was determined my voice wasn't going to crack, and I continued. "Mammy and Papa are already on it, and Daddy, you have taken care of everything." I wanted so much to settle Daddy's account with his conscience for any past action where he might still feel concern or remorse. I didn't know if he could feel any peace at this late hour, but I wanted so much to give him some. I wanted to let him know that loved ones were waiting for him. Later I regretted I didn't touch his hand. I guess I was afraid to. "It's time for you to get on that train now." Fearing my mother might awaken, I didn't dare linger, although later I regretted that my fear of her drove my actions rather what might have been best for my father – just as it had most of my life.

The nurse and I tiptoed out of the room. My mother never knew we were there. The nurse hugged me. "I think he heard you," she said. "Because of the shift in the gurgle?" I asked. She nodded. "I believe he needed that, but you needed it too," Effie said encouragingly. I thanked her and asked her to telephone me when Daddy died. But I knew that the request was redundant, and that she would indeed telephone me the minute Daddy passed away.

When I got home, I returned the call from my pastor, who prayed with me that my father would now pass into heaven, and I telephoned the preacher at Daddy's home church, Salem, where I was determined to hold his memorial service. He also prayed with me for much the same and for peace for me. After I hung up the phone, I picked it up again to telephone my neighbor and realized from my voice mail that there was a message from Effie Reed asking me to telephone her. I knew before I returned her call that Daddy had finally left this world. "Ms. Huddleston, your father passed away a few minutes ago, and I was holding his hand as I was giving him his last shot of morphine." "Oh, thank you Ms. Reed, thank you for being with my father when he died, for holding his hand, and praise God." Daddy was finally in a place where time, pain, and sorrow are unknown. He was in heaven, his "home," where he so longed to go, and no one could hurt him there. He and I were finally free.

CHAPTER 34

There the wicked cease from troubling, and there the weary be at rest.

—Job 3:17

THE JOURNEY ENDS

B reathing a sigh of relief since I would no longer have to put on a happy face, I walked out of the little country church in Cookeville where Daddy's Memorial service had been conducted. Salem Church was the church to which both he and I had been taken as youngsters by my grandmother, his mother. It was there that we both had experienced the sweet spirit of God's love which dwelled in the hearts of rural, sometimes poor people. Daddy and I had frequently attended its services during the past years prior to his becoming too sick to travel. He loved the church because the people spoke to him as they always had – not over him or around him. He had known their fathers, and he had still known some of them. He knew the hymns they sang. His great grandfather had given the land for both the cemetery (which held the graves of his parents) and the church, so there was much history for him there. Consequently, I decided I must hold his memorial service there.

It was just at the time when the sun began to peak through the clouds on what had started out as a cold, bleak day in early November. Daddy was finally home, away from all the malevolence and insanity. Over the past preceding years both of us had been forced to daily navigate through the many evil mine fields in a family which had become dominated by greed and power. It surely was God who had helped me carry out this final mission for my father, even though it meant a total separation from the rest of my family. My mother had insisted from time to time that I get and stay out of their lives, and now I could. Likewise, Daddy's death was his escape from a two-fold bondage which had held him captive for many years – the bondage resulting from his own scrambled brain and the bondage resulting from another mind, one so severely deranged that most would never believe it could exist, belonging to one who had controlled his life for so many years. And I no longer had to pander to anyone for fear of reprisal on him. So in one major way I was also now free, and at that moment, felt relatively peaceful knowing that God knew I had done my best for my father. But my liberty sat uneasily on me, not really having processed all that had gone on during the previous five years.

During those years, particularly, there had been so many battles fought on his behalf. I didn't know now what to do "next." There was always an urgent *next*. I had watched this little courageous man, afflicted with serious heart conditions and Alzheimer's, endure so much physical and mental pain, while surviving the *other* mental illness in the family, even in his final hours. This was a father whom I had hardly known until he became an Alzheimer's victim. At that time, I believed that the battles were finally over and God had taken him to heaven, his eternal home. God had given me confirmation on Daddy's death bed that he was on his way there. But I felt I had one more mission: that his memorial service was held at the place he always considered his *earthly* home.

It *had* to have been God who gave me the determination and strength to perform the various tasks needed for this service to come off as Daddy would have liked, given the events of the preceding two weeks. So I thanked Him for enabling me to prepare the service, in spite of exhaustion and lingering bronchitis. Although I had only slept four hours during the final week, the adrenalin kept pumping because I knew this was my last battle for my dad, even though I believed he was finally home safe in his eternal home.

I had spent a day and a half trying to discover exactly when and where my father's funeral was to be held so the timing wouldn't conflict with my memorial service and to enable anyone coming from East Tennessee to have the opportunity to attend this service as well. I could also get the word out to Daddy's relatives who would want to attend the memorial and his burial service. After finally discovering from the paper that the funeral was to be held about 80 miles from Daddy's hometown and where his memorial and burial service would be, I still didn't know the date or time.

I made several calls to the funeral home and each time was given ambiguous information. Maybe the funeral director didn't even believe my father had a daughter, or maybe he was told not to tell me. In any event, I finally found out from one of Daddy's cousins that it was being held on election *night!* I could hardly believe it. But why wouldn't I have? This ensured that my mother's friends could attend and most of Daddy's couldn't. The weather forecast was for a rainy, foggy, and cold night, and his elderly friends and relatives simply couldn't feel safe driving across the Cumberland Mountain and returning to their homes, especially with anticipated drunken drivers celebrating or decrying election results. Still trying to find out the exact time the ambulance would be coming to the cemetery where Daddy was to be buried so I could plan the time of his memorial service around it, I telephoned the funeral home one more time. This time the seemingly nervous funeral director said, "Your mother's here; you can speak directly with her." Not really wanting to, I had no choice. In my typical, quaking, timid voice I so despised, I asked, "Mother, could you tell me the approximate arrival time of the ambulance at the cemetery so that I may coordinate the memorial service with it?" "Oh, we're not certain...You just do your little service in Cookeville and my friends will come to mine," she sighed.

With my own physical condition, not only would Daddy's relatives in Cookeville and Nashville not be able to attend, but neither did I have the energy required to make it up and back to my home to prepare his memorial service. I was afraid that Mother would try to disrupt my final tribute to my father, so I was trying hard not to inconvenience her.

During my entire life I had always been trying not to inconvenience her. It was always and forever about Mother. "The ambulance can't wait very long; I'm having to pay for it," she added. It was always and forever about money.

As I sat there alone on the front pew, listening to the song, "Precious Lord, Take My Hand," I prayed hard that I wouldn't break down in tears during my eulogy. This was a song from the CD recorded at my church in Nashville when Daddy and I had attended the taping, and he had responded aloud to the singer. Actually, I was beyond tears and in somewhat of a dazed state, staring at the urn on the altar which held the now drooping red, white, and blue flower arrangement I had brought from Nashville. Since it was too tall to stand upright on the inside of my friend's SUV, we had to lay it on its side, so the flowers were a little bent over. But it served well enough to remind everyone of his wartime service and patriotism. This service was about the one thing that I had known about his past before our journey together.

This was one of those times when you appear to others to be functioning, but it feels to you like someone else is performing the needed tasks. Every time I heard the door to the small sanctuary open, I jumped, fearing someone might barge in to abort this last little activity for Daddy.

My associate pastor in Nashville, assisted by the Salem Church pastor, conducted some of the service. Several of my friends, who had become Daddy's friends over the past several years, and his Nashville cousins drove from Nashville early that morning to the small town church.

My mother, brother and his sons chose not to attend, though they were on the premises, waiting to bury my father's body, because Mother had created yet another competition between the services for the guests. She had given friends and relatives a choice: they could either attend *her* service *or* the one at Salem. I had telephoned my brother's home the morning of the memo-rial service and asked Marie to urge my brother to attend and to convince our mother to attend as well. He told Marie that his mother had said "no," so he couldn't attend either. I was so thankful I had only to respond to God, and that I was not bound in the chains of fear that he was.

I knew Daddy had so yearned for peace within the family and for them to stop hating and resenting me. He knew there was refuge from "the storm," and it was to get your family together and get them into the House of the Lord. He had said so to the hospital chaplain just months before his death. But it was not to be. So I just prayed that those whom God wanted at that ser-vice would be there and that He would keep evil out of it. Though my father's brother staggered in drunk at one point, after he realized that I was speaking, he cursed and left.

Somehow I got through the service, delivering the eulogy without tears, because I knew I had to perform this final mission for my father. I felt hon-ored to do this, because he had never really been recognized in or for his life. I was almost numb, and it was only on my trip back to Nashville that I began to feel deep pain and a tragic loss. It wasn't about losing an elderly parent. It was about losing a parent I had the opportunity to know only a short time, after he lost his "other mind." It was the pain of knowing how many years my mother had kept my father and me apart by creating rifts between us. It was pain that resulted from realizing that no one else in the family had ever bothered to know my father, and therefore could not really see his value. It was realizing what he had been forced to endure. It was the pain of not knowing the "next" thing to do. At that time I didn't have any strength left to feel pain about how much the family had hated me. I didn't even feel the emptiness and coldness that would follow.

CHAPTER 35

...I press toward the mark for the prize of the high calling of God in Christ Jesus.
—Philippians 3:14

CONTINUING STORMS...
THEN THE RED SKY

The will of God is supreme and everything else disappears in light of this truth. But to know this will requires much prayer and reflection. After five years of depression following my father's death, thinking that God had abandoned me, just as my family had, I finally recovered the belief that my life really did have a high purpose, to love and care for those who have been abandoned by others or who have become invisible in our society. But it took a long time to get it back.

Up until two years ago, I found myself wryly smiling about the difference in my objectives ten years ago and the objectives during those five years following my father's death. For years before the journey with my father, I had measured my success largely by the evaluations from my adult audiences and how they implemented the training into their jobs, as my trainers and I taught managers and team leaders all over the world how to write long-term objectives and weekly actions to support a continuous improvement culture. I slightly remember the joy I felt as I read their evaluations after a week of training. And then following my father's death, my skeletal pain had reduced my daily objectives to a little tutoring and writing, teaching Bible, and visiting the elderly in nursing homes.

Shortly after Daddy died, I became determined to refocus my life and return to my work. A few friends who had known a little about the journey with him had admonished me to do just that. What they and even I did not fully know at the time was that there actually was not much of a life left to get on with. Six months after my father died, my mother died, and it was then that I finally received a copy of my father's will, which my attorney had asked for several times since his death. I knew that death doesn't necessarily ensure that no one can hurt you anymore, but I really hadn't processed how much I had been resented until then. I had been robbed of my inheritance. Daddy's will appeared to have been tampered with shortly after his death, because his signatures weren't the same on every page of his will, and the signatures on this document didn't match the signatures I had of his on his Social Security card and in his Bible. This malevolent deed confirmed that my mother and brother were certain I would never again dare think that I was a real part of their family. It was, indeed, a setback. I thought about challenging it, but my attorney advised against it since this latest action increased my physical challenges, and I was just about financially broke, having had very little gainful employment for the previous few years while attending to my parents. "Kathryn, you've been through too much to have this on you; don't do it." So I just tried to push one more awful thing out of my mind. One more awful thing pushed aside surely wouldn't do me in.

I suspected that it would be the end of any interaction with my biological family since they now had more than enough money to meet their needs and wouldn't need anything else from me. I was right. It has been over seven years now since I have seen or heard from any of them. One of Daddy's cousins, whose family was very kind to Daddy *and* me, informed me some time ago that my last uncle had died. But this was the uncle who had stumbled into Daddy's little memorial service, cursing after realizing I was performing the service. He was also the one who had scowled at me during my grandmother's service. So he certainly wouldn't have wanted me at his funeral nor left me any assets. My brother and Jenny Dillon's daughters, his other nieces, were probably his heirs.

But work would be the key to forgetting the painful past and earning some money again to ameliorate some of my financial losses incurred while taking care of my parents. I would just "reinvent" myself. At the time of Daddy's death, I still believed that God's Providence could draw a good outcome from any circumstance, if it is for His purposes. He would do this even for me.

My skeletal pain had become exacerbated by the stress of the previous five years, especially my mother's latest action, so I realized I couldn't perform the same *type* of work I had done before becoming involved with my father. But I also knew that some sort of work was needed to help me refocus. So almost immediately after both parents died, I jumped back into college teaching. I had been a writing professor before beginning my training business and thought that this job would compel me to think about something else and therefore reduce the effects of stress and grief, responsible for much of my pain. I was not about to allow myself any time to reflect on the previous painful years, especially on the last few months, because I would then have to relieve the trauma. I was determined to put it all quickly out of my mind and immerse myself in something that wouldn't remind me at all of those years. I swept my grief quickly underground.

So shortly after both parents died, I had the opportunity to teach writing at an Ivy League university where I had earlier taught. Instead of it relieving my pain, there I encountered a similar scenario to the one many years earlier at the community college. Only this time it concerned football players and the chancellor's determination that they would all graduate with high grades.

Some of them in one class were writing at about a third grade level, talking in class about their outside activities and calling up pornographic material on their laptops. Their grades reflected their weaknesses. So began trumped-up accusations that I had a prejudice against athletes. But one student athlete, a Christian and a good student, stood up for me, telling the coach and the players' tutor that I was the best English teacher he ever had. I told him he had done the right thing for the class and for God. Though at the time he suffered some reprisal for his action, later he became a star quarterback on that team. Also, I had some basketball players in another class who were among my best students, receiving grades which confirmed their achievement. None of the accusations were borne out, and neither the coach nor the writing program director was able to make any of the charges stick. However, I remained under constant pressure to figure out a way for some students to make a B grade. So I began tutoring a few of the weakest ones, without charge, so they and I could legitimize a decent grade. Even with that, not all students did get high grades, and I knew I couldn't take the pressure of tossing my integrity away another semester. Besides, the stress had contributed to my skeletal pain. The good news is that I received a fair number of e-mails and notes from students who thanked me for caring enough to uphold high standards and maintain academic integrity.

But the most significant good that resulted from my return to that university involved a freshman female student in another writing class who had written very good essays. From the beginning of the semester, though, I had detected some depression in her non-verbal language, and I could tell from her writings that she was a Christian. After the class ended one day, I asked her if she had a few minutes to talk. She seemed eager. I mentioned my concern about what I had perceived in her countenance. She broke down in tears and said she had never realized how hard it would be on Christians at this school. I totally empathized with her tears, because I knew that I was probably the only conservative teacher in the Humanities Department and had received pressure myself for mentioning tenets of Christianity in response to one of the readings in our text about another religion. "Jill, I truly understand how tough this is for you, but there really are Christian students here; you just have to find them." We talked for about an hour, and later I learned that this hour may have saved her life. I came to discover she was on the brink of suicide, and that hour and some more counseling had given her hope. At the time I had no idea her depression was this great, but I did understand how God's children are often alienated. She wrote me a letter after the semester, telling me what a difference I had made in her life. Knowing that I had saved the one student's life was worth the harassment I had endured.

Even though an ultimate good came from that semester of teaching, my physical pain became greater in part because I had not taken time to grieve and in part because of the pressure to maintain some academic integrity. I was forced to address it, and as a result of several medical tests, I discovered that my scoliosis, osteoarthritis, and osteoporosis had worsened, and I needed a hip replacement.

So the attempt to recover my sense of self and forget my past was thwarted. The images of the agonizing phases of my father's illness I was determined to get out of my mind made their way back into my head with a vengeance. Except to those with whom I interviewed for just some part-time work and to those I was still trying to serve, like my elderly Bible students, I gave up my enthusiastic mask of cheeriness and optimism I had worn throughout most of my life. It appeared that God had entirely cut me off, so why should I pretend any more that He was there for me or try to show any joy that I didn't feel? But I *was* determined to keep it on in the presence of my older friends because I didn't want to take away *their* joy and optimism stemming from *their* belief that God would never leave them and would supply all their needs, especially since they were nearing death themselves. I continued to pray that God would send me confirmation that He claimed me and confirm what I had always thought was His mission for my life. But for years I received very little signal of this.

Therefore, I re-wrote my will and funeral plans and just prayed that somehow God would allow me to squeak into heaven, realizing that if He didn't, then heaven had always been only an elusive hope, just like so much of my life had been. I had longed to be there for most of my life, but it seemed there was always someone who needed me to stick around in this world because there was no one else to count on. Well, now I had a window; everybody was taken care of.

Again, I was wrong. What I became reminded of is that all the inner suffering for and response to those abandoned or invisible was, evidently, intended by God to be my life...*still*. Several events have especially helped me know this and believe that maybe He hasn't left me after all nor is He entirely finished with me.

THE RETURN OF ALECE'S CANCER

Within a year after my parents' death, I noticed that my deaf friend Alece was suffering from something other than digestive problems, for which her internist had prescribed over the counter medicines. Timmy was still recovering from a drug and alcohol addiction but had checked himself into a treatment program. I supported him in this effort and took his mother with me to his meetings until she became too sick to go. With both of them ill, it was up to me to discover what was really going on. So I again became more actively involved in her life. I had frequently asked Timmy about what he thought about her illness, but he was unable or unwilling to recognize that it could be extremely serious. I finally convinced both him and his mother to see the oncologist who had treated her for breast cancer, and the tests revealed ovarian cancer. Her doctor, who remembered me from years before when she had her first cancer, told me he thought it was in a late stage, but only surgery could confirm it. The surgery verified stage four.

Following the surgery, she was very depressed and appeared not to want to see me. She had always resented me to some degree, but it didn't matter. I was the only person willing to care for her, and I continued to see her every day, facilitating getting her into a skilled nursing facility and later skilled nursing care at her home. She continued to rapidly decline, not being able to eat the food I was taking her. After only three weeks, the doctors wanted to do an experimental extremely aggressive chemotherapy protocol and convinced her she would die without it. Her handwritten note to me stated, "But chemo will melt cancer...if I don't have it, I die." I tried to convince her not to have it and the doctors not to proceed with it. I explained that she had no one to attend to her except me, and I was limited because of my own physical condition. I knew her body couldn't withstand this treatment and asked if they might refer her to Hospice. But I was not a relative, and thus had no voice in her treatment – even though I had been her voice for almost 30 years. Besides Alece being mentally challenged, deaf, and poor, Timmy was still in his treatment and couldn't process the reality.

Still highly vulnerable, he wasn't able to resist the doctors' insistence about this treatment over my pleadings. He could not and would not imagine that she was dying, and I was unable to convince him that his mother couldn't survive this aggressive protocol.

So, like his mother, he chose to listen to her doctors, who convinced her she would die without it. In spite of my urging the doctors that her body was too frail for this aggressive treatment, they began anyway. She did die, after the first round. I cleaned out her duplex, helping move the old, beaten-up furniture to a storage facility, made the burial arrangements, conducted the funeral, and paid for it. These events exacerbated my skeletal problems and contributed to my need for a hip replacement. So within a few months of Alece's death, and following the end of that stressful semester of teaching, I had the hip replacement. It took me almost a year to realize that she really was dead because I had seen about her for so many years.

But Timmy completed his program, and he has been clean now for three years. He has a good job, is married to a very smart woman, and they have a baby. I remain grieved that I was powerless to save his mother, but I realize that I was the only one she could depend on during the last stage of her life and the only one Timmy could really depend on after her death. So God knew better than me that the journey with my father was not to be my final mission.

GAINING INSPIRATION FROM OTHERS: GLEN'S STORY

Subsequent events also verified that God might have more in mind than I did for my life. Because my skeletal pain continued even following my hip replacement surgery, the close friend who had bought me a new washer and drier gave me a subscription to a water therapy program for arthritis and other skeletal-muscular conditions. This therapy enabled me to regain considerable physical and psychological strength. It gave me the opportunity to meet inspiring, caring people, a couple of whom have made me ashamed that I ever felt depressed about anything. I became acquainted with Margaret who was blind and suffering from Parkinson's disease. Having discovered that she was taking public transportation to the Center, I determined that at least this was one burden I could remove from her. So I began picking her up and gained inspiration by her courage. Another woman, Mary, 93 years old, was a regular until she broke her hip and had to move into a nursing home. Since she really had no close relatives, I began to visit her there. On Thanksgiving Day, I telephoned the facility and asked if this woman had had any visitors that day to bring her Thanksgiving dinner and was told there had not been a single one, and so I took her a plate of turkey, dressing, and the trimmings. The staff seemed grateful that someone had remembered her.

But there was one young man, 36 years old, whose story particularly reminded me of what evidently has been my life's overall mission and why I am still alive. I had only occasionally seen him in our warm water therapy pool, and we had had only brief conversations, but enough to know that he was a

Christian. Glen was always upbeat and encouraging to others, helping the other disabled people in his therapy classes. He had such hope that the water exercises would strengthen his body so he could have another kidney transplant. I would never have discovered his life of pain had I not probed one day, determined to discover more about his circumstance.

I learned he had undergone two kidney transplants, neither of which was successful and that he had been on dialysis for over 12 years. He had undergone an open heart surgery, was living with a pig valve, and had survived various other surgeries to strengthen his body to receive yet another kidney. While all this is hard for anyone to process, it was the rest of his story that had the most profound impact on me.

During the first surgery, his kidney actually clotted before the doctor put it in. Glen's body went into cardiac arrest, and he literally died. Glen related to me, "An angel came into my room, sat at the foot of my bed and told me that I had to go back to tell my story."

At the time I had completed a book on the value of warm water therapy for chronic pain from various chronic conditions in order to help the Center survive. The book was already at the press. I was prompted to self-publish it, absorbing the cost, because the Center for some time had been in deep financial trouble, and the proceeds were to be donated to warm water therapy initiatives. Many members had no other good alternative because they needed the warm water that this particular facility provided and one where the more vulnerable wouldn't feel intimidated. For some, it was like their family. The book had a chapter of "Profiles in Courage," relating some amazing stories of people whose lives had actually been saved, or who at least had gained more mobility and independence as a result of the therapy. They had inspired me to the extent that I had included their stories in the book. After hearing Glen's story, I knew I couldn't let this book be completed without integrating what he had told me. So I telephoned the press, the formatter, and said that regardless of the cost, it had to be reformatted and reprinted. When I gave a party for the members of "Water World," (as I called the water therapy center), mainly to honor those who had been so inspirational, I had asked Glen to tell his story. He was thrilled to have this opportunity, and everyone present was visibly touched. The book by this time had been printed, so his story was told aloud and in print.

He wanted a book signed for his granny, his aunt, his father, his sister, and it seemed like every other close relative. I was so grateful to God that Glen had crossed my path, because once again I realized my purpose. It had been some time since I had discovered and helped people who had been abandoned or invisible or had suffered huge pain that few others knew about. And then my interaction with most of them had been in the last phase of their lives. But now I had the chance to hope and pray that Glen could get his kidney, that his health could become better after so many years of suffering. I prayed several times a day that the warm water therapy would strengthen his body so he would be able to undergo a third kidney transplant. Having not had the chance to come to the Center for several months because of recent surgeries on his arm from the dialysis, one day he did come back! I had continued to ask his therapist about him, and had telephoned him a couple of times. But because he lived out of town and I didn't know if he felt like company, I had not gone to see him, a failure I will always regret. But I was so grateful to God that he was able to come back. Since I didn't know he was coming, I did not go that particular day, but several members told me he was in such good spirits and was hopeful about becoming a recipient for another kidney. Praise God! I couldn't wait until he could regularly return to the Center.

And then about three weeks following this one day he came, I received a telephone call early one Monday morning from his sister Missy, with whom he lived. Oh, no! From her tone, I knew before she told me that Glen had died. This just couldn't be! I had prayed passionately for him and so often, and now he was gone. He had been so hopeful. How in the world could God let this happen to a young man who loved Him and was such a great ambassador for Christ! All I could do was just say, "Oh, No"! I cried for two days straight, a reaction which was totally unbalanced with the degree of interaction I actually had from him. Could my own inner darkness be responsible for the intensity which had seemed to grow for those suffering? Why hadn't I gone to his home to see him? I am still grieved, but others have consoled me by saying that I had given him a chance to "tell his story," just like the angel had said. I have tried to rationalize his death by thinking that in God's omniscience, He must have known that a third kidney might also be rejected and Glen would have to go through so much more pain. I do know that he is in heaven and isn't hurting any more. But I am.

This last encounter with Glen confirmed to me that as long as I am on this earth, I will evidently continue to have the same mission, even though I might "feel" abandoned by Him. My reaction to and interaction with Glen increased my belief that maybe God was not quite finished with me. I told his story, and I will tell it again and again. The chapter of the book containing his story was read at his funeral. About a year after Glen died, his mother asked me to come to a kick-off for a kidney walk-a-thon and read the section from my book about the angel coming into his room, telling him he must go back to tell his story. I have given all his doctors copies for them to give to their patients. I know that nothing happens without God's permission, so if my suffering has in some way enabled an ultimate good result, it is okay. Even if this good end eludes me, so be it as well. In spite of my own suffering, I must continue to be totally available to God, and convince others of His availability to them.

ROBERT

And then along came Robert, who really brought me back full circle to the time when I believed with certainty that God had a will for my life, a will that had become submerged during the years since my father's death. He verified how the journey with Daddy would help me push through subsequent storms others were trying to survive. His life made mine look much less difficult and made me understand what it is *really* like to always have others looking over your shoulder, expecting you to mess up. I came to realize "once a prisoner, always a prisoner" in the eyes of the law and of many others. He made me understand why the recidivism rate is so high. For many minorities, it is easier to live in prison than to live outside. He has made me understand how just having the wrong name can create stereotypes within the criminal justice system which cannot be overcome. He has acquainted me with what it is *really* like to be *really* poor, living not from paycheck to paycheck, but from hour to hour. He made me ashamed that I had been grieved about losing my inheritance. I had never been without a roof over my head or enough to eat.

I met Robert when he was enrolled in a vocational rehabilitation program in a local community college where I began working as a writing tutor about five years after my father's death. I was helping him re-write a narrative essay about how anger and stress can overtake one's life and provoke him to get on the wrong track - to get out of God's will. The writing related the loss of parental support at a very young age (although there was never any blame attributed to anyone other than himself); living in various group homes; the wrongful killing of his older brother, who had pretty much taken care of him, by city policemen; and his sister becoming paralyzed in a car accident, all of which had produced such anger in him that he was determined to get back at everybody.

On his 18th birthday, Robert had ended up in a group attempting to rob a pawn shop. He did not commit the crime, but he was there with the wrong bunch of people, and because he didn't have a good defense lawyer, was convicted of accessory to robbery. Though he shouldn't have been, he was tried as an adult. Thus, he spent the next four years in prison. In response to my questions to him, he told me, "Dr. Huddleston, I was a model inmate, because God kept me out of trouble in prison, and I did everything I was supposed to do. I signed every piece of paper that was put in front of me, but I usually didn't really understand what I was signing." I came to discover that he had difficulty reading, and therefore I was certain that he, indeed, probably had not fully comprehended most of what he was told to sign. He was led to believe he was getting out after two years because of his perfect record. However, the week before he went before the judge, an African American had committed a harmful act against the judge's daughter, and she was so biased at that point that her judgment was affected. Robert was the guinea pig. She told him because he had been a model inmate, he was going to be released – in two years!

His narrative essay defined his life's goal of keeping other at-risk teens from getting on the wrong path, regardless of how difficult their circumstances may be. His paper included various statements about how God had blessed him! After reading it, I couldn't help but learn a little about the really steep hills he had climbed. Although he never asked me for help, I knew there was no way I could ever *just* tutor him in the learning center. As I talked with him, I soon became aware that he had learning disabilities, which made it difficult for him to read and comprehend subject matter in the curriculum he enrolled in. He had received inadequate counseling on those subjects that would be more apt to render him success. His incarceration and his mental disabilities had made it difficult to find employers who would hire him. But he had no difficulty recalling those experiences which had taken such a toll on his life and produced such a Christian testimony that I had rarely heard.

Having become deeply affected by what little I knew from a couple of discussions with him on campus, I just couldn't get Robert out of my head. I suppose on some level I realized that once again, I was about to enter another helpless person's world, without being invited. But I had no intention of living in it. I would just fix what appeared to be critical issues, and then be gone from it.

After learning he had been laid off from his job as a stock clerk around Christmas time because of the recession, and having no transportation, I concluded he had very little of anything, except a lot of relatives who were either incarcerated or whom he barely knew or had never met, due to a prolific father – whom he had only met while both of them were in prison. So initially my objective was just to help him write a good cover letter and résumé so he could get some sort of job and collect some nice clothes for him from my men

344 • STORM ENDS…RED SKY BEGINS

344 • STORM ENDS…RED SKY BEGINS

friends in order to at least make a good first impression in interviews. Yes, that would be it. I knew I didn't really have the resources to do much else. When I asked him over the phone what size clothes he wore, he said, "Dr. Huddleston, I think I wear a 2X." Well, I didn't think he looked that big, but I proceeded anyway to collect nice extra large sport coats, suits, and shirts from my friends who seemed eager to help. When he tried them on, he declared they were "perfect" and "beautiful." Well, they were nice, but not perfect, at least in fit. They were huge on him. But he still insisted they were perfect. Later he admitted to me that he had never really had a sport coat. Robert was then 26 years old.

After discovering his learning disabilities, including the inability to read well enough to pass college parallel courses on his own, resulting partially from his aphasia (a language disorder possessing similar characteristics of Alzheimer's), I realized that I must do a little more than dress him. Because the policy in the learning lab is to limit each tutoring session on any one assignment to 30 minutes, I knew immediately he would need much more help. So I began tutoring him on my own. In the process of helping him with his assignments, I discovered that he was trying to financially help support his mother because she didn't have a job either. Even though this was the same person who had been unable to raise him because of her own circumstances, he still insisted, "Dr. Kathryn, God intends for us to take care of our parents." So here was the beginning of a common bond: He was trying to help take care of a mother who had been unable to care of him, just as I had tried to do. Also, when he was very young, his grandmother, like mine, helped him until she passed away. But there were major differences: I had always had enough to eat, a roof over my head, my own bed, and I had never been incarcerated. I realized, though, but for the grace of God, I could have ended up either in a drug rehab program or in prison for physically assaulting someone else.

I was led to discover more about his life. I learned that he was homeless and living at first one place and then another. Having to rely on the bus for transportation, with 8:00 classes, he had missed quite a lot of school because it took him almost two hours to get to school, having to transfer buses at least twice each way. Nor had he always been able to make it to various jobs on time because of the same reason, especially during the time after he was released from prison when he was trying to work 18 hours a day. He had become mentally and physically ill, and this illness had resulted in another setback, just when he was about to get his life back on track.

He refused to take his medicine and to give documentation of his attention deficit disorder to his teachers at the community college. This documentation would have ensured that his teachers would accommodate this disability. But Robert was determined to prove that he could do as well as the next person and didn't want to be given special privileges. He took accountability for his actions. And he was embarrassed about his disability. He said to me one day, "Dr. Huddleston, my brain is just not wired like anyone else's." I came to know that he really could learn some fairly complex subjects, including engineering concepts, which somehow connected with certain synapses in his brain. On some simpler concepts, he had difficulty. Like my father, he sometimes didn't say exactly what he meant, but he *knew* what he was *trying* to say.

I came to realize one reason he couldn't read very well is that he couldn't see very well. I thought of Daddy's inability to read his Bible because no one had noticed that he had almost become blind, and after I had gotten him an eye exam and persuaded my mother to allow him to have cataract surgery, he actually could read the signs on the road. So I secured an eye examination for Robert, and he got some real glasses. That seemed to encourage him to try to read more.

Soon I found myself involved in all aspects of his life, from facilitating his getting decent Section 8 plus (subsidized) housing because he was homeless to interactions with rehabilitation counselors, to law enforcement personnel who seemed always to be watching Robert and determined to get him back into prison. I learned what it was like to be under constant surveillance and afraid to ever step outside the lines. The more I became involved with his life, the less wretched my own life seemed. It was not many weeks before my greatest pain resulted from the everlasting thinking about his condition. Robert was getting me back on the track I was on before I became side-tracked with management training, political activism, and even the torment from my own family.

He had been staying part-time with his mother in a one-bedroom apartment, owned by a slumlord who had refused to fix a heating system which had been malfunctioning for a year. The heat couldn't be turned down or off because the knob was broken, so the heat bills were just about as high as the rent. The family purchased air conditioners and ran them even in the winter just to be able to breathe. When I contacted this apartment manager and asked for some rent adjustment for the 11th month of residence because of exorbitant heating bills, I was cursed and threatened about ever visiting the family again. They were unaccustomed to dealing with anyone other than their most vulnerable tenants. This was not my first involvement with slumlords, as years earlier I had discovered that a slumlord was taking advantage of Timmy and Alece who were also living in substandard housing. But even though both slumlords were corrupt, there were different circumstances. This situation with Robert and his family involved direct interactions with people other than slumlords, including warrant officers, bondsmen, public defenders, policemen, and judges. I was moving in unfamiliar waters. Contrary to a few friends who admonished me to keep some distance between myself and the family, I just couldn't seem to discover a stop sign. Though I never intended to become involved with the whole family, I just couldn't find a way to disconnect because Robert felt such a responsibility to help take care of all of them.

After I contacted the landlord, both his family and I were continuously harassed. On one particular day the husband slumlord tore the latch off and broke down the door to their apartment – with Robert's mother and brother inside. The mother, suffering from cancer, was terrified and telephoned the police. She then telephoned Robert and told him the landlord was threatening to put their things on the street. At that time, the rent was not even late. He urgently telephoned me, asking me to please come to get him from school and take him to his mother's apartment because he was afraid for her life. Racing from the dentist's chair to get him, I needed to reassure him that everything was going to be okay, realizing that everything was anything but. I had been going to their apartment every day for a couple of months to pick him up for school, determined that he would not miss any more class because of unreliable public transportation. He had failed a couple of courses the previous two semesters because of absences and was in danger of losing his vocational rehabilitation loan. So I was determined to get him to all his classes this particular semester. It reminded me of my interaction with Timmy many years ago when I moved him in with me, determined he would study and get his G.E.D.

As I drove up to the parking lot, the husband slumlord screamed at me that he was calling the police to have me arrested for trespassing. He was holding up a plank at the time, trying to frighten me. I said probably a little too nonchalantly, "Go ahead," as I went to Robert's crying mother and put my arm around her shaking body. The policeman, who had already left the property, came back when the slumlord telephoned him, and he, likewise, told me that he had telephoned the sergeant and I was about to be handcuffed and taken to jail. I knew I had done nothing to be arrested for, and this was just one more bullying tactic. So I just stood there between the slumlords and police and the family, almost immobile. The policeman said that the landlord could do anything he wanted to because it was his property. This was the same policeman who was a participant in a training seminar on customer relations I conducted some years back, and I remembered his racist and sexist remarks then. "Dr. Huddleston, that bad cop hates you; be careful," Robert whispered, as I had just stood there in front of the family. I said nothing but didn't leave, knowing there were no grounds for having me arrested and also realizing that if I *did* leave, the family would have no witness and would probably be in jail that evening for some trumped up charge.

There seemed to be no way to cut back on my involvement, because just about the time we would get some good news, Robert would get arrested on some bogus charge and have to be bailed out – which meant more money to pay the bondsmen and less money for other necessities. Being on a fixed income at the time reminded me of the days when I was a graduate student, leaving on a meager income and had "adopted" people like Mr. Felts. The patience and perseverance required for my father and mother enabled me to better help Robert. His learning disabilities caused him to often contradict himself, not remembering what he might have just been said, similar to my father. Both had short-term memories and difficulty focusing, and any person really wanting to help them had to enter their world, to have any success. Although neither was aware he was doing it, both controlled every situation. I recalled the times when Daddy's attention would wear down after a few minutes, and he would say, "I'm ready to get out of here." Likewise, when Robert said, I TOLD you I don't want to hear about that," I quit trying to persuade him, regardless of whether it was for his own good or not.

I established rapport with the executive director of Section 8, the subsidy program, apartment managers of reality companies who were Section 8 approved, rehabilitation counselors, and his teachers. On one particular day, with sleet and snow falling on the streets of Nashville, I took Robert to a reality company and paid the deposits for keys so he and I could look at various Section 8 approved residences. I was told that once he received his voucher, already having made application for an apartment might speed the process up. The day was stressful, as were most interactions with him, and his mental challenges caused him to become upset if things didn't go exactly the way he wanted them to go. He had told me for some time that he needed a two bedroom place to live, but I feared that a one-bedroom might be all that he would eventually be eligible for, since one woman at Section 8 had told me that. So I begged him to just look at a one-bedroom. "Dr. Huddleston, I TOLD you I'm not looking at a one-bedroom," he insisted, and then he disappeared for what seemed like a long time. I found myself screaming for him, and temporarily forgot about the neighbors. They probably thought crazy people were about to live next door, and for a brief moment, I thought they might be right. Then I remembered what I was doing and stopped screaming. It dawned on me how his different moods were connected with his learning disabilities and they would require patience, just as my father's Alzheimer's had required it. There was nothing to do, but just wait, so I sat down on one of the steps with the sleet and snow coming down, praying that Robert hadn't wandered off too far or that he hadn't been picked up by the police. He finally reappeared, but because of his outburst about the one-bedroom plea, I dropped that subject and just prayed that somehow the qualifying authority might change her mind and grant him a subsidy for a two-bedroom. He frequently said, "Dr. Kathryn, you worry too much; God is going to take care of this." We then looked at a two bedroom which he really liked, and his good mood returned. After weeks of my interaction with the director of section 8 and the reality company, expressing my willingness to pay the cost difference for a two-bedroom, he actually did end up getting this apartment some two months later.

Having helped Robert write a resume, I began the challenging task of discovering those who would at least offer him an interview. He was willing to work at virtually any job. The process of discovering regular work continues to be an uphill battle because even though the law forbids organizations discriminating against candidates unless their felonies relate to the vacant job duties, they find other ways to filter out anyone with a record. Though Robert had been released for four years and had worked well at many temporary jobs, we still had not landed a permanent job. His mental challenges made it harder.

But things were at least a little better for him. He had gotten a little part-time work, was doing better in school, and had received his voucher for his apartment.

Though he had not yet gotten into that apartment, I didn't think it would be very long before he did, and I thought we would be more apt to get a favorable ruling from the judge about his mother's eviction if I could get them out of the slummy apartment before the end of the month and before our court date. So I asked a friend of mine if he would help them move a couple of days before our court date. I rented a moving truck, the only size that was available, but it was too small for Robert, and he became upset and disappeared again. He finally reappeared and the move was going well enough until this young woman showed up, screaming one minute, laughing the next, revving her car engineer, and blocking our moving truck. That evening I learned that this was a young woman Robert had briefly dated but from whom he was trying to extricate himself because of her drug involvement and severe mood swings, which had led to some violent behavior. He was deeply embarrassed because she created a spectacle for everyone around the apartment, including my friend who had given him some part-time work and me. However, we finally managed to get the family's things to a storage unit, and I had already rented Robert a room in a hotel near the school for that week. Sometimes I feel like I have been moving poor people half of my life.

Two days later his mother and I went to court about the eviction. I was puzzled why Robert wasn't there, because he was always defending his mother. But I put it out of my mind for the moment. Although we had no attorney, I wasn't worried about the outcome because the slumlords had none either, and I had proof of the damages to the family. I had researched tenants' rights and knew his family had not had "peaceful possession" for several months. I had the original inspection sheet on which Robert's mother had one year earlier noted all the malfunctions (which still had not been addressed) and the "doctored-up" one which the slumlord had given to his mother just days before the court date. She had whitened out all the specifics that his mother had written in, left his mother's signature and date, and then copied it, trying to make it look as if nothing had been noted on the original one. Until then I had not at realized just how unjust our criminal "justice" system can be. Though I was sworn in as a witness, the judge didn't call me to testify. As the slumlords left the courtroom, they gave me the finger and told me to buy some prosaic. I learned from Robert's mother that the judge merely looked at the two inspection sheets and said, "This is too confusing," and ordered not only the amount being claimed by the slumlords to be paid, but damages as well! This was only the beginning of various court incidents where I learned about the unfairness that minorities and the poor often must endure. Instead of encouraging those who have been incarcerated to make a better life for themselves, "the system" is often determined to get them back into prison.

It was only after court that I learned he had been arrested the day before. Fearing the next move of the young woman who had created such havoc on the day of the move, Robert visited her the following day, hoping to persuade her to never do anything like this again and to come to some sort of peaceful agreement. She didn't want him to leave her apartment when his brother said they needed to be going, blocking the door, trying to keep him from going. Finally getting loose from her, he began walking down the stairs when he saw about 15 policemen at the apartment complex. Robert actually had no idea that they were there to arrest him, because he only discovered later that the daughter of this young woman had been programmed to phone the police upon hearing certain words from her mother, one being "scratch." Even though three witnesses told the police that Robert had not touched this woman, the police paid no attention to any of them and wrote down none of their statements. They asked leading questions of the young woman, after she herself even stated that no one had scratched her. Nor were there any pictures taken of the alleged "scratch" on the informant's finger. But they arrested him anyway. After having made bond and being released that night, less than five minutes afterwards, he was re-arrested, being told that the police had received a phone call, claiming he had violated the restraining order! The so-called "informant" admitted that the phone call came from a third party, but again it didn't matter. We had to find more money to make another bond. I received an education during this time about what a racket this "domestic violence" has become among people who want revenge. A case like this really hurts all those women who really are victims of this crime.

It was Robert's interaction with this woman that led to a deeper involvement than I would have preferred with the criminal *justice* system. Though I had previously experienced some negative behavior from some of the police officers in leadership training I had conducted for the Police Department, those training sessions had been my only association with them until I met Robert and his family. Through trying to help him, I came to learn far more than I ever could have learned in a book about the justice system. For example, I came to learn that any "confidential informant" can have anyone arrested, because "probable cause" doesn't require any evidence to be submitted on the informant for the judge to issue a warrant to have the accused person arrested. The informant can be on drugs, in prison, hired to telephone the police, or have a record of doing this many times in the past. It makes no difference. So the poor and minorities, the most vulnerable, often have to spend what money they have to get out of jail, even though they may have committed no crime.

At least Robert was going to get housing. That was one big bright spot during all this. Being excited about him getting approval for his section 8 apartment voucher, I never anticipated that it would be another *six* weeks before he would actually get his apartment. So after that first week, I put him and his mother up in mediocre hotels, which was all I could afford, each week thinking that surely this would be the last and he would get his apartment any day. At long last, he received the call, and he was actually going to get the apartment he wanted. I quickly gave him the deposit money, and he ran it over to the reality company. But there was still a hitch. With Section 8 there are actually two inspections required, so we had to wait on the second, because the first one uncovered a problem with the water pipe. But he finally got in and was thrilled to at last have a closet and a bathroom of his own, for the first time ever, so he didn't have to carry his clothes around in a garbage bag. God worked another miracle for us. It is amazing how much most of us take for granted, like having our own bedroom and a closet.

Before I realized it, I was feeling almost like a surrogate mother to a 26 year old African American male, indigent, with learning disabilities...and a record! I was interceding with lawyers and bondsmen on his behalf. I was going to bat for him with his professors. I was selling him to realty companies. I was trying to get my friends to discover odd yard jobs for him. Though friends continued to warn me to keep my distance, fearing something bad might happen to me, and not really able to understand my degree of involvement in this young man's life, I was never afraid. Frustrated, but never afraid because I knew Robert was a Christian. Though rarely ever acknowledging my efforts, one day he actually said to me, "Dr. Kathryn, I would probably be dead if you hadn't come into my life."

We spent months in court over the bogus charges brought against him by the unstable, dangerous woman who was determined to extract revenge for Robert trying to leave her. Sometimes we would wait hours for a hopeful ending, only to hear confusing statements from the judge like, "The plaintiff, Ms. Bartinez, isn't here because she didn't have to be. Your client pleaded guilty." Our attorney said he didn't know where that idea came from. Robert educated me as to how many cases the DA must win, and he understood that often the outcome is decided before the judge hears anything from anybody. Anyway, eventually Robert was offered a second deal. If he would plead guilty, attend a class on domestic violence for sixteen weeks, and serve four hours of community service, the charges would be deleted from his record. He took the deal, even though the class was at night, had to be paid for, and he would have to take the bus. The first deal, which he rejected, involved the same requirements, but the charges would have stayed on his record. I thought how sickening it would be to plead guilty to something I didn't do. But Robert was advised to do this even though he wanted to go on to trial. His attorney thought there were just too many unknowns in a jury trial, and I agreed. At least the worst was over. I came out of all that experience thinking that if I weren't so old, and didn't already have so many seemingly worthless degrees, I would go to law school and become a public defender. Also, since becoming Robert's advocate, I thank God every night that I have reliable transportation, a roof over my head, enough to eat, and a bed to sleep in. Before this involvement, I really had not detailed such blessings in my prayers. For the first time ever in his life, Robert has a new, nice bed, which I purchased for him, and a *real* mattress set. My, oh my, what so many of us take for granted. Things were finally looking up until six gang members followed him off the city bus and beat him up on school property when he was headed toward his math class. So clearly my journey with Robert must continue, and it will because of the strength, endurance, and patience I gained from the journey with my father.

THE SAILOR'S RED SKY

Although I had thought the journey with my father was my final battle for the helpless, I was wrong. It was by far the fiercest one I had encountered, and at the time it did take most of my energy and reserves to withstand it. But it wasn't the last. I understand why my friends can't understand my troublesome habit of getting so deeply involved with people who, without intending to, take over my life. I myself am often annoyed by this propensity and wonder why I just can't send some money to help out, spend a little effort on their other needs, and then move on like normal people do. I have never been certain why I have this extreme pain for others' suffering. Some of it may stem from the void left by my nephews seven years ago when they deleted me from their lives because my financial help was no longer needed. Or from Timmy from whom I rarely hear because he also is financially secure now and has a family of his own. Or from the emptiness I still have from the loss of my father, whom I only knew for a few short years. Or from my own mother who abandoned me when I was young and the obstacles I had to overcome to survive her mental disorders. But whatever the reason, God continues to place in my path those who can never love me back, those who are so needy that others have run from or ignored them, those who have been abandoned, or those who have been held captive either by an evil person or by an evil system. And I know for certain, in spite of what the world says, that He expects me to take care of them because there is no one else on this earth that will. I learned from the stormy voyage with my father that though the path will continue to be inconsistent and I will meet with unexpected waves, God will protect me in this moving sea.

Deep down inside I believe that God will ultimately steer me safely to shore. My faith will not be wrecked by turbulent winds. My cargo will deflect evil. My interaction with others is always only for a season, some seasons lasting longer than others. That's okay, because it is God's will that shall be done on earth. I do know it's not about trying to be good. Or earning my way to heaven. What I do believe to be true is that God has confirmed through these people who have crossed my path since my father's death that God's purpose for my life remains. I was born for His reason, no one else's. And though I suffered for years from my father's death, feeling totally abandoned by Him, during these last two years He has restored my soul. He has brought me to the point that I can predict where the waves will break more than I could before. Just as my experiences with Mammy, Timmy, Alece, Mr. Carter, and so many others strengthened and helped me overcome many hardships and evil mine fields during the journey with my father, that journey in turn gave me even greater strength to help others who are also facing their own fierce storms and are in need of a refuge. I can know that there will eventually be the "red sky at night" even while in the storm's midst. Praise Him. Thank you Mammy. Thank you Daddy. Thank you Robert. Thank you God.

GENERAL INDEX

ABOUT THE AUTHOR

Kathryn Huddleston owned and operated a leadership training business, Kathryn Huddleston & Associates (KHA), for 23 years, supplying services to profits, non-profits and government agencies throughout the United States and in Japan. Specific clients included Motorola, Sara Lee, Whirlpool, Du-Pont, GE, Saturn, HCA, The United Methodist Publishing House, Southwestern Company, and the U.S Department of the Army, USACE, to which KHA earned the status of preferred supplier. She also served as Quality Manager for Square D-Groupe Schneider, North American plants. In 1998, God handed her a new mission, the care of her father, afflicted with Alzheimer's and aortic stenosis, in order to bring him a higher quality of life than he could receive in a facility. After his death, she returned to her earlier career as writing and human resources management professor which she held prior to beginning KHA. Dr. Huddleston, author of *Back on the Quality Track: How Organizations Derailed and Recovered* and *Beyond the Title: Matching People with Jobs*, holds the Ph.D. from Vanderbilt University and the Ed.S. from Peabody College. She has been a professional speaker for the past 25 years and has taught Bible for the past 16 years. A life-long advocate for the elderly and disabled, today she devotes considerable time to mentoring at-risk youth who have too many obstacles to make it on their own.